THE WENTWORTH LECTURES:

HONOURING FIFTY YEARS OF AUSTRALIAN INDIGENOUS STUDIES

Edited by Robert Tonkinson

ABORIGINAL
STUDIES PRESS

First published in 2015
by Aboriginal Studies Press

© in the collection, Aboriginal Studies Press 2015
© in the individual chapters and Introduction, the relevant authors 2015

All rights reserved. No part of this book may be reproduced or transmitted in any form or by any means, electronic or mechanical, including photocopying, recording or by any information storage and retrieval system, without prior permission in writing from the publisher. The Australian *Copyright Act 1968* (the Act) allows a maximum of one chapter or 10 per cent of this book, whichever is the greater, to be photocopied by any educational institution for its education purposes provided that the educational institution (or body that administers it) has given a remuneration notice to Copyright Agency Limited (CAL) under the Act.

Aboriginal Studies Press is the publishing arm of the Australian Institute of Aboriginal and Torres Strait Islander Studies.
GPO Box 553, Canberra, ACT 2601
Phone: (61 2) 6246 1183
Fax: (61 2) 6261 4288
Email: asp@aiatsis.gov.au
Web: www.aiatsis.gov.au/asp/about.html

National Library of Australia
Cataloguing-In-Publication data:

Title: The Wentworth lectures : honouring fifty years of
    Australian Indigenous Studies / editor,
    Robert Tonkinson.

ISBN: 9781922059734 (paperback)

Subjects: Wentworth, W. C. (William Charles), 1907-2003
    Australian Institute of Aboriginal and Torres Strait
    Islander Studies.
    Aboriginal Australians--Archival resources.
    Aboriginal Australians--Politics and government.
    Aboriginal Australians--Social conditions.
    Aboriginal Australians--Social life and customs.
    Aboriginal Australians--Land tenure.

Other Creators/Contributors:
    Tonkinson, Robert, author, editor.
    Jones, Rhys, 1941-2001, author.
    Berndt, Ronald M. (Ronald Murray), 1916- author.
    Hiatt, L. R. (Lester Richard), 1931-2008, author.
    Mulvaney, D. J. (Derek John), 1925- author.
    Colbung, Ken, 1931-2010, author.
    Peterson, Nicolas, 1941- author.
    Langton, Marcia, 1951- author.
    Dodson, Michael, 1950- author.
    French, Robert Shenton, 1947- author.
    Marika-Munun?giritj, Raymattja, author.
    Dodson, Pat, 1947- author.
    Sutton, Peter, 1946- author.
    Nakata, Martin N., author.
    Tonkinson, Robert, 1938- author.
    Janke, Terri, author.
    Kirby, M. D. (Michael Donald), 1939- author.
    Davis, Megan, 1975- author.
    Australian Institute of Aboriginal and Torres Strait
    Islander Studies, issuing body.

Dewey Number: 305.89915

Printed in Australia by SOS print + media Pty Ltd

Contents

The Wentworth Lectures		v
Note to Readers		v
Presenter Biographies		vii
Introduction *Robert Tonkinson*		xiii
1	Calories and bytes: Towards a history of the Australian islands *Rhys Jones*	1
2	Looking ahead through the past *Ronald M Berndt*	25
3	Aboriginal political life *Les Hiatt*	59
4	'A sense of making history': Australian Aboriginal studies 1961–1985 *DJ Mulvaney*	75
5	Not land rights but land rites *Ken Colbung*	90
6	'Studying man and man's nature': A history of the institutionalisation of Aboriginal anthropology *Nicolas Peterson*	102
7	Aborigines and policing: Aboriginal solutions from Northern Territory communities *Marcia Langton*	125
8	The end in the beginning: Re(de)finding Aboriginality *Michael Dodson*	145
9	Native title: The beginning or the end of justice? *RS French*	163
10	An Arnhem Land story *Dr Marika*	180
11	Beyond the mourning gate: Dealing with unfinished business *Patrick Dodson*	192
12	Unusual couples: Relationships and research on the knowledge frontier *Peter Sutton*	204
13	Indigenous Australian Studies and higher education *Martin Nakata*	225

14	'Difference' and 'autonomy' then and now: Four decades of change in a Western Desert society *Robert Tonkinson*	242
15	Guarding ground: A vision for a National Indigenous Cultural Authority *Terri Janke*	258
16	First Australians, Law and the High Court of Australia *Michael Kirby*	281
17	To recognise or not to recognise: The place of Aboriginal and Torres Strait Islander peoples in the Australian Constitution *Megan Davis*	298
Index		312

Aboriginal and Torres Strait Islander people are advised that this publication contains names of people who have passed away.

The Wentworth Lectures

In 1959, Mr William Charles Wentworth prepared a document entitled 'An Australian Institute for Aboriginal Studies'. Inspired by UESCO developments overseas, it argued for a comprehensive and coordinated effort by the Australian government to record for posterity what remained of the culture of the Australian Aboriginal peoples. This objective, Mr Wentworth believed, was probably the most important specific task currently facing Australian scholarship. If it was not undertaken immediately, he said, 'humanity will lose something of permanent value and we Australians, as its custodians, will lay ourselves open to perpetual reproach'.

Mr Wentworth's initiative led to the establishment of the Australian Institute of Aboriginal Studies by act of Parliament in 1964. There is no doubt that when, in 1959, he identified 'we Australians' as the custodians of Aboriginal culture, he was referring primarily to European white Australians. That would have been the enlightened concept of the times. Few could have imagined then that twenty-odd years later a number of members of the Institute would be of Aboriginal descent and that the Institute itself would have become a rallying point for Aboriginal dignity and pride, and a source of hope for a future in which the achievements of the first inhabitants of this country would be regarded not just as subjects of scientific curiosity but as objects of genuine admiration.

The Wentworth Lecture was inaugurated in 1978 to pay tribute to his vision, and simultaneouly to bring to a wider public the findings and viewpoints of scholars eminent in particular fields of Aboriginal studies.

Notes to Readers

The chapters in this volume were originally presented as spoken lectures. These written versions come from a variety of different transcriptions – some provided by the lecturers, and some taken from recordings of the original lectures. They were not originally intended for publication, and in some cases have had to be amended slightly to make them suitable for this purpose. All such alterations have been kept to a minimum.

Some of the speakers have since passed away, and every effort has been made to take a culturally sensitive approach to naming any deceased person, and to respect every presenter and their original lectures.

Presenter Biographies

Ronald Murray Berndt (1916–90) was an Australian *social anthropologist*. In 1963 he became the inaugural Professor of Anthropology at the *University of Western Australia*. Professor Berndt and his wife, *Catherine Berndt*, maintained a close professional partnership for five decades, working among *Aboriginal Australians* at Ooldea (1941), on Northern Territory cattle stations (1944–46), at Balgo (1957–81) and in New Guinea (1951–53). They wrote two very successful books, *The First Australians* and *The World of the First Australians*. Professor Berndt's sole-authored monographs include *Kunapipi* (1951), *Djanggawul* (1952) and *Man, Land and Myth in Northern Australia*. He founded the Anthropological Society of Western Australia in 1958 and the scholarly journal *Anthropological Forum* in 1963, and was a foundation member of the Australian Institute of Aboriginal Studies in 1964. He was a prominent commentator and political adviser who took a keen interest in political developments, and an early advocate for legal recognition and protection of Aboriginal sacred sites.

Kenneth Desmond Colbung AM MBE (1931–2010), also known by his Indigenous name Nundjan Djiridjarkan, was an Aboriginal Australian leader who became prominent in the 1960s. Mr Colbung took on many senior roles in the Aboriginal cause, including land rights, conservation, education and preserving cultural identity. He was instrumental in the development of the *Aboriginal Heritage Act*, which protects and preserves material of cultural significance. He played a significant role in the campaign to return the remains of Nyoongar warrior Yagan to Western Australia in 1997. In 1982, he was awarded an Order of Australia for his services to the Aboriginal community.

Megan Davis is Professor of Law and Director of the Indigenous Law Centre in the Faculty of Law at the University of New South Wales. She is a Commissioner of the New South Wales Land and Environment Court and a Fellow of the Australian Academy of Law and a UN expert member and Chair of the United Nations Permanent Forum on Indigenous Issues. Professor Davis is an international human rights lawyer and has worked in the UN system for over a decade, including being awarded a UN Fellowship in the Office of the High Commissioner for Human Rights, Geneva. She is a solicitor of the Supreme Court of the Australian Capital Territory. Her primary research focus is in constitutional law and Aboriginal women's political participation. She is currently leading a national research project at the Indigenous Law Centre on the experiences of Aboriginal women and children before the courts in sexual assault cases.

Michael 'Mick' Dodson is a Yawuru man from the southern Kimberley region of Western Australia. He is Director of the National Centre for Indigenous Studies at the Australian National University and a Professor in the ANU College of Law. He was formerly the Director of the Indigenous Law Centre at the University of New South Wales.

Patrick Dodson is a Yawuru man from the West Kimberley region of Western Australia. Patrick lives in Broome, where he is Adjunct Professor at the University of Notre Dame, Chair of the Yawuru Native Title Company 'Nyamba Buru Yawuru Ltd' and a Director on the Yawuru PBC. He is a former Director of the Central and Kimberley Land Councils, Chairman of the Council for Aboriginal Reconciliation, a Commissioner of the Royal Commission into Aboriginal Deaths in Custody and Co-chair of the Expert Panel on the constitutional recognition of Aboriginal and Torres Strait Islander peoples. In 2008, Patrick was awarded the Sydney Peace Prize for his distinguished leadership of the reconciliation movement, advocacy of human rights and commitment to peace with justice through dialogue.

Robert Shenton French AC is the twelfth and current Chief Justice of the High Court of Australia. He was appointed to the position in 2008, and is the first Chief Justice from Western Australia. He was admitted as a barrister and solicitor in Western Australia in 1972, and was appointed to the Federal Court in 1986. Justice French has served on numerous bodies, including the Australian Law Reform Commission, the Supreme Court of the ACT, the National Native Title Tribunal and the Australian Institute of Judicial Administration. He has also been a Justice of the Supreme Court of Fiji. In the early 1970s, he helped found the Western Australian Aboriginal Legal Service. He was also the first president of the National Native Title Tribunal.

Lester Richard (Les) Hiatt (1931–2008) was a scholar of Australian Aboriginal societies who promoted Australian Aboriginal Studies within both the academic world and among the wider public for almost fifty years. He was also one of Australia's leading anthropologists. Dr Hiatt was Reader in Anthropology at the University of Sydney and President of the Australian Institute of Aboriginal Studies, which he helped to establish, from 1974 to 1982. In addition to his detailed ethnographic records, his written work inquires into, questions and sometimes challenges some of the more conventionally 'received' anthropological knowledge held by academia and the general public about Australian Aboriginal peoples.

Terri Janke has over seventeen years of practice experience in intellectual property, and is recognised as a leading international authority on Indigenous cultural and intellectual property. She established her Sydney-based IP law firm in 2000. She has been on a number of boards, including non-government organisations. Past directorships include National Indigenous TV (Chair), the Australian Institute of Aboriginal and Torres Strait Islander Studies, the Museum of Contemporary Art and the Collections Council of Australia. She is currently on the Board of Tourism Australia and the Jawun Board, and is also a member of the National Australia Bank Indigenous Advisory Group. Awards include the John Koowarta Law Fellowship, Emerging Indigenous Business Award. In 2005, Ms Janke was listed on the NSW Women's Honour Roll. She was awarded the Highly Commended Aboriginal Justice Award from the Law and Justice Foundation of NSW in 2007, was named NAIDOC Person of the Year in 2011 and won the Attorney-General's National Indigenous Lawyer of the Year Award in 2012. Her first novel, *Butterfly Song*, was published in 2005.

Rhys Jones (1941–2001) was Emeritus Professor and a Research Fellow in the Department of Archaeology and Natural History, Research School of Pacific and Asian Studies at the Australian National University. He was also an Honorary Professor of the University of Wales, Newport and a Fellow of the University of Wales, Lampeter. Professor Jones was a central figure in dating the arrival of Indigenous Australians, first with radiocarbon dating and then with luminescence techniques. He was also central to study of the archaeology of Indigenous Australians. Each year, the Australian Archaeological Association awards the Rhys Jones Medal – its highest accolade.

Michael Kirby was Australia's longest serving judge when he retired from the High Court of Australia in 2009. He had been appointed to the High Court in 1996, and was twice Acting Chief Justice of Australia. Justice Kirby served as Chancellor of Macquarie University from 1984 to 1991. He also served on the World Health Organization's Global Commission on AIDS; as president of the International Commission of Jurists; as UN Special Representative for Human Rights in Cambodia; as a member of the UNESCO International Bioethics Committee; on the High Commissioner for Human Rights' Judicial Reference Group; and on the UNAIDS Reference Group on HIV and Human Rights. Since 2009, he has served as a member of the International Bar Association's Human Rights Institute Council and on a number of UN bodies, including the Human Rights Council's Commission of Inquiry on North Korea. He is Editor-in-Chief of The Laws of Australia and has been appointed Honorary Visiting Professor by twelve universities. He was a member of the Eminent Persons Group investigating the future of the Commonwealth of Nations, and has been appointed to the UNDP Global Commission of HIV and the Law (2010–12). He was awarded the Gruber Justice Prize in 2010. In October 2014, he received the Leo Nevas Award for human rights from the United Nations Foundation of the United States of America.

Presenters Biographies

Marcia Langton AM is an anthropologist and geographer, and holds the Foundation Chair of Australian Indigenous Studies at the University of Melbourne. She has produced a large body of knowledge in the areas of political and legal anthropology, Indigenous agreements and engagement with the minerals industry, and Indigenous culture and art. Her role in the Department of Prime Minister and Cabinet-sponsored Empowered Communities project, as member of the Expert Panel on Constitutional Recognition of Indigenous Australians and the Forrest Review, is a recent demonstration of Professor Langton's academic reputation, policy commitment and impact, alongside her role as a prominent public intellectual (e.g. her 2012 Boyer lecture titled 'The Quiet Revolution: Indigenous People and the Resources Boom'). In the private sector, Professor Langton serves on a number of boards, including as Chairperson of Guma ICRG JV Pty Ltd, as a director of the Indigenous Construction Resource Group Pty Ltd and as a Co-Chair of Cape York Partnership. Professor Langton has been awarded a BA(Hons) from the Australian National University and a PhD from Macquarie University. She is a Fellow of Trinity College, Melbourne, a Fellow of the Academy of Social Sciences of Australia and a member of the Australian Institute of Aboriginal and Torres Strait Islander Studies.

Dr Marika (1959–2008) was a member of the Rirratjingu clan of the Yolngu people. She was an Aboriginal leader, scholar and cultural advocate. She was a Director of Reconciliation Australia and a member of the Australian Institute of Aboriginal and Torres Strait Islander Studies. She was also a director of the Yothu Yindi Foundation and a participant in the 2020 Summit. Marika advocated understanding and reconciliation between Aboriginal and Western cultures. She taught at Charles Darwin University, which awarded her an honorary doctorate, and was considered a leading expert in Yolngu customs and languages in north-east Arnhem Land. She co-founded the Dhimurru Land Management Aboriginal Corporation with her late husband. In 2006 she was named Territorian of the Year award and was nominated for the Australian of the Year Award.

Derek John (DJ) Mulvaney OAM is an Australian archaeologist who is known as the 'Father of Australian Archaeology'. He is also a teacher and a staunch advocate of cultural heritage management, and the author, co-author and editor of twenty-one books. He served on the executive of the Australian Institute of Aboriginal Studies (now the Australian Institute of Aboriginal and Torres Strait Islander Studies) from 1964 to 1980, and was chair from 1982 to 1984. He was a Commissioner of the Australian Heritage Commission from 1976 to 1982. In 1974, he became a member of the Committee of Inquiry on Museums and National Collections. In the 1980s and 1990s, he was instrumental in the campaign for World Heritage Listing of culturally significant sites, including Willandra Lakes and Kakadu National Park, and the fight to protect Tasmania's Franklin River. He received the Order of Australia in 1991, and is the recipient of several other major awards. He is a Fellow of the Australian Academy of the Humanities and a Fellow of the British Academy.

Martin Nakata is a Professor at the University of New South Wales, where he is the Director of the Nura Gili Centre for Indigenous Programs. He was the first Torres Strait Islander to receive a PhD in Australia. His mother is an Indigenous person from the Torres Strait Islands, and his father was born in Kushimoto-cho, Japan. His current research work focuses on higher education curriculum areas, the academic preparation of Indigenous students, and Indigenous knowledge and library services. His book, *Disciplining the Savages – Savaging the Disciplines*, was published in 2007 by Aboriginal Studies Press and has recently been translated into Spanish. He has served on the Council of Australian Institute of Aboriginal and Torres Strait Islander Studies and several other bodies.

Nicolas Peterson is Professor of Anthropology and Director of the Centre for Native Title Anthropology in the School of Archaeology and Anthropology at the Australian National University. His main areas of fieldwork have been in the Northern Territory. Research interests include land and marine tenure, and 'fourth world' people and the state. Since working for the Royal Commission into Aboriginal Land Rights, he has been involved in the preparation of several land and native title claims.

Peter Sutton FASSA is an Australian social anthropologist and linguist who has worked with Australian Aboriginal languages, cultures, art and systems of land tenure for almost four decades. He has increasingly come to focus on the role of public policy in governing Aboriginal Australians. In 2004–08, Peter Sutton held an Australian Research Council (ARC) Professorial Fellowship at the University of Adelaide's School of Earth and Environmental Sciences, and within the South Australian Museum's Division of Anthropology. He has also been an Honorary Research Fellow at the Institute of Archaeology, University College London.

Bob Tonkinson is Professor Emeritus and Honorary Senior Research Fellow in Social Anthropology at the University of Western Australia. His work over the past five decades has focused on Aboriginal Australia and insular Melanesia. His recent writings include direct comparisons of aspects common to both fields, particularly the uses and politics of tradition in relation to political action and issues of personal and group identity. He continues to work in both academic and applied areas of anthropological research on Aboriginal Australia. Emeritus Professor Tonkinson was Editor of the journal Anthropological Forum (2000–11). He is a Fellow of the Academy of the Social Sciences in Australia, and a Life Member of both the Association for Social Anthropology in Oceania and the Australian Anthropological Society. He is currently Deputy Chair of the Council of the Australian Institute of Aboriginal and Torres Strait Islander Studies.

Introduction

Robert Tonkinson

William (Bill) Wentworth (1907–2003) played an important role in the establishment of the Australian Institute of Aboriginal Studies (AIAS) in 1961. He had a long-term and intense interest in the origins, society and culture of the continent's first pioneers and settlers, the Aborigines, and believed that the study of Aboriginal people would throw light on human origins. Dr Jacquie Lambert, in her excellent ANU doctoral dissertation on the history of the Institute, refers to Wentworth as its 'founding father' and, as you will note in the following compilation, every Wentworth lecturer pays homage to this great Australian. His was a major contribution to what has become the world's primary repository of knowledge concerning the cultures and achievements of Australia's two Indigenous groups: the Aboriginal people and the Torres Strait Islanders.

As the late Professor John Barnes, distinguished British anthropologist, noted at the first major gathering of scholars of Aboriginal Australia in 1961 (see Sheils, 1963) the predominant view of the participants was akin to a rescue mission, to make haste and 'get it all down before it is too late'. Their overriding perception was of a continuing and accelerating loss of 'traditional' Aboriginal culture in the face of assimilatory pressures wrought on a very small, encapsulated minority. However, by the time of the inaugural Wentworth Lecture, delivered in 1978 by eminent archaeologist, Dr Rhys Jones, the field of Aboriginal Studies was burgeoning. In the thirty-six years since, there have been eighteen Wentworth lecturers, whose diverse topics amply demonstrate the dynamism and resilience of Aboriginal culture.

The task of choosing Wentworth lecturers was (and still is) undertaken by the Institute's Council from an ever-increasing pool of people having special interests and expertise in one or more area of Indigenous Studies. The Council's choices provide an indicator of expanding disciplinary foci of the Institute, and, in some instances, of what was happening in Aboriginal Australia generally at the time. In some cases, the decision also reflected an acknowledgment by Council of the significant contribution of the nominee to the Institute. Beyond an expectation that the lecturers' particular field of experience and/or scholarship will be reflected strongly in their presentations, all have invariably dealt to some extent with wider political, social, economic or religious factors or developments that bear on the chosen topic or theme of their lecture.

Appropriately for the inaugural Wentworth Lecture, *Calories and bytes: Towards a history of the Australian islands*, archaeologist Rhys Jones (1941–2001) set out to provide a big-picture overview of the state of our knowledge about the Aboriginal people, which had been exciting the world archaeological community with revelations emphasising the immense length of tenure of Aboriginal people on this continent. He quotes Lucretius and his imaginings of the earliest humans, and comments: 'Such was the cultural memory with which to try and comprehend the vast forests of the New and Pacific worlds with their mirrors of mankind staring back from the edge of the trees'. He points out that the larger mass of Sahul, which included New Guinea and what is now the island of Tasmania, existed until relatively recent times, in terms of archaeological reckoning. Summarising what is known of Australia's prehistory, Jones proposes that typology, the study of artefacts, is in fact the study of entropy. He then reviews some major excavations, such as those at Lake Mungo in New South Wales, noting that, despite the crude state of early archaeology of the Stone Age, it carried a profound message: that technology was changing in the direction of increased organisation, efficiency and miniaturisation. He suggests a modern-day equivalent in what happened to computers over a mere thirty-year period hence the 'bytes' in the title of his presentation. Jones goes on to discuss some provocative findings in both Tasmania and Arnhem Land, where he had led important digs. He also discusses exciting new data from the Wahgi Valley in Papua New Guinea, which revealed an ancient but well-developed horticultural system based on taro. He argues that this discovery in turn raises significant questions as to whether or not climatic or cultural factors prevented taro from spreading south. Jones ends with the insightful suggestion that one distinctive Aboriginal contribution to history is their success in increasing social intensification without a concomitant degradation of resources.

Margaret Valadian's 1980 Lecture, *Aboriginal education by Aborigines for Aborigines* (which was unfortunately not available for inclusion in this collection), compares Aboriginal life-long education, delivered by the adult members of the community in a disciplined and caring environment, to conventional European systems. She notes that Australians have rarely appreciated the proficient nature of that system in producing mature, disciplined and assured adults who could participate in daily activities and contribute to the social, spiritual and cultural life of the community. She points out that the new settlers and policy makers did not recognise anything akin to a 'system' in the way Aboriginal children were socialised, and criticises anthropologists and others for this shortcoming. The result of European attempts to 'educate' Aboriginal people using European models was a failure. However, Valadian points to indications of change where policy makers at both national and state levels have come to acknowledge past failures and, increasingly, recognise and value greater Aboriginal participation in the provision of educational services for their own people. This trend has been complemented in recent decades by rising Aboriginal aspirations for increased involvement in their own education. She notes that only time will tell whether these initiatives reflect a genuine desire for change aimed at facilitating a more responsive education system, one that incorporates greater Aboriginal involvement in its planning, design and delivery.

Ronald Berndt (1916–1990) was a distinguished researcher and scholar who in 1961 founded the disciplines of anthropology and sociology at the University of Western Australia (UWA). In collaboration with his wife and colleague, Catherine Berndt (1919–1994), he conducted research over several decades in many and varied locations in Australia, and in the New Guinea Highlands. Berndt's lecture, *Looking ahead through the past*, is thematically centred on the continuing significance of the past for both present conditions and future possibilities. His presentation exemplifies his skills as an observer and recorder. He includes wonderful examples of song poetry and myths to illustrate the major enabling 'vehicles' (to borrow Professor WEH Stanner's apt term) so essential for the intergenerational transmission of huge amounts of religious lore. The lecture reflects his lifelong interest in cultural dynamism and innovation, and his sensitivity to the fact that Aboriginal people have managed to retain much of their cultural knowledge in the face of enormous assimilatory pressures. Another of his major themes is the vital importance of education, which looms large in this lecture; for example, Berndt urges the establishment of multidisciplinary Aboriginal Studies units in Australian universities. Were Ron Berndt still with us today he would, I am certain, be impressed and delighted to see how amply this wish is being fulfilled.

Aboriginal political life is the subject of the 1984 Lecture, delivered by Dr Les(ter) Hiatt (1931–2008), Reader in Anthropology at the University of Sydney and President of AIAS between 1974 and 1982. He had undertaken extensive research among the Gidjingali people of northern Arnhem Land, and his monograph *Kinship and Conflict* (1965) became an important reference work. One of the major themes of his lecture centres on the fact that in small-scale societies important questions inevitably surround the origins of power, how and by whom it is exercised, and why people are persuaded to conform in the absence of centralised authority. Hiatt examines anthropological writings on this subject, by Edward John Eyre, Baldwin Spencer and Frank Gillen, Lauriston Sharp and Mervyn Meggitt, and from these the centrality of kinship and associated obligations and responsibilities emerge as major mechanisms for social integration. However, he also notes that, despite a dominant egalitarian ideology, there is male competition for prestige; and here he identifies a need for more data on male oratory and debate and on the undoubted influence of ecological factors. (Thanks to the pioneering work of Julian Steward and others from around the 1950s, ecological anthropology had become a well-established subfield.) Hiatt cites more recent criticisms of the egalitarian view and addresses relevant writings by Athol Chase, John von Sturmer, Peter Sutton, John Bern, Fred Myers, and Ian Keen. In his concluding comments, which focus on the status of women, Hiatt endorses Gillian Cowlishaw's view that their resistance to male hegemony can lead to the kind of 'collective autonomy' noted by Annette Hamilton and Diane Bell.

In his 1986 lecture, Professor John Mulvaney, who was Chairman of the AIAS Council from 1982 to 1984, discusses the development of Aboriginal Studies since the inception of the Australian Institute of Aboriginal Studies (AIAS) in 1961. As Professor of Archaeology at ANU, and internationally respected for his pioneering research and writing on Aboriginal Australia, he was well placed to address the emergence and growth of the field of Aboriginal Studies. Mulvaney notes the importance of external funding, which, beginning in 1926, superceded self-financed amateur research. Two US foundations, Rockefeller and Carnegie, gave crucial financial support via the Australian National Research Council, and the Sydney Department of Anthropology began providing both 'direction and theoretical shape' to research. The Second World War brought a dramatic decline in research activity, and it was not until 1964 that the Social Science Research Council of Australia's project, 'Aborigines in Australian Society', began, with substantial funding from private foundations. This initiative was welcomed by the Institute as complementing its work. Mulvaney views the establishment of AIAS as a watershed in the systematisation of data on Aboriginal Australia, with huge potential to contribute to administrative policies by changing the focus to social change and its inherent adaptational problems for those most adversely affected. The remainder of Mulvaney's lecture is devoted to archaeological research in Australia and, despite a degree of Aboriginal resistance to elements of such research, the global archaeological significance of major 'digs' for enhanced understandings of the prehistoric record.

Widely known and respected Nyoongah elder and Korean War veteran Ken Colbung, AM, MBE (1931–2010), the Institute's Council's first Indigenous Chair, delivered the 1988 Wentworth Lecture. Ronald Berndt, who introduced him, felt moved to interpret the title, 'not land rights but land rites', as reflecting Aboriginal peoples' long-held spiritual affinities, customary practices and attitudes relating to the protection and conservation of the natural environment. Colbung talks briefly about land reform and poverty in England, and issues surrounding the alienation of Indian land for National Parks in the USA. He then considers the declaration of reserves for Aboriginal people in Australia at a time when they were widely considered 'a dying race'. He notes that, by the 1970s, land rights had become property (rather than customary) rights, suggesting there was a growing risk that the enrichment of a few would occur at the expense of the many. He lauds the 'de-exoticisation of Aboriginal traditions', led by scholars and politicians, and the role of the Institute in this. He condemns both essentialism and the borrowing of elements from other peoples' cultures. For Colbung, the big question concerns the durability of distinctively Aboriginal cultural traits in the face of poor living conditions, diseases, the effects of alcohol and difficulties attendant on migration and urbanisation. More positively, he suggests that an Aboriginal ethic of egalitarianism in meetings and decision-making reveals a conservatism that gives his people a 'special humanity'. Also, the 'cultural revolution' that has fostered Aboriginal art, craft, and performance demonstrates that his people are active, creative and resilient 'culture makers' in their own right.

Professor Nicolas Peterson (ANU) studied anthropology at the University of Sydney and carried out research among the Warlpiri people. He chose the history of the institutionalisation of Aboriginal anthropology as his topic for the 1990 lecture, so some of his observations about the Institute complemented those of John Mulvaney four years earlier. Peterson argues that academic neglect of Aboriginal Studies prior to the Institute's establishment resulted from a necessary focus on applied research outside Australia, which had proved useful to colonial administrations in New Guinea and the Pacific. Earlier research was largely underpinned by social evolutionary theories and became influential in European circles, which in turn led to research expeditions. Anthropology's establishment in Australian universities after the Second World War occurred in an atmosphere that could be characterised as 'before it's too late'. Peterson explains why Adelaide held strong claims to be a centre for Aboriginal research, which, had these been realised, would have strongly favoured biological studies. He suggests that the dominance of functionalist theory could explain why anthropology in the Australian context was not valued for its potential administrative applications, in contrast to New Guinea. Greatly improved outback communications during the Second World War enhanced prospects for research in remote Australia, but the rapid rise of the Australian National University post-war, with its Research School of Pacific Studies in place, saw the vast majority of RSPacS scholars conducting research outside Australia. Peterson notes that the need for an Aboriginal Studies institution emerged against this background, with Wentworth providing the catalyst in his short but persuasive document proposing an AIAS.

For her 1992 Lecture, anthropologist and activist Professor Marcia Langton (then based at Macquarie University and Chair of AIATSIS, now Foundation Chair, Australian Indigenous Studies at the University of Melbourne) chose as her subject Aboriginal people and policing in the Northern Territory (NT). She cites disproportionately high rates of Aboriginal arrest, imprisonment and deaths in custody, and discusses the work of the Australian Law

Reform Commission (the recommendations of which she refers to later in the lecture). Langton outlines other issues, such as including Aboriginal ill-health, high mortality rates and levels of alcohol misuse, and asks what can be done about this lamentable situation. She goes on to describe Aboriginal initiatives in community policing, education and crime reduction, citing Nancy Williams' groundbreaking research. Langton's case examples, drawn from six NT communities, provide strong evidence for a link between effective community justice strategies aimed at reducing police interventions and the amelioration of police--Aboriginal relations. She notes a huge fear of police going back to frontier days. (This reminded me of what I observed in the early 1960s at Jigalong Mission, where dawn raids by dog-shooting police engendered abject terror among the Martu people, who were convinced that these *mantamarangka*, 'handcuffs', could also murder them with impunity. In her concluding discussion on conflicts between Aboriginal Law and the law, Langton notes that most offences committed by Aboriginal people are minor, often relating to vehicles, or to unpaid fines, and that arrest and jailing are no deterrent compared to the strictures of Aboriginal Law. Clashes between the two systems are routine; for example, fulfilling Lawful responsibilities connected with conflict resolution can lead to the imprisonment of the punishers rather than the offenders. She also draws attention to a troubling correlation between police numbers and rates of arrest and imprisonment. Langton concludes with a set of specific suggestions drawn from Aboriginal people. These proposals are aimed at improving police practices and levels of training in dealing with Aboriginal detainees and prisoners.

Professor Michael 'Mick' Dodson AM, then Aboriginal and Torres Strait Islander Social Justice Commissioner, is one of Australia's best known and respected Indigenous leaders. He was honoured as Australian of the Year in 2009. He has a long, close and continuing relationship with AIATSIS, and has been Chair of Council since 1999. He begins his 1994 lecture by quoting a range of adverse commentaries, dating from the earliest days of the European invasion, on Australia's first people. The European construction of them was as 'innately obsolete', using wildly varying criteria but with consistency as to their alleged primitivity and parasitic nomadism. This Hobbesian characterisation easily overwhelmed strains of the Noble Savage trope. Worse, classificatory schemes were employed linking 'blood' quotients to hierarchies of intelligence or assimilability based on unfounded assertions about differences, innate and cultural, between groups. Moving closer to the present, Dodson outlines the cultural relativist stance of the United Nations as to the inherent rights of encapsulated minorities to define themselves. He notes, however, that the struggle to make self-definition the dominant criterion must still do battle on two fronts: negative impositions from the non-Indigenous majority and divisions and antagonisms internal to Aboriginal society. The association of nomadism with characteristics alien to European views of property implies exclusion, well exemplified in commonly seen warnings such as 'Private Property. Keep Out' and 'No Trespassing'. The very early declaration of *'terra nullius'* underlined the intimate association in European minds of ownership with law, order and transformative work. For Dodson, closer understanding of what motivated historical constructions of Aboriginality, and the subversion of this position, are imperative for Indigenous Australians. He notes the poisonous consequences for Tasmanian Aborigines of the enshrining of Trucanini as 'the last Tasmanian Aborigine'. Likewise, 'Aboriginal Protection Acts' guaranteed regimes of separation, surveillance, paternalism and control, which fostered passivitiy and dependence. Escape was possible, but at the price of one's public Aboriginality. Moving to the present, Dodson concludes by reminding us that the past is 'dynamic, active and potentially revolutionary', and points to AIATSIS as 'a resource of freedom', enabling Indigenous Australians to experience the liberating power of remembrance, and for all others, from here and abroad, to learn and understand. As my high school motto has it, 'savoir c'est pouvoir': knowledge is power.

Justice Robert French, then President of the Native Title Tribunal, now Chief Justice of the High Court of Australia, understandably chose native title as his topic for the 1996 Lecture. His subtitle poses the question of whether it would be the beginning or end of justice, such that even if native title was declared invalid legally, 'country and its concerns remain'. He establishes the overriding significance of land and the pervasive ills inherent in the alienation of Aboriginal people from it and the paternalism that infantilised them. The converse of protection was a suffusing domination and control, along with the alienation of Aboriginal lands. French notes, however, the positive role played by Indigenous activism and advocacy of many kinds, particularly in the last half-century. He traces the evolution of statutory land rights, and exemplifies this progress by referring to the percentage of Aboriginal freehold land in each state and the Northern Territory. Many in the wider population who opposed land rights asserted unfair discrimination, discounting historical truths. They viewed Native Title as an unearned benefit accruing to the undeserving. Yet, as French notes, surveys of public attitudes around that time indicated considerable support for land rights. He described the Mabo High Court decision as immensely consequential: 'the catalyst for political and legislative action and the reordering of the place of indigenous people in our society'. He outlines the doctrine of extinguishment of native title and explains how it has been legislatively fettered by the Commonwealth's *Racial Discrimination Act 1975*. French notes the explosive growth of applications to the National Native Title Tribunal (established in 1994) and the rise of mediation, which has required innovative approaches. He refers briefly to the Waitangi Tribunal in New Zealand and to legal decisions in British Columbia to indicate the lengthy and difficult (and, for some, rewarding) processes inevitably entailed in indigenous land rights.

Prominent Yolngu identity, Dr Marika (1959–2008), began her lecture in her language, then translated her biographical sketch, describing childhood in north-east Arnhem Land: how she learned to hunt and gather, her love of books and learning, and her language work as a pupil, then later a teacher and author. Attending ceremonies and listening to songlines enriched her worldview and taught her the importance of Yolngu values and traditions. In her brief review of contact history, Marika talks of Macassan influences, Yolngu conflicts with them and with Japanese who came to harvest bêche-de-mer, and the coming of anthropologists and Methodist missionaries. In the 1960s, bauxite mining on the nearby Gove Peninsula prompted a protest by Yolngu leaders, who, fearing disruption and cultural loss prepared and despatched to Canberra the now-famous Bark Petition in 1963. Notably, the Yolngu sought a writ against the miners and the Commonwealth. They lost the case in 1971, but continued their concerted struggle for land (and sea) rights. Marika goes on to talk about multilingualism, the 'Aboriginalisation' of Northern Territory school curricula and the employment of Yolngu aides working side by side with non-Aboriginal teachers. She uses audiovisual materials to bring the Yolngu school-learning experience to life. As a teacher-linguist, she worked on culturally appropriate assessment measures, a difficult task given that 'our children are learning in and through two languages, and learning about two knowledge systems or traditions'. She concludes by questioning the Northern Territory Government's commitment to bilingual education, and calls for continuing Territory and Federal support for these unique Yolngu school programs.

In 2000, the Wentworth Lecture, entitled *Beyond the mourning gate: Dealing with unfinished business*, was given by Professor Patrick Dodson, prominent Yawuru elder, ex-priest and Inaugural Chairman of the Council for Aboriginal Reconciliation. He is also Director of the Kimberley Institute, based in Broome, WA, and the Lingiari Foundation, and Professor in the Social Policy Research Centre at the University of New South Wales. He begins with an account of Sydney's Australia Day Aboriginal protest in 1938, which attracted many Aboriginal people from along the eastern seaboard, and entailed calls for respect, equality and recognition of 'full citizen status'. As with the multitude of protests that have followed, the crucial demand was Indigenous rights. Dodson asks why real and lasting change has taken so long, and why governments have been so slow to react and take steps aimed at enhancing Aboriginal freedom and dignity. He cites the 1967 referendum as a step in the right direction, pointing out that governments have been better at political posturing than delivering results that address Aboriginal rights and responsibilities to both law and land, and in maintaining their unique traditions. He then turns to the specifics of Reconciliation Week, which would deliver a national (rather than an Aboriginal) agenda for reconciliation. Dodson accuses the then federal Coalition Government and its leader, John Howard, of cynical manipulation of the process. He lists the core principles for a legislated framework agreement or treaty, but considers the federal government incapable of grasping possible consequences of the continuing denial of the rights of the first Australians. Dodson calls on the powers that be to have the courage and the will to change course, and ends with a warning against being trapped in our history, since, as the Irish have it, 'Bigots and begrudgers will never bid the past farewell'.

In anthropologist Peter Sutton's 2002 Lecture, *Unusual couples*, he discusses relationships between several historically prominent researchers and their Indigenous collaborators, as pairs of distinct characters. Although time constraints limited his talk to just four such partnerships, he expanded his examples in a subsequent publication, *The politics of suffering* (2009), which spans more than 160 years of Australian history. In this work, Sutton provides visual portraits of Johnny Flinders and Peter himself, Biraban (John McGill) and Lancelot Threlkeld, Tulaba (Billy McLeod) and Alfred Howitt, Harry Mahkarolla and Lloyd Warner, Billy Mammus and Ursula McConnel, Smiler Durmugam and Bill Stanner, Raiwalla and Donald Thomson, Lazarus Lamilami and Ronald Berndt, Mick McLean and Luise Hercus, Ellen Atkinson and Diane Barwick, Peret Arkwookerum and John von Sturmer, and Topsy Nelson and Diane Bell.

All of us who have done fieldwork must have, at some stage of our research, pondered how and why our 'key informants' found us, and about the huge spectrum of initial responses we receive, ranging from strong interest, even fascination, to utter indifference. Sutton notes that researchers may become objects of competition, potentially at least a source of good things (money, goods, a 'boss'; or perhaps mediators between our subjects and the wider polity or potentially as 'kin', with all its implications for reciprocity, trust or manipulation). He also suggests that the anthropologist often came off well in remote situations when compared to other frontier types, though, in the case of missionaries or government employees, there may have been antagonism directed against them as inevitably subversive and anti-authoritarian. Sutton also observes that little is said by researchers about how those among whom they study interpret the meaning of 'friendship'. In conclusion, Sutton lauds these close friendships as part of a 'rich fabric of understanding and appreciation of Australia's cultures that we enjoy today'.

The 2004 Wentworth Lecture is notable as the first to be given by a Torres Strait Islander, Professor Martin Nakata, then Director of Indigenous Academic Programs at UTS, and now the Director of Nura Gili at the University of New South Wales. His presentation focuses on the topic of Indigenous Studies as scholarly and intellectual activity occurring within the realm of higher education. He stresses that, as well, these activities 'must always remain articulated to community concerns and sensibilities'. There is a resulting tension in this balancing act that can lead to a questioning of loyalties, so the challenge is how to maintain solidarity while producing useful knowledge and strategies for Indigenous communities. As content evolved and insights derived from within Indigenous culture were included, 'Aboriginal Studies' attracted more and more non-Indigenous students. This new field also increasingly critiqued and challenged existing stances. The use of materials from other countries, notably New Zealand and North America, added to the cross-disciplinary nature of these programs. Nakata talks at length about the problems inherent in trying to develop 'Indigenous' paradigms; he notes efforts to create 'Indigenous spaces' in universities wherein allowance for cultural differences is made. For him, hopes that 'Indigenous meanings' will predominate and be the medium in which to couch solutions to social problems, constitute 'flawed thinking', given the dominance of non-Indigenous systems of thought. There is of course a space for 'Indigenous knowledge', he says, but there are inevitably issues surrounding intellectual property and how it is modified when employed in teaching. In Nakata's view, accommodation between Indigenous and non-Indigenous understandings is achievable. He uses Indigenous health-worker education as a case example n to illustrate 'the constantly shifting and intersecting' sets of understandings entailed and the need to align them in practice. His final call is for Indigenous people to abandon narratives of cultural loss, and engage with an increasingly complex 'knowledge landscape' so as to protect their future interests.

In 2006, I was honoured to be the Wentworth Lecturer. My talk focused on the Martu, a Western Desert people with whom I have worked as a social anthropologist since 1963. Moving from the desert and settling at Jigalong, which became a Christian mission just after the Second World War, the Martu had little choice about conceding their former autonomy to the state and its agents. The lecture's theme centred on 'difference' and 'autonomy', concepts which aptly describe Martu adaptive strategies that have accommodated missionaries and other outsiders while insulating core values and activities from damaging interference. They strongly resisted alien intrusion into their cultural domain, exemplified by 'the camp' and the secret-sacred ideas, paraphernalia, and rituals which comprise 'Martu Law', clearly differentiated from whitefella institutions and spaces, such as the clinic, office and school. Although 1970s 'self-management' policies broadened Martu understandings of the world beyond their own experience, and provided some new skills, these did not entirely mitigate the loss of employment on pastoral stations and did little to ameliorate entrenched disadvantage. They had an elected Council, but seemed content to have non-Martu manage 'whitefella business', notably administration, finance and the day-to-day running of the community. The establishment of the mining town, Newman, suddenly brought the wider world and its attractions and dangers, notably access to alcohol, much closer; deaths from traffic accidents and violence, and encounters with the criminal justice system, rose dramatically. The establishment of two new Martu communities back on desert homelands enhanced autonomy, greatly strengthened regional cultural networks and facilitated 'Law business' and political developments. In recent decades, Martu exposure to the wider world has broadened: many now live in towns and in Perth, expanding their horizons but also bringing new challenges, including a high incidence of 'lifestyle diseases'. However, the lives of most Martu still revolve around key cultural institutions, notably kinship, country, and their Law, as well as values such as sharing, nurturing and compassion.

Ms Terri Janke, of the Meriam people of the Torres Strait Islands and the Wuthathi people of Cape York Peninsula, is an arts lawyer, writer and consultant. A leading specialist on Indigenous cultural and intellectual property rights, she is a former AIATSIS Council member. In her 2008 Lecture, Janke discusses the rapid rise of Indigenous cultural production, which has spawned 'unreasonable commercial practice' entailing rip-offs by Australian and overseas companies. After summarising the history of Indigenous cultural rights advocacy, she notes the outcome of her major 1999 Report, *Our Culture, our Future* and its 115 legislative and policy recommendations. The bulk of her lecture concerns six notable case examples of copyright breaches and their aftermath. Two involve currency: in the first, unauthorised use of one of David Malangi's bark paintings resulted in his receipt of $1000, a fishing kit and a silver medallion; the second case went to court but failed, prompting Justice French to criticise national copyright law for its inadequate regulatory powers in the case of Aboriginal community claims. The Bulun Bulun t-shirt case resulted in an out-of-court settlement and a $150,000 damages payment to the Northern Territory artists concerned, and raised important broader copyright issues about fiduciary duty to all traditional owners in the case of clan- or community-owned designs. The unauthorised use by a t-shirt manufacturer of an Institute-funded researcher's drawings and photographs (published in an AIAS book) of Deaf Adder Creek rock art in the NT resulted in cessation of production, damages and a public apology published in *The Australian*. After outlining her vision for a national Indigenous cultural authority, empowered to encourage the fair and authorised use of Indigenous products and property rights, Janke concludes with a discussion about what can be learned from 'prior informed consent' models that have been developed internationally.

The National Library was the venue for the 2010 Lecture, *First Australians, Law and the High Court of Australia*, delivered by the then High Court Justice, Michael Kirby. He begins by outlining the great significance of the *Mabo* decision, and noting the many dire prognostications that failed to materialise in its wake. For him, *Mabo* laid down a new principle that required readjustments of Australian law. In his exposition of the *Roach* decision, pertaining to the rights of prisoners to vote in the Federal Election of 2007, he deems the judgment as rightfully bringing this nation into line with major international legal precedents. Kirby devotes considerable attention to the momentous 1996 *Wik* decision, which happened not long after his appointment to the High Court, and in which he cast a deciding vote. This landmark case was vigorously opposed by pastoralists and others for whom the very notion of Aboriginal land ownership was anathema. By the narrow margin of four to three, the Court upheld the Wik people's assertion that pastoral leases came under the ambit of the *Mabo* principle. Reflecting on the Northern Territory 'Intervention' and the failed 2008 High Court challenge to its constitutional validity, Kirby, although on the losing side, nevertheless felt that there were strong precedents favouring his arguments against that legislation. He cites strong opposition to the 'Intervention' from many quarters, including the former Prime Minister, Malcolm Fraser, and former Governor-General, Sir William Deane. Internationally, there was also a detailed examination of the situation by a United Nations official, James Anaya, whose investigation and subsequent damning report (2010) pointed to haste and inadequate prior consultation. Justice Kirby closes with the hope that Australians will read *This is what we said*, a book in which Aboriginal people and others discuss the Intervention.

The 2012 Wentworth Lecture was presented by Dr Megan Davis, whose ancestral country is in southern Queensland. As a member of the UN Permanent Forum on Indigenous Issues and Director of the Indigenous Law Centre at the University of New South Wales, she has a strong interest in constitutional reform. Moves to advocate for constitutional change regarding Australia's Indigenous minorities can be traced back to the 1970s. For Davis, such reforms should reflect both the unique status of the nation's First Peoples and respect for its Indigenous cultures. She was nominated in 2010 to membership of a panel to consult with the Australian community (including Aboriginal and Torres Strait Islander communities) on constitutional changes that would recognise the unique status of Indigenous Australians. Davis deftly summarises the formation, methodologies and recommendations of this panel and the significance of its contribution in clarifying some of the finer points and vagaries of how constitutional change could affect Indigenous Australians. She concludes that the Constitution is well crafted and in general fulfils its purposes, but is less than fair in its treatment of Indigenous Australians. She notes that Indigenous political and legal concerns are far outweighed by the principle of the greatest good for the greatest number; and recent history (here she cites the Native Title Act as a clear example) shows that such rights can be easily abrogated. In the second half of her lecture, Davis gives an outline of the panel's inception and objectives, followed by a compelling, sometimes moving, sometimes hilarious, detailed and always insightful account of its nationwide travels and experiences. To her final question as to how can we persuade Australians to engage with the complexity of the Constitution, her answer is: 'first you get the nation — Aboriginal and Torres Strait Islander people and everyone else — to engage with, recognise and understand the complexities and nuances of the relationships that they already have with one another'.

In addition to the diverse and always engaging content, the collected Wentworth Lectures provide insights into the Institute's history and the development of Aboriginal Studies more generally. For example, in the early years of the lecture series, the Institute's Council, membership and staff were almost entirely non-Indigenous. While most of the lecturers in that period were non-Indigenous academics, there was an early recognition of Indigenous voices. In recent years, the preponderance of lecturers have been Indigenous scholars. On the whole, their presentations have tended to reflect sociocultural trends and concerns manifest in the wider Australian society at the time. Increasingly, the lecturers have been Indigenous and have also come from the professions, particularly law.

It is striking that many of the Aboriginal and Torres Strait Islander people who later became presenters went on to make their mark in the Academy. In most cases, they continued to maintain strong ties with their communities of origin, and some have become prominent voices in support for Indigenous advancement, both on the national scene and in the international Indigenous Peoples arena. Some regularly command attention and comment in the Australian media, and one of them, Mick Dodson, joined the exalted ranks of the 'Australian of the Year' award winners.

Bill Wentworth and his fellow founders of the Institute would, I am certain, be surprised and delighted that, far from being a salvage mission, the Institute has come to facilitate and promote a breadth of scholarship concerning Indigenous Australia. More than this, the lecture series has supplied a showcase for scholars, an increasing number of whom are Indigenous. The success of the WWL Series provides confidence that for as long as the unique institution, AIATSIS, endures, it will retain its pre-eminence as a vibrant, world-class repository of knowledge about Australia's First Peoples.

Reference

Sheils, H (ed.) 1963, *Australian Aboriginal Studies*, Oxford University Press, Melbourne.

1

Calories and bytes: Towards a history of the Australian Islands

1978 Wentworth Lecture

Rhys Jones

As Mr Wentworth (1819, p. 115) said in his first book, written while still an undergraduate at the University of Cambridge: 'The Aborigines of this country [Tasmania] are, if possible still more barbarous and uncivilised than those of New Holland. They subsist entirely by hunting, and have no knowledge whatever of the art of fishing.' Published in 1819, this was not of course the work of William Charles Wentworth the Fourth, in appreciation of whose contribution to Aboriginal studies this lecture series has been inaugurated, but of William Charles Wentworth the First, another 'Great Native'. He continues, saying of the Tasmanian Aborigines:

> Even the rude bark canoe which their neighbours possess, is quite unknown to them; and whenever they want to pass a sheet of water, they are compelled to construct a wretched raft for the occasion ... The woomera, or throwing stick, which enables the natives of Port Jackson to cast their spears with such amazing force and precision, is not used by them. Their spears too, instead of being made with a bulrush, and only pointed with hardwood, are composed entirely of it and, are consequently more ponderous. (1819, pp. 115–16)

Exactly 150 years later, in 1969, in his Presidential address to the Anthropology Section of the Australian and New Zealand Association for the Advancement of Science Congress in Adelaide, Mr Wentworth touched on similar matters, but within a different perspective: one that offered to us by contemplating Aboriginal society on a continental-wide basis and with the bright shafts of prehistoric sunlight beginning to illuminate its vast history. How did people make the minimum 60-kilometre water crossing that existed among the water gaps on the way from Asia? Were the Tasmanian reed boats some last remembrance of the original machines that had allowed woman and man to claim 10 million square kilometres of empty space? Had there been in Australia a technological blossoming 20 millennia ago? Australia, an island and largely isolated, offers the best situation in the world to study a society of man under an economic regime of hunting and gathering, one in which 'humanity has passed most of its existence ... the post-agricultural phase, with its larger units and depersonalised orientations occupying only less than one percent of human history', so that 'if there is an ingrained human propensity for organisation, it must relate to man's experience in that other 99 percent of his time' (1819, p. 6).

In Mr Wentworth's view, in its broadest context the study of Aboriginal society (its economy, genetics, language, music, art and prehistory) 'places upon Australian Anthropology its unique responsibility and makes it, from a world standpoint, by far the most important academic project in Australia' and, furthermore, that 'the loss from the failure to record the facts of Australian Aboriginal life is irreparable. Because of this, humanity may lose forever the best chance of an insight into the forces which guide all human societies; the real nature of men everywhere' (1819, p. 8).

The early men of Saint Germain

In 1753, while walking through the forest of Saint Germain, Jean-Jacques Rousseau sought and found the primitive times, the history of which he proudly traced, the result being his great *Discourse on the origin of inequality among men*, one of the foundational works of prehistory. The first men, said Rousseau, 'wandering up and down the forests, without industry, without speech and without a home', produced a situation where 'every art would necessarily perish with its inventor; and generations succeeded generations without the least advance ... each always setting out from the same point, centuries must have elapsed in the barbarism of the first ages; when the species was already old, and man remained a child' (1753, p. 72).

This brilliant vision, which has been seared onto the European imagination ever since, does however, run afoul of the Second Law of Thermodynamics, since it postulates a cyclical process running through time but returning always to its initial state — a situation never found in nature.

A carnot cycle tour

In every change in a closed situation from one state to the next, there is always an increase in entropy. Entropy measures the amount of unavailable energy in a system. That is, whereas hot and cold water mixed together always results in tepid water, we never get the reverse: a situation of a bowl of water, half of it spontaneously boiling so that the other half freezes. Since irreversible processes are continually going on in nature, energy is continually becoming unavailable for work — what is idiomatically termed 'running downhill'. Entropy can also be thought of as a measure of the degree of disorder, and since a state of order in nature is highly unlikely, energy in Boltzmann's general formulation (Hasenöhrl 1909) is a function of the probability of a given state, a general philosophical concept of enormous scope, as well as formally defined as a law in physics.

Information, the transference of a set of messages — a series of binary choices, one-two, one-two, one-one, one-two, one-one, two-one, etc. — from one centre to another without loss of initial order (what in human terms you might call 'meaning') is a highly improbable situation. The more complex the information, the less probable is its state. Information can be thought of as analogous to negative entropy, a measure of order or organisation, and which in a closed system will always tend to move towards less order and more disorganisation.

Biologists are faced in nature with highly complex living systems, indeed ones which through time have become more complex, not less as expected from the Second Law. They have the dilemma solved when it is realised that entropy like mass can be added or taken away. In an open system, the system itself can lose entropy; that is, become more complex, but only at the expense of a wider universe where the total entropy of system and universe has increased. Eating a steak to power myself to transfer this message involves the degradation of low-entropy chemical energy through to high-entropy heat, which is why I am sweating here to-night! The initial organisation of that chemical energy was, however, bought at the price of a total increase of entropy in the processes of photosynthesis, the digestive systems of the bullock, and so on.

Archaeologists can study energy in the past by analysing middens, converting bone counts to the original animals and hence their calorific value. Shawcross (1967) had the combined shellfish of his Galatea Bay midden powering a Boeing 707 through take-off for a few seconds until it ran out of the shellfish (pipis). In Meehan's (1975) study with the Anbarra Aboriginal community of Arnhem Land, we see the flow of 14 million shellfish from their beds through a human society to power the 35 people for some 7 per cent of their energy needs; and then, like the waste gases of some industrial process, proceeding to a state of maximum disorder as 10 cubic metres of scattered midden heaps on the landscape. This is the stuff onto which we archaeologists must re-impose some analytical order in order to perceive a dim history.

The second half of my title, 'bytes', refers to a unit of computer technology consisting usually of eight 'bits', the basic unit of information: the zero/one, the yes/no of the binary system. But, veracity as usual being sacrificed for art, I have decided to maintain a consistent gastronomic flavour. To make tools requires a body of organised information: ideas inherited from the past, copied from neighbours and transferred to future generations. Archaeologists study changes in the form of ancient tools and from consistent patterns of their shapes in postulating the existence of traditions and cultures. Typology, the study of artefacts, is an analysis of the coherence of the transfer of technological information from one generation to the next. It is a study of entropy.

Chaos

Chaos was the ancient European model for the hunting world. Lucretius 2000 years ago, when imagining the earliest men, said that:

> they lived out their lives in the fashion of wild beasts roaming at large ... stayed their hunger amongst the acorn-laden oaks ... lived in forests and hillside caves and stowed their rugged limbs among bushes when driven to seek shelter from the lash of the wind and rain. Here were no rules governing location and no social constraints. Venus coupled the bodies of lovers in the greenwood. Mutual desire brought them together, or the males' mastering might and over-riding lust. (1951, pp. 219–20)

Such was the cultural memory with which to try and comprehend the vast forests of the New and Pacific worlds with their mirrors of mankind staring back from the edge of the trees.

> Dy gastell ydyw'r gelli,
> Derw dol yw dyrau di.
> Da yw ffin a thref ddinas,
> Gorau yw'r glyn a'r graig las.
> Gwylia'r trefydd, cynnydd call,
> A'r tyrau o'r arall.

So sang the 15th century poet, Tudur Penllyn (cited in Parry 1962, pp. 169–70) to the Lancastrian bandit David Jenkins of the Conwy Valley:

> Your castle is the copse,
> Oaken glade your towers.
> Good the urban edge of cities,
> Better the glen and the shining rock.
> Watch those towns, formal and fat,
> And turrets from inside out.

This verse shows rare appreciation that landscapes can be conceived of in obverse ways, depending on the point of view of the observer. Yet to most travellers on the alien beaches, it seemed as if they were witnesses of primeval anarchy, the natal soup of man.

The process of imposing order on 'tumult and confusion', as Governor Phillip put it, gave no greater satisfaction than when 'a settlement of civilized people is fixing itself upon a newly discovered or savage coast. The wild appearance of the land, the close and perplexing growing of trees, bare rocks, weeds, flowers, flowering shrubs or under wood, scattered and intermingled in the most promiscuous manner' (1789, p. 132).

As with the backdrop, so too with the actors: President de Brosses of Dijon (1967) wrote of Tierra del Fuegians that they were 'without religion or policy or the least regard to decency' and Crozet, remembering the killing of his leader Du Fresne in the Bay of Islands, satirised the 'Children of Nature now so much extolled and praised as having more and less than those we called cultured' as 'within the same quarter of an hour ... chang(ing) from childish delight to the deepest gloom, from complete calmness to the greatest height of rage, and then bursting into immoderate laughter the moment afterwards' (1891, p. 87). We are with the Marquis de Sade's fellow inmates in some ethnographic madhouse, laughing as the oblique iron blade drops at the capricious whim of a Committee for Public Safety.

In Sydney, at Government House in 1811, the convict poet Michael Massey Robinson (cited in Mackaness 1946) declaimed in his 'Ode for the Queen's Birthday' that in Australia over a vast period: 'Nature scarce owned the unproductive waste' and the Aborigines had been:

For Ages Doom'd in Indolence to roam,
The rocks their Refuge and the Wilds their home!
Lost to each social Interchange of Thought,
Their Youth neglected and their Age untaught.

In its moral aspects, this is a view of man without social rules and in its spatial manifestation we have men wandering about without pattern or purpose, like molecules of gas according to the kinetic theory in perpetual random motion. Knowing the number of men within the Australian container and the velocities of their travel, one could calculate the probable frequencies of their collisions that in such a state of disorder would pass for social intercourse. This view of man — *'sans roi, sans loi, sans foi'* (without king, law or faith) — was a postulation of humanity in a state of maximum entropy.

Crystal society

Very quickly after the establishment of the British settlement at Sydney, however, it became apparent to the more perceptive observers, such as Hunter (1793) and Collins (1802), that the movements of Aborigines along the shores of the harbour and past the outlying farms, while irregular in detail, did indeed have an underlying pattern and consistency to them. In Tasmania, that prince of historians, John West, said in 1852 of the by then almost vanished Tasmanians that 'the tribes took up their periodic stations, and moved with intervals so regular, that their migrations were anticipated, as well as their return. The person employed in their pursuit, by aid of his native allies, was able to predict at what period and place he should find a tribe, the object of his mission' (1852, p. 3).

We now realise that Aboriginal society was bound to the land by profound religious ties, that there was and is an intensity of knowledge about place and ownership, resources and their flux through the seasons, such that people who do not live by hunting have forgotten. Only in Australia are we given that overview of the relationship of hunters to landscape on a continent-wide scale.

In his 1953 paper, Birdsell showed that a highly significant negative correlation existed between areas of inland Australian tribes and rainfall. Since tribal populations were normally distributed with a mean of some 400 to 500 people, this meant that Aboriginal population density was roughly related to the rate of primary production of plant material. Despite all the glosses and errors of the original data, this is a profound statement, especially if we add the rider 'and not technology'.

The highest population densities of all were found along rivers and inland lakes, and around that part of the coastline where the land behind is well-watered, so that there are numerous river mouths, lagoons and other wetlands with a high biomass and great diversity of species of plants and animals. These areas were omitted from Birdsell's study because these biological factors were then considered to be too difficult to measure.

Tasmania

For Tasmania I calculated the Aboriginal population density using the numbers and locations of named Aboriginal bands according to field journals of George Augustus Robinson (as analysed by Plomley 1966), together with other information from Péron (1809), Labillardiere (1800) and general estimates of settlers and other scholars. In my opinion, there were some 4000 people in Tasmania and that the basic social and ecological unit was the band of some 50 people (of whom half might have been adult), there being 80 such bands in the whole of Tasmania.

Each band on average had primary ownership of 500 to 600 square kilometres of land, or on the coast they were spaced out every 50 kilometres or so in a remarkably regular pattern. These bands were agglomerated into larger social units that spoke the same language, shared the same material culture and other traits such as art and burial customs. They had a pattern of cooperation, marriage and seasonal movements within, as opposed to non-cooperation and even of enmity without, so that we may legitimately think of them as 'tribes' in the loose Aboriginal sense of the term. There were nine such tribes in Tasmania, ranging in size from 175 to 500, but most of them averaging about 450.

In relating such population densities to resources we have two kinds of ecological zones to consider, namely, the land and the seashore. For each tribe I examined the area of land per person against the length of coastline per person. This calculation showed a strong negative correlation that was significant. With no coastline it took 20 square kilometres to support one Tasmanian, and with no land — that is, purely the strand itself — it took two kilometres to support one person. It appeared that these different resource potentials were added up together, like bricks of two different sizes, to form total units; that is, 'tribes'. These were relatively uniform in final size. Tribes with large inland areas had small coastlines, while those with long coastlines were small in land area. What is fascinating here is that, in terms of spatial organisation, it is as though this society tried to maintain a uniform tribal population as a prime objective.

Add to this Peterson's (1976) demonstration that Tasmanian tribal boundaries corresponded extremely well with some of the major drainage basins, and that other factors such as access to important resources like ochre and shells, or the location of main seasonal travel routes, tended to give, as Tindale once suggested, maximum access with minimum trespass, then in Tasmania we have this beautiful pattern of the integration of cultural imperatives onto a mosaic of land and sea. Yet the crucial point remains that, although human population density is a function of bio-production, the organisation of social groups, as much as possible, conforms to our own template to meet our own social and cultural needs.

Arnhem Land

The same is true of Arnhem Land. The relationship of population density to coastline and area has the same form as in Tasmanian, except that the actual number of people is some four times as great (eight people per kilometre of coast in places), reflecting not only the greater biological richness of this tropical coast but also the more even distribution of resources throughout the year, which is highly important to an economy without much capacity for storing food. This high population density is, however, deployed on the ground in terms of many small units rather than a few large ones. It is reflected in diversity — linguistic, genetic and in kinship terms — not in size.

Calories

A kilocalorie is the heat required to raise the temperature of a kilogram of water by one degree Celsius. On average, a person needs to obtain some 2000 to 2500 kilocalories of energy per day to live. That is more or less the heat required to raise the temperature from 0°F to 100°F of 20 kilograms of water, some 4 gallons.

Relating this to the Tasmanian demographic pattern described earlier, this means that along the coasts the Aboriginal society was extracting energy to drive itself at the rate of 1 kilocalorie per day per metre of coast (say, one fish a year); or, taking the land itself, 1 kilocalorie per 10,000 square metres per day. This is only one part in 100,000 of the total plant primary biomass production.

To calculate the total energy requirements of Tasmanian hunters, we would also have to take into account their use of firewood for heat and cooking which, if it was used at the same rate as amongst the Anbarra of Arnhem Land, would be some 20–30 kilograms per hearth group per day, indicating a figure of the order of some 10,000 kilocalories per head per day. That is something like five times the energy used in the body's internal chemo-dynamic processes. This total of about 12,000 kilocalories per head per day can be compared with the 200,000 kilocalories per head per day of modern industrial societies.

This energy was obtained from killing animals and digging and collecting edible parts of plants. The Anbarra in 1972–73 ate some 120 species of fish, shellfish and crustacea, fifty species of land animals and birds, and fifty to seventy species of plant foods. In terms of calorific intake, shellfish contributed some 7 per cent, fish 24 per cent, the reptiles, birds and mammals some 16–17 per cent, fruits and nuts 2 per cent and vegetables 5 per cent (Meehan 1976). The remaining 40–50 per cent came from carbohydrate foods that were bought from the supermarket at Maningrida, mostly flour and sugar. Before the arrival of Europeans some twenty years ago, the Aborigines said women used to get this fraction from collected vegetable foods. Nowadays they work less hard than they used to. Even so, roughly half of the energy came from animal flesh, and Meehan (1977) thinks that the present fashionable trend towards seeing Australian hunters as largely vegetarian is a gross exaggeration.

Aborigines were to a substantial extent meat-eaters, the Anbarra men, women and children eating over one kilogram of meat per head per day. According to our friend, the Second Law, it is obvious that meat, being higher up the food chain, is less plentiful in absolute terms; however, more highly concentrated, red meat has 3000 kilocalories per kilogram as opposed to shellfish at about 800. To obtain this energy, work must be done. The yield in terms of kilocalories gained per person hour of effort for various targets can be calculated against the probability of success on any particular trip aimed at getting food. These calculations are based on data collected by Meehan (1975) and Jones (1975) with the Anbarra over one year. There is a strong inverse correlation between a high yield and the probability of getting it. Men get those foods that usually require highly athletic activities involving physical power and skill: the difference of a few centimetres in trajectory or a few seconds' hesitation in throwing of a spear can mean no food or a glut. On one foray there may be only one such occasion of opportunity, lasting for just a few seconds. The women, on the other hand, have a lower yield per effort but their work is highly reliable and its yield is almost directly proportional to the effort invested.

The best combination of high yield and adequately high reliability was fishing with fish traps (*an-gujechiya*). These were owned and used by mature or older men, who also had a monopoly of the strategic places on tidal creek banks where the traps could function efficiently. The Anbarra hunting strategy was to combine the two types of foraging: high yield/low probability with those giving low yield but high probability of success. This mixing took place on a daily basis, with people of different sexes and ages embarking from camp on their various kinds of tasks. On average, roughly half the food energy was contributed by men, but their actual work input in terms of hours was much less than that worked by the women. Three types of women's work — collecting shellfish, digging for yams, and the collecting and processing of Cycad fruits (*Cycas angulata* or *C. ngacha*) — gave remarkably similar results, roughly 1000 to 1400 kilocalories per woman hour. Even this, the lowest result, meant that a woman could feed herself with two hours of work per day.

The total amount of food energy potentially available in vegetable food is much greater than in the animals that feed from it and, in the case of the Anbarra landscape, there were several suitable edible plants. *Cycas media* in Cape York, according to Harris (1975), has a potential yield from its kernels of 130 kilocalories per square metre and such trees exist on the eastern bank of the Blyth River as the dominant under-storey of eucalypt forests extending over an area of some 25 square kilometres. These lie within easy reach of the Anbarra and other Gu-jingarliya camps offering enough food there to feed some 5000 people. One limiting factor in the processing of Cycad might be the lack of water during the late dry season for leaching the kernels, but there are other foods such as the spike rush (*Eleocharis dulcis* or *E. gulach*), which forms a dense mass filling in all the prior ancestral meandering stream beds of the Blyth River. In addition to these are Dioscorea yams, the Polynesian arrowroot (*Tacca leontopetaloides*), a species of true rice (*Oryza rufipogon*), some Ipomoeas, possibly taro (based on a single identification) and the trees Pandanus, Terminalia, Eugenia and several palms, all of which are either staples or important domestic foods amongst the horticultural peoples of the coast of Melanesia, the Pacific and parts of South East Asia.

The question as to why the Aborigines did not have agriculture is too vague for investigation, but it can be re-phrased. What were the mechanisms that allowed Aboriginal foraging strategies to reap continually a substantial part of their food from the high-value, high-weight spectrum, meaning that high-labour input was restricted largely to women and even then was kept within reasonable bounds?

It is with the aid of technology that we gain energy from the environment and, viewed as a whole, wandering through ethnographic rooms of museums we are presented with Aboriginal technologies as if they related to specific areas and problems: the nets, the stone fish traps of the Darling River for Murray cod and black duck; the boomerangs and grinding stones of Cooper's Creek for desert euros and the seed *nardoo*; the multi-pronged fish spear and the light spearthrower of Arnhem Land coast as a machine to impale and disable a barramundi, until a fist can be inserted through its gills and its paroxysms stilled by a blow to the skull.

Subtler are the refinements. When the lightwood tree (*Acacia sophorae*) flowers, it is time to go to the Tasmanian islands for mutton bird. On the one day of the year at the end of the wet season in Arnhem Land when the new moon high tides correspond to the last draining of fresh water back to the rivers, the marine Striped Butterfish (*jingol* or *Selenotoca multifasciata*) is plucked from between aerial roots of mangroves by excited hunters; knowing when an arm is fully committed down a hole whether it is a king brown snake or a goanna that one is feeling; tying a spider's web onto a bee's foot so that it may guide the hunter, gossamer like, back to the hive. None of these strategies requires material objects. They are the result of knowledge stored in the brain, not lumps of wood wielded by the hand.

Given that a single type of spear does an effective job, why therefore have five or ten, all slightly differently barbed and named? Why all the variation in clubs and baskets? There is a bewildering redundancy in Aboriginal technology, particularly the technology of men, which cannot be explained in simple ecological terms. A clockwork view of Aboriginal economy is not a sufficient explanation.

An outline of Australian prehistory

Australia is an island and therein is the key to its prehistory. It is not a single island but, rather, an archipelago on a continental shelf dominated by the huge mainland. Yet Tasmania, New Guinea, Kangaroo Island, the Furneaux Group, Deal Island, the Torres Strait Islands and Aru all share a common historical heritage: periodically, during times of low sea level at the height of the last Ice Age, they were all joined into a single continuous land mass. These Australian islands form but the southern half of the greatest archipelago in the world extending 8000 kilometres to the south-east of Asia. However, between the Australian and Asiatic islands are a series of deep sea channels which have not been dry for many tens of millions of years. This great sea barrier blocked the southward thrust of the placental mammals and allowed in relative isolation the continued evolution and radiation of the marsupials. Only rats, mice, bats and humans on their own made this crossing.

However, even the smallest probability of success, given enough time, eventually becomes a certainty. We may have to think of the initial colonisation of Australia in terms of a large number of random and probably accidental aquatic departures from the mangrove shores of Asia, perhaps over a period of tens of thousands of years until finally the right combination occurs. This would comprise a safe journey, two sexes and — if the colonising group is very small, a few individuals only — a great deal of good luck in sex ratios of the children born, the fertility of the mothers and a minimum of accidents over a period of many generations, perhaps hundreds of years, until a demographically viable group is established on the new continent. The first Australians, like most of the first European Australians, probably came here involuntarily.

At least 35,000 years ago and probably considerably earlier, humans had, through a combination of technological advancement and chance, claimed Australia — 10 million square kilometres of empty space — one of the great leaps in the expansion of the human geographical range. Birdsell (1953) has shown that it would have been possible to fill this space with people in a few thousand years, especially if, initially, some degree of differential preference was shown for the better-watered areas first, as Bowdler (1977) has suggested. Certainly, by at least 25,000 years ago people were occupying the entire southern swathe of the continent and, in the opposite direction, at 2000 metres in the New Guinea highlands. Such is the span of time involved that man was the witness of great climatic and environmental changes, even to the shape of the land itself — all aspects of the vast energy oscillations of the last Ice Age.

Some 25,000 to 30,000 years ago on the shores of Lake Mungo, then full of water, we get a glimpse of men and women camping on the beach and catching fish, mussels and crayfish, collecting emu eggs and hunting a range of small marsupials. They use ochre and cremate their dead by smashing the bones and burying them in shallow pits near the camp. Did they also hunt the three-metre-high giant Procoptodon, now known from the work of McIntyre and Hope (1978) to have shared their dunes with them (see also Hope 1978)? Were they indeed responsible to some extent for the extinction of the giant marsupials (some rhinoceros- and bear-sized creatures), which comprised one third of all genera and which had up to then, or a few thousand years before that, lived on this continent? How long previously had their ancestors lived here? Were the people of Kow Swamp a genetic memory of an earlier phase of colonisation from that of the Mungo people? And did the modern Australian race spring from a union between these two groups? These questions, which deal with crucial adaptations of early humans to this continent, arise in the context of a rapid pace of discovery and are obviously beyond the scope of this paper. Their resolution, however, is essential to our understanding of what happened afterwards.

At Mungo, people left their kit of stone tools, consisting of heavy, domed, horse-hoof shaped core tools and scrapers with steep, tough edges, and planes to chop and smooth wood. Some of these scrapers have rounded edges and others are notched — they are perhaps, spokeshaves. Studies on sites as far apart from each other as Lake Burrill on the New South Wales coast and the Dampier Archipelago 5000 kilometres to the west, from Tasmania in the south to Cape York, the Arnhem Land escarpment, and even in the New Guinea highlands in the far north, reveal that similar tools were made throughout the continent and over a time scale of 30,000 years. The 'Australian core tool and scraper tradition' was one of the major technological provinces of the Late Stone Age world, ranking in terms of space and time on the same scale as the European Upper Palaeolithic and carrying information of the same cultural magnitude.

Kangaroo Island has always been a problem in Australian archaeology. It was uninhabited when Flinders (1801) and Baudin (1974) saw it in 1802, yet strange stone tools have been found in its ploughed fields: very large horse-hoof cores and pebble choppers, called 'Kartan industry' by Tindale (1937) and Cooper (1960), who carried out pioneering studies there. Recent research by Lampert (1972) has confirmed the integrity of this industry and has shown that it must date from a period considerably older than 16,000 years, for it has never yet been found in situ. Along with these core tools, Lampert (1975) also found large flat roughly bifacially-flaked objects with a pair of indented waists on opposite sides. These 'waisted blades' as they are called are also found in the 26,000-year-old site at Kosipe in highland New Guinea, and in many Late Pleistocene sites in South East Asia. They show that this ancient Australian 'legacy' industry must be seen as part of a broader province which encompasses also parts of South East Asia, and that the first colonists across Wallace's Line, hazardous though the journey was, brought substantial parts of their technology with them in their minds.

We can trace a lineage from these waisted blades to similar objects where the edges themselves are ground. Typologically similar are hatchet heads of igneous rock, with ground-down cutting edges and again with a waist or groove around their middle. Such axes, found in 23,000-year-old levels in several sites at the foot of the Arnhem Land escarpment, together with typical steep-edged scrapers, were for many years by far the oldest examples of edge-ground axes in the world (White 1975). Similarly-aged ones have now been found in Japan, suggesting that right throughout East Asia a high antiquity for this technique was a general Late Pleistocene development.

Based on the size and shape of the tools and general stratigraphic considerations, Lampert (1975) considers that the Kangaroo Island or Kartan type of industry, especially as now quantitatively defined by him, is either ancestral to or represents the initial phase of the Australian core tool and scraper tradition. This is a re-formulation of what Tindale (1937) said originally. The implication is that it is older than 30,000 years, perhaps much older.

Looking at various assemblages of the core tool and scraper tradition on a continent-wide basis, we can see over a span of 30,000 years what Lorblanchet and I (1979) have called 'direction of the evolutionary trend'. Over time, there is a shift from horse-hoof and other core tools towards scrapers. There is also a shift within the scrapers from the more ad hoc, steep-edged ones to the finer-made round-edged types and the concave and nosed varieties. Thirdly, there is a diminution in the size of individual tools. All these are but different aspects of the same thing; that is, efficiency as expressed in terms of millimetres of edge per gram of material. Millimetres of edge per gram of scrapers, millennium after millennium, slowly and surely increased at roughly the same rate throughout the Australian continent: approximately half a millimetre per gram 30,000 years ago, doubled to one millimetre per gram at 10,000, 2 millimetres per gram at 5000 and maintained its accelerated rate to 4 millimetres per gram 1000 to 2000 years ago (Allen 1972). There is a similar trend in Tasmania over the last 8000 years, but the final figure reached is only about 55 per cent of that achieved on the mainland.

The tools themselves remained the same shape, with their proportions the same, so the tiny domed horse-hoof core scrapers from Burke's Cave in western New South Wales 4000 years ago look like miniatures of the Mungo examples in the same region that are 20,000 years older. The question arises: how was it that cultural information was maintained and transmitted through time, that man fashioned such brute objects of stone to such well-defined average templates of design that the strike of an artisan's hand 10,000 years ago produced an edge twice as effective in terms of unit weight as some ancestor 800 generations before him, and yet only a quarter as effective as his descendants 400 generations still to come?

Archaeology of the Stone Age is crude, yet its message is profound. We are seeing but one tiny aspect of the fundamental discovery of prehistory: that human technology has been proceeding generally in one direction, towards increased efficiency, increased organisation and, in analogous tools, towards miniaturisation. What happened to the horse-hoof cores of the Darling Basin over 30,000 years was simply an ancient manifestation of what has been happening in the last 30 years with our computers.

These tools were but tools to make tools: the wooden artefacts of the chase and the dig. They were multi-purpose, often with different kinds of edges on the same blank. They were designed to be versatile and therein lay their functional robustness. They were effective enough to carry men through the great environmental changes which, geomorphologists and biogeographers are now telling us, occurred during the time under review without having any appreciable effect on their design. Some 20,000 to 18,000 years ago, the lakes of Mungo dried up. At Lake George, the temperature became so low that the evaporation decreased, causing the lake level to rise and the water to flow out at Geary's Gap. There were no trees then, only grassy plains and relentless cold winds from the west in winter that whipped up sand and mantled it on the lee shore. Seventeen thousand years ago mobile desert dunes were active on Kangaroo Island, in western Victoria and in north-eastern Tasmania. So also with the major economic shift in Papua New Guinea, which Golson (1977, p. 154) says gives 'no hint in [the] stone tool technologies of basic changes in substance, from hunting and gathering to agriculture'.

These tools belong to a design strategy Lévi-Strauss (1966) called 'bricolage' —
that is, a handyman's understanding that a single object can do many things with
minimum alteration rather than (as with the contemporary stone-tool strategy
of Western Europe from 30,000 to 10,000 years ago) where for every different
purpose a different object was made. This was a gadget strategy which, although
typologically dazzling, proved in terms of long-term survival vulnerable to the
environmental changes at the end of the Ice Age. These changes were similar in
scope, though slightly different in time, to the ones ridden by the users of the
Australian scrapers. We must not allow the monotony of shape, as White (1977)
has reminded us, to lead us into the trap of assuming inefficiency.

The small tools

Some 6000 to 4000 years ago there suddenly appears, in sequences all over
mainland Australia, a plethora of new stone tools (points, backed microliths
and adzes) that did not replace the scrapers but was added onto inventories.
These small geometric objects with blunted backs suddenly appear all over
southern Australia at approximately the same time. The dates from the east
coast and those from the west near Perth and Dampier are very close. Given
the so far inadequate sampling and inherent problems of charcoal dating or the
possibility of small tools being trodden down into deposits of soft sand, they
are almost archaeologically instantaneous, though 5000 kilometres apart. In
addition, the structures of the industries are very similar indeed, containing
scrapers and the 'little tools' (as Gould 1968 called them), points, backed
blades and small adzes. Three sites in Western Australia, one at Burke's Cave
near the Darling River in western New South Wales, and one on the east coast
are dated to the same time and show almost no differences in assemblages.

In environmental terms, these small backed-blades are found on the beaches
of Bondi (hence the Bondi Point), in the Blue Mountains, west of the Darling
River to the dry saltpans of Lakes Frome and Eyre and beyond, to the coastal
plains of the Swan River and the salty mangrove shores of Dampier Archipelago
in Western Australia. Yet these same tools, possessing such catholic adaptability,
were not found on the east coast of Queensland, the desert region of Tennant
Creek, rich Arnhem Land or in Western Australia along the north coast of the
Kimberley. Why, if so efficacious along the southern half of the continent, across
almost the entire range of Australian environments, are there not analogues of
them in the north? We could argue the same for the points which are found
in northern Australia from Arnhem Land right down the Centre to the south
coast, but not east or west; small adze slugs are found in the Centre but not on
the coast — and so on.

Microliths were set in gum onto a handle as elements of composite tools.
They mark, not as Mulvaney (1961) had originally postulated, the introduction

or invention of hafting in Australia, but as Dickson (1976) pointed out, a new technique of hafting, holding the bit securely in its handle in a bed of gum allowing a much higher pressure to be exerted on a much smaller stone than can be done if held by the fingers alone, or even in a thong made from a vine. In terms of efficiency, these tools allow (through successive re-sharpening of, for example, the adze flakes) a much greater amount of cutting at high pressures to be done from a unit weight of stone than with hand-held scrapers. They increase the efficiency improvement curve I have discussed earlier.

In other cases, however, it is difficult to see how their performance was better than the tools they replaced. As Peterson (1971, p. 53) pointed out many years ago, a wooden spear is just as penetrating as one tipped with a stone point. Furthermore, it does not shatter so easily if the throw misses its target. If backed microliths were so efficient, why did they disappear from the New South Wales inventory over the past 2000 years?

To make these small tools, new sources of excellent raw materials were sought, and these materials (cherts and chalcedonies) were carried and traded scores and sometimes hundreds of kilometres from quarries to places of manufacture. Local materials such as quartzite continued to be used for the scrapers. Mulvaney's paper in *Tribes and Boundaries* (1976) contains relevant examples of such trading networks, and it may be that these expanded in association with the appearance of the small tools.

Mulvaney (1976) has characterised these changes as marking a period when Australian society was 'quickened and transformed'. These transformations can probably be seen in art and disposal of the dead, two of the few aspects of intellectual and religious life capable of being investigated directly by archaeological methods. In Pleistocene Australia, as in Tasmania throughout its prehistory, the dead were disposed of according to what Hiatt (1966) and Meehan (1971) called 'simple disposal'; that is, through cremation or inhumation or perhaps abandonment. In all cases, the act of disposal was a single activity that took place more or less on one occasion, presumably soon after the death of the individual. By contrast, compound disposal involved many different activities, often separated by long periods of time, and required not only the co-operation of many individuals but the maintenance of those links over time for performance of ceremonies, which lay at the very core of the Aboriginal religious system. Meehan (1971) has argued that archaeological evidence for compound disposal is restricted to the period of the small tools, and, indeed, that examples of such tools are found in the same layers as the funerary evidence. New data from Broadbeach (Haglund 1976) in Queensland, and Roonka (Pretty 1977) in South Australia, provide profound demonstrations of the association.

In Arnhem Land the components of a spear not uncommonly originate in widely-separated locations. The stone tip comes from a certain quarry, the gum from a forested area some distance away, the binding from the coastal hibiscus plant, the ochre from a mine perhaps 100 kilometres away in one direction, and white clay from 20 kilometres away in the opposite direction. The stone, wrapped in paper bark from a swamp, has travelled along a trade route from one person's curatorship to another's and may be used in men's secret ceremonies. The spear has this in common with compound disposal: in both cases, what previously could be carried out by one person, or a small group within a short period of time in one location, is transformed into the cooperative work of many people, who are separated in time and space. They both mark the same phenomenon: that there has been a transformation of the organisation from simple to complex, that entropy has been reduced and that, consequently, the amount of available work put into the system has been increased.

Tasmania

To reach an understanding of Australian prehistory, we must turn to that brooding island to the south, Tasmania. At the height of the last Ice Age, some 24,000 years ago, the sea had dropped sufficiently to expose a salty and dry road to the southern mountainous peninsula. Traces of human occupation of the Bassian plain have been found on its high hills, still above the sea now on Erith, Flinders, King and Cape Barren Islands (Orchiston & Glenie 1978; Jones & Lampert 1978). By 23,000 years ago, people were camping in Cave Bay Cave on Hunter Island, and we have evidence from several sites in Tasmania for human occupation there in glacial times. Tools were of stone and bone, typical of the Late Pleistocene Australian core tool and scraper tradition, and people carried over with them other aspects of that cultural tradition, such as cremation of the dead and art style motifs. Their art (geometric motifs and tracks) is found at Mount Cameron on the north-western coast of Tasmania.

With the later melting of the ice the sea rose, and 12,000 years ago the Tasmanian part of Bass Strait between Wilson's Promontory and the Kent Group was cut off from the Australian mainland. Men situated on the southern side of this rapidly widening strait were then doomed to the longest period of isolation of any people ever recorded in history. Between Australia and Tasmania lie large blocks of land, some with mountains 700 metres high, that never became flooded. These could have supported between 300 and 500 people. Yet when Matthew Flinders saw them they were empty of people and their works. Archaeological research on the islands of Bass Strait indicates the absence of shell middens on the present shore and no sites younger than 8000 to 6000 years old. This suggests that no *significant* relict group was left behind, stranded on the islands. These islands were abandoned when the water crossing to Tasmania became too dangerous.

We have then a situation where groups of the same order of size as a modern Tasmanian tribe made a conscious decision not to be split off from the main bulk of the slowly retreating population. My analysis here is that wherever the seasonal movements of bands of a tribe were cut off or the straits became too difficult to negotiate, the people themselves decided to relocate on the larger or higher of the two pieces of land being severed. By being unwilling to divide their perceived minimum acceptable social group, they consigned a total of some 10,000 square kilometres of prime coastal country, both in actual and symbolic terms, to the domain of the dead.

Kangaroo Island is a marginal and subtle example of this same process in action. Meticulous fieldwork by Lampert (1972) has shown that some half a dozen sites on this island date from 8000 to 3000 years ago, thus postdating its separation from the mainland (Lampert pers. comm.; cf. Clark and Lampert 1981, Appendix 1, based on an unpublished paper given at the 48th ANZAAS Congress, Melbourne 1977). Do these represent the tenuous hanging on of a slender strand of humanity, never bigger than a few families or a band, its lines of culture and genes stretched taut for thousands of years, like a spider escaping a predator down a long sliding thread until its snaps because of the whims of cruel chance? Or, as I feel was the case, do we have here an example of an island not quite big enough for people to stay on it and thus abandoned at its severance from the mainland; yet close enough (14.5 kilometres) to receive over thousands of years the odd random human visitor or refugee?

A few months ago on Steep Head Island, less than one square kilometre in area, the mutton bird yield for six weeks work was 107 kilocalories, enough to feed fifty people for one year. On the Bass Strait islands, there were plenty of calories but not enough bits!

Tasmania was big enough not to be abandoned by its human population on its severance from the mainland, but in cultural terms its inhabitants paid a penalty for their separation in two ways. First, they were cut off from the developments on the continent in mid-recent times — no small tools and associated cultural richness, no dogs. Secondly, during their long stay away from the rest of the world, there was a steady loss of technology, a diminution of foods eaten and a constriction of the intellectual matrix. What a terrible fate! Of the things lost in Tasmania somewhere between Pleistocene Australia and the 18th century AD, we might infer the concept of hafting, of edge grinding axes, boomerangs, barbed and composite spearheads. We might explain these reductions by reference to a general theorem that the number of ideas is proportional to the number of minds interacting or, on a more general note, that a closed system will, according to the terrible Second Law, move always towards increased entropy and reduced coherence. This has been the fate of all isolated island groups. Cassels (1984) has argued that the distribution of domestic animals in Oceania is better explained by their tendency to go extinct on small and remote islands than by their failure ever to have been brought there by humans; and the same, he says, applies to pottery (within the limits of its spread). A similar process happened on the island of St Kilda, until one day half the population decided to move to a place on Port Phillip Bay.

Entropy increase is the fate of all isolated human systems. This is the profoundest message that Tasmanian prehistory can give us. Here in Tasmania, with the longest isolation we also had the simplest technology of any known human group. Yet there remains a paradox: despite the vast quantum of difference between the technologies of 18th century Tasmania and the Australian mainland, the absolute numbers and the organisation of Tasmanians and Australians on the ground, in similar ecological areas, were within the same order of magnitude. What therefore was the role of the basic toolkit of the Tasmanians? And what was the role of that elaboration on the mainland subsequent to the separation of the two blocks of land?

I appreciated Lourandos' (1977) important paper in *Archaeology and Physical Anthropology in Oceania*. He showed that population densities in the western districts of Victoria are much higher than in Tasmania. (You could also show they are much higher than, say for example, on the southern coast of New South Wales.) He has also shown that the population of western Victoria is similar to those in the tropical north.

In Tasmania there is one fundamental absence: the great religious ceremonies, the elaboration of dance and art, the convolutions of the mortuary process, and the lack of designs engraved onto the objects of the chase. Here there are no vistas of hundreds of men acting out vast allegorical plays, no songs in the night under a full moon that control half the hunting capacity of the society for months, no times when the entire society is engaged in the consummation of a single act at the very core of its intellectual creative and emotional energy, an act which reverberates through relationships, tools, ideas and social needs over an area of thousands of square kilometres. These things are here in Tasmania but in a terribly attenuated form, like a coastal pine tortured and bent against its growth by the wind.

Jim Allen has asked the rhetorical question: What was it like to be a Tasmanian, knowing your world was finite and knowing about every other person in it? Perhaps there had even been a loss of cultural memory that another world had ever existed, so that it seemed their small finite universe consisted of the entire limit of mankind.

I have tried to quantify the size of the Tasmanians' social matrix. The total number of potential face-to-face contacts of adults in Tasmanian society during an annual cycle of seasonal movements, as calculated using all the possible combinations of one against one, was some 300,000. This is the same number as all the handshakes of everybody shaking hands with everybody else in a room containing 650 people. This is the total maximum potential social matrix in Tasmania, year after year and millennium after millennium. If the total number of different face-to-face contacts — 10 to the 3rd, 10 to the 4th, 10 to the 5th — is plotted against different sorts of organisation of 1000 people, a long curve is produced. If you have 200 groups, each one like a family, separate, in space, then calculate all the face-to-face contacts of five people against one another; or you have 20 groups of 50 people, or you have five groups of 200 people (which in the Tasmanian situation is the maximum), or you have 1000 people, which is what Lourandos (1977) has shown for western Victoria (and is also partly the case in Arnhem Land), keeping 1000 people solid, the total of face-to-face contacts rises in an exponential curve.

There is an exponential relationship between the internal organisation of a single, total-sized group of people and the total number of possible one-by-one combinations. The genius of Aboriginal society was to invent a system of intensification which, while allowing the population to remain more or less constant, invested the necessary energy gained by technological development into an internal re-organisation that satisfied the higher needs of the intellect, art and religion. This lies at the very crux of our understanding of Australian prehistory.

Such a re-organisation or intensification of organisation, which involved bringing the maximum possible number of people together in one place for a socially significant period of time, was powered in a number of different ways. Seasonally rich and locationally concentrated resources were exploited, as was the case with the Bogong moth in the Snowy Mountains (Flood 1973), with elements of tribes coming together from hundreds of kilometres east and west. Sometimes such resources did not occur every year but intermittently, as is the case with the Bunya pine of south-eastern Queensland (Sullivan 1977).

Technological investments were made in the construction of structures or machines which enabled a lot of food to be captured at one time and place: the stone fish traps of Brewarrina in western New South Wales, woven fish traps of the tropical estuaries, the earth dams in western Queensland and, most fascinatingly, the kilometre-long ditches and associated traps for facilitating the movement, catching and perhaps even breeding of eels, which Lourandos (1977) has demonstrated for western Victoria. All of these required cooperative action by many people and forward planning to make the device 'now' for some future time. There was nothing of this planning in Tasmania.

Macrozamia nuts, leached and baked, were the carbohydrate staple all down the east coast of Australia. A similar product from the related *Cycas armstrongii* grows in Arnhem Land and is so identified with the staff of life that its name in various dialects — *ngacha* or *ngathu* — is also the name for all carbohydrate food and the slang name for European flour and bread. Current work by Beaton (1977) has pointed out the terrors of this plant in its unleached form: it not only causes what is called 'zamia staggers', a paralysis of the central nervous system in cattle, but is also probably the greatest cancer-forming agent known in the natural world. There is no question of a gradual adaptation to the use of this plant. Once the detoxifying technique is acquired, however, the yield in terms of Aboriginal requirements is almost unlimited, being a function only of the work invested. Beaton (1977) has found husks of Macrozamia right to the base of rock shelters in the southern Queensland highlands, back to about 4000 years. These are associated with backed microliths and other small tools, and the deposits mark the first substantial and general occupation of the region. Beaton's (1977) theory is that knowing how to treat Macrozamia enabled large numbers of people to congregate periodically in this previously rather intractable area; and that the associated microliths and the exotic raw materials from which they are made are, in a sense, just the debris of communication, symptoms of the enlargement of the social network powered by Macrozamia.

Meehan and I could see all these processes at work between July and August of 1972 at the great camp at Ngalijibama near the mouth of the Blyth River (Jones & Meehan 1989, pp. 123–24). On this sacred ground a small number of men initiated a Gunabiba ceremony, their numbers swelling to hundreds at the climax, including representatives from most languages on the north coast of Arnhem Land. Women were responsible for feeding this multitude. Shellfish were gathered on some 70 to 80 per cent of days, compared to only 55 per cent in the later domestic dry season camp (Meehan 1975). Women working eight hours a day gathered, de-husked, dried, smashed, leached, ground and, finally, baked the *ngacha* bread from Cycad. This process produced an average of 1400 kilocalories per woman hour. Some women produced 45 kilograms of bread in four or five working days. Men not engaged in the ceremony dug the wells in which the *ngacha* was leached, and also engaged in low-key activities such as fishing with hooks and lines.

The main limitation on the annual yield of cancer-free bread was a shortage of water for leaching purposes in the late dry season. Manpower could have been invested in the construction of dams for the storage of water from the wet season surplus, or even the building of aqueducts from the freshwater stretches of the Blyth River, only 15 kilometres away. Because this was not done those people (mostly women and some men who for a few weeks or months had laboured like agricultural peasants) were released from their voluntary bondage. The men, having fulfilled their religious obligations, returned to society and shifted the centre of gravity of the chase back to what it had been prior to the ceremony. The frequency of shellfish gathering dropped and *ngacha* became a rare delicacy, like pieces of a wedding cake.

Rousseau (1992) said that:

> so long as men undertook only what a single person could accomplish and confined themselves to such arts as did not require the joint labour of several hands, they lived free, healthy, honest and happy lives. But from the

moment one man began to stand in need of the help of another; from the moment it appeared advantageous to any man to have enough provisions for two, equality disappeared, property was introduced, work became indispensable and, vast forests became smiling fields, which men had to water with the sweat of their brow, and where slavery and misery were soon seen to germinate and grew up with the crops.

In the ecological world an Aboriginal man could [and can] do all things: get his foods, make his tools. He is self-sufficient, yet in the religious world he can do on his own almost nothing. In the world of the intellect he has defined himself into a system of reciprocal inequality. Here is an intensification that did not lead to degradation or a diminution of resources. It was an intensification that did not lead to tyranny.

The Wahgi Valley

A year ago I would have finished at this point. However, recent discoveries by Golson and Hughes (1977; Philip Hughes, pers. comm. 1977) have altered our whole interpretation of Australian prehistory. In the Wahgi Valley in Papua New Guinea, dominated by mountains rising to some 3000 metres, they have found deep in a swamp a large ditch that they have traced over some half kilometre of its length. It is two metres wide and a metre and a half deep. This ditch is well dated to 9000 years, and Hughes thinks it must extend another one and a half kilometres to an outfall at the Wahgi River. Associated with it are other structures, again dating to 9000 years, almost certainly indicating the horticulture of taro. This was a drainage ditch of huge scale that deflected water away from the swamp.

This complex system must have required a much longer period of adjustment before arriving up in the mountains. Indeed, Hughes (Golson & Hughes 1977, p. 20) has argued that there is very little possibility that it could have arrived there before because of the Ice Age. We do not know how long horticulture has been practised in New Guinea, but soon after the ditch had begun operating, there is evidence of clay washing down from the hills of the swamp catchment as a result of classic Brandwirtschaft or slash-and-burn cultivation. Here we have evidence of coordinated horticulture, probably based on the imported plant, taro.

What does this mean for Australian archaeology? At the time these drainage ditches were constructed in the Wahgi Valley, there was a substantial land bridge linking northern Australia to New Guinea. Aboriginal people were living on the plain that was then the northern part of Australia, and in New Guinea there existed a fully-functioning taro-producing horticultural system.

In Australia, we have for a very long time been able to shrug off the problem of why horticulture did not occur here: the continent was isolated, the plant did not come across because of the sea. However, at the time of the Wahgi Valley developments, 9000 years ago, the same situation as this existed in the Fertile Crescent in the Middle East. The archaeological problems associated with having a range from full horticulture through to hunters in the high altitude regions are precisely the same for Australia as for the Middle East and Europe. The question then has to be formulated: Did horticulture, and all that it meant in terms of a different style of intensification, not come to Australia because of ecological factors, because we lie south of the closed tropical rainforest? Is it a situation just of time, that is, as intensification was about to sweep across, sea levels rose and saved Australia, as if the sea had made the Bosporus too wide for boat crossings? Or do we already have within this continental landmass the distinctive Aboriginal contribution to history: a method of increasing its social intensification that does not lead to a degradation of resources? As we observe Tasmania on a larger scale, this is probably the most important thing that Aboriginal history has to tell us.

Acknowledgments

This lecture was delivered by Emeritus Professor Rhys Jones (then Dr Rhys Jones) in 1978, while he was a Research Fellow in the Department of Prehistory, Research School of Pacific Studies, Australian National University. When he died in 2001, he was Emeritus Professor in the same department, which by then had been renamed the Department of Archaeology and Natural History, Research School of Pacific and Asian Studies. Unfortunately, he never revised it for publication. This text has been prepared from good original drafts, research notes and a transcript of the spoken lecture by Betty Meehan, with a great deal of help from Dr Les Hiatt, Emeritus Professor Jack Golson, Emeritus Professor Erich Weigold and Ms Barbara Lewincamp and other AIATSIS staff. Every effort has been made to keep the text as close as possible to the original and no ideas contained in the original lecture have been knowingly altered.

References

Allen, HH 1972, 'Where the crow flies backwards: Man and land in the Darling Basin', unpublished PhD thesis, Australian National University.
Baudin, N 1974, *The journal of Post Captain Nicolas Baudin, Commander-in-Chief of the Corvettes Geographe and Naturaliste, assigned by order of the government to a voyage of discovery*, translated from the French by Christine Cornell, Libraries Board of South Australia, Adelaide.
Beaton, JM 1977, 'Dangerous harvest', PhD thesis, Australian National University.
Birdsell, JB 1953, 'Some environmental and cultural factors influencing the structuring of Australian Aboriginal populations', *American Naturalist*, vol. 87, pp. 171–207.
Bowdler, S 1977, 'The coastal colonization of Australia', in J Allen, J Golson & R Jones (eds), *Sunda and Sahul: Prehistoric Studies in Southeast Asia, Melanesia and Australia*, Academic Press, London, pp. 205–46.

Cassels R 1984, 'The role of prehistoric man in the faunal extinctions of New Zealand and other Pacific islands', in PS Martin and RG Klein (eds), *Quaternary extinctions: A prehistoric revolution*, Arizona University Press, Tucson, AZ, pp. 741–67.

Clark, R and Lampert, R 1981, 'Past changes in burning regime as markers of man's activity on Kangaroo Island, South Australia', *Terra Australis*, vol. 5, pp. 1–86.

Collins, D 1802, *An account of the English colony in New South Wales, vol. 1*, Cadell and Davies, London.

Cooper, HM 1960, 'The archaeology of Kangaroo Island, South Australia, *Records of the South Australian* Museum, vol. 13, pp. 481–503.

Crozet, JM 1891, *Nouveau voyage a la mer du Sud*, Truslove and Shirley, London.

de Brosses, C 1967, *Histoire des Navigations Aux Terres Australes*, Da Capo Press, New York.

Dickson, FP 1976, 'Australian ground stone hatchets: Their design and dynamics', *Australia Archaeology*, no. 5, pp. 33–48.

Flinders, M 1801 *Observations on the coasts of Van Diemen's Land, on Bass Strait and its Islands, and on part of the coasts of New South Wales*, John Nicholls, London.

Flood, JM 1973, 'The moth-hunters', PhD thesis, Department of Prehistory, Australian National University.

Golson, J 1977, 'No room at the top: Agricultural intensification in the New Guinea Highlands', in J Allen, J Golson & R Jones (eds), *Sunda and Sahul: Prehistoric Studies in Southeast Asia, Melanesia and Australia*, Academic Press, London, pp. 601–38.

Golson, J & Hughes, P 1977, 'Ditches before time', *Hemisphere*, vol. 21, no. 2, pp. 13–21.

Gould, RA 1968, 'Living archaeology: The Ngatatjara of Western Australia', *Southwestern Journal of Anthropology*, no. 24, pp. 101–22.

Haglund, L 1976, *An archaeological analysis of the Broadbeach Aboriginal Burial Ground*, University of Queensland Press, Brisbane.

Harris, D. 1975, *Traditional patterns of plant-good procurement in the Cape York Peninsula and Torres Strait Islands: Report on fieldwork carried out August–November 1974*, AIATSIS, Canberra, pp. 32–61.

Hasenöhrl, F (ed.) 1909, *Wissenschaftliche abhandlungen*, 3 vols, Leipzig.

Hiatt, LR 1966, 'Mystery at Port Hacking', *Mankind*, 6, pp. 313–17.

Hope, J 1978, 'The late Pleistocene and Holocene vegetational history of Hunter Island north-western Tasmania', *Australian Journal of Botany*, no. 26, pp. 493–514.

Hunter, J (1793), *An historical journal of the transactions at Port Jackson and Norfolk Island,* John Stockdale, London.

Jones, R and Lampert, RJ 1978, 'A note on the discovery of stone tools on Erith Island, the Kent Group, Bass Strait', *Australian Archaeology*, no. 8, pp. 146–9.

Lévi-Strauss, C 1966, *The savage mind*, University of Chicago Press, Chicago.

Jones, R & Meehan, B 1989, 'Plant foods of the Gidjingal: Ethnographic and archaeological perspectives from northern Australia on tuber and seed exploitation', in DR Harris & GC Hillman (eds), *Foraging and farming: The evolution of plant exploitation*, Unwin Hyman, London, pp. 120–35.

Labillardière, M 1800, *Voyage in search of La Pérouse*, John Stockdale, London.

Lampert, RJ 1972, *A preliminary report on some waisted blades found on Kangaroo Island, South Australia*, Flinders University, Adelaide, viewed 20 June 2015 fat <http://dspace2.flinders.edu.au/xmlui/bitstream/handle/2328/200/1975002045048_final.pdf?sequence=3>.

Lampert, RJ 1975, 'Kangaroo Island', *Australian Archaeology*, no. 3, p. 39.

Lorblanchet, M & Jones, R 1979, 'Les premieres fouilles à Dampier (Australié occidentale), et leur place dans l'ensemble Australien', *Bulletin de la Société Préhistorique Française*, no. 76, pp. 463–87.

Lourandos, H 1977, 'Aboriginal spatial organization and population: South western Victoria reconsidered', *Archaeology and Physical Anthropology in Oceania*, vol. 12, no. 3, pp. 202–25.

Lucretius, 1851, *Lucretius on the nature of things: A philosophical poem*, trans Rev. John Selby Watson, Henry G. Bohn, London.
Mackaness, G 1946, *Poets of Australia*, Angus & Robertson, Sydney.
McIntyre, ML & Hope, J 1978, 'Procoptodon fossils from the Willandra Lakes, Western New South Wales', *The Artefact*, vol. 3, no. 3, pp. 117–32.
Meehan, B 1971, 'The form, distribution and antiquity of Australian aboriginal mortuary practices', PhD thesis, University of Sydney.
Meehan, B 1975, Shell bed to shell midden, PhD thesis, Australian National University.
Meehan, B 1977, Hunters by the seashore, *JHE*, no. 6, pp. 363–70.
Mulvaney, DJ 1961, 'The Stone Age of Australia', *Proceedings of the Prehistoric Society*, no. 4, pp. 56–107.
Mulvaney, DJ 1976, *Tribes and boundaries in Australia*, AIATSIS, Canberra.
Orchiston, DW & Glenie, RC 1978, 'Residual Holocene populations in Bassiania: Aboriginal man at Palana, Northern Flinders Island', *Australian Archaeology*, no. 8, pp. 127–41.
Parry, T 1962, *A history of Welsh literature*, trans HI Bell, Oxford University Press, Oxford.
Péron, F 1809, *A voyage of discovery to the Southern Hemisphere, performed by order of the Emperor Napoleon, during the years 1801, 1802, 1803 and 1804*, Richard Phillips, London.
Peterson, N 1971, 'Open sites and the ethnographic approach to the archaeology of hunter-gatherers: Aboriginal man and environment', in DJ Mulvaney & J Golson (eds), *Australia*, ANU, Canberra, pp. 239–48.
Peterson, N (ed.) 1976, *Tribes and boundaries in Australia*, AIATSIS, Canberra.
Phillip, A 1789, *The voyage of Governor Phillip to Botany Bay: With an account of the establishment of the colonies of Port Jackson & Norfolk Island*, John Stockdale, London.
Plomley, NJB 1966, *Friendly mission: The Tasmanian journals and papers of George Augustus Robinson 1829–1834*, Tasmanian Historical Research Association, Hobart.
Pretty, GL 1977, 'The cultural chronology of the Roonka Flat', in RVS Wright (ed.), *Stone tools as cultural markers*, AIATSIS, Canberra, pp. 288–331.
Rousseau, J-J 1992 [1753], *Discourse on the origin of inequality among men*, Indianapolis, IN: Hackett.
Shawcross, W 1967, 'An investigation of prehistoric diet and economy on a coastal site at Galatea Bay, New Zealand', *Proceedings of the Prehistory Society*, vol. 33, pp. 107–31.
Sullivan, H 1977, 'Aboriginal gatherings in south-east Queensland', BA (Hons) thesis, Australian National University.
Tindale, NB 1937, 'The relationship of the extinct Kangaroo Island culture with the cultures of Australia, Tasmania and Malaya', *Records of the South Australian Museum*, vol. 6, pp. 41–60.
Wentworth, WC 1819, *A statistical, historical and political description of the colony of New South Wales*, G. and WB Whittaker, London.
West, J 1852, *The History of Tasmania, vol. 2*, Dowling, Launceston.
White, IM 1975, Sexual conquest and submission in the myths of Central Australia', in LR Hiatt (ed.), *Australian Aboriginal mythology*, AIATSIS, Canberra, pp. 123–42.

Original lecture available at:
<http://aiatsis.gov.au/publications/presentations/calories-and-bytes-towards-history-australian-islands>

2

Looking ahead through the past

1982 Wentworth Lecture

Ronald M Berndt

Foreword

LR Hiatt

In 1959 Mr WC Wentworth prepared a document entitled 'An Australian Institute for Aboriginal Studies'. Inspired partly by UNESCO developments overseas, it argued for a comprehensive and coordinated effort by the Australian Government to record for posterity what remained of the culture of the Australian Aborigines. This objective, Mr Wentworth believed, was probably the most important specific task currently facing Australian scholarship. If it was not undertaken immediately, he said, 'humanity will lose something of permanent value and we Australians, as its custodians, will lay ourselves open to perpetual reproach'.

Mr Wentworth's initiative led to the establishment of the Australian Institute of Aboriginal Studies by Act of Parliament in 1964. I have no doubt that when, in 1959, he identified 'we Australians' as the custodians of Aboriginal culture, he was referring primarily to European white Australians. That would have been the enlightened concept of the times. Few could have imagined then, that twenty odd years later the Principal of this budding Institute, and the Deputy Chairman of its Council, would themselves be of Aboriginal descent. Nor would it have seemed credible that the concept of custodianship, as epitomised by the Institute, might become a rallying point for Aboriginal dignity and pride, and a source of hope for a future in which the achievements of the first inhabitants of this country would be regarded not just as subjects of scientific curiosity but as objects of genuine admiration.

This, in fact, is how it has turned out, and the first to acknowledge and applaud it would be that most progressive of Australian citizens WC Wentworth. The Wentworth Lectures were inaugurated in 1978 to pay tribute to his vision, and simultaneously to bring to a wider public the findings and viewpoints of scholars eminent in particular fields of Aboriginal studies.

This is the third Wentworth Lecture, the first having been given by Rhys Jones on Australian prehistory, and the second by Margaret Valadian on Aboriginal education. My duty tonight in introducing the Wentworth Lecture for 1982 is a pleasant but quite unnecessary one. Professor Ronald Berndt needs no introduction from me or anyone else. He is undoubtedly the foremost living authority on the social and cultural life of the indigenous inhabitants of Australia. In collaboration with his wife Catherine, he has published works on all aspects of the subject on the basis of their firsthand experience of Aboriginal communities in various parts of Arnhem Land, and the Northern Territory, Western Australia and South Australia. Their writings are standard references at all levels of teaching and research from primary school to postgraduate scholarship, and in all parts of the world where there is an interest in the Australian Aborigines. It is a massive and unprecedented achievement in Aboriginal Studies and one unlikely to be repeated.

*****

It is an honour of which I am deeply conscious to have been asked to give this third Wentworth Lecture, as one of the ritual features of the Australian Institute of Aboriginal Studies' biennial meeting. I do not know just when Mr WC Wentworth — that incorrigible backbencher, as he then was — had his original vision of a national body which would be dedicated to Australian Aboriginal research. We first met Bill in 1958 when he discussed with us what he had in mind. I must admit that initially we thought his vision to be simply that — idealistic, but no more than a pipedream. Yet that was in those far-distant pre-ABINST days, which I may be excused for characterising as an anthropological age of innocence. The plans were, however, one product of his fertile imagination which, happily, led to positive results, in the face of some opposition and a great deal of indifference. How far the emerging reality coincided with what he had seen in his vision is another matter. That is for him to tell us. What is more immediately relevant to us here is that quality we call imagination. In a sense, this is the underlying theme or implication of my talk, taking 'imagination' as what the Oxford Dictionary calls a 'creative faculty of the human mind stimulated by and inseparable from enquiry'. I don't mean simply 'curiosity'. Curiosity can be a trigger, or an incentive. It can provide motives for enquiry, prompting questions about who and when and how and why. However, enquiry implies a more or less systematic follow-through, going beyond mere curiosity rather like the contrast between a preliminary hunch and a serious investigation.

The 1961 Conference on Aboriginal Studies which preceded the formation of the Institute was concerned with collating and assessing previous research in this field, in order to plan what needed to be done next. The Conference tried to look ahead through the past as a guide to action in the future. All people, everywhere, are bound to their own past in one way or another, and to some awareness of that past; and it is this perspective, perhaps more than others, which qualifies them to be regarded as human. Both Alfred Radcliffe-Brown and (long before his anthropological articulation) Australian Aborigines recognised the social value of the past in the present: not the past per se but particular elements of that past, including the inevitability of change. Wentworth, drawing on evidence from the past, had the imagination and ability to conceptualise an approach which looked ahead to the future. That was not done without enquiry. A basis must be established if imagination is to take successful flight.

Throughout the course of my fieldwork and anthropological writing, two primary aspects have interested me. One is the issue of innovation in Aboriginal society. Very early in my first research period at Ooldea, I rejected the view that traditional Aboriginal life was static, with little or no room for flexibility or innovation. Of course, cultural imperatives did limit the range of opportunities for both of these, but were present nonetheless. Imaginative ingenuity was, and is, manifested most obviously in the field of the arts, and not only the visual and dramatic arts. It is conspicuous in myth and song, especially in terms of variations on specific themes, which in turn are linked to familiar surroundings or familiar situations and interests.

Think of the deep concern for land among Western Desert people. Many of their verbal and non-verbal comments on life are expressed in relation to country and to the natural environment. Yet that apparent simplicity masks considerable complexity. In north-eastern Arnhem Land, in contrast, complexity is much more visible (and audible); and, continuing the theme of people and their environment, in western Arnhem Land hundreds of myths and quasi-historical accounts and contemporary warnings about the Rainbow Snake suggest that people were victims of an almost unpredictable fate or destiny and there was little they could do about it. This view has been borne out by the impact of the massive uranium mining in that region. Such themes, and many others, have not been adequately explored anthropologically, although some beginnings have been made. If they were considered in conjunction with attempts to identify particular cultural style, or ethos, they could reveal interesting insights into how members of Aboriginal societies traditionally saw themselves and how they envisaged the meaning of life. It is within this area of endeavour that Aboriginal imagination flourishes: imagination as opposed to fantasy, which is so often confused with it.

The other complementary aspect concerns the general issue of enquiry. The questions people ask, and how they ask them, and with what expectations, provide an evaluative grid that should help us to understand a people's adaptation to changing circumstances.

Asking questions

Aborigines did not live at one of the cross-roads of the world, and only fairly recently were they subjected to large-scale alien intrusion. This meant that, on the whole, they had to rely on what was available within their own continent, and especially within their own regional zones of interaction, including their range of trade and exchange and religious linkages. In other words, they themselves were mostly responsible for their own civilisation; they had to rely more on themselves than on others. Because of the nature of the environment, particularly in less fertile areas, personal and social security were matters of major concern. Up to a point, everything else had to be subordinated to them. Consequently, enquiry in a more general sense was at a minimum. It would have been risky to ask too many open-ended or change-oriented questions, because the structure of consensus was, and had to be, upheld if the way of life that had proved more or less satisfactory in the past was to continue to be so in the future. Superficially, all this is true. Yet it is a half-truth and as such has engendered such comments from teachers as 'Aboriginal children just don't ask questions'. Knapp (1981, p. 6) quotes statements to the effect that 'Why'-type questions were discouraged in traditional contexts. That assumption (false, in my experience) led to a more far-reaching claim which postulates cognitive differences or differences in modes of thinking between Aborigines and (for example) Europeans. As Knapp notes, if there really are any such differences, they are over-emphasised. The issue, of course, is not a cognitive one (not in relation to what can be called deep-seated differences in the processes of thinking) but a social one, and is a matter of culturally-based differing premises.

When discussions take place between traditionally-oriented Aborigines and outsiders, Aborigines have sometimes shown a lack of sustained curiosity about the outside world, except in regard to individual persons, or scenes that link with their own experiences. Concern for their own affairs and their own local interests seems to discourage broader enquiry outside their own areas of direct experience. Yet this is a special case. The problem is one they perceive as being relevant to themselves, having a bearing on their own lives.

In the give and take of everyday living, especially in northern areas, questions are an accepted part of conversation and discussion. It is, therefore, more about whether people ask questions than the type of questions, and the expectations they may have about obtaining answers and the kind of answers elicited. The most common questions are those which are expected to bring a more or less immediate response; for instance, where so and so is to be found, the identification of particular things and persons, and other matters of practical concern. Even if people already know, or think they know, the answer, this in itself is not a deterrent to asking.

Some myth and song-sequences provide conventionalised examples. At the mythological level, in the great Dja 'gau song epic of north-eastern Arnhem Land, one of the characters, the 'stooge', Bralbral, continually asks questions of the two Sisters and the Dja 'gau Brother. I take a few of lines from each of two songs belonging to the 188 that make up the Yirrkala version I recorded in 1946–47. For example:

> What is that, waridj, before us?
> Drag the paddles, rest the paddles.
> There before us, waridj Bralbral,
> That is the morning pigeon, [calling out] as it saw
> the darkness clearing.
>
> na digam waridj adjil
> *danar wariyuwa danar uyu*
> adjil ali waridj bralbral
> *da um djigaina druban na al...*
>
> Primary singer Mawulan, Riradji u *mada, dua* moiety
> (R Berndt 1952, song 22, p. 76).

And:

> What is this, waridj Dja 'gau?
> That crying, waridj [from the sacred tree],
> that is a parakeet,
> Murmuring, red breast feathers gleaming [in
> the sunlight].
>
> *na digam waridj dja ' gau*
> adi duwanma waridj dwibim-manalri
> ulugdun-nanyin gwoyum in dalwarara ...
>
> Primary singer as above (R Berndt, 1952, song 33, p. 97)

This stylistic device in the song cycle permits information about the travels of the mythic Dja 'gau to unfold at the level of action rather than description. There are many such instances of this. For example, in one *dua* moiety bushfire song sequence in that region, a singer asks, 'Who lit that fire?' 'Who set the grass alight so that the flames sweep across the face of that country?' And he answers these questions himself, singing their names: 'It is the spirit people of that country, always there, looking after it ...' (C & R Berndt 1971, pp. 56–7). The answers are straightforward, even though they allow symbolic allusion to be revealed. Nevertheless, these responses are circumscribed, and already known. They resemble *ex cathedra* statements that do not ordinarily provoke additional queries and are designed as final answers. Apart from practical matters, most answers are of this kind. The reasons are obvious, in that such discourse takes place within a closed system and is essentially conservative.

However, there do seem to be examples which allow an element of speculation to appear. 'Gossip' songs in western Arnhem Land provide such an avenue, at two levels. At one, interpersonal events and attitudes are revealed in song, while listeners try to identify the characters involved. At the other level, within the content of a song, the unnamed character himself or herself asks questions, not necessarily expecting a reply.

In the following example, although a man sings, the speaker in the song is a woman.

> Good, good, [is] his [body] ...
> I long for him.
> Oh, where has he gone, my own one?
> If only I could see him returning,
> I would be happy! Ah!
>
> *gunmag gunmag nuye*
>   arowerowe nuye
> *a a bale'nug adug wam*
>   anayi gumbebmenin
>   awanmag-niwerin a a
>
> > Mariwa singing by 'Singlet' Miilil a Gunwi gu (book 14, song 60, 13 March 1950).

Next, again a woman speaks in the song, although the singer is a man.

> Where are they camping now?
> They're making a travelling-camp at Ma arubu.
> Day after tomorrow they'll be returning!
> *bale'nug bolgimi gabiriyu*
> *gabiriwo'yu ma arubu*
> *malewi-bwiyiga gabirimdunde*
>
> > Guri singing by Paddy Bull (Wogiman 'tribal' origin), in Gunwi gu (book 9, song 19, 4 February 1950)

These are very simple examples. Nevertheless they indicate that, apart from the question that is asked, there is an incipient element of speculation which goes beyond — but not too far beyond — the ordinary process of observation and comment.

There is a danger in making such an assumption, especially when we consider Western Desert song productions. For instance, the following six songs, from Balgo in the eastern Kimberley, come from part of a *di ari* cycle which begins in the west and moves across the country to the east. In mythic context, it concerns Djilgamada (Echidna), who has stolen secret-sacred *darugu* boards from a Diyari ritual group (see R Berndt, 1970, pp. 226-7); here, *Di ari* are following Djilgamada's tracks to recover the *darugu*. The spears referred to in the songs are really *darugu*. The first six songs are sung in the main camp.

(a) Di ari lighting their way as they walk [at night], with firesticks.
(As they go along, the *Di ari* kill small creatures with their *darugu*.)
(b) Carrying bundles of spears.
(c) Carrying spears across their shoulders,
(d) Spear bundles rattling as they walk,
(The *darugu* rattle together.)
(e) Spear bundles knocking against the trees,
(The Di ari are angry because branches knock them.)
(f) Moving through patches of bloodwood trees.
(They name the various trees.)

(a) di arindi djinindi-nindila wuna-djundju ara
(b) yalwePu gulimanu gulada gulada
(c) gandjuma gandju-bundju ura gulada-yalindjara
(d) djilbarin-djilbarindjara
(e) djugu djugubu u yalweru yalinbana
(f) birlmadji waru-warula djalidjali birlmadj waru-warula
     Di ari cycle, Balgo (R Berndt, songs 1 to 6, 15 March 1960).

While such songs appear to be explicitly descriptive, they are actually just as cryptic as the more elaborately structured Dja 'gau songs. At face value, a song of this kind makes sense in its direct meaning. It does have other things to say, but these cannot be anticipated unless the wider context is known, as well as the particular clues necessary for interpretation. One point is clear. Speculation rarely enters into this kind of picture because the clues are conventional. With 'gossip' songs, speculation is not so formally limited.

Directions in inquiry

In Arnhem Land, more obviously than, for example, in the Western Desert, there were more opportunities for interpretation than speculation or, to put it another way, for variations on well-known themes. This was a recognised activity, and did no violence to established convention and literary style. Therefore, it allowed some scope for what we can call a traditional breakthrough. Opportunities were more circumscribed in song poetry than in the telling of stories, recalling historical events, or reporting contemporary ones, where there was more room for manoeuvre.

 The first real insight I had into this process was when I recorded hundreds of dreams at Yirrkala in 1946–47 and at Oenpelli in 1950 (see R Berndt 1980, pp. 285–7, 290–91). By the time I became interested in these, I already had a reasonably good knowledge of symbolic representations expressed through song cycles and in ritual. Such symbolism was readily identified by knowledgeable men and women. In north-eastern Arnhem Land, songs included different words that could refer to the same phenomenon or creature. These could imply different levels of meaning; and labels such as 'singing words', sacred (in contrast to ordinary words of everyday speech, and so on) were in common use.

One set of problems that interested me was how interpretations were made (that is, on what basis), how were they justified, and, importantly, the degree of personal involvement of the singers. One thing that concerned me was the conceptual separation of social structure from the ongoing process of events, and the interrelationship of these two dimensions, as keys to understanding more clearly how internal changes were taking place. Looking back on this, it is obvious to me that several important implications were involved. One I already mentioned was the continuing significance of the past for the present and for the future. Another was that a step forward had been taken by the people themselves, not as something imposed on them by an outsider, such as an anthropologist: a step forward from direct interpretation to an intellectual appreciation of ideas. Although such a procedure is not equivalent to a systematic enquiry, it nevertheless points in that direction. Within the realm of knowledge, this assumes a development of great importance. While dreams led me to that assumption in northern Arnhem Land, it is quite possible that, for example, the 'travelling cults' and different *di ari* traditions of the Kimberley could do, or would have done, the same.

It will provide some indication of what I have in mind, and for this purpose I have chosen two versions relating to a similar theme, from the *Dja 'gau* cycle, which I recorded at Yirrkala, Milingimbi and Elcho Island at different times and from different dialect-speakers. These concern the great mythic scene which dramatises an important statement about role reversal between women and men. In the beginning, the Dja 'gau Sisters — and by extension, all women — possessed unquestioned authority to organise all major ritual sequences and to be custodians of all secret-sacred emblems. Men gained that authority by subterfuge, and for all time. This momentous event is mirrored in other Aboriginal areas (see C Berndt 1965, especially pp. 265–81). The first example here is one song and the lines are numbered. This was sung at Yirrkala by Mawulan (see R Berndt 1952, p. 232–3). I begin with the general translation. This translation has been slightly altered from the one originally published. Also, many of the words included here are in sung, not spoken form.

> 1. We move quickly, hips swaying, shaping the landscape with the point of the *mawulan* emblem ...
> Carefully, buttocks swaying, filling our bags [baskets] with shellfish...
> We move quickly, with the aid of the *mawulan*.
> We [must] go to look at our things — the long cry of the *djunmal* bird warns us, maybe the fire has burnt them ...
>
> The younger Sister speaks:
> 5. Yes, yes, yes, Sister, we'll go and look!

Looking ahead through the past

Hurry, indeed, go and look!
Not here, Sister! Everything gone [the sacred bags] that we left hanging here!
Only that tree, the claypan tree, is standing alone!
Hurry, quickly, with the aid of the *mawulan*, hips swaying, shaping the landscape. They must have fallen, burnt in the fire.

The elder Sister speaks:
10. Yes, Sister, truly, they must have fallen!
Quickly, run fast to look for our bags ...
They must have gone, burnt in the fire. Nothing, Sister!
Here inside are these footprints — our Brother Djag'gau and the *galibiyu* novices, *they* may have taken them!

15. Hurry, pour the shellfish from our bags on to the glowing coals [of the fire]
But why did they take our sacred bags, leaving only the shellfish?
Pour them on to the glowing fire, the smouldering claypan wood ...
We leave them, to look for our sacred bags ...
Why did they take them from us, like [children] playing?

20. We move quickly with the aid of the [*mawulan*] emblem, prodding the ground, we drag it along

The younger Sister speaks:
Yes, Sister, truly, we'll ask them — why did they take them? Why do they act like [children] playing?
Why didn't they ask us? Why did they do it?
Our [sacred bags] — they came sneaking and stole them, quietly, without asking!
Where is the sacred shade? There, Sister, on the wooden posts, hanging within the shade...

The Dja 'gau Brother speaks:
25. [Coming] quickly, with the aid of the *mawulan* — truly, [our] Sister[s]!
Hurry, young Brother!
Get those clapping sticks [says the Dja 'gau Brother]? They are coming closer!
Those sticks, clapping them carefully, rhythmically beating, sound echoing from the mouth of the shade ...
Singing, clapping the sticks, from the sandhill mound in the sacred shade
30. They are coming close! Hurry, start the *nara* ritual, make the sound of the roaring sea, waves breaking and splashing.
For those two are coming closer!
Clap the sticks fast, make the sound of the roaring sea, of waves breaking and spraying.
Carefully, make the sound of the roaring sea, for the sacred *ra ga* people who came from the transverse fibre of the uterus-mat ...

Clap the sticks fast, rhythmically clap them!
35. They hear it, they're coming closer! They slacken their pace as they hear it, young Brother!
They can knead the cycad nut for us, whitening their hands, carefully [kneading] — it is proper, that way!

The elder Sister speaks:
Oh, stop, Sister! What's happened?
We'll get down in the mud, crawling along!
We leave it for them, for our younger Brother(s), it's proper that way.
40. We shall knead the cycad nut for them, for our younger Brothers(s).
We'll whiten our hands, kneading carefully — it is proper that way ...
With our hands we'll hold the stone, crushing the cycad. We'll hang our fibre bags from our foreheads, collecting foods ...
We leave the ritual for them, carefully, it is proper that way.
Yes, yes, Sister, truly, we shall whiten our hands with cycad nut, grasping the transverse fibre of our uterus-mat, our sacred shade.

1. ah anagan naru a lamindjuna dawalyi-yarbum dawalyi-yaralman djina gai duldjiyuldji
   uwargay galanyimbduwa dareyuma
   ali aragan gurundun naru a
   ali galag-naman ali gan da um an wigara adin bayi -bai'eid ragaran an nunu baya-da aldun da ulda

5. yu-yu-yudamu yaba ali naman-yudun
   gaidju hi na un-galag
   aganbai yaba baiir un gwoyumam ug gwayumun
   unam darbam wo gainna daya djulumbal mal umbam
   gaidju araga gurundun lamindjun dawalyi-yarbum bi an da aldu-wan-yul um da ulda

10. yu yaba bugudjil i bi baya-galag yubduwan
    gaidjuwala maramia- aria gaindjaryu-yuduwa anal bi badjiwi
    an baii unan da aldun-da ulda
    baii un yaba
    djina alin gumbuwanin da um nugum dja 'gauwun galibi un milwumbuwan

15. gaidju djulu'yuwan dambal guldwililwi djambala rindjareilil
    bill nalbian danal alin milwumbuwan ganagan
    djulu'yuyuwa daenbal eiawiral male umbal djulumbal
    ganagan ali naman badjiwum gundau'marauwum
    bana-danal ali gu wogai-yuwun- aidj

20. ali aragan narur a guruduna guna ei-yarbum guna a-wariyun
    yu yaba bugudjil i ali danalin gwumbun bana danal wogalyuwun- aidj
    bana-wari alin danal da agara dawuldji

ali gu yululdjiwaram gayulma a g'dunda- ara yumara
ala djarbulma gwoyum unawei balman-balman gwoyum unamu yawu-
lyawulma bal'marayum balman-balman gwoyum yaba

25. araga gurundun djoii yaba bugudjil i
gaidju yugulyuma
maia an-banyadi u da u galgidina
da umgai bilmi - uram bilman bildji-wuldjin uwarga liwa da a djarbul a
marag-maragduwa djinala a dunarwolabu- ara a balimar a unamu a

30. galgidina gaidju muriyuwan guluwu an gulgayu galara an
bili dubal da u galgidina
maramia muriyuwa gabun yaguma wuluwu yambarwo an ia
gulgayu-galara
uwarga muriyuwa malararei u malararagu gwoiii yandal-yandal
malawul-malawul
buyuwoi wogulwogulwi
maramia liwa bilma duwan bilma ura

35. dubal ama da u galgidina dubal ibaliyuldun ama duwan yugulul
dubal ali gu damar gadan-go lurayamir uwargarga -manmu
wai yaba nafan
alim naru galgian dambal gawul ali galyu a
baia an galag- uwarga -mana gudayan

40. alim darnar a gadan dubali gu gudawul
alim galag go duriyabmii uwarga min
bana gor an galag alim woadjuruman damar a alim danali gu badji-war-
iyuna arlgan gadan dul ayuna
baian bana- uwarga an ali gwumbuwan
yu-yu yaba bugudjil i alim galag gon luraya- iyin da um gadan boyum
wogulwogulna yelagandjan

                      Riradji u *mada* (dialect), Yirrkala (R Berndt, song 140,
                                                book 28, 7 April 1947).

This song is longer than most in this cycle, which are all rather long when contrasted to those in other parts of north-eastern Arnhem Land. For the second example, we have a Milingimbi version of the Dja 'gau given by Djunmal and Yilgali (both Liagalawumiri *mada, dua* moiety). The events pertaining to the theft of the sacred dilly bags, treated in one song in the Yirrkala version, are expanded to five songs in this Milingimbi version.

The two Dja 'gau Sisters speak:
Song 1. We hang our things, our sacred bags, on the sacred trees [posts of the sacred shade]
We go down for shellfish, many different shellfish [named] …

Song 2. We heap them up as we go. Here we heap them up [carelessly], mixing them
The elder Sister speaks:
I think of my things, my sacred bags there — someone may take them!
From among the white mangrove roots, we collect [shellfish]...
We leave the shellfish, we move along quickly.
Maybe they've taken our things.
Those *wo ar* men of the Feathered Armband, of the Feathered String, of the Eye ...

The two sisters speak:
Song 3. We hear that bird speaking, that blackbird...
We hurry along, hips swaying, with our sacred [*rnawulan*] poles.
We [must go and] see our feathered string bags, our sacred emblems...
Like a spirit, it warned us, that *djunmal* bird.
Here is the tide flowing in, bubbling, the pleasant sound of water.

The younger Sister speaks:
Quickly, hurry! Where have they taken them?
Who starred this fire, burning along? Maybe they were the ones!

Song 4. These are the tracks, maybe, of those who took them ...
Wo ar men of the Feathered String, of the Eye, of the Feathered Armband
Our red-feathered strings, our sacred belongings.

The leader of the men speaks:
Song 5. We took them, the feathered armbands, the feathered bags and the emblems, they are ours!
You will walk by the water, for us \...
You are not to look at [your emblems], I'll keep them; for you are women, I am a man!
You are not to come near our sacred shade;
You, close your ears, hold them, you're not to hear! I've taken over from you!

The elder Sister replies:
And the sacred rock ... ! I shall make many people. Good! I will collect food.

1. ah al'maram ra gain giwilildja dial duga gurum darba ur mara ada ur djuda ur ali yawalgduna meibalgu dudjumu walawun bunjbu ma au dugureigu badjimuru u
gagar ma algur.

2. ali durbmaram-mardji maibalndja dibal ali nirban-nirban wa gain manaban
bili aragu marnabunan bala woral una badin-djau'yun
lugubi djabalawi eialuwirawoi mal umbalwi
duwali ali ganana ali mardjin bundin

bala ayi djau'yun lidjala
mayilwara guliguli wongidjdu geialwal uru mil ani ai

3. alin duwal waragan wor an gawudalbudal
ali bundin lamindjuna ali gaman
ali badin nama giwililna ra gan dagalgalbinalwi djuribirin bili i-lidjalain
mali galabu al djunmalyu gawudalbudal gawul
duwal ayi gabu urudun bulbulyuna maralbindjuna
bundi gaindjaryun wunan bili walal djau'yun
yoldu nara-mardji gurda bala mag urunudi

4. duwalna waialwul mag-dia -djau'yur
guliguli gaialwal urwi mil ani awi wongidjdu buralgi mil ani ai
ganbalaidjna
lidjala yiriyirin gunbug'gun guliwona guligulin gundamarain yanayanan

5. bili anabur djau'yuna ganbalaidjna giwililndja yiriyirin ra gain guli-wonain anaburu oina
numainralna anabura gin
yaga numadu naman aiadamduga bili mialg ni duwali arain diramun
yaga nidu guwaidjman araburin
nindu budurun mandain aiadamamir yaga nidu ama
aradu yub'maraman nu u
manbun manburuwoina araindu malabumd mainmag araindu ralmina

Liagalawunuri mada, Milingimbi (R Berndt, book 24,
songs 85–89, 12 May 1950).

In comparing the two song versions, it is obvious that the structure is very similar in each case, but the content varies a little. More information is given in the Milingimbi version, and extra details, but there is also a different emphasis. I should say that the songs as they are read present what we can call a manifest meaning; as they are sung and heard by Aborigines they are dense with latent meaning. In these two versions we have a mythic account which explains and justifies contemporary male–female relations in religious and economic terms, plus interpretation that provides an insight into the nature of human behaviour and the place of men and women in the natural order. I would also hold that this is a further process exemplifying a conscious intellectual approach to the realm of ideas.

Like all forms of language, songs communicate messages which have to be understood; otherwise, they don't perform the job for which they are designed. In Aboriginal Australia, effort was not knowingly wasted in this or in other activities, so that what was conveyed had to be explicable to the listeners. Certainly, not everyone was expected to know all the meanings, symbolism and allusions involved. The message for a number of listeners could well be, in some circumstances, 'This is something you don't understand. You understand the circumstances and the general relevance of these songs, but that's all.' Or, 'You don't understand these yet …' Or, 'You know about one level of meaning, but you realise also that there are other levels, which we know and you don't.' And so on. Such understanding rested, traditionally, on the processes of socialisation in a particular community, including information about how religious knowledge and action were both compartmentalised and complementary.

This aside, such songs demonstrate that song poetry is, within a certain range, dynamic, flexible and subject to personal (and social) treatment. Provided a story has coherence and conforms with cultural expectations regarding content, it does not have to adhere to rigid rules about word-for-word accuracy. It is not a question of 'whose version is right?' because all usually are, if designed for local hearers and not for alien consumption, in which case liberties outside local cultural taste may be taken with it. What can be said about these songs may also be said about others, and about the great heritage of oral literature which is current in Arnhem Land as well as in other parts of Aboriginal Australia. While all this is an example of the past being used for the present and future, the major point is how such processes reveal the realm of ideas. In recognising this, we draw closer to understanding Aboriginal intellectual treatment of such material. Is it possible to see in this a kind of enquiry, in a relatively systematic way, tempered by aesthetic considerations?

External enquiry

Much enquiry in Aboriginal Australia was far from being systematic, from both Aboriginal and outsider points of view. In my experience, traditionally-oriented Aborigines involved in early contact with strangers were fascinated by what they took to be basic differences between those strangers and themselves, and curious about what they regarded as strange or unusual behaviour. In 1939 and 1941, the Aborigines who were still coming south across the Great Victoria Desert into the Ooldea mission settlement and to the transcontinental railway line had not seen or interacted with Europeans before. North-eastern Arnhem Landers were (in 1946) quite blasé in this respect, perhaps because their earlier curiosity had been satisfied by Indonesian contact, and later by the presence of an air force base at Gove during the Second World War. They already knew the answers, or thought they did, and had little need to ask questions.

The people coming in to Ooldea did not know what questions to ask, and by the time they learnt enough of outside affairs to frame meaningful questions, it was almost too late. Yet within their own setting, they were moderately interested in people who inhabited areas outside their own 'country'. (I use 'country' to indicate a stretch of land wider than is implied by the current term 'homeland'. I speak here of areas where mobility was limited and strangers, Aboriginal or otherwise, were rare.) Usually, they had information (mostly speculative) to impart about these other people, often disparaging, highly discriminatory, and not necessarily based on observation. They were apt to regard strangers living outside their own known country as being almost non-human. And they often spoke of themselves as 'people', or human beings, and all others as something quite different.

From the standpoint of any one Aboriginal community, Europeans who came to this land of 'others' behaved and thought in this respect very much like the Aborigines, but much more assertively. Europeans, too, regarded those 'others' (in their case, Aborigines) as non-human; but, unlike the Aborigines, they did not follow the precept of 'live and let live'. Or rather, if they did, it was 'live and behave in our terms, or do not live at all!' How consistently this principle was adopted is well documented in our Australian history. What comes as a fresh shock is the attempted vindication by Patricia Cobern (1982, pp. 32–3) of Australia's classic example of the systematic virtual extermination of the 'traditional' Tasmanians, in spite of the overwhelming evidence to the contrary. Rather than elaborate on what she said, pernicious as it is, I quote her two last lines: 'My research has shown that the only massacres that were carried out were those on white people by the natives. The killer that stalked the Tasmanian Aborigine tribes was the traditions and customs of the race, its face was not white.' Although her article could well have been said or written 50 or 100 years ago, in differing contexts and in different words, it was published in 1982! In one respect this Tasmanian statement does not diverge too markedly from Blainey's thesis in his *Triumph of the Nomads* (1975, p. 228). Although less bluntly put, for Blainey, too, the dice were loaded for the Aborigines long before the 'Sails of Doom' appeared on the horizon (see R Berndt 1978, pp. 530–3).

These claims are a deliberate or careless distortion of the past. They are designed, perhaps, to 'whitewash' and redefine the course of past events, to justify European actions and European settlement of this country, and to ease any feelings of guilt that non-Aboriginal Australians might have about those earlier happenings. Such a stance goes along with an essentially negative attitude toward Aboriginal culture, however much this is concealed under what appear as positive comments in the Blainey study. The negative assessment is much more obvious in the Tasmanian example. Also interesting is the way Cobern has written about Aborigines. It is little different from many accounts by European settlers, who were often meticulous in describing their own life and activities but hopelessly biased and ignorant even when referring to Aboriginal behaviour observed at first hand.

There are obvious pitfalls in trying to compile a social history of Aboriginal life from the reports of untrained observers, who usually evaluated what they saw through their own cultural vision and limited understanding. The result has been some almost incredible misrepresentations. The errors are compounded when ethnographic material is taken out of context and misinterpreted. Of course, not all of the early reports were of this order. Many included instructive insights into Aboriginal society and culture, yet these were rare. Up to the days of Baldwin Spencer and Herbert Basedow, and even a little later, they were the ethnographic forerunners of anthropologists. Nevertheless, Aborigines did not really speak through the voices or writings of outsiders until the advent of professional social anthropologists. Some time afterward, however, the Aborigines began to speak directly to the outside world through their own voices, and were heard.

Speculation and casual observation were with us from the commencement of European settlement. Yet enquiry in a systematic fashion, heralding *relative* objectivity came only slowly — and has struggled for its very existence, even within anthropology. Nevertheless, it has achieved outstanding results that are not adequately recognised. One has to remember that for a long time professional anthropologists were very few in number. Moreover, professional anthropology, from the time of its inception in Australia (in 1925–26: see R & C Berndt 1981, p. 539), concentrated on Aboriginal research within a broader comparative frame. In fact it was the only discipline which did focus on Aboriginal research, apart from occasional ventures by some others. My point here is that, although Australian anthropological research was carried out in a number of areas within and outside this country, by far the most substantial part, in aggregate from 1925 onward, related to Aboriginal Australia. Detailed information about many Aboriginal cultures was being accumulated, and, importantly, the way this was done differed considerably from how it was done in the past. Through improved techniques and methods, including working through local languages, it became possible to draw closer to Aboriginal reality. Moreover, through the analysis of material collected, a greater understanding could be reached about the nature of Aboriginal cultures: how they functioned, and something of people's underlying interests and motivations. Much depended on the training of the anthropologists concerned, and on other factors too: for example, how well they could cope with cross-cultural situations, their personalities, and the degree of their commitment to the research. Other things being equal, what we may call a scientific approach was directly in contrast to anything which had been operative within the contexts of traditional Aboriginal societies.

One point needs to be made quite clear. Studying Aborigines, like studying any peoples, does not depend or being Aboriginal or non-Aboriginal. There are advantages and disadvantages in physical and cultural identification between the person studying and those being studied. The colonial experience simply adds another dimension to this more general issue. Certainly, a fully-socialised participant in a particular society could be expected to know a great deal more about its everyday running than an outsider. However, without appropriate training, he or she would not be able to carry out the tasks usually associated with an anthropologist. Such research is, or should be, a collaborative undertaking, with Aborigines participating along with research workers. Ideally, it has always been like this, and still is. Ideally, also, Aborigines themselves should be research workers, trained as anthropologists, working either among Aboriginal people, or in other situations, in Australia or elsewhere. In any circumstances, personal involvement on the part of an anthropologist is a natural and realistic outcome, unless the anthropologist is a machine-like creature intent only on extracting information for his or her own purposes. Fortunately, this is not too common. It is a good thing that the interests of anthropologists and their co-workers, in this case, their Aboriginal colleagues and teachers, should converge. Nevertheless, this must be counterbalanced by the research worker being able to stand to one side from time to time and examine what he or she is doing in a broader perspective. There is some truth in the statement that outsiders, persons not immediately involved, can see most of the game; and, certainly, social systems are not necessarily explicable in their own terms.

Having said this, I should add that social anthropologists have not been very adept at coping with change, less so than Aborigines themselves. They have, of course, along with others, written a great deal about changes taking place in Aboriginal Australia, but often this is a matter of documentation rather than analysis. The reasons are obscure, but may have something to do with not coming to grips with variations, and trends toward innovation, in traditional Aboriginal society itself; not recognising, for instance, that several versions of a myth, song, ritual performance, an ordinary event and so on can exist simultaneously and all be correct.

There is also the problem of particular information being recorded by one anthropologist at one point in time, and then enquiries being made by another anthropologist about the same material at another time, producing a different account from the first. Whose version is correct? Comparisons of this kind are made frequently, and have been the cause of much heartburn, if not controversy. It is often a personal affront to learn that another anthropologist has found what you have recorded to be different from what he has recorded at another period. Your immediate response is likely to be that the other person must be wrong, you yourself are right. Sometimes this is undoubtedly the case. Just as frequently, however, there is a lack of willingness to acknowledge that 'times have changed', that particular information has been given a different emphasis, or simply that there are different ways of looking at an issue. Perhaps the most obvious examples refer to delineating land ownership and usage. Yet times have not always changed so radically; and even if they have, there is likely to be some continuity of theme that can be readily identified.

Providing information

Traditionally, Aborigines did not lead a hand-to-mouth existence, living one day at a time. They looked ahead and planned for the future. There is plenty of evidence for this: in religious rituals, especially those concerned with species renewal; in betrothal and marriage arrangements; and in everyday domestic affairs (see C & R Berndt 1978, pp. 41–60). They drew upon information from the past in their approach to environmental management, and to the ideals and actualities of relationships between people. Interpretation of the past in the light of present circumstances helps people to predict, at least roughly, the outcome of future events. The intergenerational flow of information was of vital concern, and was regarded as an inbuilt assurance that their way of life would be carefully perpetuated. This information flow was found wanting when the nature of alien impact became obvious, and when time-honoured solutions were applied but proved inadequate. Additional information was needed, though this need was not always recognised. Mostly, the necessary information was not forthcoming. If it was, it usually took a form that could not be readily understood, or was downright misleading. This is how things were at the onset of alien settlement. And, to some extent, this is how things still are today.

The fact that this situation has not radically changed for very many Aborigines has meant that, especially in outback areas, they are forced to rely on their own resources, while coming to realise that their own intellectual frontiers are narrowing. In traditional settings, this means that there is a growing scepticism, and not only among young people. One consequence is a hardening of conservative views and a greater reliance on past precedents not necessarily applicable in changing conditions. In some areas it has taken the form of a closing of the ranks; for example, an accentuation of religious secrecy. In others, the response has been more outward-looking. The people involved in the Elcho Island (Galiwinku) 'adjustment movement', of the late 1950s and early 1960s posed questions and attempted to answer them. The primary intention of its leaders was one of conscious re-formation, or reorganisation. In contrast, the *djuluru* ritual of the eastern Kimberley, at least in its ritual manifestations known to me, was widespread and syncretic. It sought to come to terms with alien elements by placing them within a traditional setting. Much of the information used was incomplete, and in the process was re-digested and reinterpreted but nevertheless regarded as stating eternal 'truths'. Certainly, it has or had the function of creating a protective screen, providing a feeling of security against a potentially hostile world, one not of their own making yet capable of transformation into manageable and known dimensions. That such an institution may be based on inadequate information and misinterpretation, with little opportunity for people to check if they wanted to (and most do not), creates a kind of artificiality. For the people of the particular area I am thinking of, Balgo, who are surrounded with mining ventures, there is little doubt that today they are more vulnerable than before, and than they need to be.

In a rather different setting, urban and in country towns, Aborigines were, in the early part of their history, faced with the cumulative disappearance of their traditional, lived-in present, which rapidly became their traditional past, very much in the background. It was replaced or integrated with non-Aboriginal materials, within the context of the policy and practice of assimilation, and reframed to accommodate to their own social demands, or those imposed upon them. For them, there were rather more opportunities to check the inflow of information. The upsurge of Aboriginal identity that became apparent in the early 1970s was far more relevant to urban than to 'traditional' Aborigines, who had been able to maintain continuity with their traditional past. Yet this development provided an opportunity for information to flow back to Aborigines generally. The ethnographic reservoirs of anthropological knowledge were available, but Aboriginal access to them was limited. The question was how to use them in practical terms, how to transform them to a level of practical communication.

Information flow is vital. Put simply, information obtained in the course of social anthropological research in traditional and urban-rural Aboriginal settings is increasingly believed to be directly relevant in contemporary circumstances, and should flow back into these settings. There are, however, several difficulties. First, most detailed ethnographic information has been obtained at times different from the time of its anticipated return. When it does flow back in that form, it re-enters an area under changed conditions: and its re-integration can pose problems. Second, as far as non-traditional Aborigines are concerned, their interest in such material has to do with a generalised view of Aboriginal cultures rather than with a specific Aboriginal culture — although there are some who want to know about their own particular culture (when it is identified), which is no longer a living reality. Often their own background of knowledge depends almost entirely on 'memory culture'. That is, it comprises either information which has passed from one generation to another by word of mouth or what can be gleaned from indifferent and often inaccurate sources about Aborigines. This involves a kind of re-education, in contrast to re-absorption, as is the case with Aboriginal people raised in an actively continuing traditional setting.

It is important to recognise the highly complex nature of the information referred to here, especially where it concerns the question of feedback. Where processes of re-education and re-absorption are to be taken into account, probably a major issue is what form(s) it should take, what kinds of information, and in what degree of detail. The likely return flow of anthropological materials is minor when compared with the overwhelming impact of all sorts of non-Aboriginal materials, including those purporting to be Aboriginal. I am thinking here of the mass media and the schools. We must also take into account the multitude of European advisers, consultants, lawyers, tourists, welfare officers, government agents, school-teachers and so on, all of whom are caught up in the communicatory game.

The constant flow of information into Aboriginal communities far exceeds what comes out of them. Because of this truly overwhelming situation, virtually uncontrolled, or uncontrollable, it is no wonder that the normal receptivity of Aboriginal people becomes choked and often blocked; no wonder that resistance builds up, and many Aborigines consciously adopt a closed and negative or self-protective stand against all this. If they did not do so, if they did not set up metaphoric filters through which such information can flow, 'mental indigestion' would inevitably follow — as has been the case in a number of examples I know.

I would regard two channels as primary: one is the anthropological channel and the other comprises the information-exchange systems operating over wide areas through face-to-face contact (that is, the informal or 'grass-roots' approach) between Aborigines, which has been effective since first contacts. In both of these, Aboriginal receptivity is at a maximum, so we must take seriously the content of such information, because the future social incorporation of Aboriginal Australians depends on it.

Schools

The tapping of anthropological resources is most notable in our schools. Early school texts were notorious, either for the misinformation they supplied about Aborigines or their failure to refer to Aborigines at all. They are only gradually being replaced by more informed views. There are also school 'kits', which are focused on particular Aboriginal societies or on particular culture areas or regions. Some of these are good. Probably one of the most ambitious is the series edited by Williams and Fidock (1978 onward) on north-eastern Arnhem Land. Such kits are not intended solely for Aboriginal school use. Ignoring, however, non-Aboriginal usage, it is interesting to speculate on the likely results of information feedback of this kind through a school system that differs from traditional systems of teaching and learning, into the same community from which it originally came (and where, ostensibly, the same material is a part of the living culture). In a sense, depending on the period of time during which such texts may be used, and the degree of receptivity on the part of the schoolchildren, along with the proficiency of the teacher, we are faced with two simultaneously effective guides for action. One, in the schools, is relatively static. The other relates to an ongoing society, subject to changing directions, with some degree of flexibility built into it, and some expectation of improvisation. Issues of cultural lag, cultural survival, and conflicting values are inherent in the presence of two such differing models, however closely they may seem to converge. Further models are being advocated within the Aboriginal context, as people continue to cope with non-Aboriginal contact.

These problems are not peculiar to Aboriginal schools in which Aboriginal curriculum content has been introduced. They are apparent also in other Australian schools, where changing perspectives are recognised unevenly or only obliquely, and where the heritage of the past (usually a very limited segment of that past) hangs heavily over planning for the future. Some Aboriginal people would argue, 'Why shouldn't it?' Many other Australians would hold that such an approach is retrogressive. Some anthropologists would remark that the past is never very far away from the present.

There is another facet, among others, which deserves consideration. Texts about specific Aboriginal cultures as presented in schools where Aboriginal students come from different traditional backgrounds may result in blurring of socio-cultural differences. These add to a socio-cultural mix that contributes to a generalised view of an Aboriginal heritage. The information supplied, whether specific or general, is taken to apply to all Aborigines and, to some non-Aborigines, this means that it must apply to all urban Aborigines as well. One of the major questions today, over and above those of land rights, political equality, and socio-personal identity, is what Aborigines themselves mean when they speak of nurturing an Aboriginal heritage. The answers are not at all clear. Ironing out socio-cultural differences between Aboriginal groups may well mean achieving, eventually, pan-Aboriginality; but that achievement has certain implications, which make it plain that the result will be a very different Aboriginal situation from what it is today, and very different persons whom we will call Aborigines and whom Aboriginal people will themselves identify as Aboriginal.

The amount of time devoted in schools (Aboriginal and otherwise) to a consideration of Aboriginal-oriented subjects is small, compared with educational aims relevant to the wider Australian society. Aboriginal people are no longer isolated, not even in the so-called remote areas of Australia, nor even in their decentralised homeland communities. Many Aborigines are thrust into close interaction with non-Aborigines, whether or not they want this, and many mining companies operate literally on their doorsteps, if not within their home ground. These are facts of life for many Aborigines. The Social Impact of Uranium Committee (Northern Territory), functioning with federal funds under the auspices of the Australian Institute of Aboriginal Studies, is probably one of the most significant units in recent times, set up to monitor changes taking place in Aboriginal western Arnhem Land. Its researchers have clearly demonstrated that a people subject to such an impact cannot evade the social consequences, which are very far-reaching indeed. The same is the case, in differing degrees, in other mining and resource development areas in the Northern Territory, Queensland, Central Australia and Western Australia. A pivotal consideration is Aboriginal education. With few exceptions, Aboriginal schools have been ill-served in regard to financial support, curriculum planning, general provision of facilities, and the availability of anthropologically sophisticated teachers.

It takes only a little stretch of imagination to understand, now, why Dhupuma Aboriginal College near Yirrkala (in north-eastern Arnhem Land) was arbitrarily closed by the Northern Territory administration a couple of years ago — ostensibly because money was not available to refurbish it and to keep it going. Despite this excuse, it has recently been replaced by the Nhulunbuy High School, designed to serve children of the Nabalco mining town. According to official reports (New Schools 1981, p. 197), 'a small number of Aboriginal students attend' the school. Another striking example is the new Jabiru Primary School, established to cater for secondary students from the 'Uranium Province' until a secondary school is constructed (1981, p. 20), while the Aboriginal school at Oenpelli languishes. These are by no means isolated cases.

It is fairly well recognised that Aboriginal schools must include an appreciable proportion of Aboriginal material, and that Aborigines themselves should have a greater part to play in these institutions. There is similar recognition that Aboriginal people need to be better informed about the wider society, if only to help them survive in relation to it. There are of course difficulties in integrating these two dimensions, which do not necessarily have complementary aims. The question of balance here is crucial if Aboriginal identity is to be maintained in more than nominal terms.

Television programs are already operating in a number of areas where Aborigines are living. These are geared to non-Aboriginal audiences, and their programs are the same as those available to most Australians. This uniformity, with its contra-ethnic emphasis, will eventually be reinforced by Australia's domestic satellite-bounced programming, which will be available to most Australians in 'outback' areas, including school-children. As adults we are, ideally, in a position to switch off, whereas children exposed to school programs produced for general consumption will not have that choice. What is desperately required in all the main Aboriginal language areas are small radio and/or television stations run by trained personnel, including Aborigines. Programs produced in these contexts would not only provide general educational and local cultural materials, including entertainment sessions for adults, consisting of Aboriginal music, story-telling, drama, dancing, visual art, etc, but would also provide local and general news items with commentaries in the local language. The Aboriginal background could thus be sustained in a changing, realistic fashion, making effective communication possible. A project of this kind for western Arnhem Land, supported by the Australian Institute of Aboriginal Studies, has been before the relevant authorities for over two years now, without any indication of its acceptance and implementation, even in a modified or in an experimental form.

The communication flow between Aborigines and other Australians is just as significant as communication among Aborigines themselves. Aboriginal people are talking publicly more than at any other time since Europeans settled in this country. Although it is difficult not to find a reference to Aborigines in the daily newspapers across the continent, it is questionable whether they are really being heard — and if they are heard, understood. Perhaps this could be slightly overdrawn, but I don't think so.

An academic pursuit

Thinking back to scenes of one's fieldwork is like an imaginary cine film arbitrarily arrested for inspection at various points, and more vivid and penetratingly alive than the cold words of one's notebooks. There are flashback images of naked desert men singing to the accompaniment of clapping boomerangs, marking the complex patterning on the windbreak-shaded sand in illustrating the content of their songs. A dilapidated tin and hessian shack a stone's throw from the Murray water's edge in South Australia, where an old man, the last fluent Yaralde speaker, sits among the debris of what to him was still an alien culture; and in this squalor telling me the myths of his now-almost-forgotten gods. A rubbish-strewn creekbed on a central-western Northern Territory pastoral station, where young men sit with bowed heads before a line of emblem-bearing and decorated ritual dancers. Orderly rows of tin and bamboo huts arranged within a wartime army settlement, where the night echoes resonantly with the rhythmic sounds of competing ceremonies, enticing us with glimpses of an assortment of different cultures. Scenes, hundreds of scenes crowding and jostling each other, as that imaginary film runs on and on through the past into the present, breathing life into events which are gone; in that sense, gone, yet enshrined in words written in one's notebooks along with the knowledge they conveyed — still living, awaiting (as it were) an act of revival.

How far all this is from the cold portals of academia where the pursuit of knowledge is supposedly divorced from the dangers of subjectivity! Which is the real source of intellectual understanding? Scenes vibrant with emotion, with faith and feeling, or the translation of those scenes into words, measured and analysed, their implications spelt out for inspection by the profane eyes of (perhaps) anyone who cares to read them. Of course, the answer must always be, both. But how, and in what sense, both? Too often, we forget that behind our notebooks are people, living and dead, who lived and thought and felt the things we write about.

Aboriginal studies as an academic pursuit is as old as professional anthropology in Australia. An immense amount of raw material has been gathered over the years and great is the extent and range of subsequent publications. The 1961 Conference on Aboriginal Studies (which preceded the setting up of the Australian Institute of Aboriginal Studies), in its assessment made that point. Since that time, the accumulation has galloped ahead. Yet among this plethora of studies few stand out as landmarks. This aside, a great deal of the work which has been carried out in the universities (and much of it has been done there) was framed within the context of disciplinary dictates that have been more or less obligatory. In spite of this, or because of it, most such studies have been tempered by a consideration for the people who supplied the basic information. This was certainly the case in Sydney when Elkin held sway. For him, as for many of his students, the pursuit of knowledge for its own sake was not the end-all of anthropology. People were equally important. His *Citizenship for Aborigines* (1944) alone demonstrated that; and so did the arrangements he made with the Australian Investment Agency and the Northern Territory administration for my wife and me to examine problems of Aboriginal labour on pastoral stations. Elkin did this with the express intention and expectation that we would produce realistic recommendations that could be activated to the advantage of Aboriginal people. This traditional commitment on the part of social anthropologists vis-à-vis Aborigines themselves is a continuing one, whether or not they were trained in, or associated, with the Sydney Department.

'Practical' or 'applied' anthropology, an important area of the discipline, has been slow to develop in Australia. Perhaps this is because it has appeared less precise in its approach than what is thought desirable in the non-social sciences, and also because it is open to subjective evaluation. Nevertheless, in spite of its limitations, the demands for applied anthropology are inseparable from the kind of society we live in. Among many social anthropologists there is a strong interest in current Aboriginal affairs, and in the problems that face Aborigines. Yet the number of persons professionally trained in anthropology who are directly involved in such activities is really quite small. This is in fact one of the 'grey' areas. Increasingly, Aboriginal communities and organisations are being crowded with anthropologically untrained advisers, consultants and other directive-oriented and service-motivated personnel. Government-imposed economic constraints are being felt in Australian universities. Staff mobility is restricted, and younger graduate trainees in anthropology, for example, are often forced to ply their skills in a hostile open market against severe competition from untrained personnel focused on similar employment goals. One inference here could well be the need for wider recognition of the significance of practical anthropology, and the registration of professional anthropologists. The situation which obtains today in this field of activity would not be tolerated by a truly professional association.

When the Australian Institute of Aboriginal Studies began, it was concerned with filling gaps in systematically recorded knowledge of traditional Aboriginal cultures that had largely defined by the 1961 Conference. Only through the relative strong-mindedness of the small pocket of social anthropologists were we able to broaden the mandate so that more attention could be paid to changing

Aboriginal conditions. Even so, it was some years before the Institute was able to sublimate its reluctance to deal with what can be called contemporary social issues. Interest in these has since grown, and is now taken very much for granted. They cannot be ignored, being a part of the current scene and thus also part of any field situation in which research is carried out.

One major move in this respect was the arrangement made between the Institute and the Northern Territory land councils for nominating anthropologically trained persons to prepare ethnographic substantiation for the Aboriginal land claims that would be brought before the Land Rights Commissioner administering the Northern Territory Land Rights Bill (see R Berndt 1981, pp. 5–20 for some attendant implications). Two points of relevance here: firstly, the inflow of information, from anthropological sources past and present, including direct and indirect Aboriginal interpretation of immediately past events and what they mean, when Aborigines are faced with what is, from their perspective, the unprecedented situation of having to articulate their demands for something they have always regarded as implicitly their own; and secondly, while a person engaged to undertake such a task is carrying out an exercise in 'practical' anthropology, this task is not an 'applied' one (except in the sense of applying information within a specific, practical problem area) because what anthropologists seek is 'facts'.

Facts, however they are defined, are likely to change in shape or content in today's fluid situation, in regard to how they are framed, what information is either included or excluded, and how they are interpreted. In land claim cases, there is an additional perspective on interpretation because this takes place in a court of law (often with the aid of an anthropological adviser) by a Land Rights Commissioner who subsequently passes judgement. Furthermore, land councils and appropriate administrations do the 'applying' of it. In this rather laborious process, there is considerable room for distortions of 'facts', including the submergence of Aboriginal (and anthropological) opinion. As I have said elsewhere, there are more non-Aborigines (and institutions) standing between Aborigines and what they themselves now want than at any other time during their experience with Europeans — much more than during the so-called colonial period. The position in which they find themselves is by no means unique; most or all of us seem to be caught up in a 'no-win' situation. This aside, it does seem to be the case in regard to Aboriginal affairs generally.

I note two examples in which I am personally involved. One is in Western Australia: the Aboriginal Cultural Material Committee, which is empowered by the State government to recommend the protection and preservation of Aboriginal sites of significance. The other is the Institute's project on the Social Impact of Uranium Mining, which I already mentioned. This project, concerned with monitoring social pressures being brought to bear on western Arnhem Landers, not only takes into account the views and attitudes of Aborigines but is expected to present these in a strongly supportive way. The obstacles that are encountered in connection with straightforward recommendations are formidable, whether or not necessarily intended. They seem almost to be built into government administration, social welfare, educational planning, community organisation and political requirements, among others, as part of their structure or nature.

For good or bad, anthropology has entered (not deliberately, but because of its research imperatives) a potentially controversial arena. This potential is exacerbated when it entails the many representatives of non-Aboriginal organisations, such as mining companies, which have vested interests in Aboriginal affairs. The fiction of Aboriginal self-determination is (as it is for most of us) as far away now as it ever was in the heyday of assimilation. One thing is clear: if only in the interests of Aborigines, anthropology cannot retreat, and there is no indication that it would want to do so. In fact, I can see only greater involvement on its part in a continuing collaboration with Aboriginal people. While our analytic tools are being sharpened by participation in today's events, a great deal has remained unchanged or is apparently changing very slowly indeed. The shadow of the past falls firmly across Aboriginal cultural perspectives, indicating directions which remain familiar to the majority of Aborigines: shadows that do vary in shape, since so many different factors of a non-Aboriginal nature are increasingly impinging.

The involvement by anthropologists in practical matters has, on the whole, strengthened their ties with Aboriginal people. Ties of friendship, of varying degrees of closeness, do not necessarily detract from our scientifically-oriented research. One is a necessary component of the other. However, there are difficulties which must be faced if we are to help in providing reasonable solutions to immediate issues, solutions that Aborigines themselves can consider further, then make decisions and take appropriate action. Apart from this matter of expediency, we are concerned with far-reaching issues more in line with traditional anthropological perspectives. For instance, there is a vast array of socio-cultural material displayed before us, through which anthropologists must find their way and reveal their ever changing patterns. The exploration of these brings us back again to those 'cold words' of which I spoke earlier: words recording what we have seen and what we have heard; words which, when connected one with another, form interrelated shapes, providing meaning, bringing 'blood and flesh' to our understanding of a living people.

It was within this context that Aboriginal studies developed. Yet as a subject in its own right it has only recently (as late as 1974) entered Australian universities. The reasons for its introduction are varied. I see its primary function as being a contribution to living in Australian society (R Berndt 1979, p. 512), over and above its provision of more opportunities for students to understand Aboriginal life, past and present, in a manner more detailed and systematic than can be attained in another context. However, a year-long course can take into account only a fraction of the available significant Aboriginal material. There is insufficient teaching time to consider specific problems in more than a cursory way or to cover practical issues. Even the introduction of short courses of this kind at other academic levels, and the fact that so many of our MA and PhD theses (in the Department of Anthropology, University of Western Australia) are written on Aboriginal topics, have done little to remedy this state of affairs. Few of us realise the magnitude of this task until we commence to teach and write, and to talk with students (and here I am thinking only of my own discipline, not of what others have accomplished and could conceivably do).

One significant task before us is to make the material we talk and write about warm and rich with life and meaning. To some extent this is achieved by our emphasis on fieldwork. However, the atmosphere of the field is not easily transferred to the classroom or lecture theatre, whether or not Aborigines are involved. Some of us speak of 'hard' and 'soft' sciences. Aboriginal studies is neither 'hard' nor 'soft', but 'warm', and at times it is only lukewarm, or downright cold!

The next step

The idea I mentioned at the outset of this lecture related to the utilisation of the 'faculty' of imagination. For this to become a viable proposition within the context of enquiry, a recognised frame of common cultural understanding is required. Such understanding has its basis within a particularised past, since any form of imaginative endeavour must commence with what is known: it may then proceed with reassembling elements from that past in order to plan for the future. To some extent, this is latent in so much of traditional Aboriginal mythology, where the frame is known, but innovative expansions provide opportunities for interpreting fundamental 'truths' within changing social situations. I don't want to overemphasise this issue of imagination, since I am really using the term in two ways. In each, however, I presuppose what is often vaguely called the creative faculty of the mind, or the realm of ideas.

In one way, to introduce the question of imagination is almost tantamount to declaring support for something that might be regarded as the antithesis of social scientific enquiry. In another way, if properly confined, the use of imagination enables us to perceive relationships between facts and to underline probable implications arising from them. Both aspects are present, and are indeed often warranted, in any piece of social anthropological writing that goes beyond the purely ethnographic descriptive level. With the first way, it is not solely the question of speculation which is at issue. Often, it emphasises an aesthetic quality in particular events, where explanation in these terms is paramount. There are areas of socio-cultural life, whether they be Aboriginal or otherwise, which are more responsive to such treatment than are others (in oral literature, song poetry, storytelling, music, drama, dance, values, innovation, personal approaches, and so on). In the broadest terms, these display distinctive qualities, enabling us to see and understand both differences and similarities between particular cultures.

Such concerns are not so easily transferred to what we can call the practical dimension. If we are interested in transforming 'cold' words into 'warm' ones, it is necessary to bring things together, to see them in relationship to one another, and discern whether or not they express elements of complementarity or contrast. The question of integration, of things being put together into patterns and working, or being made to work, is of major interest to anthropology, certainly in Aboriginal studies. As an example, I mention two common anthropological approaches: one studies a particular Aboriginal society or community according to a special focus or theme (which can constitute a problem or a theoretical issue). How would this society look, anthropologically, if several different foci or themes were adopted: what degree of sameness would be apparent? A second kind of study may focus on Australian Aborigines in general terms, subsuming differences between cultures and subcultures to achieve a comprehensive view. Depending on the methodology adopted, the end results could vary quite considerably.

One of the most surprising things, in view of the importance of Aboriginal studies to all Australians, is to find that there is no department of Aboriginal studies within an Australian university. If any next step is required, this is one. Such a department should ideally be multidisciplinary, drawing into its orbit the varying expertise which may be harnessed to serve in understanding Aborigines and their social systems; and its practical component would be significant. The Australian Institute of Aboriginal Studies has it within its power to establish such a body, since most if not all the disciplines that have shown concern in the past and in the present for Aboriginal issues are represented on its Council and committees, as among its members. Despite difficulties inherent in forming an integrated body such as this, cross-disciplinary communication must be at a maximum. If we are to seek such an integrated approach, this seems to be the only viable way in which it can be done. It is unlikely, in the present climate of economic stringency, that a response will be forthcoming from an Australian university unless initial developments are specifically stimulated. I do not see this as what is popularly called a 'Centre of Excellence'; any department or centre that has to resort to such a device to advertise its wares is not worth its salt. Any department or centre should by definition be as good as it possibly can be; and if it isn't, mechanisms exist to bring it to an end.

One positive step has been the growing acknowledgement of the need for the intellectualisation of Aboriginal studies, so that it becomes the concern and interest of all Australians as a significant field of study in its own right, and no less important than others. For some of us, in our European past, study of the classics (deriving from ancient Greece and Rome) was what defined an educated person. Since those days, the vacuum which was left was filled to some extent, and nominally, by a broader cross-cultural view of the world, on the assumption that the more people know of how other peoples lived and thought, the more hope they have of settling disputes amicably (or of exploiting them economically, or politically). While the cross-cultural perspective is somewhat tarnished these days, it is still important. However, we must not lose sight of our own Australian roots, actual or putative. The Aboriginal heritage remains a force in the land, and gives every indication of continuing to be so as a unique body of Australian knowledge.

This heritage, since the time of early European settlement, has been there for sharing, but not for taking over. Some Australians have disparaged it, and cast it aside unthinkingly. It has taken them a long time to realise the richness of Aboriginal culture and what it has to offer, and to recognise the stamina of Aboriginal people in the face of enforced changes and the occupation of their own land. The tide is gradually changing. There is every reason to hope that all Australians will have more than a passing acquaintance with changing Aboriginal cultures, not for the purpose of becoming professional Aboriginal-Australianists, or becoming scholars in the field, but to round off their own education, and in doing so to enrich their own intellectual development.

To accomplish this would involve a concerted effort, taking into account all the available formal and informal educational avenues. There is also a mutuality about all this since I am not thinking solely of Europeans making this effort, but of Aborigines sustaining the knowledge they already possess, supplementing it and getting to know a great deal more about European cultural backgrounds, with each group safeguarding its own cultural integrity.

Whichever way we turn, the past exerts its influence over us. Aboriginal people found this out and utilised it to their advantage, to plan for the future in a straightforward way. This is not just a lifting of the past, or a relevant part of that past, into the present. It can only be a past seen through the eyes of the present generation, yet in one sense its transmutation makes it an element of the present, whatever that 'present' may be.

Aboriginal wise men, cultured in their own terms, have always had much knowledge and experience to impart to oncoming generations of youths emerging as social adults. These elders were not necessarily conservative and retrogressive in their views. They weren't living in the past, and are not doing so now. Aboriginal youth of today, however, sometimes characterises them in that way. Yet what those wise men and women have to offer concerns the present far more than it does the past, and is relevant to their future. The past becomes irrelevant only when it can no longer be communicated to a living people, or where the channels of communication are closed.

The Australian Institute of Aboriginal Studies is symbolic of those wise men and women, although by no means a substitute for them. It has a particularly important task to perform; and I sometimes wonder whether this is sufficiently realised by people within as well as outside the Institute. The Institute is concerned with holding and safeguarding the Aboriginal past for the future. The use which can potentially be made of all this accumulated knowledge, in its varying forms, is far greater than could have been possible without the active cooperation of Aborigines. With their participation, the steps which it is now necessary to take are more likely to be taken and will, consequently, be more effective.

The Institute of Aboriginal Studies (and I stress the word 'studies') has a special mandate, and a special responsibility. It needs to foster the development of systematic enquiry, with an appropriate mixture of imagination and dedication. This must be done with total integrity, honesty, and commitment, in a context free from political pressure and political manoeuvring. Only in these conditions can it help Aboriginal people to preserve, for Aborigines as well as for others, the heritage that is uniquely theirs, and to use the past for the benefit of their own future.

Postscript

It is two years since I prepared this lecture. Within that period governments have changed and to some extent so have their policies. A Labor government is now in power at the federal level, and the Labor-government states now include Western Australia. What I have discussed, though, remains just as relevant today as it was in 1982. Some of the points I raised continue to need urgent attention. Nevertheless, a few additional comments are necessary.

I mentioned under the subheading 'External enquiry' the prevalence of careless distortions of the Aboriginal past, as well as some of the pitfalls inherent in reconstructing or reinterpreting the social history of Aborigines. There are very real issues here, which have crucial implications for the Aboriginal future, not least in political terms. While the prejudice in past events involving Aborigines as portrayed by European writers needs to be rectified and the record put right, there is no guarantee that Aboriginal views of social history will be less prejudiced. Distortions on both sides of the ethnic fence do not necessarily balance out to provide a more positive assessment. In such matters, differences between truth and falsity can be a matter of judgment; and where 'the facts' are not recoverable or only partially so, the outcome can depend on who is making the judgment and in what circumstances. In the lecture I spoke of imagination as being an integral part of approaching certain types of material. Yet this is not the same as using one's imagination deliberately to create a view of the Aboriginal past and present, not for the historical record, but as a political device to achieve particular ends. The bases of evaluation differ considerably on both these scores.

One significant aspect is the concern of Aborigines with their own affairs. This in itself is a good thing and, increasingly, Aborigines are managing their own concerns and making decisions on a wide variety of matters. Many have little interest in the wider society except where it impinges on their own, or where it is not possible to avoid its influence. In a sense this 'localistic' view is a heritage of the past which has persisted into the present, most notably among people of Aboriginal descent whose traditional cultural continuity has been at a minimum. This is understandable where they have been threatened, or felt threatened. It is also, for those whose socio-cultural as well as physical background is partly European, a way of rejecting the wider society that rejected them in the past. Nevertheless, their overt or covert 'identification against' the wider Australian population and its ideas and beliefs can be a negative factor in the present socio-cultural climate. This requires serious consideration by Aboriginal people. It is undoubtedly linked to the communication channels I mentioned (under the subheading 'Providing information'). Insufficient general information is reaching Aborigines, or 'getting through' to them; and there are too few opportunities for stimulating varying lines of enquiry. Ways and means must be explored to remedy this situation. Information about the practicalities of socio-economic living is only one element here. Equally important are the possibilities of creating an awareness of intellectual pursuits both within and outside the Aboriginal context.

Intellectual considerations have suffered more acutely in the now relatively long history of intercultural clash of ideas. Responsibility for this state of affairs does not belong directly within the political arena, but falls squarely within the context of schools and academic institutions, which should have been in a position to consider it more seriously, comprehensively and with greater comprehension. The answer to cultural survival and identity is not to be found in dichotomising Aboriginal from non-Aboriginal features, even if that were possible. An intelligent appreciation of common interests and lines of approach is, in the long run, developmentally more valuable. This should in no way prejudice the unique contribution which Aboriginal people can make in respect of themselves and others. It is more likely that, such circumstances, Aboriginal distinctiveness can be maintained as a dynamic force in both thought and action. Certainly, there is more chance of these surviving than there is through an escape into a closed system. Closed systems of any kind are intellectually limiting.

Anthropology, or rather that special branch of anthropology which is committed to Aboriginal studies, has a much more active part to play in the present and the future than it had in the immediate past. Anthropologists have not had time or incentive to give serious thought to new directions; and

Aborigines, in their turn, have not understood sufficiently (or had presented clearly to them) what anthropologists can or should do. In emphasising practical aspects of anthropology, the vital significance of research per se, or of research which may conceivably have no direct practical relevance (in short-range terms) should not be ignored. Aborigines have not been slow in recognising the actual or potential advantages of specific practical anthropological research within their communities, particularly that concerning particular social issues that they face.

Some Aboriginal individuals and organisations have been less receptive to research that seems not have direct practical advantage to them. This attitude, when it is expressed, may give rise to restrictions imposed by Aborigines on anthropologists, approving or disapproving particular research projects, attempting to control their direction, and reserving the right both to 'vet' and to censor what an anthropologist writes. The reasons for such moves are partially understandable in the light of previous experiences not necessarily associated with trained anthropologists. Responsible academic and professional research workers cannot accept such injunctions, whether they come from Aborigines or from anyone else. They do, however, take into account the opinions and attitudes of the persons with whom they work. Difficulties that may arise in this connection can mostly be traced to an inadequate information flow. Another reason is that not enough Aboriginal people have received a tertiary education and not enough have entered the various professional fields, including anthropology.

I mentioned the importance of 'practical' or 'applied' anthropology. Recently, the Australian Anthropological Society discussed setting up a professional body and framing a code of ethics for anthropologists. A Professional Association of Applied Anthropology and Sociology has been established in Western Australia, along with a (national) Australian Association of Applied Anthropologists (which is to have its inaugural meeting in May 1984).

In my lecture, I mentioned the Western Australian Aboriginal Cultural Material Committee. Originally this was located in the Western Australian Museum, in order to administer the Aboriginal Heritage Act (1972), which concerns the protection of Aboriginal sites of significance. Difficulties which arose during the Noonkanbah crisis (1979–80) led to resistance on the part of the Museum's Trustees to being involved in political issues. In December 1983, this Committee and its Department of Aboriginal Sites were transferred to a government building, pending decisions on their future role. A Labor government in Western Australia has honoured its pre-election promise to legislate on Aboriginal land rights. With that intention, it set up an Aboriginal Land Inquiry (in 1983) under Mr Paul Seaman, QC, with an Aboriginal Liaison Committee (under the chairmanship of Mr E Bridge, MLA). The future of the Aboriginal Heritage Act and the role of the Aboriginal Cultural Material Committee are included in the Seaman brief. Of particular importance is a Workshop on Aboriginal Land Rights held at the University of Western Australia in December 1983, under the auspices of the Australian Institute of Aboriginal Studies. This was designed to provide an anthropological input to the Seaman Inquiry.

On another topic: The initial five-year period of the Institute's Social Impact of Uranium project draws to a close in 1984, but it is expected to be continued. Its significance should not be underestimated. There is an urgent need to establish similar projects in other areas of Australia where 'resource developments' are occurring in proximity to Aboriginal communities or on their lands. While it is too early to gauge the results of changed federal policies in relation to Aboriginal affairs, there are indications that major efforts will be made to ensure that there is a more direct involvement of Aborigines in matters that concern them, and to achieve a greater degree of uniformity throughout the country in relation to Aboriginal land rights and guidelines for resource developments on Aboriginal-owned, held or occupied land.

To keep pace with current developments, a greater degree of financial commitment on the part of government to tertiary institutions is needed — if Aboriginal studies is to be developed along the lines I have suggested and if many more Aborigines are to be encouraged to enter universities than has previously been possible. There is one thing that *all* Australians must recognise: both Aboriginal and other Australians have much to contribute in relation to each other; and the future for both lies in mutual support framed in positive terms.

References

Berndt, CH 1965, 'Women and the "secret life"', in RM & CH Berndt (eds), *Aboriginal man in Australia: Essays in honour of Emeritus Professor A. P. Elkin*, Angus & Robertson, Sydney.

Berndt, CH & Berndt, RM 1971, *The Barbarians: An anthropological view*, Pelican, Harmondsworth.

Berndt, CH & Berndt, RM 1978, *Pioneers and settlers: The Aboriginal Australians*, Pitman, Melbourne.

Berndt, RM 1952, *Djanggawul*, Routledge & Kegan Paul, London.

Berndt, RM 1970, 'Traditional morality as expressed through the medium of an Australian Aboriginal religion', in RM Berndt (ed.), *Australian Aboriginal Anthropology*, published for the Australian Institute of Aboriginal Studies by the University of Western Australia Press, Perth.

Berndt, RM 1978, 'Review of *Triumph of the nomads* by G Blainey', *Historical Studies*, University of Melbourne.

Berndt, RM 1980, 'Looking back into the present: a changing panorama in eastern Arnhem Land', *Anthropological Forum*, vol. IV, nos 3–4.

Berndt, RM 1981, 'A long view: Some personal comments on land rights', *Australian Institute of Aboriginal Studies Newsletter*, no. 16.

Berndt, RM & Berndt, CH (eds) 1979, *Aborigines of the west: Their past and their present*, University of Western Australia Press, Perth.

Berndt, RM & Berndt, CH 1981, *The world of the first Australians*, Lansdowne Press, Sydney.

Blainey, G 1975, *Triumph of the nomads: A history of ancient Australia*. Macmillan, Melbourne.
Cobern, P 1982, 'Who really killed Tasmania's aborigines?', *The Bulletin* (Sydney), 23 February, pp. 32–3.
Elkin, 1944, *Citizenship for Aborigines*, Australasian Publishing Co, Sydney.
Knapp, P 1981, 'School, cognition and the Aboriginal child', *Developing Education,* vol. 9, no. 1, pp. 5–10.
New Schools 1981, *Developing Education*, vol. 9, no. 1.
Williams, D & Fidock, A (eds) 1978 onward, *The Aboriginal Australian in north eastern Arnhem Land* series, Curriculum Development Centre, Canberra.
—— c. 1981, *Exploring Aboriginal kinship*, video recording, Curriculum Development Centre, Canberra.

Original lecture available at:
http://www.aiatsis.gov.au/lbry/dig_prgm/wentworth/m0035082_a.rtf <http://aiatsis.gov.au/publications/presentations/looking-ahead-through-past>

3

Aboriginal political life

1984 Wentworth Lecture

Les Hiatt

In 1841 Edward John Eyre took up a selection on the Murray River at Moorundie, a few miles south of what is now Blanchetown. He was twenty-six years of age and had just returned from his heroic journey from Adelaide to Albany. In acknowledgment of his achievement, the Governor of South Australia appointed him Resident Magistrate and Protector of Aborigines on the Murray River.

At Moorundie, Eyre found himself in a region 'more densely populated by natives than any in [the] colony, where no settler had ventured to locate, and where, prior to my arrival ... frightful scenes of bloodshed, rapine, and hostility between the natives and parties coming overland with stock, had been of frequent and very recent occurrence' (Eyre 1845, p. 317). Over the next three years Eyre travelled widely among the Murray and Darling tribes and evidently established a humane and peaceful relationship with them. He resigned as Protector late in 1844 and soon afterwards returned to England. On the voyage home he drafted an account of his expeditions of discovery, together with a description of the manners and customs of the Aborigines. The work was published in two volumes in 1845.

On the question of Indigenous government, Eyre's view was that there was none. The natives of Australia, he thought, recognise no authority apart from time-honoured traditions: 'Through custom's irresistible sway has been forged the chain that binds in fetters a people, who might otherwise be said to be without government or restraint' (Eyre 1845, p. 384). Admittedly, he said, men of influence exist: they are typically individuals from 45 to 60 years of age, possessing strength, courage, energy, prudence, skill, and so on, and often belonging to powerful families (Eyre 1845, p. 307). Male elders discuss and decide upon matters of importance, and influential men may address the community. But, 'though at such times a loud tone and strong expressions are made use of, there is rarely anything amounting to an order or command; the subject is explained, reasons are given for what is advanced, and the result of an opposite course to that suggested fully pointed out' [Eyre 1845, p. 318). After that, people are left to form their own judgments and to act as they think proper.

In Eyre's opinion, then, talking things over and offering advice do not amount to government. Government means the power to give orders and have them obeyed. Years later, as Governor of Jamaica, Eyre demonstrated executive powers in their most awesome form. Following a massacre of whites at Morant Bay in 1865, he declared a period of martial law in the course of which 439 people were executed and 600 flogged. I put the matter curtly to make an analytical point, not a moral judgment; many of you will be familiar with Geoffrey Dutton's sympathetic account of Eyre, *The hero as murderer* (1967).

Some years ago John Mulvaney praised Eyre's contribution to Aboriginal studies and expressed regret that it had 'never emerged from its oblivion as an appendage to his exploration memoirs' (Mulvaney 1958, p. 146). By then Eyre's description of government had been superseded by formulations attributing to Aboriginal social organisation a greater degree of hierarchy and centralisation of power than Eyre had been able to discern at Moorundie. However, in that same year (1958), in a symposium entitled 'Systems of political control and bureaucracy in human societies' organised by the American Ethnological Society, Lauriston Sharp gave a paper on the Yir-Yoront of Western Cape York Peninsula, and Eyre, had he been present, would certainly have applauded, even if he might not have been able to understand all of it. Sharp, who had carried out fieldwork in the Mitchell River area in the early 1930s, referred to a number of concepts that had, as he put it, 'seeped into and seriously rigidified much of the discussion of Australian Aboriginal social structure' (Sharp 1958, p. 2); these were concepts such as 'chief', 'headman', 'council of elders', and 'gerontocracy'. Yet, he went on, in the whole of north Queensland no such institutions or structures are to be found.

To the European mind, accustomed as it is to positions of authority and hierarchies of command, a state of ordered anarchy poses a set of intellectual and emotional problems: how do people know what to do? Who punishes wrongdoers? How are the weak protected from the strong? Who organises the community's defence against its enemies? Who takes responsibility for the society's religious life? And so on. Eyre, as we have seen, attributed the performance of such civic tasks to the invisible hand of custom. Sharp, with the benefit of a century of ethnography, sought to give flesh to this notion by locating it in the domain of kinship: 'As an orderly organization of a very limited number of highly standardized roles which an individual plays over and over again in almost all his interactions with others, the Yir-Yoront or any other Australian kinship system constitutes an extremely simple but almost complete social system' (Sharp 1958, p. 4).

What Sharp meant was something like this. In accordance with well-understood principles of classification, each individual in an Aboriginal community stands to every other individual in one or other of a limited number of relationships stated in the idiom of kinship. For example, approximately one-eighth of the males in my social universe may be classified as my 'fathers', one eighth of the females as my 'mothers', and so on. All my rights, privileges, and obligations are defined on the basis of kinship, either actual or classificatory; and as I grow up I also learn rules of etiquette which constrain or shape my behaviour towards others according to my predetermined relationship with them. In short, kinship rules provide a total framework for social interaction.

So far the formulation is more or less classical Radcliffe-Brown (see, for example, 1952, p. 79). Sharp, however, made two interesting additions. First, all kinship relations among the Yir-Yoront (or, at any rate, Yir-Yoront males) are characterised by an imbalance of status, that is to say, one party to the relationship is superior or superordinate, the other is inferior or subordinate. The basis of this asymmetry has to do either with the giving and receiving of women in marriage (that is, the gift of a bride and its attendant obligations) or with relative age. The important point is that, while no man has dealings with any other man on exactly equal terms, in half of his relationships he is superior and in the other half inferior. In such circumstances, Sharp argues, no one can be absolutely strong or absolutely weak. A fixed hierarchy of authority is an impossibility. In point of fact, 'the Yir-Yoront cannot even tolerate mild chiefs or headmen, while a leader with absolute authority over the whole group would be unthinkable' (Sharp 1958, p. 5). If authority above the level of the family is a necessary criterion for true political organisation, then the Yir-Yoront are 'a people without politics' (Sharp 1958, p. 7).

Sharp's second point was that kinship roles have an aggressive or punitive aspect as well as a benevolent one. Normally the altruistic or supportive aspect is uppermost. But kinsmen also exercise some surveillance over each other's behaviour, and they may take measures against neglect of duty, breach of promise, or other delinquencies. Although there is no judiciary or police force as such in Aboriginal societies, these surveillance and disciplinary components in kinship roles serve a quasi-legal function (Sharp 1958, p. 7).

Sharp concluded that Aboriginal society lacks special institutions or organisations existing for the purpose of government. A few years later, MJ Meggitt independently advanced a similar viewpoint. In a paper entitled 'Indigenous forms of government among the Australian Aborigines' (1964), he described Aboriginal society as 'intensely egalitarian' (Meggitt 1964, p. 176) and maintained that 'although the local communities that made up the Australian tribes were the significant political and administrative units, they had no formal apparatus of government, no enduring hierarchy of authority, no recognized political leaders' (Meggitt 1964, p. 178). In support of this proposition he made three main points. First, religious precedent as conceptualised and articulated within the framework of the Dreamtime provided a moral master plan for behaviour that largely obviated the need for chiefs or headmen (Meggitt 1964, p. 174). Second, although men gained ritual knowledge and ceremonial status as they grew older, authority and prestige of male elders in the sacred sphere did not carry over into the secular sphere (Meggitt 1954, p. 176). Third, the organisation of cooperative undertakings such as initiation rites, death rites, or revenge expeditions was not the prerogative of a chief, headman, or council of elders, but (depending on the circumstances) of any and every man of mature age in the community (Meggitt 1964, p. 178).

In the following year, I supported Meggitt's proposition on the basis both of a critical appraisal of the previous literature and of my own research among the Gidjingali (Hiatt 1965). In speaking of the latter, I gave details of an ethic of generosity regulating access to resources, and I tried to bring out the importance of a set of common values and formally defined rights and obligations operating within a political system lacking institutionalised authority. In 1972 Maddock, in his general work on the Australian Aborigines, described the traditional polity, with its freedom from institutions of enforcement and its stress on self-reliance and mutual aid, as a 'kind of anarchy, in which it was open to active and enterprising men to obtain some degree of influence with age, but in which none were sovereign' (Maddock 1972, p. 44).

One aspect of Meggitt's formulation about which I had some reservations was the significance he attached to the notion of a transcendental master plan. Undoubtedly, Aboriginal conceptions of correct behaviour have a basis in those cosmological and metaphysical speculations that have come to be known collectively as the Dreaming; furthermore, sanctions are certainly believed to issue from the transcendental here and now. But the existence of a supernaturally sanctioned moral code does not imply the non-existence of a governmental authority; indeed, there are innumerable instances in which the two flourish side by side. A second point is that Dreamtime heroes, like those in many other mythologies, are not always heroic, nor are they always punished for setting a bad example. As the late Professor Strehlow once commented, 'the lives of the totemic ancestors are deeply stained with deeds of treachery and violence and lust and cruelty: their "morals" are definitely inferior to those of the natives of today' (Strehlow 1947, p. 38).

In short, Aboriginal religious beliefs are not so explicit and unequivocal, nor sanctions so unerring, as to constitute a set of instructions which people follow automatically. Indeed, Dreamtime formulations often manifest a deeper concern with understanding what man is than with prescribing how he ought to behave. If traditional Aboriginal society truly lacked government, the reason is unlikely to be found in the content of the traditional religion (see Sackett 1978, p. 42; Hiatt 1975, 1983).

Putting this particular issue to one side, the common ground between me and Meggitt, and between us and Sharp, is clear enough: Aboriginal political life is characterised by a uniform distribution of rights, privileges, and duties throughout a social order based on kinship and suffused by an egalitarian ideology. In recent years this position has been assailed from two directions: on the one hand, there has been what we can refer to as 'class-oriented' Marxist critique and, on the other, a kind of Hobbesian individualism. Let as begin with the second.

*****

After Sharp left Mitchell River in 1935, no further anthropological research was carried out in western Cape York until 1968, following the establishment of a chair of anthropology in the University of Queensland. John von Sturmer and Peter Sutton, who worked at Aurukun and Cape Keerweer respectively and who submitted important doctoral theses in 1978, have both explicitly challenged Sharp's formulation. Sutton underscores the point by referring to Aborigines as 'people *with* politicks': In his thesis on Cape Keerweer he reported that each clan usually has a senior man or woman who is unambiguously the spokesperson for that clans country; that 'big men' or 'bosses' occur at a regional level, encompassing numerous clans; and that the success of these leaders depends on qualities such as political astuteness, skill in argument, fighting prowess, and the ability to mobilise large numbers of kinsmen and kinswomen as supporters. In a recent paper (Sutton 1982), written in collaboration with Bruce Rigsby, he argues that traditional Aboriginal political life has been misrepresented because anthropologists have preferred to believe that Aborigines lack the competitiveness and shrewdness of urban industrial peoples.

Political life among the Kugu-Nganychara, as described by von Sturmer (1978), revolves around the pursuit of pre-eminence as a ceremonial 'big man' or 'boss'. Two vital ingredients for success are an aptitude for ritual discipline and control of an important totemic site. While all men of normal intelligence and ability graduate to the status of *pama manu thaiyan* (a man of thick or strong neck), only some are singled out for the special training necessary for big-man status (*pama kathawawa*). This involves periods of celibacy and fasting, undergoing various other mental ordeals and indignities, as well as instruction in the performing arts. But talent and special training, while necessary for pre-eminence, are not sufficient. Ceremonies focus on particular sites, and to be boss of a big ceremony one has to control a big site. Ownership is normally transmitted from father to eldest son, but unless an inheritance is actively protected and reaffirmed it may be lost to more forceful rivals. In short, land tenure is subject to competition, and von Sturmer surmises that over time the most powerful individuals and their supporters will gravitate towards the most important sites.

Important ritual sites are often located at or near favoured camp locations (for example, at the mouth of a river, offering ready access to ample water and food resources). They constituted the premium ecological vantage points along the coast, and in von Sturmer's judgment there would have been a tendency in pre-European times for the boss of such a focal site to have become the focal male for a whole riverine community. There can be no question, he says, 'that certain individuals ... achieved a level of eminence and prestige beyond that enjoyed by their peers [sic], and wielded authority at a supra-familial level' (von Sturmer 1978, p. 421). The nature of this authority is a question I shall return to.

In 1974, in his thesis on political struggle and competition in south-eastern Arnhem Land, John Bern advanced a similar analysis of the relationship between land, ritual, and politics. According to Bern, 'Control of the major rites is based on the custody of the ritual estates, and both are subject to competition. Success in this competition confers prestige on the victor, a prestige whose relevance is largely restricted to ritual performances and associated activities. The competition for prestige is a major interest in the holding of the ceremonies' (Bern 1974, p. 217).

Subsequently, Bern was led to consider whether Aboriginal political life is amenable to analysis within a 'Marxist problematic'. And in 1979 he published in *Oceania* a critique of the Sharp/Meggitt/Hiatt position in which he asserted that not only were the conclusions false but the wrong questions were being asked. According to Bern, the representation of Aboriginal politics as an embodiment of ordered anarchy and equality can be sustained only by pretending that the female sex and the junior half of the male population do not exist. In addition, we must assent to an analytic division of the social milieu into secular and ceremonial activities as though they constitute two separate and unconnected domains. On the contrary, Bern argues, religion is the ruling ideology where the relations of domination in the Aboriginal social formation are articulated and justified. The dominant category in traditional society is made up of senior males. It is they who control the secret religious cults, from which women are excluded and into which junior males are inducted through elaborate initiation procedures. And it is they who control female reproductivity through the institution of bestowal. Typically, young women marry senior males who not uncommonly acquire a plurality of wives as they grow older. Young men are thus deprived of wives and, moreover, are officially expected to remain celibate throughout their bachelorhood (which roughly coincides with the period of their induction into religious mysteries).

*****

Now, the immediate question is whether these three formulations represent contradictory viewpoints or whether in fact they are mutually compatible statements about different aspects of a complex field of inquiry. I want to argue for the latter alternative, but let me straightaway dispose of what I consider to be a non-issue: the question whether Aborigines have or do not have politics (spelt with a 'k' or without one). We could agree about the facts of Aboriginal social life, yet continue to disagree about whether or not Aborigines have politics simply because we disagree about the definition of politics. I do not intend to get into an argument about terminology. I see no special virtue in the evolutionist taxonomy accepted by Sharp for the purposes of his discussion in 1958, and I am perfectly happy with the broad usage advocated by Sutton and von Sturmer. Indeed, from 1962 onwards, following Hart and Pilling in their book, *The Tiwi*, I have regularly used the expression 'politics of bestowal' to refer to strategies used by bestowers and seekers of wives to advance their interests in a context of scarcity. In short, I do not argue, and never have argued, that Aborigines are 'people without politics'.

In making a retrospective evaluation of Meggitt's paper on Aboriginal government, we should remember that its objectives were largely set by programs established within the British structuralist school of social anthropology, then still flourishing. Meggitt refers at the beginning to two exemplary collections of essays on African political systems, one edited by Fortes and Evans-Pritchard (1940), and the other by Middleton and Tait (1958), and his own paper can be fairly described as a contribution to what Radcliffe-Brown called 'comparative morphology' (1952, p. 195). 'In the political structure of the United States', Radcliffe-Brown wrote, 'there must always be a President; at one time it is Herbert Hoover, at another time Franklin Roosevelt, but the structure as an arrangement remains continuous' (Radcliffe-Brown 1952, p. 10). The question Meggitt therefore asked himself was whether in traditional Aboriginal society there is a structure of government which can be described independently of the individuals who, as it were, pass through it.

Against this background it is clear that when Meggitt concludes that Aboriginal communities have no enduring hierarchy of authority, the critical word is 'enduring'. With respect to the administration of public affairs, he is asserting that there is no single articulated set of superordinate and subordinate statuses which operates from one situation to another and which persists as a system over time in accordance with acknowledged rules of recruitment. In these terms, the Aboriginal polity would seem to be morphologically distinct from, say, a Polynesian chiefdom, which comprises a pyramidal structure of positions filled by a formal process of installation, designated by titles, and carrying with them as an inherent feature authority over a wide range of public matters.

From such a viewpoint, statements about relations of domination and subordination on the basis of age and sex differences, as well as about individual differences in achievement and prestige, might be regarded as true but irrelevant. To make a simple analogy, the author of an essay on school government might consider it important to describe the prefect system (the duties and privileges of office, method of appointment, powers of the head prefect, and so on) but regard it as outside the scope of the analysis to investigate bullying and bastardisation of juniors by seniors or competition for success in various spheres of activity such as scholarship, sport, performing arts, and so on.

For my own part, I see no logical difficulty in maintaining simultaneously that traditional Aboriginal communities lack enduring hierarchies of authority for the administration of public affairs; that individuals, especially senior males, compete for control of scarce natural and metaphysical resources in order to gain or enhance reputations as ceremonial big men; and that, collectively, senior males exercise a degree of domination over junior males and females, especially in the sphere of religion. Furthermore, I believe that all three propositions are substantially true. In that case, however, what do we make of Meggitt's description of Aboriginal society as 'intensely egalitarian'? Was he mistaken? Or are we confronted here in this Wentworth Lecture of 1984 with a version of Orwell's paradox 'all [men] are equal, but some are more equal than others'?

Now, as it happens, Fred Myers has argued in a recent series of papers (1980a; 1980b; 1982) that a central paradox of Pintupi political life is the co-existence of hierarchy and egalitarianism; furthermore, the traditional resolution of this problematic, as Myers phrases it, comes remarkably close to the Orwellian formula. He says, 'The content of this mediation might be summarised as the statement that while all men are ... equal because all are subordinate to the same moral imperative, those who came before [that is the] (elders) hold and represent The Dreaming for those who come after' (Myers 1980b, p. 312). What the elders hold in trust is esoteric knowledge, deemed necessary for the attainment of full manhood. The only legitimate way to procure it is through initiation. Therefore, to put the matter somewhat more bluntly, while all men are subordinate to the transcendental, those who need the word are subordinate to those who have it (see Kolig 1982).

The disciplines imposed by Pintupi men are sustained and severe. They include tooth avulsion, nose piercing, circumcision, subincision, fire ordeals, and the removal of fingernails. Novices may be beaten for too much talking, inattention, or insolence. They may be awakened at any hour of the night and chased with bullroarers. From time to time they stand in a line with heads bowed, signifying subordination, and during ritual performances senior men shout orders at them and threaten them with violence. Indeed, according to Strehlow, 'Executions of younger males, especially of those who were considered to be disrespectful to the authority of their own elders, on charges of sacrilege were ... a feature of the accepted penal systems of all ... tribes in the Centre' (1970, p. 120).

This may seem a harsh regime. Yet, by focussing upon the Pintupi concept of 'holding' or 'looking after', Myers is able to show how the conservation and transmission of transcendental knowledge is represented as a kind of nurture. Within the context of the secret cult, initiated men act symbolically as 'male mothers' who pass on to neophytes the wherewithal for spiritual development. The subordination of young men and their maintenance in a protracted state of immaturity and bachelorhood is conceived as a necessary condition for the discharge of a sacred duty: the custodians of esoteric knowledge act out of a loving responsibility for succeeding generations and for the cosmos itself.

This profound and pervasive paternalism would hardly seem to provide a fertile ground for the development of egalitarianism. Yet, according to Myers, egalitarianism is a central value in Pintupi culture. He speaks of 'the contemporary community at Yayayi with its egalitarian ethos' (1980b, p. 313), of the Pintupi as a 'society of autonomous, egalitarian actors' (Myers 1980b, p. 311), of 'the over-riding concern of individuals with "egalitarianism"' (Myers 1980b, p. 315), and so on. In essence, Pintupi egalitarianism means 'no one is better than me', and it is common for men to say such things as 'he's only a man like me'. From Myers' account, it would seem that the concept embraces both a sentiment of equal intrinsic worth and a notion of an equality of rights and privileges (compare Jayawardena 1968). The question is, how can it flourish side by side with religious authoritarianism?

Meggitt's answer, as we have seen, is that religious authority is non-portable. To quote his precise words:

> no matter how, much authority people conceded to a ritual leader in the sacred sphere, it did not as a rule extend at all into secular affairs ... the religious expert did not on this account derive any special freedom from social conventions in the secular world. He had no immunity from criticism or from open violence in everyday disputes. Away from the ceremonial ground he was but another member of an intensely egalitarian society ... (Meggitt 1964, p. 176).

Strehlow (1970) has challenged this formulation on empirical grounds, asserting that in pre-European times ceremonial leaders and old men of authority terrorised whole communities through their monopoly of cult-based power. However that may be, Meggitt's final sentence now seems unsatisfactory to me on logical grounds, since it leaves the existential status of the ceremonial ground completely obscure: is it part of Aboriginal society or not? Assuming that it is, and that the values in force there are non-egalitarian, the description of Aboriginal society as intensely egalitarian is clearly in need of some correction.

Myer's argument, so far as I can follow it, is not merely that hierarchy and egalitarianism flourish together in Pintupi society but that, in some sense or in some degree, the latter is actually a product of the former. Like others before him, he contrasts the severity of initiation procedures with the lack of discipline in childhood. To an American observer, he says the freedom enjoyed by Aboriginal children is truly remarkable. Nowadays Pintupi youths refer to the period of seclusion for initiation as 'high school' (thereby alluding to its educational content), but also as 'prison'. The newly initiated are said to be 'free men', What we have, then, is a transition from the irresponsible freedom of childhood to the responsible freedom of adulthood, mediated by a period of humiliation, suffering, and subordination. The experience certainly induces an abiding respect for seniority, and for years to come the initiates will be inhibited and unassertive in the presence of their male elders. But, according to Myers, through the laying on of hands and the gift of the spirit, it also provides a foundation for the development of personal autonomy and self-respect.

As it is only a year since we celebrated the 500th anniversary of the birth of Luther, there is no need for me to remind you that the mediation of man's relation to God by religious hierarchies has a long and complex history. Much as I am impressed by Myers' empathy with Pintupi culture, I am not convinced that Aboriginal egalitarianism depends on paternalism and graded access to the transcendental. If personal autonomy means independence, as I should suppose it does, it is hard to understand how it is promoted by cultivating in grown men a spirit of dependence upon authority. Unless, of course, authoritarianism has a tendency to create its opposite. Perhaps this is the due. After the indulgence of a mother-focussed infancy followed by a permissive boyhood, Aboriginal youths are suddenly confronted by father figures in whom threat is dramatically magnified at the same time as benevolent paternalism is proffered in return for obedience. Within the context of the cult, the only option consistent with survival is submission. Outside the cult, however — back in the general community — a compensatory anti-authoritarianism takes hold. Egalitarianism becomes 'intense' (Meggitt 1964), the notion of a chief 'intolerable' (Sharp 1958).

I place no great weight on this speculation. The essential point is that the indigenous Australian polity was neither wholly authoritarian nor wholly egalitarian. Rather, both elements coexisted in strong measure. It may be (and here I offer a further speculation) that the tension between them helps to explain some of the characteristic adaptations of Aboriginal society to European hegemony. On the one hand, traditional egalitarianism militates against the emergence of black political leaders. According to Myers, rank-and-file Pintupi regard decisions by the village council not only as having no authority but as lacking respect for the autonomy of others: as one man said after the announcement of a no liquor law, 'It's only their idea; they are just men like me' (Myers 1982, p. 7; compare Sackett 1978). On the other hand, traditional religious authoritarianism may perhaps pave the way for a ready acceptance of paternalism emanating from an external source. A white 'boss' is conceived as a person who 'looks after' Aborigines in return for deference and obedience. As Chris Anderson notes, 'Aboriginal people today in south-eastern Cape York Peninsula speak of "my old boss", often with a great deal of humour and affection, sometimes even when he had been "hard" or "cheeky"'.

One man said sorrowfully of another, 'Poor old fella, he got no boss' (Anderson 1984, p. 228).

*****

Let us move from the corporate power of senior males to the question of individual 'bigmanship'. At the outset I should make it clear that, when I refer to egalitarianism in Aboriginal society, I do not in any sense imply that individuals are endowed with a natural disinclination to excel or to be admired or to gain ascendancy over others, nor do I imply that Aborigines are by nature unselfish when I draw attention to the importance they attach to generosity. It would be more accurate to say that in both instances we are dealing with cultural values directed against natural tendencies. Traditionally, public disapproval of selfishness and self-importance reinforced the distributive effects of the laws governing land tenure and marriage and inhibited the emergence of marked differences in wealth, status, and power. To inhibit ambition is not, however, to remove it and, as Eyre acknowledged when he spoke of 'powerful families', the status profile of an Aboriginal community is not entirely flat. Probably everywhere, through a combination of genealogical good luck, enterprise, and energy, some men acquired more wives than others and raised more children. Ian Keen has recently argued that, on this basis, certain kinship systems may generate a higher degree of social inequality than others (Keen 1982). Some Yolngu men, for instance, are able to acquire unusually large harems (Berndt & Berndt 1964, p. 172). Such achievements tend to produce fast-growing clans through positive feedback (that is, success tends to breed success), and flourishing clans may acquire the estates of dying clans through a process, well described by Howard Morphy (1977), of ritual custodianship and accretion. The senior men of such clans, with their ample resources in land, wives, and warriors, are well placed to become citizens of note and, not uncommonly, they embellish their reputations by becoming patrons and practitioners of the religious arts.

A long-standing problem in the study of Aboriginal religion is why certain totems become more important than others. For example, in their great work of 1899, Spencer and Gillen described the Engwura ceremony, the final and most important of the four rituals constituting the male initiation complex among the Aranda. It lasts about four months and consists of a long series of totemic rituals culminating in the revelation of a particularly sacred icon symbolising female generative powers. The totems represented vary from one Engwura ceremony to another, depending on which local groups happen to be present. But one totem, the ancestral Wild Cat, is always pre-eminent. According to Aranda mythology, all totems and totemic sites were created in the Dreamtime by a supreme superhuman ancestor called Numbakulla. Numbakulla's first creation was Wild Cat. Before disappearing forever, Numbakulla gave the sacred icon to the first Wild Cat man, and the Engwura ceremony as performed today is said to reproduce in all essentials the Engwura ceremony performed by the Wild Cat ancestors in the Dreamtime.

Spencer and Gillen describe the Engwura as the 'great central ceremony of the whole tribe'. When Durkheim wrote *The elementary forms of the religious life* not long afterwards, he viewed rituals like the Engwura as constituting an evolutionary step towards a higher level of social integration: initially, so the argument goes, there were totems symbolising the unity of the individual clans; subsequently, one of these totems came to symbolise the unity of the whole tribe (Durkheim 1961, pp. 320–1). What is unexplained, however, is why it was this one rather than that one (that is, why Wild Cat rather than Kangaroo, or Eaglehawk, and so on?). Spencer and Gillen indicate that the Engwura, though performed by all initiated Aranda men, belongs primarily to the people of the Wild Cat totemic group, who officially control the ceremony (Spencer & Gillen 1899, p. 233). Although the authors give the mythological ratification for Wild Cat supremacy, they are unable to provide any sociological clues as to how this may have come about historically. No doubt any such clues are lost forever in the case of the Aranda. But the trend of recent research suggests that, whatever integrative function Aboriginal religion may have, it also constitutes a major domain in which men compete for prestige. It is a reasonable speculation that, within this arena, the pre-eminence of particular rituals and supernatural conceptions may represent the success of particular mortal aspirations and energies.

Although a man may try to become a 'big name' through the deployment of artistic, administrative, and political talents in the religious life, we should note that the religious and artistic forms as such do not glorify individual human achievement or reputation. Men may become great singers, but singers do not sing the praises of great men. Furthermore, the extent to which individual achievement in ceremonial matters confers authority over other mature men in non-ceremonial contexts remains a vexed and unresolved issue. Von Sturmer says that 'the "big man" is not only the major decision maker and instructor in matters of ceremony, he is also the arbiter of what constitutes correct or incorrect knowledge. While every individual has the right to air his or her views on all issues of moment, the "big man" speaks only after all others have spoken. His is literally the final word. While others speak, he is heard' (von Sturmer 1978, p. 450). But, having heard, do people obey? Or, to recall Eyre's words, do they 'form their own judgments, and ... act as they think proper' (Eyre 1845, p. 318)? And if actions regularly conform to the 'big man's' prescriptions, is it because of his position and power, or is it because, having listened to everyone, he articulates a consensus that has already been reached? Or is it a combination of both? Unfortunately, we know little more about the forms and effects of traditional oratory and debate than did Eyre (compare Thomson 1956, p. 91), and I sincerely hope that this aspect of Aboriginal political life will attract the attention it deserves as a matter of urgency.

Years ago my colleague Frank Gurrmanamana explained to me how, in northern Arnhem Land in pre-European times, an assembly of men might reach a decision to execute an individual whose violence had become a matter of deep public concern. Gurrmanamana invented a scenario in which a man he described as 'the oldest brother, an old man, a really important man' opens a meeting with these words (I translate from the Gidjingali). 'You who are assembled here, I speak to you all. Perhaps you will agree with me.' Someone replies, 'Tell us what you have to say. Then we will tell you whether we agree with you.' The senior man speaks of two killers whose violence has terrorised the whole community, and he suggests that they should be assassinated. 'Talk it over among yourselves', he says, 'and if you decide to do it, we must not say a word about it.' Two men volunteer and, with the moral backing of the meeting, carry out a surprise night attack, and the deed is done.

Although I realise that such a slender piece of evidence proves nothing, I offer it as an example of a style of 'big man' oratory more in keeping with a secular polity structured around consensus than with a system geared to a hierarchy of command. It may well be that in western Cape York the style is more authoritarian and consensus less important. In a recent paper, Athol Chase states that at Lockhart River in eastern Cape York, 'There can be a "big man" for ceremonies, and a "boss" for sites and country, but rarely a "boss" for people ... The ethos is that to set oneself up as a spokesperson or a leader of people against others is an act of foolhardiness, and one which will lead to public humiliation ... Leadership, if it occurs, is covert' (Chase 1984, p. 117).

Chase suggests that the uniform spread of natural resources along the east coast inhibits the emergence of economic and political inequality, whereas the special importance of estuarine sites on the west coast facilitates it. This close-grained analysis of the role of ecological factors in determining cultural variation is obviously important and deserves to be pursued further. But a similar point also needs to be made about historical factors: some of the forces emanating from white Australia may inhibit 'big man' tendencies, while others may strengthen them. As Rolf Gerritsen has argued in two recent papers (1981a, 1981b), a combination of white patronage, ceremonial prominence, and 'traditional owner' status under the Northern Territory Land Rights Act 1976 is producing a category of, to use his words, 'dominant men' in Aboriginal communities who are able to magnify their importance by controlling the distribution of new wealth. It would appear that in some instances such individuals have consolidated their positions to the extent that they are no longer susceptible to constraining or levelling forces inherent in the traditional polity (Smith 1984).

In this review of perceptions of Aboriginal political life, I have spent my allotted time talking about issues of egalitarianism, authoritarianism, and careerism among men. I regret that I have said nothing about women, apart from alluding to their alleged subordination. Although individual women display leadership and initiative in the organisation and performance of women's secret ceremonies (see, for example, Kaberry 1939, pp. 253–68), no one yet has spoken of ceremonial 'big womanship'. Nor has anyone reported that induction into women's cults is accompanied by disciplines of the sort that characterise male initiation. In many parts of Australia, women are expected to act as junior partners to their menfolk (White 1970, p. 26), and often their labour and ideologically cultivated nurturing responsibilities are exploited for the purpose of sustaining male cults (Hamilton 1975, p. 170). The reverse seems not to occur. Indeed, from the viewpoint of gerontocratic polygynists, women's so-called love magic rituals may seem more like hotbeds of subversion than adjuncts to orthodox religion, in so far as they glamorise inclinations towards sexual infidelity (Kaberry 1939, p. 267; C Berndt 1965, p. 245; Reay 1970). For the most part, women are not in the business of domination but of resistance (Cowlishaw 1978, 1979), through which in favourable circumstances they may achieve the kind of collective autonomy so well described in the recent work of Annette Hamilton (1980) and Diane Bell (1983). I see women, therefore, as contributing more to the egalitarian and anarchistic tendencies in Aboriginal society than to its authoritarian components, though it should be acknowledged that they may also feel obliged to support the ambitions of their menfolk.

As John Bern (1979) has remarked, Meggitt's paper for a time was regarded as the definitive statement on traditional Aboriginal political life. Its publication coincided with the formal establishment of the Australian Institute of Aboriginal Studies. Practically all the work I have surveyed in the second part of my paper has been carried out under the Institute's auspices and, if I have done nothing else, I hope I have demonstrated that our understanding of Aboriginal political life has been considerably advanced as a result of it. Far from being settled, the topic is in a state of ferment. That in itself must be a source of satisfaction to the man in whose honour this lecture is named, since intellectual ferment is the state he probably relishes most.

Acknowledgments

For comments and suggestions I am particularly grateful to Margaret Clunies Ross, Jeremy Beckett, Gillian Cowlishaw, Diane Bell, John Bern, Jan Larbalestier, John von Sturmer, Peter Sutton, and Fred Myers.

References

Anderson, C 1984, 'The political and economical basis of Kuku-Yalanji social history', PhD thesis, University of Queensland.
Bell, D 1983, *Daughters of the Dreaming*, McPhee Gribble, Melbourne.
Bern, J 1974, 'Blackfella business, whitefella law', PhD thesis, Macquarie University.
—— 1979, 'Ideology and domination: Toward a reconstruction of Australian Aboriginal

social formation', *Oceania*, vol. 50, no. 2, pp. 118–32.
Berndt, C 1965, 'Women and the "secret life"', in R & C Berndt (eds), *Aboriginal man in Australia*, Angus & Robertson, Sydney.
Berndt, R & Berndt, C 1964, *The world of the first Australians*, Ure Smith, Sydney.
Chase, AK 1984, 'Belonging to country: Territory, identity and environment in Cape York Peninsula, Northern Australia', in LR Hiatt (ed.), *Aboriginal landowners*, Oceania Monograph No. 27, Sydney University, Oceania Publications, Sydney.
Cowlishaw, G 1978, 'Infanticide in Aboriginal Australia', *Oceania*, vol. 48, pp. 262–83.
—— 1979, 'Women's realm: A study of socialization, sexuality, and reproduction among Australian Aborigines', PhD thesis, University of Sydney.
Durkheim, E 1961 (1912), *The elementary forms of the religious life*, Collier Books, New York.
Dutton, G 1967, *The hero as murderer*, Collins, Sydney.
Eyre, E J 1845, *Journals of expeditions of discovery into Central Australia and overland from Adelaide to King George's Sound 1840–1*, vol. 2, Boone, London.
Fortes, M & Evans-Pritchard, EE (eds) 1940, *African political systems*, Oxford University Press, London.
Gerritsen, R 1981a, 'Thoughts on Camelot: From Herodians and zealots to the contemporary politics of remote Aboriginal settlement in the Northern Territory', paper presented to the Australian Political Studies Association, 23rd Annual Conference, Canberra.
—— 1981b, 'Blackfellas and whitefellas: The politics of service delivery to remote Aboriginal communities in the Katherine region, NT', paper presented at North Australian Research Unit, Darwin.
Hamilton, A 1975, 'Aboriginal women: The means of production', in J Mercer (ed.), *The other half*, Penguin, Harmondsworth.
—— 1980, 'Dual social systems: Technology, labour and women's secret rites in the eastern Western Desert of Australia', *Oceania*, vol. 51, no. 1, pp. 4–19.
Hart, C & Pilling, A 1960, *The Tiwi*, Holt, Rinehart & Winston, New York.
Hiatt, L 1965, *Kinship and conflict: A study of an Aboriginal community in northern Arnhem Land*, Australian National University Press, Canberra.
—— (ed.) 1975, *Australian Aboriginal mythology*, Australian Institute of Aboriginal Studies, Canberra.
—— 1983, The relationship between Aboriginal religion and Aboriginal customary law, *Law Reform Commission Report (Aboriginal Customary Law)*, Australian Law Reform Commission, Sydney.
Jayawardena, C. 1968, Ideology and conflict in lower class communities, *Comparative studies in society and history*, vol. 10, no. 4, pp. 413–46.
Kaberry, P 1939, *Aboriginal woman: Sacred and profane*, Routledge, London.
Keen, I 1982, 'How some Murngin men marry ten wives: The marital implications of matrilateral cross-cousin structures', *Man*, vol. 17, no. 4, pp. 620–42.
Kolig, E 1982, 'An obituary for ritual power', in M Howard (ed.), *Aboriginal power in Australian society*, University of Queensland Press, Brisbane.
Maddock, K 1972, *The Australian Aborigines*, Allen Lane, London.
Meggitt, MJ 1964, 'Indigenous forms of government among the Australian Aborigines', *Bijdragen tot de Taal-, Land-en Volkenkunde*, vol. 120, pp. 163–78.
Middleton, J & Tait, D (eds) 1958, *Tribes without rulers*, Routledge & Kegan Paul, London.
Morphy H 1977, 'Too many meanings: An analysis of the artistic system of the Yolngu of north-east Arnhem Land', PhD thesis, Australian National University.
Mulvaney DJ 1958, 'The Australian Aborigines 1606–1929: Opinion and field-work', *Historical Studies*, vol. 8, no. 1, pp. 131–51.

Myers, F 1980a, 'The cultural basis of politics in Pintupi life', *Mankind*, vol. 12, no. 3, pp. 197–214.
—— 1980b, 'A broken code: Pintupi political theory and contemporary social life', *Mankind*, vol. 12, no. 4, pp. 311–26.
—— 1982, 'Ethnography, language, and social value among Pintupi Aborigines', paper presented in honour of Mervyn Meggitt, American Anthropological Association Meeting, 1982.
Radcliffe-Brown, AR 1952, *Structure and function in primitive society*, Cohen & West, London.
Reay, M 1970, 'Decision as narrative', in RM Berndt (ed.), *Australian Aboriginal anthropology*, University of Western Australia Press, Perth.
Sackett, L 1978, 'Clinging to the law: Leadership at Wiluna', in M Howard (ed.), *'Whitefella business': Aborigines in Australian politics*, Institute for the Study of Human Issues, Philadelphia.
Sharp, L 1958, 'People without politics', in V Ray (ed.), *Systems of political control and bureaucracy in human societies*, University of Washington Press, Seattle.
Smith, D 1984, '"That register business": The role of the Land Councils in determining traditional Aboriginal owners', in LR Hiatt (ed.), *Aboriginal Landowners*, Oceania Monograph No. 27, Sydney University, Oceania Publications.
Spencer, B & Gillen, F 1899, *The native tribes of Central Australia*, Macmillan, London.
Strehlow, TGH 1947, *Aranda traditions*, Melbourne University Press, Melbourne.
—— 1970, 'Geography and the totemic landscape in Central Australia: A functional study', in RM Berndt (ed.), *Australian Aboriginal anthropology*, University of Western Australia Press, Perth.
Sutton, P 1978, 'Wik: Aboriginal society, territory and language at Cape Keerweer, Cape York Peninsula, Australia', PhD thesis, University of Queensland.
Sutton, P & Rigsby, B 1982, 'People with "politicks": Management of land and personnel on Australia's Cape York Peninsula', in N Williams and E Hunn (eds), *Resource managers: North American and Australian hunter-gatherers*, Westview Press, Colorado.
Thomson, DF 1956, 'The Aborigines of Australia', in *The Australian junior Encyclopaedia*, Australian Educational Foundation, Sydney, pp. 70–97.
von Sturmer, J 1978, 'The Wik region: Economy, territoriality and totemism in western Cape York Peninsula, North Queensland', PhD thesis, University of Queensland.
White, I 1970, 'Aboriginal women's status: A paradox resolved', in F Gale (ed.), *Woman's role in Aboriginal society*, Australian Institute of Aboriginal Studies, Canberra.

AIATSIS Library, S06.1/AIAS/10 **PMS 3985**
'Aboriginal Political Life', paper presented at the Wentworth Lecture.
(m0036843_a.rtf)
To cite this file use:
http://www.aiatsis.gov.au/lbry/dig_prgm/wentworth/m0036843_a.rtf
Dr L R Hiatt

Original lecture available at:
<http://aiatsis.gov.au/publications/presentations/aboriginal-political-life>

4

'A sense of making history': Australian Aboriginal Studies 1961–1985

1986 Wentworth Lecture

DJ Mulvaney

Exactly a quarter of a century ago, on 15 May 1961, 55 scholars assembled in University House to discuss the future of Aboriginal Studies. Stimulated by the prospects, Bill Stanner (cited in Sheils 1963, p. xiv) later remarked that the participants 'had a sense of making history'. As convener of the meeting, Stanner (cited in Sheils 1963, p. xii) enunciated the following criteria for attendance. 'Everyone should be invited who had authoritative knowledge of any relevant field of research; all appropriate academic disciplines should be represented; the sole concern should be with problems of fundamental study; and the approach should be truly national.' By 1964, the Act which created the Institute [of Aboriginal Studies — AIAS] was operating and I was elected to its first Council. As I have served on Council for all but two years since that time, I decided to reflect upon the Institute, its achievements and its critics over its first quarter century, as the first major theme in this lecture. Then follows some consideration of archaeology, its achievements and some of its problems.

We are here, however, to honour Bill Wentworth, to whose energy and vision we owe so much. There must be few senior researchers who, over the years, have not been challenged by Bill Wentworth to develop some new line of research on the instant. Others have been visited by him in the field, with searching demands to explain or to justify their projects. This happened to me in 1966, when Bill and Mrs Wentworth arrived at the Ingaladdi excavation, Northern Territory. That they were over 30 kilometres off the beaten track from Willeroo station did not deter them, despite the lack of a spare tyre and tools on their hired vehicle. We walked miles around the bush, inspected the excavation, and over steak by the camp fire, defended the importance of archaeological research well into the night. If WC Wentworth IV has ranged widely over matters Aboriginal or scientific with unbounded enthusiasm, it is interesting to reflect that he has emulated the first of the WC Wentworth dynasty. His ancestor was one of the party that first crossed the Blue Mountains; in 1824 he published a 900-page book on Australia. His 1819 *Statistical, historical, and political description of the colony of New South Wales* was shorter, but it anticipated one of the problems which was to concern 'our' WC Wentworth. He observed (1819, p. 5) that the Aborigines:

> bear no resemblance to any of the inhabitants of the surrounding islands, except those of New Guinea, which is separated from New Holland by a narrow strait. One of these islands, therefore, has evidently been peopled by the other; but from whence the original stock was derived is one of those geographical problems, which in all probability will never be satisfactorily solved.

It is appropriate at this chronological landmark to also acknowledge the contribution of Kim Beazley, Sr, in ensuring that the Institute was founded in a spirit of bi-partisan political co-operation. Let it be stated clearly that, despite fluctuating fortunes and funding, this has continued in large measure in Institute affairs. Before 1964, Professor John Barnes acted as chief executive officer and it is good to welcome him, as another founding architect, back to this biennial meeting. For his assistance in arranging the conference, Stanner acknowledged young Mr LR Hiatt. Les Hiatt went on to play a key role in Institute affairs and was last year's Wentworth lecturer. Diane Barwick was another major assistant at the 1961 conference. To the sadness of us all, and a serious loss to scholarship, Diane died suddenly a few weeks ago. I owe her a deep personal debt for her assistance. With the passage of time, I note the forlorn statistic that one in every three of the persons present in 1961 is no longer living.

Over the years, the Institute has been subjected to periodic official review and frequent criticism by members, by the general academic world, and by Aboriginal communities. Much of this criticism was constructive, although unfortunately Institute staff have been at the receiving end of much misdirected, unjustified and personalised criticism and rudeness, which, if directed anywhere, should have been addressed to Council. Despite the fact that the Institute is under almost perpetual criticism from some quarter, it has been more open to new ideas and change, in my opinion, than are most academic or statutory institutions. Understandably, reformers are constitutionally impatient and they seldom set their immediate concerns within an historical context. In human affairs, however, a quarter of a century is a long time — time sufficient for seven Prime Ministers — and my first purpose is to sketch something of the context, in order to credit the Institute with its due.

In the years before 1926, when the teaching of anthropology commenced at the University of Sydney, virtually all research into Aboriginal society was performed in a voluntary, self-financed capacity, mainly by amateurs. AW Howitt, Spencer and Gillen, RH Mathews and John Mathew are notable examples. After 1926, the new Sydney Department of Anthropology provided some direction and theoretical shape to research. While much outstanding research had been reported by 1940, it is interesting to record the basis of funding for that fieldwork.

Before Radcliffe-Brown was appointed to the Sydney Chair of Anthropology, the Australian National Research Council, which sponsored it, estimated total departmental costs at £1800 (£1100 for the professor's salary and £350 for a lecture room assistant): Even in 1933, costs were estimated at only £2500. Half of this sum was paid annually by the Commonwealth government, in return for training 'colonial' administrators, particularly for Papua New Guinea service. (In 1933, according to the *Sydney Morning Herald* of 8 February, there were 2126 applicants for six New Guinea cadetships.) The other half was met by some of the states, chiefly NSW and Victoria. There was no provision for any research component.

Until the outbreak of the Second World War, the universities of Sydney, Adelaide and Melbourne contributed small amounts to various research projects. However, the basic funding for all Australian and New Guinean research was the American Rockefeller Foundation. Between 1926 and 1949, the Rockefeller Foundation subsidised research through the Australian National Research Council (ANRC) to a total of £52,500, while the Carnegie Foundation provided £3000. (Elkin 1945). There was value for money here, for the 30 anthropologists or institutions involved in the 42 funded projects included Radcliffe-Brown, Elkin, Stanner, Lloyd Warner, Ralph Piddington, CWM Hart, Ursula McConnel, Phyllis Kaberry, Donald Thomson, TGH Strehlow, Reo Fortune, Raymond Firth and the notable series of South Australian expeditions, involving Tindale, Cleland and others. Their combined field terms amounted to more than 70 years. In addition, *Oceania*, an important journal, was subsidised heavily from these funds.

Fieldwork diminished upon the outbreak of war and funding sources dried up for long after its duration. Some research was supported by the ANRC, including that by our illustrious members, Ronald and Catherine Berndt, evidently using the residue of the Carnegie Grant. Typical of the late forties' funding drought was Elkin's 1949 report to the ANRC as chairman of its Anthropology Committee. 'The Anthropology Research Committee is not active for the simple reason that we have no money for research purposes and at present no problems have been referred to us.' At that time Sydney University provided Elkin's department with £1000 for research.

When the Australian Academy of Science was established, the Australian National Research Council went out of existence in 1955, at a period when Elkin was its chairman. Its Committee on Anthropological Research had ceased to function in 1951. The ANRC's administrative role was assumed by the Social Sciences Research Council (SSRC) of Australia, established in 1952. During that Council's first five years the Carnegie Corporation provided £40,000 to promote social science research, from which four projects by two anthropologists received a total of £1800 (SSRC, 1956). Around this time the Nuffield Foundation also supported fieldwork, and both FD McCarthy and I were recipients in the period preceding the 1961 meeting.

The decades following the 1926 Sydney chair, therefore, would have been bleak in the annals of field research without American Foundation funding, both in Australia and New Guinea. Although the results of much research became the stuff of classics, the number of projects was few. The contribution of governments appears minimal, although the establishment of anthropology at the Australian National University (ANU), with funding of posts from 1948, represented a major investment of Commonwealth funds. As the first annual report of the AIAS (1965, p. 8) observed, when the ANRC terminated its activities, 'the number of anthropologists making field studies decreased to a point where, at times, there were none in the field at all'.

Of course, until the early sixties, the number of anthropologists in academic employment was few in any case. Radcliffe-Brown had recognised the problem in 1930, when he wrote to the ANRC as follows (National Library, ANRC Ms482 Box 60./849, to Osborn, 4 Dec 1930):

> We must either find salaried appointments for the anthropologists we have trained, or they must abandon anthropology. If no salaried appointments are available we cannot, in fairness to them, permit any more students to devote themselves to anthropology as a career — Hogbin and Hart will be returning from abroad well trained in anthropology. They cannot depend for a livelihood on occasional research grants from the Australian National Research Council. Nor can we find room for them in the University. The Council must therefore recognise that if anthropological research in Australia is to proceed — some provision must be made for salaried research appointments ...

Wise words, but their author had clay feet. At this time, Radcliffe-Brown, the only tenured anthropologist in Australia, was negotiating for a post at Chicago.

The research funding drought broke around 1964, when the Social Sciences Research Council sponsored the 'Aborigines in Australian Society' project, under Charles Rowley's wise direction. Its scale of funding was unprecedented, as the Myer Foundation and the Myer Charity Trust contributed $78,000, while the remaining quarter came from the Council's own resources. Public sector sponsorship also took an equally dramatic leap forward in that year, with the formal commitment to the AIAS. Funds available in the 1964–65 financial year were over $135,000; by 1969–70 the grant was $400,000. Much too little, many complained, but when seen in historical perspective, it constituted a brave new research world.

I have compiled a summary of Institute funded projects 1961–85. During the period 1926–61, it seems improbable that more than 75 research projects were undertaken from Australian institutions into Aboriginal society (around 25 per cent of ANRC projects were centred in New Guinea). No matter how the statistics are counted over the Institute years, over 1300 Institute funded projects are numbered, presumably representing several hundred person-years of research. Whether quantity has swamped quality is a question to ponder, but in most cases the answer is, I believe, in the negative. To this research must be added Australian Research Grants Scheme sponsored projects; those funded by government departments, such as Health or Education; or Commonwealth scholarship recipients.

An accurate tally requires detailed research into all Institute research files. I used my thumb as a rule. Accounting procedures varied between annual reports; committee names and functions have changed; 1976–81 saw the category 'Aboriginal requested' cross many subject boundaries and range beyond them; special funds were earmarked 1972–75 for site recording. At times 'limited' or 'emergency' grants have varied in size and scope, and at times were not listed separately. The 1961–72 figures are adapted from the 1971–72 annual report. Taking my table as a general guide only, however, it makes the point. Participants at the 1961 conference were correct in their sense of 'making history'. The creation of the Institute was a watershed in developing a systematic corpus of information about Aboriginal society and, despite its critics, this data is not a non-Aboriginal monopoly. My summary table does not include all those other resources which make the Institute an archive of the Aboriginal heritage for all Australians: the sound and pictorial archives, the ongoing film program, the bibliographical records and the library, with its 1206 theses and the world's best assemblage of written records on Indigenous Australia.

Not everybody has been optimistic about the direction or nature of Institute policies. Too often, it has been regarded as some monolithic and inflexible body. Let us return to the 1961 conference, and set it into its context.

Not surprisingly, this meeting reflected many perceptions of that period which appear unduly restrictive today. Hindsight may encourage criticism, but it must be tempered by praise for what it represented and what Wentworth and Stanner achieved during less enlightened times. Three aspects of that conference are relevant here. Although 55 scholars assembled, not a single Aboriginal person was present; 20 papers were discussed across diverse disciplines, but the detailed history of Aboriginal society since 1788 was not amongst them; policy formulation was dominated by a sense of urgency — it was a race against passing time, which, it was assumed, shortly would extinguish traditional culture — and 'salvage' was its ethos. This was a gathering of scholars to discuss scientific and cultural problem in a backward-looking manner; its problems virtually excluded current welfare or politics. The reason is not far to seek.

Listen to the future Prime Minister, Senator John Gorton, introducing the Bill into the Senate on 7 May 1964:

> I think it is important to clarify to the Senate the Government's concept of the role of a permanent institute of aboriginal studies. The permanent institute will not be concerned with current problems as they affect the Australian aborigine. Its work will be scientific and anthropological. This is made clear in the bill in the section dealing with the functions to be assigned to the institute; but I think it is important to stress the academic nature of the work of the institute. I should add that it is not the Government's intention that the institute should become a super department of anthropology with a large research programme in its own right and conducted by its own professional staff. It is not intended that the new institute should rival existing institutions, or do work which properly and conveniently lies within the appropriate departments of universities and similar institutions. It will exist to complement the work of these institutions, to work through them, and to strengthen them by its activity' (Australia, Senate 1964, no. 19, pp. 1027–8).

Although Gorton asserted that the Act 'made clear' that 'current problems' were excluded from its functions, the Act (Sect. 6) does nothing of the sort. Yet this was government policy and the Institute during its infant years felt constrained to keep within those limits, presumably under ministerial advice.

Even its twin proponents, Mr Beazley and Mr Wentworth, specifically referred to these constraints in their speeches in the House of Representatives on 20 May 1964. In that political climate, not to have done so would have courted disaster. They both hinted, however, at the difficulty of keeping within those limits.

Mr Beazley said:

> I hope that the respect for the aboriginal people that this legislation implies carries over into other items of policy. I know that it is not a function of the Australian Institute of Aboriginal Studies to make any comments on aboriginal policy. It is not a policy-making body; it is a scientific body. But it is inevitable, if the government is enlightened, that what the institute does will affect policy, even though that is not its primary aim. Already the work of the institute has very clear implications for education. It has very clear implications for psychology. It has very clear implications in understanding the whole question of linguistics — that is, how languages came into being. It has very clear implications in health policy: All these studies, I hope, will affect policy, though the institute does nothing to set out to suggest policy. (Australia, House of Representatives 1964, no. 21, pp. 2161–2)

Mr Wentworth agreed:

> entirely with the point made by the honorable member for Fremantle that, although the intentions of this institute are academic, it will help

us to handle the problems, whether they be in regard to assimilation or anything else, of our relations with aborigines a little better than they have been handled. Understanding of aborigines has been lacking in the past. I find myself in complete agreement with the statement by the honorable member for Fremantle that this institute will help in the administrative policy although the Institute itself will have, and should have, nothing to do with policy in the first degree. It is an academic organization which may provide instruments for other people to use, but in itself should have no part in policy. (Australia, House of Representatives 1964, no. 21, pp. 2166)

The Institute's brief, therefore, was defined more narrowly through its first decade. Its research and recording were of fundamental importance, but it focussed exclusively on traditionally oriented people, defined as 'tribal' and assumed to preserve pristine traditions or customs. The study of urban or fringe dwelling communities, or the history of Aboriginal people since 1788, or of cultural adaptations in the face of white domination, were excluded as subjects beyond its scope. This policy contrasts with the ANRC funding phase, when considerable research was attempted on such matters.

The 1960s coincided with the terminal phase of the publicised but unsuccessful government assimilation policy, based on its paternalistic Eurocentric assumption that the amalgamation of the two races constituted a virtual one-way transformation which would convert 'them' to 'us'. Quite apart from the political expedient of urging action in a crisis situation, this ethos served to underline the 'salvage' emergency mentality, before ancient traditions were assumed to all perish with the present generation of elders. In retrospect, there was a strong covert element of sexism in this salvage program, because there was little emphasis upon females as repositories of tradition. Anthropology remained a predominantly male preserve, and senior anthropologists stressed the role of 'the old men' as the fount of arcane knowledge.

During the 1960s, many members sought to expand the Institute's brief away from exclusive concern with traditionally oriented societies. Remember that the political and intellectual ferment of this period coincided with the Freedom Rides, Wattie Creek, the 1966 Pastoral Award and the 1967 referendum. Early in Peter Ucko's Principalship, important changes took place. In the 1972–73 Annual Report (pp. 7–8), the first of his administration, he noted that 'urban and semi-urban Aborigines' had been neglected and that 'Council has now agreed that the Institute should carry out research in the "contact" situation'. In the meantime, of course, the Whitlam government had assumed office. In a review of 1973 activities, published in the January 1974 *Newsletter* (p. 14), Ucko observed that it was essential to 'convince those in power that research and Aboriginal indigenous activity are not separate activities but are intimately connected, and inextricably bound together'. This rethinking was therefore in place before the biennial meeting in May 1974, which witnessed successful demands for greater Aboriginal participation in Institute affairs.

It did *not* require any changes in the Act to bring these new research directions into operation, or to arrange for Aboriginal participation in decision-making. Many consider that the adaptations over the past decade have been too slow or merely token. Again, however, they need to be set into their historical and political context. The comparison is best made between the 1961 conference and those themes and participants which today would constitute a comparable conference of assessment. Events during the past decade or so are too close to pursue here.

In Elkin's paper at the 1961 meeting, he referred to the needs of archaeology. 'The future is brightening', he observed (in Sheils 1963, p. 23). 'The University of Melbourne has a prehistorian on its History staff, and the Australian National University and the University of Sydney has each appointed an archaeologist — These specialists, the students whom they will train and the fellow workers whom they will attract, will be able to work on the numerous and varied sites which are there for the searching. The rewards will be great'.

Well, a quarter of century on, those rewards have added a new dimension not only to Australian history, but to world prehistory. Let us turn to the significance of these discoveries. I summed the matter up for European Australians in 1969, when I challenged conventional explanations of our history. The opening sentence of my *The Prehistory of Australia* asserted that, 'the discoverers, explorers, and colonists of ... Australia, were its Aborigines' (1969, p. 12).

This is not the place to attempt a critique of prehistoric research, but it is necessary to highlight some issues of significance. The first is the chronological revolution, which the Institute assisted by promoting the foundation of the radiocarbon laboratory at the ANU, and by funding the costs of sample dating at other laboratories. In 1961 there were chiefly three places where claims were made for human occupation earlier than 10,000 years ago, the conventional end of the Pleistocene epoch, or ice age. These were Kangaroo Island, where Norman B Tindale worked; Keilor, under investigation by Edmund D Gill; and Koonalda cave, where Dr Sandor Gallus claimed the presence of Pleistocene artefacts and mural art. Later research and radiocarbon 14 dating established the validity of their claims, but at that time stratigraphic evidence which included artefacts or other associated cultural material was lacking.

The dating of the Kenniff cave sequence during 1962 placed Australian settlement and recognisable artefacts within the context of Late Pleistocene times. Dating of Koonalda, Keilor and Alligator River sites by 1966, with artefacts associated in stratified context, pushed a human presence back to around 20,000 years ago. At this time sea level was at its lowest, and New Guinea, Tasmania and Kangaroo Island all formed part of the continental mass. Within another five years, dates from Lake Mungo pushed the human time range beyond 30,000 years. After excavations there during 1973, age estimates resulted in a possible 40,000 years occupation. Comparable antiquity was established subsequently for sites on the upper Swan River, WA, and on the Huon Peninsula, Papua New Guinea. With the development of more refined dating techniques, there are revisions likely which may render these dates too conservative. Ages of 50,000 years or more are possible. Two sites on the Hopkins River, Warrnambool, have been claimed by Edmund D Gill as possessing even greater antiquity, but further research is necessary to establish positive human associations.

Even if the current minimal date of 40,000 years is taken as the established figure, consider the dramatic implications. Within only twelve years, archaeological research added 30,000 years to Australia's human past. No parallel exists elsewhere for such an expanded time dimension for modern society. The further back into the past that a human presence is extended, the more remarkable becomes the sea crossing which enabled the first colonisation. Whatever its motive or means, it ranks as the world's earliest major sea voyage.

Around 20,000 years ago, when the Australian climate was at its coldest, people had entered widely diverse environments. These included the arid Mt Newman region of the Pilbara and the Arnhem Land escarpment, an area then far inland. The New Guinea highlands and remote caves in south-west Tasmania also were occupied, within sight of glaciers. Colonists evidently adapted to regionally diverse and unfamiliar flora and fauna, and they co-existed for thousands of years with the now extinct giant marsupial fauna, including diprotodon.

Further testimony to the adaptive and creative spirit of these ancestral Aborigines is indicated by a number of inventions. Across the cold south-east, bone tools resembling awls were manufactured, possibly used to sew pelts together for clothing during those cold times. The points were manufactured through rubbing on abrasive stone. A comparable grinding technique was applied to stone tools, because Arnhem Land hatchet blades are older than 20,000 years. Along with Japanese examples, these constitute the world's first evidence for shaping stone by grinding. Some specimens possess hammered or pecked grooves, a device for holding the handle firmly in place, again the earliest evidence for hammer dressing. Recently, even older examples have been recovered from a 40,000 years old context on a former shore line on the Huon Peninsula.

Another grinding technique was the employment of flat slabs, or mortars, for grinding dry grass seeds to flour. Dates of over 12,000 years have been claimed, although this antiquity is disputed by others. Whatever its origin, the technology of flour production was a vital strategy for survival in arid lands.

Wooden tools survive less frequently, but in a swamp near Mt Gambier fragments of boomerangs and barbed wooden spears have been excavated, indicating their use over 8,000 years ago. Paintings in different styles are superimposed upon rock walls in Arnhem Land. This visual evidence indicates that there were periods when spear-throwers were fashionable, sometimes boomerangs, and at other times, hand-held spears were carried. The analysis of stone tools from excavations also demonstrates that there were both regional differences in technology and chronological changes in the types of artefacts used.

Apart from such material evidence for change through time, Lake Mungo provided insight into the symbolic world. Red pigment fragments were carried there and left at lakeside camps even before 32,000 years ago. The purpose of the ochre is unknown, but an extended male burial was interred about 30,000 years ago, with powdered ochre dusted over the corpse. Less than a kilometre away, but dating from some 4000 years later, was a cremated female. This is the world's oldest recorded cremation, and it was a complex ritual in which the burnt bones were smashed and the ashes buried. Archaeology demonstrates that the practice persisted throughout prehistoric times in south-eastern Australia, including Tasmania.

The hints of body decoration implicit in the ochred burial are amplified by later finds. At Devil's Lair, WA, marsupial bone beads were recovered, dating prior to 12,000 years ago. Various burials in the Murray valley, including examples at Kow Swamp, were interred with ornaments or wearing necklaces or chaplets of marsupial bones or teeth. The most notable find was the necklace worn by the Nitchie male, buried in western New South Wales over 6000 years ago. It consisted of 178 pierced Tasmanian devil teeth. Significantly, this man had lost his upper incisors during his lifetime. As a number of other burials in the Murray valley dating from the last few thousand years also show a similar condition, it is reasonable to infer that it resulted from ritual tooth avulsion. This was the most widespread Australian initiation rite in 1788, so its origins are remote.

Aboriginal people are sensitive to archaeological investigations involving human remains. Archaeologists, however, can derive vital clues to ancient ritual life and cognitive systems and so increase Aboriginal knowledge concerning their spiritual life and increase general community respect for Aboriginal society. Material proof of the continuity of spiritual values and ritual practices could become invaluable 'deeds' to land title. For the increasing number of Aboriginal children being educated in the general Australian community, and lacking direct contact with traditional communities, such evidence provides invaluable documentation of their cultural heritage.

The art on rock surfaces offers another set of glimpses into ancient creativity and belief systems. Engravings at the Early Man shelter, near Laura, are positively older than 13,000 years. Wall markings in the darkness of Koonalda cave may have survived for 20,000 years. Astonishingly similar designs have been discovered in a number of caves near Mt Gambier through the enterprise of RG Bednarik and GD Aslin (1985). Research here may confirm this antiquity.

There are numerous paintings of thylacines (Tasmanian tiger) in Arnhem Land and engravings of the same species occur in the Pilbara. As thylacines were extinct everywhere but in Tasmania when Europeans arrived, these pictures must be ancient. The arrival of the dingo from Asia, possibly about 3500 years ago, may have caused their extinction. Tasmanian devil species also were extinct on the mainland in European times. Remembering that Nitchie man had a necklace requiring almost 50 animals to produce the necessary teeth, it is a reminder that the combined onslaught of human hunters and predatory dogs may have affected the distribution of animal species during prehistoric times.

Even this selective sketch suffices to establish the importance of Australia as a focus for technological invention and for distinctive artistic and conceptual systems. Their origins are so remote in time that this continent ranks amongst the oldest and most significant creative regions of modern humanity. Ancient Australia is endowed with a dignity, therefore, and modern Aboriginal Australians are correct to be proud of their cultural inheritance. Despite contemporary tendencies towards claiming a unitary culture, however, the extent of distinctive regional variation in Aboriginal culture during recent centuries needs stressing. That there existed no single Aboriginal Way is reflected in the regionally diverse archaeological remains and the technological and aesthetic variation reflected in material culture and art forms. The extent of linguistic differences is another striking indicator of diversity. Any assessment of Australia before the Europeans must take this into account, just as the extent of Aboriginal contact with Papuan and eastern Indonesian peoples is another factor fostering innovation and local variation.

Another complex reality in the pattern of human settlement was the extent of environmental fluctuation which communities faced. Seas retreated some 140 metres below present sea level and surged back again; freshwater lakes in the interior were transformed into saline or dry basins and massive rivers ceased to flow; volcanoes erupted and died; numerous animal species became extinct, especially larger forms; many landscapes changed because of the human practice of regularly firing vegetation; forests retreated and advanced following temperature and rainfall fluctuations. Research during the past 25 years has documented these changes and demonstrated the contemporaneity of humans even with massive environmental changes. Consequently, just as Aboriginal societies were dynamic and regionally complex through time, environments and ecological niches were never static.

If the state of prehistory was in flux, so is the contemporary archaeological scene, no more so than in the relationship between archaeologists and Aborigines. I can claim to be the first of the few archaeologists in academic employment in 1961, so as an elder today I feel astonished by the rapid expansion in knowledge and numbers involved. I am deeply disturbed, however, by the loose use of data by prehistorians, myself included, and by the reception of this knowledge by many prominent Aboriginal leaders. At the risk of prompting criticism, I feel obliged to voice my problems. Note that they apply equally to practitioners and to Aboriginal people.

Prehistorians and historians must maintain their academic objectivity and standards, even in the face of unpopularity or criticism. They cannot maintain their academic integrity if they board the latest bandwagon and mouth popular sentiments simply to curry favour. I note that Diane Barwick, always an outspoken scholar, voiced similar worries concerning historians in one of her latest publications. Barwick (1985, p. 221) remarked that 'revisionist accounts of Aboriginal history are now fashionable, but their writers seem to commemorate examples of confrontation with more eagerness than they describe the process of accommodation. They commend Aborigines ... who returned violence for violence. They ignore, or else dismiss as turncoats, "trusties" and "Uncle Toms", those Aboriginal men and women who were apparently willing to negotiate with the invaders — and sufficiently wily to exploit them.'

Although the following comments also apply to my own writings, I am motivated by doubts similar to Barwick's, concerning archaeological explanation and Aboriginal interpretations of prehistoric data.

The 'ethnographic present' has become a useful resource for prehistorians as a model for the explication of archaeological data or situations. The literature is extensive and much benefit has been derived. Yet, given the cultural and environmental changes outlined previously, I suspect that the model derived from recent ethnographic situations is an oversimplification. Inherited human experience is another factor to be taken into account, making later situations more complex than earlier ones. I suspect that the use of ethnographic analogies serves to exaggerate the extent of general continuity, thereby minimising more detailed change. If this applies to archaeological reconstruction, it relates even more emphatically to some Aboriginal conceptions of the past. My earlier outline of changes in salient cultural and environmental factors makes it obvious that conditions in some earlier Dreaming time *cannot* have persisted unchanged into the present. Neither the laws of nature nor the rules of Dreaming ancestors were immutable.

Accepting the conservative estimate of a human arrival in Australia at least 40,000 years ago, it is valid to claim that stone tools and the use of fire extends back to that period. Until older human remains, artefacts or other evidence for cultural activities are isolated and dated, claims for earlier occupation are unsubstantiated and best ignored. On the other hand, the first dated and published human bones comprise both the Mungo inhumation and the cremation, circa 30,000 and 26,000 years old respectively. No other human remains are dated earlier than 15,000 years ago. Allowing a generous 25 years per human generation, this means that there are no human bones for the first 10,000 years or more — possibly a minimum of 400 generations. Our sample from the following 600 generations consists of one male and one female. How reliable are inferences drawn from a sample size of two persons in 1000 generations? Is it an act of faith rather than scientific proof to claim the first colonists as ancestral Aborigines?

There are claims in the media that *Homo sapiens* originated in Australia. This may prove to be correct, but it lacks foundation or logic at present. The earliest toolmakers in Afro-Asia are over 2 million years old, and fire was used some million years ago. *Homo erectus*, evidently an efficient hunter-gatherer, colonised widely and reached China and Java possibly 1.2 million to 800,000 years ago. Neanderthal people possessed a complex stone technology, comparable to the early Australian practice, and adopted complex burial rites almost 50,000 years ago in the Middle East. Anatomically-modern *Homo sapiens* remains occur in burials in France and in the Middle East at least as early as the Mungo burials. Present evidence from South Africa and Ethiopia suggests that *Homo sapiens* may belong to the period 60,000 to 120,000 years ago (Klasies River mouth; Border cave; Omo), supporting claims that modern people evolved in Africa.

In island south-east Asia (Palawan, Borneo, Java, Sulawesi) there is evidence for the presence of *Homo sapiens* during the period c.40,000–20,000 years ago, associated with a stone technology which bears comparison with that of the earliest Australian industries. Taking all this data into account, the most economical hypothesis is to assume that human society developed outside Australia and that the first colonists brought with them invisible baggage which included a stone techno-complex and a knowledge of fire.

Despite the vehemence of Aboriginal assertions to an origin within this continent, such inferences need not conflict with Aboriginal beliefs. This is a subject meriting joint Aboriginal and anthropological discussion. I note that there are numerous Dreaming creation-time stories in tropical Cape York and Arnhem Land, involving the arrival of beings from the sea, or from the north. On the other hand, creator-beings in the arid interior frequently moved along those Dreaming tracks which crisscross the Centre. Many of these beings in the tropics or in the desert simply did not emerge in situ, but they travelled long distances to get there. It is interesting to reflect that the earliest radiocarbon dates available today are peripheral to the Australian heartland.

I am concerned that an undue emphasis upon a separate origin for the Australian race could produce unforeseen political consequences. Obviously, if scientific evolutionary theory is rejected by Aboriginal creationists, who also ignore the archaeological evidence for human antiquity in south-east Asia, the claim is lodged for a separate human origin within Australia.

Multi-racial theories of creation are not new. Before the American Civil War the theory of polygenesis became popular for sinister reasons. In order to demonstrate that Negro slavery was justified and not a violation of human rights, some theorists postulated that the Negro race was created separately from the Caucasian. The conclusion was obvious: the Negro race was inferior and unconnected with 'normal' humans. The appeal of this doctrine is indicated by the popularity of a prominent American exposition of polygenesis. When Nott and Gliddon published *Types of Mankind* in 1854, it went through three editions by 1857. Human rights are universal to all people, races and creeds. If the separateness of the Aboriginal race from the rest of humankind were seized upon by opponents as a political or land rights issue, it could prove unfortunate.

A group of Aboriginal historians recently defended the proposition that 'Aboriginal history should be written by Aboriginal people', implying that nobody else may do so validly (Atkinson et al. 1985, pp. 38–9). From comments made to me by Aboriginal people, I deduce that some believe that this applies also to the study of prehistory, which, they insist, should be termed history. I am willing to accept the latter redefinition and call that period prior to 1788, 'Ancient Australian History'.

Naturally, I urge Aboriginal people to write history of their people or to become archaeologists of their past. However, I reject emphatically the notion that learning can be a monopoly based solely upon racial grounds. In my opinion, these historians confuse the collection and custodianship of a corpus of source material (in their case, chiefly oral, but if it is to be used by others over time, necessarily material committed to paper), with its interpretation. Addressing a planning conference for a history of a Australia to celebrate the bicentenary of European settlement Marcia Langton (cited in Broomfield 1997, p. 23) states that 'white people would not tamper with the structure and form of the Iliad ... or Shakespeare'. Quite so, although I spent some years lecturing on Greek history, using the Iliad as a text for studying social and economic history, and its form and structure were irrelevant to my purpose. For example, I selected those sections which described burial rituals and, having explicated them, compared the data with archaeological evidence obtained from Bronze Age tombs, both in the Aegean area and in western Europe. My interpretation may have erred, but the scholarly apparatus used is international in character. My interpretation could be refuted if somebody disagreed, for the texts remained intact. Significantly, I did not have to be a Greek in order to study them, and I used prehistoric Greek evidence to interpret and explain western European cremation burial practices.

Along with the Aboriginal historians, I accept that Aboriginal people are the guardians and custodians of our history and culture, and it is our responsibility to pass onto future generations our set of truths. If, however, those guardians and custodians also act as gaolers, while claiming infallibility in interpreting their source material based upon race, totalitarianism is just down the road.

References

Atkinson, W, Langton, H, Wanganeen, D & Williams M 1985, 'A celebration of resistance to colonialism', in M Hill & A Barlow (eds), *Black Australia*, AIAS, Canberra.

Australia, Senate 1964, *Debates*, no. 19, pp. 1026–8.

Australia, House of Representatives 1964, *Debates*, no. 21, pp. 2160–73.

Australian Institute of Aboriginal Studies 1965, *Report of the Australian Institute of Aboriginal Studies for the period*, AIAS, Canberra.

Barwick, DE 1985, 'This most resolute lady: A biographical puzzle', in DE Barwick, J Beckett & M Reay (eds), *Metaphors of interpretation*, ANU Press, Canberra.

Bednarick, EK and Aslin, GD 1985, 'The parietal markings project: A progress report', *Rock Art Research*, no. 2, pp. 71–4.

Broomfield, J 1997, *Other ways of knowing: Recharting our future with ageless wisdom*, Rochester, VT: Inner Traditions.

Elkin, AP 1945, National Library, ANRC, MS 482, Box 32/99, 16 October.

—— 1949, *Report to Australian National Research Council*, NL, ANRC MS482, Box 35/538.

Gorton, J 1964, House of Representatives *Hansard*. 7 May.

Mulvaney, DJ 1969, *The prehistory of Australia*, Thames & Hudson, London.

Nott, JC & Gliddon, GR 1854, *Types of Mankind*, Philadelphia.

Sheils, H (ed.) 1963, *Australian Aboriginal Studies*, OUP, Melbourne.

Social Science Research Council of Australia, 1956. *Annual Report*.

Wentworth, WC 1819, *A statistical, historical and political description of the colony of New South Wales*, London.

Original lecture available at:
<http://aiatsis.gov.au/publications/presentations/sense-making-history-australian-aboriginal-studies-1961-1985>

5

Not land rights but land rites

1988 Wentworth Lecture

Ken Colbung

Foreword
Ronald M Berndt

A Wentworth Lecture is a prestigious event, not only for the person who is to deliver it but also for the Australian Institute of Aboriginal Studies. On this particular occasion, the recipient of this honour is Ken Colbung, who has chosen a title that is certainly provocative. The subject matter he provides concerns some issues of considerable complexity.

If I understand correctly the drift of his theme, he is taking as a baseline the well-known assumption that traditionally oriented Aborigines have a close and intimate spiritual affinity to their land; and that that assumption may be applied more generally to encourage attitudes relating to the protection and conservation of the natural environment; in turn, he suggests, the general adoption of that view could conceivably lead to a greater understanding and appreciation of Aboriginal and other (for example, European) cultures. Perhaps I am putting the thrust of his argument too simply — but I have not yet had the advantage of reading or hearing his lecture.

In this short paper I propose to examine the theme, or themes, in a preliminary way, recognising that most of what I have to say would really require considerable elaboration. Before I can do this, we need to look at Mr Colbung's Lecture title. As it stands it is rather ambiguous. In view of the Aboriginal land rights platform, we can suppose that he does not intend to deny that aspiration. Rather, the title reminds us that religious rites concern the land, and are in themselves substantiation of specific socio-personal ties with the land — as well as being direct and indirect statements about land 'ownership' and use. One point here is that the emphasis on 'land rites' invites us to espouse a religious approach to the land in order to nurture that land. How far this is possible for the majority of us, in practical terms, is open to question. So is the assumption that the more we know of a culture other than our own, the less tension will exist between members of those cultures, and the greater the likelihood of a better understanding between them. Nevertheless, there are ingredients in all cultures that could conceivably be drawn upon, to lead to a more general rapprochement between the cultures concerned.

One of the problems in discussing a theme of this kind, involving traditional Aboriginal societies and cultures on one side, and non-Aboriginal societies and cultures, mostly of European-origin, on the other, is that the differences between them are quite obtrusive in almost all respects — not least in politico-economic and technological frames of reference, including, among other things, such fields of thought and action as the physical and social sciences. Beyond the dimension of social relations, and basic physiological concerns, there is, or has been, little in the way of common ground. Where there is commonality of intention, this is often wrapped up in such differing cultural packages, in relation to practices and values, that it is not always easily identified.

The issue, however, is really much more difficult. As you will appreciate, I am making artificial contrasts, using a generalised concept of traditional Aboriginal society, and coalescing a range of cultural and subcultural patterns that are often arbitrarily categorised as 'European'. That is social-anthropologically indefensible. The reality, in regard to Aboriginal Australia, is that while modified traditional socio-cultural frames of reference continue to exist in some parts of Australia, the range of people and groups identified as Aboriginal is now wide and varying, embracing many who are only partially Aboriginal in socio-cultural terms and are indeed very closely involved in what is called 'the wider Australian society'. While many Aborigines at the latter end of this continuum emphasise their Aboriginal heritage, that heritage has assumed the perspective of being a kind of Aboriginal 'Golden Age' that is far removed from the reality of what is categorised as being a near-traditional Aboriginal heritage. I don't want to labour this point, but it is one which should be thoughtfully recognised.

* * * * *

My theme in this historic lecture, and historic year, will be 'Not Land Rights, But Land Rites'. This theme is both controversial and idealistic. The controversial aspects are bound up in the way I will be using the words 'rights' and 'rites'. My use of the word 'rights' will be obvious to most people, and it relates to the political and legal rights in our everyday lives. However, this use is not so simple because it has something to do with ritual or spiritual actions of a customary or cultural nature. The idealistic aspects of this paper are not something I want to evade. Nor do I want to run away from this problem because I happen to be looking into the unknown. Making predictions about the next two centuries might present, to some, an impossible task; however, I do have a bias, which encourages me to go ahead and give the message contained within the theme of this lecture. My lecture tonight does have a message both for Aboriginal and other Australians. In giving it, while I have a debt of gratitude to the AIAS staff and the many inspiring comments received from people to whom I wrote, I accept full responsibility for the ideas I am about to present.

The task I have of encouraging Aboriginal people to set their own social and cultural agenda far into the next two centuries is an important exercise, for two reasons. The first is that Aboriginal people are too often led up political blind alleys. Although it may appear to Aboriginal and non-Aboriginal supporters of 'land rights' that I am arguing in direct opposition to what they believe, or think they believe, that is not the case. What I am doing is clearing some of the dead wood away in order for us all to see more clearly into the future. The second reason is that there are many Aboriginal and non-Aboriginal Australians who hold little or no concern for protection of the environment, and for its enjoyment by others. What I am talking about is two great themes of the past and two groups of people living in the one society. I will talk about Aboriginal society first, then about Australian society, and my focus is on customs and beliefs about our society. It is impossible to talk about the next two hundred years without making some reference to the past. While the references will be brief, I think they are important because some Australians have failed totally to take account of them. It is my hope, and from those I know here tonight it is their hope, that a change will take place in human consciousness about our habitat.

Current knowledge shows clearly that human beings have been living on this continent for 40,000 years and, a recent report indicates, perhaps even 80,000 years. Those human beings, we now appreciate, had an extremely good record of living in a very harsh natural environment without wreaking havoc, either on the human beings they lived with or on nature. Furthermore, those same peoples, we now know, cooperated with groups at great distances from the areas in which they themselves lived. Today we look back in wonder at such an achievement: that people were able to solve what is to us such unsolvable problems, in a seemingly simple way. It is true that just 200 years ago the two greatest obstacles to European occupation were that they couldn't communicate with Aboriginals or the environment. Likewise, when we look back to the late 1960s and early 1970s, it was a simple matter to talk about 'land rights', and to think in terms of either a solution to the need for resources (and this means money capital) or the ownership (and this means owning large areas of property, of land). It may appear to some here (and I know it has a reality for many short-sighted Aboriginal political and moral activists in Australian society) that we had discovered something new about what Aboriginal people had been thinking about, or the way they acted, over the past 200 years, and that the solutions would rest on money and property. This was an illusion, because if we look briefly at how the issues of land management and land distribution affected other countries we might see some similarities with ourselves.

European and American dilemmas: Land management and distribution

I want to suggest that the reform movements of the nineteenth and early twentieth century had to face very similar questions to the kinds of problems faced by Aboriginal society, such as, poverty, dispossession and environmental mismanagement.

If we look at England in the mid-nineteenth century we can see that poverty and land shortages were closely related, For example, the growth of industry and the movement of populations into towns and the cities meant growing health problems. When town populations and the areas of land they lived on expanded, more food was needed and, in turn, more land was needed by the farmers to feed these populations. This process began earlier but showed up in the 1830s. By the 1840s, the conditions were created which gave almost everyone a better standard of living. The point to be made here is that human problems have always revolved around space, wellbeing and cooperation: here was a victory for conservation.

America is not noted, especially if we take a guide from the last two or so decades, for human-social management, but in the 1930s it was the leader of the world. In that period the emergence of huge areas of common land, together with huge resources for both indigenous peoples and other Americans, had been set aside as a heritage for use by today's society. This type of action, and earlier human activity in England, can be seen as humanitarian acts by past societies out of concern for present-day peoples. The actions of those idealists were sufficiently realistic to make some lasting impact for the common good. I want to ask the question: what has been the Australian experience?

The Australian Experience: space, wellbeing and cooperation

If we look closely at Australian history in this century we can see that reserves (that is, land set aside for use and benefit of Aboriginals by governments or even church lands used as missions) have been the history of my own, and many other, Aboriginal people, a Welfare throw-back from old colonial times. It should not be forgotten that huge areas of land have been set aside for common use by federal and state governments since the First World War. By this I am saying that providing land to certain groups in society for one reason or another is not unique, because for land to be set aside for use by Aboriginals has been part of our history since about the 1820s. Aboriginals, like anyone with a legitimate or proven case of need and entitlement, may require government to provide for their needs. Aboriginal political, social, economic and cultural needs are, for the most part, common to those needs of the general society: in other words, Aboriginal needs are both common and special, but they all fall into the area of space wellbeing and cooperation.

On the issue of the need for space or land, I want it clearly understood what I am saying. Now, Justice Woodwood stated what the land rights debate, and the concept, were all about. The issue, as we know, arose out of the *Gove Case*. But the two issues are, in one sense, separate, because one was concerned with sacred sites and rites associated with traditional understanding of caring for land; the other was concerned with political rights to land. In part, the issue has been clouded by the misconceptions of these two words. In part also, the issue has become confused by what modern political action, and the interpretation of those actions, represent. I am not against 'land rights' but I am against turning land 'rights' into material gain by a few.

Recently Professor Blainey has objected to the recognition of Aboriginal heritage being enshrined in the constitution. This is no simple question and involves dividing what is political from what is democratic. As a member of a minority of which all Aboriginal issues are intrinsically involved, Australian politics has neither protected our land rights nor our land rites. Democracy, on the other hand, can guarantee what Aboriginals are entitled to for their wellbeing.

To enshrine Aboriginal heritage within the constitutional document protects us from the 'mob' and the 'mob' from our own extreme political demands. Our wellbeing is legitimately based upon provable pre-existing rights.

On this point of pre-existing rights, I concur with Henry Reynolds, the Australian historian, when he argues that history has shown that the whole of the Aboriginal peoples possessed 'pre-existing title to the land', and other property rights, which were part and parcel of the Australian Aboriginal peoples' prior occupation. When the British unjustly, and wrongfully, claimed the continent for itself, those pre-existing rights had never been recognised nor has the question of compensation been seriously confronted. If, for example, this issue was taken seriously, the preservation and perpetuation of Aboriginal democratic rights could also be preserved by the creation of an institution which could be modelled around the kinds of democratic bodies which already exist, such as independent political bodies of the trade unions and other democratic bodies. We could, therefore, be free of governments and this would allow us to care for our own political and democratic self-determination. As it currently stands, Aboriginal organisations cannot be free of well-known Australian bureaucratisation. One could talk for some time on this issue alone, but I want to move on and talk about cooperation.

Historically, and in pre-contact history, Aborigines have been most efficient land managers. In modern times Aboriginal people have deep within their culture an obligation to protect the land upon which they have lived. Intrinsic to that obligation was the right to occupy land and that right was recognised by all who lived near and far. If the land was not cared for or managed to the satisfaction of all then it was taken over by people who could do so. Cooperation, therefore, by land managers was an essential humanness of my people. It is important for us here today, and in particular for those political conservatives like Professor Blainey and Aboriginal political extremists, to understand this most important concept of cooperation. It involved cooperation between land managers with their traditional obligations and with other human beings.

In the 1920s, a great deal of land was provided for reserves. At this time Aboriginal people were thought to be a 'dying race', and the mentality was one of 'welfare'. Likewise, other Australians have sought land for common use, and it was not long ago when national parks were something used only for respites on picnic days. In other words, there was a social, political, economic and spiritual consciousness based more on the political expediencies of the day, rather than upon any consciousness which saw something of value in the preservation of the balance between humans and nature.

The long view of Aboriginal social, economic, political and spiritual relationships to the land has only emerged in the past two or so decades. Since the 1920s the thinking was that land upon which Aboriginal people lived would ultimately return to the wealth-stock of the dominant society. Thanks to democracy and not politics we are able to share in the long-term possessions of Australia rather than simply be a short-term social problem. By the 1940s, which was a time when it became widely accepted by the authorities that Aboriginal populations were increasing, forests and pastoral properties were seen as a way in which lands were purchased for habitat and employment reasons. For those who have this long view, the events and attitudes of the period 1972 to 1976 were not new; it was the old story with a new slant: Land rights had become property rights and not customary rites.

It is not a cynical thing to say that, 'the more things change the more they remain the same'. Looking back to the 1960s, land rights ideology, particularly as portrayed by young Aboriginal people in New South Wales, was to became a political slogan which captured the imagination of many short-sighted Aboriginal activists all over Australia. It became a political and moral strategy for a great many present-day Aboriginal groupings to monopolise areas of land for material gain. The result will be, particularly in NSW, that a terrible price will be paid in the next couple of years as the dismantling of the legislation takes place. The idea that the heritage of Aboriginal society is the preserve of a few short-sighted and self-seeking Aboriginal powerbrokers is a most disturbing thought, and in my view, exposes the fallacy of 'land rights'.

Moreover, there is the idea that the ownership of land is one where a few powerful family groups are able to reside, in an attempt to be like those rural farmers around whom they had grown up, and this has been the reward of only those few people supporting land rights. What was taken to be a legitimate political strategy for cultural self-correction became a dystopian strategy for self-destruction. Also, we can say that many of the real strengths of Australian political supporters were damaged. The perspective that self-correction would come from a deeper understanding of what our immediate ancestors were trying to tell us was lost in the rush for material gain and possession of property, not heritage. The real workers who built that support, in a painstaking and methodical way, are today the most disappointed among those still living. Let me give an example to show you who those workers were.

Certain scholars, along with a small number of politicians on both sides of politics of the conservative mould, can take the credit for any gains that were won in the years since the late 1930s. Two of the founding fathers of this Institute are representative of the kind of supporters I am talking about, WC Wentworth and WEH Stanner, in particular. These individuals strove to raise the status, in the minds of Australians generally, of traditions seen by most as exotic. The de-exoticisation of Aboriginal traditions was a cooperative task by scholars and politicians in all parts of Australia. Some Aboriginal people were able to help, and they did so wherever possible.

The formation of the Australian Institute of Aboriginal Studies in the early 1960s epitomised the cooperative nature of scholarship and politics. The AIAS began at the forefront of the hardest problem, that is, the self-correction of Australian society's ignorance. In this task these workers were able to show the immense strengths of Aboriginal traditions and culture. Furthermore, these workers were able to show to the whole world (and not just to a few nationalistic Aboriginal chauvinists or local Aboriginal monopolists) the antiquity, humanity and strength of that culture. These efforts of political diplomacy and scholarship have been some of the most monumental in world history. For example, archaeology in New South Wales was followed by the establishment of the Willandra Lakes as an area of World Heritage. Without that status as a site of significance there would have been nothing of value for Aboriginals or other people in which they could feel some pride. Other scholarship in and around Australia on Aboriginal culture, in particular in the Northern Territory, has profoundly changed Australian's perception about Aboriginal people (and it has profoundly changed Aboriginal perceptions of themselves for the better in some areas). Disciplines like anthropology, ethnology, linguistics, photography to mention a few, have contributed in many ways. Arts and culture can be included in the kinds of concerns that the AIAS membership has been responsible for protecting and promoting. The AIAS membership has been at the forefront, some may say blindly, of political controversy for which no apology is given. Nevertheless, it is the area of rites which I think that we have been most successful, and it is to this concept I will now turn, as a means of carrying some ideas I have into the future.

What do I mean by the word 'rites'?

Let me say immediately what I mean by 'rites' to land. When I use the word 'rites' I mean it to be understood as a formal procedure carried out in Aboriginal communities, or in a religious or solemn observance of other human beings, living or dead. What I mean is the customary practices which people develop among themselves, but yet, not practices which are offensive to themselves or to others. In short, customary practices which are deemed an important conserving factor of Aboriginal people's community customs and manners for which they want to be able to continue to practice. Let me say also that I am not advocating the reintroduction of practices which certain groups may believe were once part of ceremonies that are no longer used. For example, it is as unnatural for people to revert to the production of stone tools as a means of replacing steel hammers, as it is for Christian groups to introduce certain rituals which are outside either the spirit for which they were originally used or the spirit upon which such custom is based. In the same way, I am not in favour, nor am I advocating, the importation of other Aboriginal people's culture from inside Australia, where we are not willing to put the time and effort into the research on what those customs and manners really meant, or to research our own culture from our own areas. In other words, I am against the importation of customs that would offend the sensibilities of those from whom such practices are taken, thereby destroying and distorting other peoples' real meaning.

Every living tradition is profoundly shaped by its own history. Through that history even those features which it considers to be non-historical are strongly affected. 'Attempts to describe the essence of Aboriginal spiritualism in terms of absolute doctrinal formulations must fail simply because they neglect the historical dimension and the development that has led to those.

It is impossible to give a precise definition of 'spirit' or to point out the exact place and time of its origin.

Contemporary spiritualism preserves many elements from various sources, differently emphasised in various parts of the country and by individual groups of people. Roughly speaking, we may identify four main streams of tradition that have coalesced to form spiritually the traditions of the original inhabitants of Australia, whose cultures have been traced back about 40,000 years and some of whose practices and beliefs may still be alive among the numerous tribes of this country, thus implying a minimum of common beliefs and practices and freedom to follow individual traditions in all other matters.

Most Aboriginals prefer even now to define their religion, lore, culture, by more restricted names and call themselves Nyoongah, Yamaiji, Wongais or whatever group they belong to. But there are others who feel the need to define the unity underlying the nationhood of Aboriginal Australia in terms which allow Nyoongahs to transcend sectarian boundaries within Australia and at the same time distinguish them from the followers of other traditions. To define such a people is impossible, just as we cannot express or define 'reality' because words came into existence after reality. Similar is the case with Nyoongah people. They existed when there was no necessity for any name. They were the good, the enlightened people. They were the people who know about the laws of nature and the laws of the spirit. They built a great civilisation, a great culture and a unique social order.

'Rites' to land not land 'rights': The next two hundred years

Aboriginal society has literally come back from the grave since the 1920s. In part, this survival is due to Aboriginal society's incredible capacity, as human beings, to withstand internal violence, apathy and ignorance, together with the tremendous pressures placed upon us from the wider Australian society. In part also, it has been the basic strength of our deep understanding of the belief in our heritage. Although we are, in reality, not the same type of people who were here when the Europeans first came, it has been the 'rites' in customs and manners which has enabled our own survival. Other individuals and institutions both good and bad (religious and secular), helped, but for the most part we and our close friends were the history makers. The big question for the future, which I have to confront, however, is: will Aboriginal people be able to maintain this pattern of doing things into the next two centuries, and what are some of the things that might threaten some of the traditions we see as important?

A number of things will most certainly take place. Aboriginal populations will continue to increase, and this has implications for Aboriginal people in the same way as it does for government. Aboriginal populations are moving both away from their own institutions into areas that require a totally different pattern of habitation and into urban areas (towns and cities). Like other times and parts of the world, Europe in the nineteenth century perhaps, mining industries are affecting those who remain in rural areas and large industry is affecting those who move to the cities. In both instances, further cultural decay will occur if some form of self-strengthening knowledge and strategy is not mounted right away. The emergence of health patterns caused by concentrated living, with poor hygiene and access problems to health knowledge and treatment, will not abate for some time. Nor will other diseases such as alcoholism and heart problems. These are some of the material effects; what about the cultural effects?

Arts and culture have gone through what some might describe as a cultural revolution, and whether this adequately describes the upsurge in interest in the 1970s and 1980s I am not sure. Nevertheless, I can say with some certainty that Aboriginal art is flourishing, and will continue to do so, due in no small measure to the AIAS's long interest. Aboriginal dance is expanding, not only within traditional society but also as a means of communicating information to others. These are powerful mediums and they should be protected, from within a self-conscious and self-strengthening intellectual strategy. One real problem is the great urban drift: the Aboriginal populations are shifting we know, the question is: what cultural baggage are they taking and what is the rate of change? Now, I do not know what the answer to that question is because I am not a social scientist, but historical archaeology or ethnographic and social anthropological accounts might be able to (do so). The AIAS might, in the future, tackle such important and necessary questions and, in this way, we can be our own research fox and not the government hound. Aboriginal arts and culture will change, as they are currently doing: we must learn to record the arts and culture we are creating today as being a record of ourselves as culture makers in whatever we do. Material gain has diverted contemporary Aboriginal society away from its basic goals of culturally and customarily self-strengthening its own knowledge, in the face of a tremendous threat from ideas which compete, and undermine, our own intellectual strengths. This will disguise and cloud our differences and uniqueness in that, as a cultural group, we will be indistinguishable from other Australians: perhaps this is what Blainey wants.

External threats are many but in the same way we must be mindful of internal threats to Aboriginal culture. For example, I am acutely aware of Aboriginal political nationalism and extremism. In relation to Aboriginal knowledge, I want to say that, like everything else, knowledge changes and grows, but only if we can share it with other human beings. Some of that knowledge will begin, and continue for an unknown length of time, as something only a few will or can know, that is the nature of things. In the fullness of time it must become common or public knowledge: that is also the nature of things. Many Aboriginal groups have the mistaken belief that, because they have a racial and cultural link with people who once lived, for example at Kow Swamp or Lake Mungo, they have a monopoly over both the knowledge itself and the material gains from that knowledge. This is the kind of materialism I was hinting at: an extreme dominance over other people who are in need of that knowledge in order to be able to understand about the humanness of those civilisations who preceded contemporary Aboriginal people. It was not long ago that Aboriginal people were believed to be a subhuman species, but recent archaeology, ethnology and anthropology has demolished that falsehood. One final point will bring together all the things I have been talking about. Essentially, they concern our similarities and, most importantly, our differences with people with whom we occupy this continent, or the people who live close to our own communities. This is an important question because underlying the points mentioned above is the question: who are the people that are most likely to be our friends, and how will we be able to identify them, over the next two centuries?

The conservation movement: A case for Aboriginal survival

Conservation movements have tended to be people with concern for other human beings and for nature. Although the AIAS has its share of conservationists it is not (necessarily) an organisation which is part of any political arm of the conservation movement. Nevertheless, the scholarship produced by the AIAS does have that wider concern for the conservation of the environment, and the way Aboriginal people fit into that picture. The workers that I have previously mentioned, the real workers of Aboriginal survival, have that kind of concern for both the preservation of a national minority and the environment as a central feature. These people had a mix of the ideas and practical solutions in which Aboriginal peoples could make a positive contribution towards others and themselves in the next twenty or so decades. A special characteristic which gives Aboriginal people their special quality is what I will call 'Aboriginal conservatism' and it stands in direct contrast to 'Aboriginal chauvinism'. It is the Aboriginal conservatism which gives our people that special humanity.

All the issues mentioned before need to be addressed with an understanding of Aboriginal political processes.

Aboriginal processes of decision making and Aboriginal attitudes towards elected representatives are markedly different from those of European Australians. Aborigines follow processes which are, I believe, basically democratic, but the concept of representative government seems alien to their culture. The basic unit of Aboriginal decision making (where the means to decision making are not clearly established by tradition or where decision making lies within the authority of individuals by inherited right) seems to be the local community or group meeting, open to all. Issues are discussed but decisions are rarely made at once if the matters are important. Discussions are often interrupted and may be spread over several meetings to allow time for discussions within families or other smaller groups or for consultation with other people of authority and influence. During these intervals, respected members of the community often move around to ensure that issues are understood, to identify the lines of emerging consensus and perhaps to support particular ones. Even when the community has an elected council, its meetings are generally open and discussion is not confined to councillors. If people are chosen to take part in discussions with other communities or with government and other agencies, it is my understanding that their nomination is not an authority to decide or in other ways to act for the community without reference back to it, but rather to act as two-way messengers on its behalf between it and the other parties.

Another important aspect of Aboriginal decision-making processes is the complementary division of ritual responsibility between separate but related groups. For example, the reciprocal relationship between 'owners' of land

and ceremonies and the 'guardians' — those with responsibility to see that traditional duties are properly performed — is now increasingly understood. It is the same expectation of reciprocity and fulfilment of mutual obligations that serves as the basis of authority and leadership in many Aboriginal societies. In particular, if individual leaders or 'bosses' are given deference or respect, then it is as a person who looks after and works for others and who will transmit to subordinates valued knowledge and experience. Authority to command or to effect decisions continues to be accorded only to those who observe reciprocal obligations, and is given within an ideology of egalitarianism — and traditionally, within the context of the 'law'. Thus conceptualised, 'legitimate authority is without despotic or personal overtones, taken on as a responsibility to ensure the security and benefit of its objects' (Myers 1980, p. 206).

Conclusion

In this 1988 Wentworth Lecture, I have attempted to bring some kind of reality to Aboriginal politics by exposing the contradictions in the symbolism of land rights and land rites. If Aboriginal people, as we recognise ourselves today, overlook the necessity for our own needs and those of others, of space, wellbeing and cooperation, then we will also overlook the underlying message I have been trying to get across here tonight. As a minority within the Australian political framework, one of the important elements of (both) our own survival since the turn of the nineteenth and twentieth centuries has been the kinds of friends we were able to cultivate in that time. In the next two hundred years I do not believe that the political situation will change. The conservation movement, and those scholars, citizens and politicians will have to play the kind of role earlier friends had to carry out. In these circumstances Aboriginal self-correction in the way they perceive the important concepts of 'rights' and 'rites' will be of the utmost importance, I hope that I have been able to throw some light on a debate which has been clouded. If I have been able to do that then the way ahead in the next two centuries will be, I am certain, a much more productive one than the preceding two centuries.

Reference

Myers, F 1980, 'The cultural basis of Pintupi politics', *Mankind*, no 12, pp. 197–213.

Original lecture available at:
< http://aiatsis.gov.au/publications/presentations/not-land-rights-land-rites>

6

'Studying man and man's nature': A history of the institutionalisation of Aboriginal anthropology

1990 Wentworth Lecture

Nicolas Peterson

On 5 March this year (1990) the new Australian Institute of Aboriginal and Torres Strait Islander Studies Act came into force, restructuring the governing body and membership of the old Australian Institute of Aboriginal Studies, established in 1964. The chief purpose of this restructuring is to ensure greater Aboriginal control over the Institute's activities now that the production and distribution of objectified knowledge about Aboriginal cultures and societies is of so much greater interest and significance to Aboriginal people than it has been in the past.

In the past the production and use of knowledge about Australian Aboriginal societies and cultures has been of major, although not exclusive, concern to anthropologists, and at certain periods it has played a central role in the creation of social theory. The restructuring of the Institute is an explicit recognition that institutional structures have an influence on the kinds of knowledge produced and the ways in which it is organised, used and distributed. Of course, such institutional structures and arrangements are themselves shaped in complex ways by historically specific conjunctures of intellectual interests, personal and public agendas, and institutional histories.

It is these issues of history that I will address here. Specifically, I consider why there was support for the establishment of the Institute, given that anthropology had existed as an independent university discipline since 1926. In providing an answer to this question I also address some other related questions that have been raised, but not dealt with, in the existing partial histories of the discipline.[1] In particular, I look at why the first chair of anthropology was established in Sydney rather than Melbourne, the home of the most distinguished anthropologist in the country at that time; why the older generation of scholars in

Adelaide believe the chair was really meant for them (Jones 1987, pp. 72–3); and why American philanthropists should have played such a key role in funding Australian anthropological research and publication prior to the war.

These four interrelated questions raise issues not only of institutional history but also of intellectual history, in particular, the extreme fascination that Aboriginal studies and cultures have exercised over the European imagination from the moment of first encounter, and the perception of each generation of scholars interested in them that they were the last ones to have the opportunity to secure authentic information about these cultures and societies for posterity.

Studying Aboriginal societies and cultures has long been seen not simply as studying another regional type of small-scale society but as confronting the primordial, 'studying man and man's nature', as Mr Wentworth put it in his original proposal for an Institute of Aboriginal Studies (1959). Aboriginal ways of life were seen as providing a privileged window onto the origins of religion, marriage and social life in a way that other societies did not. This interest drew much of its inspiration from the social evolutionary paradigm that dominated anthropology at the turn of the twentieth century. With the rejection of this paradigm such views were no longer academically respectable, although they are still a flourishing part of popular culture. Academically, they have been transformed into a more sophisticated view which sees Aboriginal ways of life as a paradigm of the relations between people and nature, and Aboriginal societies as the sociological, ecological and evolutionary prototype of the hunting and gathering existence.

The significance of research on Aboriginal cultures and societies has continually been fuelled either by the belief that Aboriginal people were doomed to extinction by the operation of natural laws or by the belief that access to the authentic pre-colonial practices was about to disappear. The former view was clearly stated by Baldwin Spencer in the preface to *The Native Tribes of Central Australia* where he comments:

> The time in which it will be possible to investigate the Australian native tribes is rapidly drawing to a close, and though we know more of them than we do of the last Tasmanians, yet our knowledge is very incomplete, and unless some special effort be made, many tribes will practically die out without our gaining any knowledge of the details of their organisation, or of their sacred customs and beliefs. (Spencer & Gillen 1899, p. vii)

Such views, as will be seen, were echoed throughout the last three decades of the nineteenth century and again in the 1960s.

I will argue that although the history of the push to institutionalise Australian anthropology was driven by the intellectual fascination with Aboriginal societies and cultures, the only way government support for the discipline could be gained was by emphasising anthropology's uses to colonial administration in New Guinea and the Pacific. Thus, from the outset, Aboriginal anthropology was always in incipient danger of being overshadowed by research outside Australia, despite the real intellectual interest of the disciplines' founders being within the country. This marginalisation did not come about until after the Second World War, when research in New Guinea and Asia came to dominate academic anthropology and Australia was no longer seen as capable of providing a privileged source of understanding about the human condition. It was in this climate of the academic neglect of Aboriginal anthropological research that the move to establish the Institute arose.

In tracing this history I will follow a modified version of Elkin's original 'periodisation' of the discipline's development.[2] I shall bypass the initial phase of unsystematic research between 1606 and c.1870, when the interest in Aboriginal life first manifested itself, and turn to the period when it blossomed in a period of systematic research c.1870–1925. The period from 1925 to 1946 saw the establishment of professional anthropology, and from 1946 to 1974 the rise of academic anthropology.

Systematic research c. 1870–1925

Aboriginal societies and cultures began to gain wide international interest with the re-emergence of evolutionary theory in the 1870s. The first 50 years of the nineteenth century had been dominated by Christian-inspired 'degenerativist' views that, for the most part, eclipsed the social evolutionary framework. Darwin's ideas fuelled the revival of social evolutionary interest but his particular views posed problems since they did not entail the idea of progress.

In 1880, Lewis Henry Morgan summed up contemporary opinion as to the significance for theory of Aboriginal societies when he commented that 'they now represent the condition of mankind in savagery better than it is elsewhere represented on the earth — a condition now rapidly passing away' (in Fison & Howitt 1880, p. 2). He made this comment in the prefatory note to the first book-length theoretical study of any Aboriginal societies, *Kamilaroi and Kurnai*, by Lorimer Fison and Alfred Howitt, which sought to fit them into Morgan's theoretical scheme. The case studies of the two tribes, whose names provide the title of the book, are used to argue against degeneracy theories and for the evolutionary view.

The first researchers to spend prolonged periods with Aboriginal people in a spirit of inquiry were natural scientists whose primary interests, at least initially, were in the collection and study of flora and fauna and who were employed in state museums and universities or came from abroad. Pre-eminent among these Australian researchers was Baldwin Spencer, a founding father of academic anthropology and Professor of Biology at the University of Melbourne. The three major volumes of ethnography he produced, two in collaboration with

FJ Gillen, Alice Springs' postmaster and Protector of Aborigines, excelled in their detailed observation and recording of Aboriginal social and religious life.

The impact of their first work, *The native tribes of Central Australia* (1899), was immense, both here and abroad. Sir James Frazer declared its authors to be 'immortal, surpassing Tacitus in their ethnographic virtues' (see Mulvaney 1981, p. 61), an admiration that was mutual (see Spencer & Gillen 1927, vol. 1, p. vii). Yet it was not only natural scientists who were publishing major ethnographic studies prior to the First World War. Other writers less involved with evolutionary theory were WE Roth, a medical practitioner and Aboriginal Protector in Queensland; Erhard Eylmann, a German ethnographer who worked in South Australia; Mrs Parker, a station owner's wife in western New South Wales; the Rev Mathew on the Kabi of southern Queensland; Daisy Bates on the peoples of Western Australia; Carl Strehlow on the Aranda; and RH Mathews on eastern Australia generally. It was in this period, also, that specifically anthropological expeditions began. The first was the Cambridge Anthropological Expedition to the Torres Strait, led by Alfred Haddon in 1898; shortly afterwards, he took up a lectureship in ethnology at Cambridge. This expedition was followed by Spencer and Gillen's second year-long expedition in 1901, financed by a Melbourne newspaper and assisted by the state governments of Victoria and South Australia, after impressive lobbying from the British academic establishment (see Mulvaney & Calaby 1985, pp. 189–90, 442). The third expedition was the Oxford and Cambridge Anthropological Expedition to Western Australia, 1910–11, headed by Radcliffe-Brown, who was to become the first professor of anthropology in Australia.[3]

This spate of research stimulated huge interest in Europe, particularly among British anthropologists. For a short period there was an active export industry in Aboriginal ethnography, in return for intellectual guidance. Howitt and Fison had early on been communicating with Morgan. Following Morgan's death, Howitt joined Spencer in corresponding with Tylor, and Spencer also maintained close contact with Frazer; Mrs Parker corresponded with Andrew Lang, who prepared her work for publication; Daisy Bates sent her manuscript to Radcliffe-Brown (White 1981); and RH Mathews corresponded very widely (Elkin 1975–76).

The impact of the Australian ethnography is evident in the role it played in the production of anthropological theory: twelve major theoretical books drawing either entirely or extensively on the Australian ethnography appeared in the first fourteen years of the twentieth century, with a highly influential set of authors: among them, van Gennep (1905), Lang (1905), Marett (1909), Frazer (1910), Durkheim (1912, see 1915), Freud (1913) and a future influential figure, Malinowski (1913, see 1963).

British anthropological interest in Australia reached its peak in 1914 when Haddon,. Rivers and Marett, all key figures in the British anthropological establishment, came from England to attend the first British Association for the Advancement of Science Meeting held in Australia. Marett brought Malinowski with him as his secretary. Grafton Elliot Smith, an Australian by birth but at that time Professor of Anatomy at the University of Manchester, also attended, as did Radcliffe-Brown, while Spencer was one of the organisers of the anthropology section.

Around this time, the first formal attempts to establish anthropology as a university discipline were taken. A research committee was set up to advance the teaching of anthropology (BAAS 1915, vol. 1, pp. xiii), but the timing was unfortunate: news of the outbreak of War reached the Association during its meetings in Adelaide.

Immediately after the War, in 1919, Haddon, at that time Reader in Anthropology in the University of Cambridge, tried to reactivate the proposal to establish some form of anthropological teaching by writing to David Orme Masson at the University of Melbourne and Chairman of the interim Australian National Research Council. Masson showed the letter to Spencer, who wrote back to Haddon saying that coincidentally he had been discussing the self-same question with the Chancellor of Melbourne University within the previous few weeks and made an offer which might enable the university to start a small department of anthropology. Spencer had decided to resign his chair of biology and devote himself to museum and anthropological work. His proposal was that he would act as Honorary Reader in Anthropology if the university would give him an assistant who would undertake the anthropometric side of research while he devoted himself to matters social and technological.[4]

Haddon, whose research interests were in the Torres Strait, had expressed a preference for the establishment of a chair in Sydney because of the Australian Museum and its holdings of Pacific Island material. Spencer pointed out that Melbourne, with Howitt and Fison, Rev. Mathew, Gillen and himself, among others, had been the home of real ethnological work in Australia, and though Melbourne Museum was not so rich in Island material, it was vastly superior to Sydney in Australian material and the university taught all the collateral subjects. 'It is true', he continued, 'that Sydney is and always must be the main port of the Pacific but after all this does not seriously affect the question of the teaching of ethnology'.[5]

Two years later Spencer wrote to Haddon again saying he had heard nothing more from the Chancellor of the University of Melbourne about his proposal and that if anything were to happen it would be in Sydney, as they had the funds that Victoria lacked.[6] Although this switch to a Sydney focus for the establishment of a department of anthropology can be seen with hindsight to have had long-term consequences for the nature of Australian anthropology, it was not at this period a simple change from an Australian to a Pacific focus. At this period the University of Sydney was a flourishing centre for research on

Australian topics; significantly, however, this research was carried out in the Department of Anatomy.

While the social evolutionary paradigm that fuelled the huge interest in Aborigines had run out of steam by the outbreak of the War, Darwinian evolutionary theory was alive and flourishing among biological anthropologists. In the first 30 years of the twentieth century, however, a rather simplistic scientific naturalism was sometimes combined with an over-enthusiastic view of the important role of heredity in human make-up and civilisation, giving rise to the eugenics movement (see Pickens 1968). Evolutionary biological interest and the eugenics movement would play a crucial role in the establishment of institutionalised anthropology.

While the demand for the support of anthropology in Australia up to the First World War had been almost exclusively in terms of the importance of knowledge about Aborigines for science, there was a dramatic shift in the basis of justification in the subsequent years, even though it was still the same set of natural scientists pushing for it. As a result of the War, Australia received a mandate from the League of Nations for the governing of New Guinea in 1920, and in 1921 the *New Guinea Act* of the Australian Commonwealth Government came into force, establishing a civil administration throughout the Territory, thus bringing the whole eastern half of the island of New Guinea under Australian control. It seems more than merely coincidental that, when the Australian Branch of the Association for the Advancement of Science held its first post-war Congress in 1921, the terms in which the Anthropology Section forwarded its resolution about the need for the teaching of anthropology made reference for the first time to the practical uses of the discipline.

The resolution supported by the Congress Council recommended:

> That there be urged upon the Federal Government the need for endowment of a Chair in Anthropology, especially in view of its value in the government of subject races. (AAAS 1921, p. xxxiii)

At this same meeting, the Australian National Research Council (ANRC), which was to play such an important role in the promotion of anthropology, was officially formed. Seeking to advance the anthropology section's proposal, the ANRC wrote to Malinowski and Seligman at the London School of Economics, Frazer and Haddon at Cambridge, and Elliot Smith at the University of London, for advice on the need for a chair, to bolster their cause prior to the 1923 Pan Pacific Science Congress, which was to be held in Australia. Although their replies display a diversity of opinion on specifics, all were uniformly enthusiastic about the general project.[7]

Malinowski (see endnote 7) wrote back with a six-page statement urging the creation of a central institute in Sydney, where the Mitchell Library (which was attached to Sydney University and had close connections to the Australian

Museum) provided an excellent reading room and library. He strongly advocated that all efforts should be concentrated on the study of cultural anthropology as the culture, customs, beliefs and organisation of the 'South Sea Islanders will disappear within decades' while the people will remain 'physically pure for centuries' (1923, p. 6). Physical anthropology, which he stated was quite independent of cultural study, required a different training regime and abilities and could be developed later.

Haddon (see endnote 7) felt there should be a concentration on Australia and New Guinea. Regarding the Australian situation, he felt that opportunities were rapidly diminishing because of acculturation but that there was 'greater hope for more extensive and precise information from the study of the natives in the unsettled areas, but even here the old conditions seem to be passing away very rapidly' (1973, p. 1). Interestingly, in the light of the correspondence with Spencer, Haddon suggested that the University of Melbourne would seem to be the most natural centre for research among Aboriginal people although this should not, he said, preclude other centres from making local or general studies, especially Adelaide, Perth and Brisbane. Sydney would also continue to do so, he thought, but 'it has another sphere of action which seems to be more pressing' (Haddon, see endnote 7). This, of course, was New Guinea and the Pacific. To the reasons advanced by Malinowski he added the fact that Sydney is the port of departure and arrival for people interested in this area. It scarcely needs emphasising that both Haddon and Malinowski had their field experience outside Australia.

Elliot Smith did not travel to the meetings but sent the lecturer in his department, W Perry. They authored a joint submission, in which they concentrated on general principles. They emphasised that researchers should be free to decide what type of inquiry they would carry out, although they should also be prepared to offer information and advice to the government on every question affecting the welfare of the population they study; they should be independent inquirers, not officials, and their work should be overseen by somebody who was not a narrow specialist but capable of taking a wide view covering physical and cultural anthropology and archaeology. At that time, this could only be done, so far as the British dominions were concerned, by someone in England (see endnote 7). Only Frazer (see endnote 7) felt that foremost place should be given to what remained of the Australian Aborigines, as yet little influenced by contact with civilization, and that on two grounds, 'first, on the surpassing interest of these natives as representing the lowest type of culture now accessible to us on the globe; and second, on the ground of the rapidity with which these people seem hastening to extinction' (1923, p. 1).

Haddon, who had travelled from England for the Congress, was chairman of a committee of the Anthropology Section charged with developing proposals for the establishment of a chair. The secretary to the committee was a bureaucrat from the Prime Minister's Department in Melbourne, underlying the good connections to the federal government (then based in Melbourne) that were enjoyed by promoters of anthropology such as Spencer and Masson. The Committee brought forward two resolutions:

> Recognising the necessity for the immediate prosecution of anthropological research in Australia and Oceania, this Congress calls the attention of governments, Universities patrons of research, and research foundations to the pressing need for this investigation.
>
> The Congress urges that provision be made for the teaching of Anthropology in the Universities of Australia. (PPSC 1924, p. 35)

The language of the detailed supporting statement is significant, since it clearly reveals an underlying concern with the collection of 'valuable scientific material', rationalised in terms of humanitarian considerations and confidence in anthropology's usefulness to colonial administrations. Further, while it articulates the utility of anthropological research in New Guinea, no such mention is made with respect to Aboriginal people in Australia (PPSC 1923, pp. 40–3). It is thus clear that as early as 1919 the academic powerbrokers, in this case particularly, Haddon, who also played a key role in establishing the Chair of Anthropology in Cape Town in 1920 (Firth 1956), had already settled on Sydney as the centre for the establishment of anthropology, specifically because of its significance for work in New Guinea and the Pacific. Only Frazer, of the people consulted, felt research in Australia to be of the first importance, whereas the others were, by clear implication, focussing on the new opportunities in the Pacific, where the impact of Europeans was so much less significant. Within Australia, only Sir Baldwin Spencer had the authority to advance the cause of Aboriginal anthropology but he was by this time ailing and ineffective.[8]

It is therefore interesting that the folklore of the Adelaide academic establishment, that the chair of anthropology should properly have been established in Adelaide — and nearly was — is so persistent, being reproduced again in a recent account (Jones 1987, 73). Certainly, if it had been, Australian anthropology would have taken a substantially different course, because the interest in Adelaide was not only firmly in Aboriginal anthropology but especially in biological anthropology. The Adelaide views arise from the conflict of intentions surrounding a crucial but neglected aspect of the founding of professional anthropology in Australia.

Establishment of professional anthropology, 1925–46

In 1925, the University of Sydney established the first Chair of Anthropology in Australia; however, the 18 months between the 1923 Congress and the establishment of the Chair were by no means smooth sailing.

Following the Congress, an ANRC delegation went to see the Acting Prime Minister to seek the commonwealth funding of a chair of anthropology at the University of Sydney. Cabinet approved the concept the same day. However, a British colonial administrator from the African Civil Service, who was later contracted by the government as a consultant on the proposal, advised against university-trained administrative officials (Mulvaney 1988, p. 207). The ANRC was unable to counter this setback and in early March 1924 Senator Pearce, the Minister for Home and Territories, wrote to the Council reversing its support for a Chair.

As is well-known, the day was saved by an American philanthropic body, the Rockefeller Foundation. Yet the reasons for its willingness to fund anthropology in Australia have not been well understood, nor the somewhat fortuitous timing of its intervention. In late December 1923, the Rockefeller Foundation received a letter from the Galton Society of New York proposing a major study of so-called primitive peoples (Jonas 1989, p. 133).[9] The Galton Society members were eugenicists devoted to the science of human wellbeing. Their central concern was with the threat that modern medicine posed to racial fitness because of the way it thwarted natural selection and allowed 'bad' genes to be reproduced. A study of contemporary small-scale societies, they argued, was a last chance to examine the human biology of people living in societies where natural selection was working uncorrupted.

Among the Society's Charter Fellows were two of the leading eugenicists of the day, Charles Davenport, Director of the Station for Experimental Evolution run by the Carnegie Institution, and Madison Grant, Vice President of the New York Zoological Society and author of *The Passing of the Great Race*. Among its ordinary fellows was Clark Wissler, Curator at the American Museum of Natural History and among its corresponding fellows, Elliot Smith, who by that time held the Chair of Anatomy at University College, London.[10] The proposal was taken up by Edwin Embree, secretary of one of the funding divisions within the Foundation, who was casting about for new projects to support, as his previous humanities-based proposal had recently been rejected by the Foundation's Board of Trustees (see Jonas 1989, pp. 138–9). Embree took up the suggestion expeditiously but the Board quickly narrowed it down to a single regional study. It will come as no surprise that Australia, home of the 'natural society', was the region chosen. The Galton Society proposed that the research be organised by the establishment of a field hospital, which would offer treatment as a means of attracting Aboriginal people for study. It would be staffed by five Americans and two Englishmen, the latter being thought desirable because 'Great Britain controls so much of the territory occupied by primitive peoples'. Somewhat surprisingly, Sir Arthur Keith and Sir James Frazer were suggested as suitable people.[11] The Galton Society quickly lost direct input into the course of the proposal, however, partly because Embree began making the project his own but also because of the Foundation's policy of working through the institutions and scholars of the countries concerned. On 19 March 1924, Embree wrote to Elliot Smith, seeking advice about the project and enquiring whether he might be available to visit Australia with a representative of the Foundation to make preliminary investigations as to the project's feasibility. Elliot Smith wrote back immediately saying he was 'keenly interested in the Australian scheme' and already had plans to visit New York within three weeks. He also endorsed Embree's suggestion that Dr Hunter of the Anatomy Department at the University of Sydney would be a good Australian-based person to direct the investigation.[12]

Thus at the very time the plans for the Chair of anthropology at Sydney University were grinding to a halt, Elliot Smith, who less than 12 months before had outlined his proposal for the kind of work that should be carried out in Australia, was being approached independently by the Rockefeller Foundation in connection with the kind of anthropological research project in which he was clearly most interested. The decision to approach him must have seemed natural: he was a member of the Galton Society, he was a respected scientist to whom the Rockefeller Foundation had already given two million dollars for his school of anatomy, and he was an Australian.[13]

Although the letter of authorisation Elliot Smith carried with him from the Foundation when he arrived in Australia was quite non-committal, the Foundation had, on 27 February 1924, already approved in principle a study in Australia and recorded in its minutes that it awaited a mature definite proposal at a later meeting.[14]

In Australia, Elliot Smith went straight to Adelaide, where the Australasian Association for the Advancement of Science and the ANRC were holding meetings, and enlisted their support for the establishment of the chair in anthropology. On 30 August 1924, Elliot Smith was received by Prime Minister Bruce who, in his own words, proceeded to 'interview' him on the need for the chair.[15] Elliot Smith reported on the meeting in the following terms:

> I took advantage of the opportunity provided by this interview to discuss the question of my mission to Australia. I explained to the Prime Minister that my purpose was merely to inquire what the attitude of the Government and the Universities would be if the Rockefeller Foundation should be asked to provide funds to help the Australian Universities, or one of them, to embark upon a comprehensive investigation of the Australian Aborigines. I made it clear to him that I was not authorised to make any offer, or to promise that any such help would be forthcoming, but merely to say that if the universities (or one of them) were to approach the Rockefeller Foundation, the appeal would receive sympathetic consideration.
>
> The Prime Minister authorised me to inform the Rockefeller Foundation that he keenly appreciated this new demonstration of the Foundation's

interest in Australia and would gratefully welcome any help the Foundation might give to promote the scientific study of the native population of Australia.[16]

Of course, this elaborate denial of commitment simply served to underwrite its existence. Shortly after the visit, the commonwealth government, and with it the state governments, reversed their earlier views and supported the chair so it could go ahead.[17]

Professor Frederick Wood Jones of the Department of Anatomy at the University of Adelaide was seen by Elliot Smith as a strong ally in the establishment of anthropology in Australia because of his biological interests. Also, Sydney University had association with at least five people working in the area of Aboriginal human biological and psychological research at that time (Drs Burkitt, Lightoller, Tebbutt, Bostick and Graham).[18] They were led by Professor Hunter, of whom many people, including Elliot Smith, held a high opinion. The presence of these people gave Elliot Smith the feeling that the choice of the ANRC to establish the chair at Sydney was compatible with the Rockefeller Foundation's proposed project, but that some way of encouraging and helping Wood Jones and his associates in Adelaide should be found. Significantly, he felt that the way to do this should be left to Professor Hunter's discretion, clearly indicating that Hunter was foreseen as having a considerable input into the course of the developments at Sydney, and even as gaining a lectureship in physical anthropology out of it if funds should prove adequate.[19] Unfortunately for these plans, Professor Hunter unexpectedly died in England in December 1924, while on a visit to Elliot Smith.

On 7 November 1924, the Foundation moved to commit itself to a maximum of $US100,000 to fund anthropological studies over a five-year period, in cooperation with Australian universities.[20] Thus what began as a proposal for an extended bio-anthropological expedition from the Galton Society ended up as an untied grant to anthropological studies, but one in which Aboriginal human biology was clearly assumed to be central. Further, the theoretical interest of the Galton Society in Aboriginal peoples fell firmly within general intellectual interests at the time in Aboriginal societies and cultures, viewed as uniquely capable of shedding light on the human condition because they most closely represented it in its natural form.

With Australian government and Rockefeller support, Sydney University moved to establish a chair of anthropology in June 1925. Events moved fast. On 14 September 1925 Elliot Smith reported that after preliminary correspondence he had met with Haddon and JT Wilson, formerly Professor of Anatomy at Sydney but at that time holding a position in Cambridge (Mulvaney & Calaby 1985, p. 147), at Haddon's house in Cambridge, to select an appointee for the chair. The main applicants were Radcliffe-Brown, AM Hocart and Arthur Grimble. Malinowski was considered in the absence of an application but it was felt certain he would not leave the LSE. It was also thought unlikely that Hocart would accept if offered the position and, given that Radcliffe-Brown had university teaching experience and fieldwork in Australia, he was the unanimous choice.[21]

Although it is clear, then, that there is no justification for the view that the chair of anthropology narrowly missed being given to Adelaide, there were clear grounds for the Adelaide University group to expect substantial support because of its members' biological orientation and their knowledge of the original ideas behind the Rockefeller funding. Oral history has in some cases further confused the issue because some members of the Adelaide group have reordered the sequence of events and viewed the visit of Edwin Embree and Clark Wissler, representing the Foundation, in October 1925 as further evidence that Adelaide was in the running for the chair: this visit was, of course, after a chair had been established at Sydney, but the confusion reflects the tension between Australian and biological interests on the one hand and Pacific and social on the other.

Embree and Wissler visited the universities and museums in Brisbane, Sydney, Melbourne and Adelaide to learn of the state of research in each. In his report to the Foundation on the visit, Wissler records that:

> No other university in Australia seems quite so intent upon research in ... [the Aboriginal] field. Yet, it is almost exclusively the medical group that is interested. This does not mean that the biological side is unduly emphasised, for a number of the men engaged are as much interested in archaeology and ethnology as in any other aspect of the subject...(Wood-Jones) is the 'best bet' to lead in anthropological research on the Aboriginal.[22]

Because both universities and Aboriginal affairs were state matters, Wissler saw this as giving a further prominence to Adelaide as a centre of Aboriginal research, which, when compared with Sydney and Melbourne, was the gateway to central and western Australia and had the easiest access to substantial populations of traditionally oriented Aboriginal people. Because Melbourne and Sydney scholars were not in contact with large Aboriginal populations, they were seen as being disposed to look towards New Guinea; so, he concluded somewhat surprisingly:

> In general, then, the University of Adelaide has first claim for support in aboriginal research, whereas Melbourne and Sydney are to be considered only in respect to more strictly biological; studies of the aboriginal, if at all.[23]

His final conclusion was that because New Guinea offered one of the few places in the world where there were people as yet uncontacted by Europeans, it was a most important area of research, but that research work in Australia should also be strengthened by a specific grant of funds for fieldwork. He proposed $US12,000 annually for research in the Mandated Territories to be administered by the ANRC, and $US4,000 annually be made available to the University of Adelaide for research on Aboriginal topics.[24]

The Rockefeller Foundation subsequently decided to channel funds exclusively through the ANRC. Embree explained the reasons for this in a letter to Wood Jones:

> Our officers and the Board in considering the matter [of the allocation of funds] felt that we would not be justified in attempting to make allocation to several institutions in Australia. In addition to the important work in Sydney and Adelaide, the claims of Melbourne were also being advanced. It seemed to us that the proper thing for such an outside organization as the Rockefeller Foundation was to carry its contribution through a central scientific body, leaving to that representative body in Australia decisions as to the allocation of the funds from time to time...I hope that this decision of ours will not be a disappointment to you. It should in no way result in fewer resources for Adelaide than might be the case by direct appropriation from the Foundation. It may in fact result in greater resources for South Australia, particularly during these early years when personnel for research is more available at Adelaide than at any other place.[25]

This analysis was incorrect for two reasons: first, the Chairman of the Anthropological Committee of the ANRC was always the head of the Sydney Department and it was always more resolutely social anthropological in orientation than biological. Although in later years the Adelaide research workers were to allege that they were not getting their fair share of the funds, figures from their own Board for Anthropological Research show that they received over 75 per cent of the cost of eight expeditions between 1927 and 1935 from the ANRC;[26] secondly, Embree's prediction failed because Radcliffe-Brown, who took up the Chair in 1926, was active in finding research workers and in expediting their fieldwork. Indeed, even on his way to Australia to take up the chair he was on the lookout for people, and upon meeting Lloyd Warner, then a graduate student at Berkeley, he immediately recruited him.

Under Radcliffe-Brown's aegis, research in Australia received some priority. The terms in which he rationalised this have a familiar ring:

> These [Australian] investigations are perhaps not of an immediate practical use, for the Australian aborigines, even if not doomed to extinction as a race, seem at any rate doomed to have their cultures destroyed. But they will provide data of the very greatest importance for a comparative science of culture. (1930, p. 3)

It is interesting to reflect on why anthropology was not thought of as having practical use to Aboriginal administrators when the New Guinea administration perceived it as useful. Not only did they appoint two government anthropologists in 1921 and 1924 but, up until the end of the Second World War, administrative officials were sent to the Department of Anthropology in Sydney for a year of training. The reason for this difference appears to relate to the dominance of functionalist theory. Although functionalism's preoccupation with how things work at the time of study reflects the interests of colonial administrators, these interests relate to indirect rule. To the extent that the work of the functionalist anthropologists was perceived to be useful to government in New Guinea, it was because government was concerned with more or less independently functioning societies. In Australia, however, even where there were people whose social and cultural orientation was close to that of pre-colonial times, the demographic and economic situation was always transformed, often radically. The pre-colonial past was close enough, however, for the changes not to challenge the functionalist paradigm within which the researchers were working, even though elements of land tenure and economy had to be reconstructed. However, the situations in which people were actually living (and, indeed, their social organisation) were not amenable to indirect rule; and in consequence it appears that the work of anthropologists was not seen as having great practical relevance.[27]

Until the outbreak of the Second World War, research in Aboriginal Australia was thus actively pursued — not under the guise of being useful to administration but for the same reason it had always been studied: for the insights it was thought to give into 'man's nature'. An editorial comment in *Nature* during the course of 1930 makes this clear:

> Spencer and Gillen saved from oblivion a vast amount of material which demonstrated the value of the Australian evidence in its bearing upon the early history of society and culture. Even now much further study is needed for which the data still exist, especially among the remoter and less known tribes. A few years more and it will be too late; the evidence will have vanished for ever (Nature 13 September 1930, p. 342. See also BAAS 1931, p. xxvi and Firth 1932, p. 6 for expression of the same sentiments).

Although Rockefeller funds ceased in June 1938, the last fieldwork they funded was not completed until June 1940. In the meantime, AP Elkin, who had become Professor of Anthropology on Radcliffe-Brown's departure, set about raising more funds for research from abroad, since such funding was not forthcoming from Australian sources. In 1940, the ANRC received $US10,000 from the Carnegie Corporation to continue research work (Elkin 1940, p. 465), but it was a lean period and the only real research lights on the anthropological horizon were Ronald and Catherine Berndt, working out of Sydney under Elkin's direction.

Establishment of academic anthropology, 1946–74

Following the war there was a change in perception and a change in institutional structure which had ramifications for the pattern of research in

Aboriginal anthropology. The threat of invasion had greatly improved internal communication in Australia, particularly in the Northern Territory, where a new surfaced road linked Alice Springs and Darwin and many airstrips had been built. Outback Australia was becoming much better known and it seems the idea of there being an internal frontier came to an end. Even though there were perhaps as many as a few hundred Aboriginal people who had not yet seen Europeans, it seems there was a widespread academic view, both within and beyond Australia, that Aboriginal societies and cultures could no longer provide special insights. A consequence of this was that working with Aboriginal people became doing anthropology at home whereas before it had been, so to speak, like working in a foreign country. The interesting and authentic non-Western ways of life were now to be found exclusively outside Australia and work within Australia became less valued professionally (see Cowlishaw 1986).

At the same time, there was a change in institutional arrangements which led to the removal of the training of administrative officers from the Department of Anthropology at Sydney to the Australian School of Pacific Administration. Although Elkin remained vitally interested in the formation of policy for Aborigines and personally played an important part in the development of that policy, the consequence of this shift of training to a non-university facility was that the Department became entirely academic, in a formal sense, and the direct relationship with colonial administration was terminated.

Ironically, however, it was the perceived usefulness of anthropology that led to the establishment of the second department of anthropology in the Research School of Pacific Studies at the newly created Australian National University. The need for such a school had grown out of the wartime awareness of the importance of an understanding of the Pacific Islands and the countries to the north. It is the department that has had by far the greatest impact on the world of anthropological scholarship outside Australia, primarily because of the large number of postgraduate students trained by it. Yet despite the early appointment of WEH Stanner to the department, little work on Aboriginal societies and cultures was sponsored by it: only seven of 56 projects up until 1977 (Review of activities 1977).

Post-war funds were being put into research outside Australia for the most part and research work within Australia appears to have been seen mainly as a training ground for advanced research: all five scholars who carried out their first research in Australia chose the Torres Straits or New Guinea for their PhD research. Only four pieces of PhD research were sponsored in Australia during the 1950s (Barwick, Munn, Hiatt and Worsley) and, at the time the moves for the Institute began, they were invisible to the wider public because three of them were still in process.

The third centre of anthropology grew out of a 1952 survey of social sciences in Australia by the American psychological anthropologists, Clyde and

Florence Kluckholn. They recommended Western Australia as the site for a new department of anthropology and with support from the professor of psychology, a senior lectureship was funded and taken up in 1955 by Ronald Berndt, who formed a separate department in 1961 (see Tonkinson & Howard 1990).

It is in this context that the perception of the need for the establishment of an institute of Aboriginal studies emerged. Little work was being done. In August 1959, Mr Wentworth circulated a nine-page document entitled, 'An Australian Institute for Aboriginal Studies'. Free from the epistemological and theoretical constraints surrounding academic anthropologists, which made Aboriginal cultures and societies undergoing rapid transformation problematic for a holistic functional approach, Wentworth espoused the view that any knowledge gained from what he described as perhaps the most interesting people in the world would contribute to a record that would be 'one of the priceless treasures of mankind'. He was fired with a sense of urgency: 'Within ten years there will be nothing but a fraction of a fraction left. It must be recorded now, or it will go unrecorded forever' (Wentworth 1959, pp. 2–3). Despite good work in the past, he wrote, the field had been inadequately covered, because of too few workers, a lack of funds, inadequate equipment and limited publication.

In an obvious and telling reference to the Rockefeller funding, he remarked: 'It is significant that Australians until recently did not always play a major part in studies of our aborigines. Funds and scholars came largely from abroad, knowledge and collections tended to flow overseas. Even where Australians themselves did the work, the necessary funds were often provided from abroad' (Wentworth 1959, p. 6). He went on to argue that:

> In view of the desirability of obtaining the whole of the finance from Australian sources for the sake of our national credit it would not be unreasonable to ask the Commonwealth to finance this, which would seem to be the most important academic project facing Australia.
>
> Should we not do so, humanity will lose something of permanent value and we Australians, as its custodians will lay ourselves open to perpetual reproach. (Wentworth 1959, pp. 8–9)

In his Second Reading speech he was to make a similar point:

> Somebody will say: 'Why bother? What does it matter? These are only the aborigines: does it matter if this knowledge is lost?' I believe that this is the crux of the matter and here we see the real importance of our study. We are not just studying aborigines although the aborigines are important people in their own right for whom we have a responsibility. We are studying man and man's nature. We are laying up the raw material for future psychologists and sociologists. (Wentworth 1964, pp. 216–7)

Here then, in this influential document, the feeling emerges yet again that Aboriginal societies and culture could provide a unique insight into the human condition and the belief that the possibility of gaining this insight was rapidly disappearing.

The conjunction of circumstances that made government receptive to the suggestion for this kind of institution is complex but the principal reasons seem evident. By the early 1960s Australia was extremely prosperous. The economic assimilation of a continuing stream of migrants appeared to have made it seem inevitable that the official government policy of assimilation of Aboriginal people would be successful. This policy stated that all Aborigines 'shall attain the same manner of living as other Australians, enjoying the same rights and privileges, accepting the same responsibilities, observing the same customs and being influenced by the same beliefs, hopes and loyalties' (see Lippmann 1981, p. 38). The success of the policy would end once and for all the chance to secure the insights Aboriginal societies and cultures could provide. With the prosperity also went an increasing interest in Australian history and culture and a loosening of the ties with Britain, which was to climax in the cultural and economic nationalism of the early 1970s. The explicit nationalism of Mr Wentworth's statement clearly resonated with these sentiments and he perceived that Aboriginal people and their cultures were a crucial icon of an independent Australian identity. But there was a firm preference for the schematic authority of normative accounts to the reality of the disorder and the poverty of many Aboriginal people's lives, which gave the lie to the success, or even the possibility, of an assimilation policy (Said 1978, pp. 92–3).

In its initial years the AIAS remained a conventional academic research institute as envisaged at its founding. The money it injected into research saw a great surge in linguistic recording and helped develop academic archaeology, but was slower to have an effect on the amount of substantive social anthropological research, because, with the exception of Western Australia, the universities did not place it high on their own teaching and research agendas.

At the Institute's 1974 Biennial Conference a group of Aboriginal people circulated a document that has come to be known as the 'Eaglehawk and Crow Letter'.[28] The immediate pretext was the cost of the Conference which the newly arrived Principal organised as a three-week international event, in contrast to the usual two-day regional affair. The authors of the five-page letter asked what benefit Aboriginal people would receive from the Conference and attacked the move to relevant research as merely influence-seeking with government to obtain further funds. They accused the Institute of conducting research on economic viability as an apologist alternative to land rights; and most significantly, stated their belief that Aboriginal communities should have commissioning rights over research and control of funding for projects carried out among Aboriginal people and on their cultural property (Widders et al. 1974). The letter was strong for its time and helped precipitate changes to the way in which the Institute was run, but only gradually. An opportunity for the Institute, and anthropologists more generally, to reposition themselves in respect to research with Aboriginal people was provided by the passing of the *Aboriginal Land Rights (Northern Territory) Act* of 1976. This Act enabled Aboriginal people in the Territory to lay claim to their traditional lands where they are unalienated Crown lands. With the assistance of their newly established and Aboriginal-controlled Land Councils, most anthropologists have been employed in the preparation of claims initially under the coordination of the Institute.

The reinstatement of a strong commitment to Aboriginal anthropology in the universities has been fuelled by student demands for courses. This demand has stemmed in part from the high profile that Aboriginal issues achieved with the federal government's commitment to land rights, and has been most enthusiastically met by the present and former colleges of advanced education.

Thus nationalism and public interest have placed Aboriginal culture and social life firmly back on the agenda of the universities. The public interest now has a dual focus: first, the original concern with the uniqueness of traditional Aboriginal societies and cultures remains powerful, often coloured by contemporary interests in conservation and rejection of materialism; second, there is also a strong interest in the present situation, its origins and what can be done to improve it.

The structure laid down in the new Act is for a continuation of the cooperative enterprise that has developed since 1974: an Aboriginal-controlled Council with a minority elected component and a largely elected Research Advisory Committee. No doubt this combination will emphasise slightly different kinds of knowledge from the previous Council. Yet it should be evident from the foregoing account that, although institutional structures and funding sources are important influences on the kind of knowledge produced, they are only one factor in a complex social process that is not easily controlled. Further, while Aboriginal people are increasingly concerned to be involved in the production and control of knowledge about their societies and cultures, their own demands that all Australians learn about them will itself generate increased interest. This is likely to widen the number of non-Aboriginal people producing knowledge about Aboriginal societies and cultures, both within and without institutional structures, thus diluting the possibilities for easily increased control.

Conclusion

At many stages in the history of anthropology certain groups have had a central place in the production of anthropological theory because of the light their social and cultural practices are believed to throw on universal questions relating to the nature of human sociality. Aboriginal societies and cultures held this place between 1870 and 1914 in the context of an evolutionary paradigm. With the demise of that paradigm international scholarly interest in Aboriginal societies and cultures declined and was further diluted locally as functionalist perceptions made it seem that it was no longer a productive area for research. Yet, among the general public social evolutionary views still had and have a firm grip on the imagination, which is in no way weakened by the claim that Aboriginal culture is 40,000 years old. For me, and I do not believe I am alone, the sense of physical and intellectual adventure occasioned by time spent with Aboriginal people in remote places still produces a palpable *frisson*. Although this may be enhanced by a romantic impulse it has a sound intellectual grounding. The history of Aboriginal Australia is remarkable: the complete occupation of a continent by people practising a single mode of subsistence for a very long time and intensified by a high degree of isolation has given involution a central place in the historical process. Clifford Geertz (1963, pp. 81–2) has characterised this process as one where cultural and social patterns:

> having reached what would seem to be a definitive form, nonetheless fail either to stabilise or transform themselves into a new pattern but rather continue to develop by becoming internally more complicated…(displaying an) increasing tenacity of basic pattern; internal elaboration and ornateness; technical hair-splitting and unending virtuosity.

Under such conditions cultural and social processes become cryptic and self-referential and the bricoleur central to creative life. Face to face with societies comprised only of people, in which everything is overdetermined, one is confronted with the enormous complexity of all human life, even in societies of the smallest scale, and by our capacity and need to generate worlds of meaning.

It has, as WEH Stanner put it, been a long hard intellectual struggle to develop an informed, detached and respectful perspective on Aboriginal society. However, in rejecting the unsatisfactory views of the past and in recognising the need to pursue new understandings that directly address issues of the day, there is no need to lose the sense of wonder at, or the self-knowledge offered by, ways of life with such unusual histories.

Acknowledgments

I have made only minor changes to the form in which the lecture was given. I would like to thank John Barnes, Athol Chase, Koko Clark, Faye Ginsburg, Chris Gregory, Jacquie Lambert and John Mulvaney for assistance and suggestions. This paper utilises unpublished material from the Records of the Australian National Research Council, held by the National Library, Canberra, and referred to by the prefix NL below; the Rockefeller Archive Center, New York, in the Record Group 1.1 Projects, Series 410 Australia, referred to by the prefix RF below; and the Haddon Collection in the University Library, Cambridge.

Notes

1. There are a number of partial histories of the discipline but for the most part they are overly dependent on Elkin's writings. See, especially, Elkin 1938, 1939, 1943, 1954, 1958, 1959, 1963, 1970; Mulvaney 1958, 1966, 1971, 1986, 1988; Mulvaney and Calaby 1985; Wise 1963; Hamilton 1982; McCall 1982; Berndt 1967; McCarthy 1946; Jones 1987.
2. Elkin's periodisation was: a phase of incidental anthropology; a compiling and collating phase; a phase of fortuitous, individual field projects; and a phase of organised, systematic research (see Elkin 1963). McCall's phases are: Development of social science phase, pre-1788; Casual or incidental phase, 1788 to mid 19th century; Compiling and collating phase, mid 19th century to late 19th century; Systematic research phase, late 19th century to 1925; Professional anthropology phase, 1925 to present (McCall 1982, p. 2). The final phase in my own sequence is Diversification, 1974 ongoing. The beginning of this phase is marked by the Eaglehawk and Crow letter mentioned below, which can be taken as more or less the start of negotiated anthropology within Australia. It also saw the beginning of a move away from the dominance of British social anthropology symbolised in a range of new appointments made in the Department of Anthropology, Research School of Pacific Studies at the Australian National University. Between 1973 and 1977 the Department made nine new appointments, six of them American trained scholars; subsequently two professors and at least a dozen other American academics have taken up anthropology positions elsewhere in Australia. This marks a weakening of the British intellectual tradition.
3. AR Radcliffe-Brown was known simply as AR Brown until 1926 when he changed his name by deed poll (see Firth 1956).
4. Letter from Spencer to Haddon, 21 April 1919 (Haddon Collection 4 – Letters).
5. See Note 4.
6. Letter from Spencer to Haddon, 15 October 1921 (Haddon Collection 4 – Letters).
7. Copies and or extracts of their advice are in the Haddon Collection. See Malinowski 1923, 6; Haddon 1973, 1.
8. At this time Spencer had a problem with alcohol (see Mulvaney & Calaby 1985, pp. 365–6).
9. There were in fact a number of separate funds within the Foundation which underwent administrative reorganisation at various times; for convenience I use Rockefeller Foundation to cover them all.
10. List of members, RF 1.1141013123.
11. Letter CB Davenport to Embree, 3 March 1924 – RF 1.1141013124.
12. Letter from Elliot Smith to Embree, 31 March 1924 – RF 1.1/410/3/23.
13. The views of Elkin and Mulvaney differ on the significance of Elliot Smith's role in this history: Elkin makes a great deal of it (1958, pp. 231 and 235) while Mulvaney (1988, p. 208) plays it down. Elkin had studied under Elliot Smith.
14. Minutes of Board of Trustees Meeting, 5 July 1924 – RF 1.1/410/3/25.
15. NL 482/61/853B.
16. Letter from Elliot Smith to Embree, 30 September 1924 – RF 1.1/410/3/24.
17. The reasons why state governments were prepared to support the chair need further investigation. If it was because they felt it would help in the administration of Aboriginal affairs it is curious that no officers who worked or were to work in Australia were sent to the Department at Sydney for training. Training seems to have been confined to people who were to work or were working in PNG.
18. Burkitt of the Anatomy Department was working on a comprehensive investigation of the physical characteristics of Aboriginal people; Lightoller, of the same Department, was working on the minute muscular topography of the face in Aboriginal and

European people; Tebbutt was investigating the precipitin reactions of Aboriginal people's blood at Royal Prince Alfred Hospital; Bostick, Assistant Superintendent of Callan Park Hospital for the Insane, was working on the incidence of insanity; and Graham, whose precise affiliation is not clear, was working on an epidemiological study of the spread of pneumonic influenza through the Aboriginal population (see Elliot Smith letter of 30 September 1924 to Embree — RF 1.1/410/3/24).
19 Letter from Elliot Smith to Embree, 5 November 1924 — RF 1.1/410/3/24.
20 Minutes of Board of Trustees, 7 November 1924 — RF 1.1/410/3/24.
21 Selection Report, 14 September 1925 — RF 1.1/410/3/27.
22 See C Wissler, 'Report of a visit to research institutions in New Zealand and Australia during the year 1925, pp. 41–4 — RF 1.1141014/42.
23 See Wissler, 'Report of a visit', p. 57.
24 See Wissler, 'Report of a visit', pp. 59, 60, 62.
25 See letter from Embree, 28 May 1926 — RF 1. 1141013128.
26 The cost figures are £2615 of £13,403 (see NL 482/32/498). Mulvaney points out that this was a small proportion of the total funds allocated by the ANRC and is not proportional to productivity, which was higher than Elkin indicated (see Mulvaney 1988, pp. 209–11).
27 Spencer, for instance, had been appointed as a Special Commissioner and Chief Protector of Aborigines in the Northern Territory for a year in 1912, following the commonwealth government taking over control of the Territory from South Australia in 1911. Although he did comment in his first report that in the interests of efficient welfare planning a systematic study should be undertaken, he also emphasised the need to do this on scientific grounds made no great issue of the applied side (see Mulvaney & Calaby 1985, pp. 264–5, 273).
28 These two birds are moiety totems in south-eastern Australia.

References

AAAS 1921, *Report of the fifteenth meeting of the Australasian Association for the Advancement of Science*, AAAS, Sydney.
BAAS 1915, *Report of the British Association for the Advancement of Science, Australia: 1914, 28 July–31 August*, John Murray, London.
—— 1931, *Report of the ninety-eighth meeting: Bristol 1930*, Office of the British Association, London.
Berndt, RM 1967, 'Social anthropology and the Australian Aborigines', *Oceania*, vol. 37, pp. 241–59.
Cowlishaw, G 1986, 'Aborigines and anthropologists', *Australian Aboriginal Studies*, vol. 1, pp. 2–12.
Durkheim, E 1915 (1912), *The elementary form of religious life*, Allen & Unwin, London.
Elkin, AP 1938, 'Anthropological research in Australia and the western Pacific', *Oceania*, vol. 8, pp. 306–27.
—— 1939, 'Anthropology in Australia', *Oceania*, vol. 10, pp. 1–29.
—— 1940, 'Notes and news', *Oceania*, vol. 10, no. 4, p. 465.
—— 1943, 'The need for sociological research in Australia', *Social Horizons*, pp. 5–15.
—— 1954, 'The Australian National Research Council', *Australian Journal of Science*, vol. 16, pp. 203–11.
—— 1958, 'Anthropology in Australia: One chapter', *Mankind*, vol. 5, pp. 225–42.
—— 1959, 'A Darwin centenary and highlights of fieldwork in Australia', *Mankind*, vol. 5, pp. 321–33.
—— 1963, 'The development of scientific knowledge of the Aborigines', in H Sheils (ed.), *Australian Aboriginal Studies*, University Press, Melbourne, pp. 3–28.

—— 1970, The Journal *Oceania*, Oceania Monographs, no. 16.
—— 1975–76, 'RH Mathews: His contribution to Aboriginal Studies', *Oceania*, vol. 46, pp. 1–24, 126–52.
Firth, R 1932, 'Anthropology in Australia', *Oceania*, vol. 3, pp. 1–2.
—— 1956, 'Alfred Reginald Radcliffe-Brown: 1881–1955', *Proceedings of the British Academy*, vol. 42, pp. 287–302.
Fison L & Howitt, AW 1880, *Kamilaroi and Kurnai: Group-marriage and relationship, and marriage by elopement, drawn chiefly from the usage of the Australian aborigines. Also the Kurnai tribe, their customs in peace and war*, G Robertson Melbourne.
Frazer, JG 1935 [1910[, *Totemism and exogamy*, Macmillan, London.
Freud, S 1963 [1913[, *Totem and taboo: Resemblances between the psychic lives of savages and neurotics*, Random House, New York.
Geertz, C 1963, *Agricultural involution: The process of ecological change in Indonesia*, University of California Press, Berkeley.
Gennep, A van 1905, *Mythes et legendes d'Australie*, E Guilmoto, Paris.
Hamilton, A 1982, 'Anthropology in Australia: Some notes and a few queries', in G McCall (ed.), *Anthropology in Australia: Essays to honour 50 Years of Mankind*, Anthropological Society of New South Wales, Sydney, pp. 91–106.
Jonas, G c. 1989, *The circuit riders*, Norton, New York.
Jones, P 1987, 'South Australian anthropological history: The Board for Anthropological Research and its early expeditions', *Records of the South Australian Museum*, vol. 20, pp. 71–92.
Lang, A 1905, *The secret of the totem*, Longmans & Green, London.
Lippman, L 1981, *Generations of resistance*, Longman Cheshire, Melbourne.
McCall, G (ed.) 1982, *Anthropology in Australia: Essay to honour 50 Years of Mankind*, Anthropological Society of New South Wales, Sydney.
McCarthy F 1946, 'Anthropology in Australian museums', *Oceania*, vol. 17, pp. 26–37.
Malinowski, B 1963 (1919), *The family among the Australian Aborigines*, Schocken Books, New York.
Marett, RR 1909, *The threshold of religion*, Methuen, London.
Mulvaney, DJ 1958, 'The Australian Aborigines 1606–1929: Opinion and fieldwork', *Historical Studies*, vol. 8, pp. 131–51, 297–314.
—— 1966, 'Fact, fancy and Aboriginal Australian ethnic origins', *Mankind*, vol. 6, pp. 299–305.
—— 1971, 'The ascent of Aboriginal man: Howitt as anthropologist,' in MH Walker (ed.), *Come wind, come weather*, Melbourne University Press, Melbourne, pp. 285–312, 323–4.
—— 1981, 'Gum leaves on the golden bough: Australians palaeolithic survivals discovered', in JD Evans et al. (eds), *Antiquity and man*, Thames and Hudson, London, pp. 52–64.
—— 1986, 'A sense of making history: Australian Aboriginal Studies 1961–1986', *Australian Aboriginal Studies*, vol. 2, pp. 48–56.
—— 1988, 'Australian anthropology and ANZASS: Strictly scientific and critical', in R MacLeod (ed.), *The commonwealth of science*, Oxford University Press, Melbourne, pp. 196–221.
Mulvaney, DJ & Calaby, JH 1985, *So much that is new: Baldwin Spencer 1860–1929, a biography*, Melbourne University Press, Melbourne.
Pickens, DK 1968, *Eugenics and the progressives*, Vanderbilt University Press, Nashville.
PPSC 1924, *Proceedings of the Pan-Pacific Science Congress, Australia 1923*, Government Printer, Melbourne.
Radcliffe-Brown, AR 1930, Editorial, *Oceania*, vol. 1, no. 1, pp. 1–4.
Review of activities from 1952 to 1977 and some Indications for the future, 1977, unpublished manuscript, Department of Anthropology, Research School of Pacific Studies, Australian National University, Canberra, pp. 1–49.

Said, EW 1978, *Orientalism*, Routledge & Kegan Paul, London.
Spencer, B & Gillen, FJ 1899, *The native tribes of Central Australia*, Macmillan, London.
—— 1927, *The Arunta: A study of Stone Age people*, vols 1 & 2, Macmillan, London.
Tonkinson, R & Howard, M 1990, 'The Berndts: A biographical sketch', in R Tonkinson & M Howard (eds), *Going it alone*, Aboriginal Studies Press, Canberra, pp. 17–42.
Wentworth, WC 1964, Second Reading Speech, *House of Representatives Hansard*, 20 May, Government Printer, Canberra.
—— 1959, 'An Australian Institute of Aboriginal Studies', unpublished paper, AIAS, Canberra, pp. 1–9.
White, I 1981, 'Mrs Bates and Mr Brown: An examination of Rodney Needham's allegations', *Oceania*, vol. 51, no. 3, pp. 193–210.
Widders, J et al. 1974, *Eaglehawk and Crow: Open letter concerning the Australian Institute of Aboriginal Studies*, 29 March, AIAS, Canberra, pp. 1–5.
Wise, T 1965, *The self-made anthropologist: A life of AP Elkin*, Allen & Unwin, Sydney.

Original lecture available at:
<http://aiatsis.gov.au/publications/presentations/studying-man-and-mans-nature-history-institutionalisation-aboriginal-anthropology>

7

Aborigines and policing: Aboriginal solutions from Northern Territory communities

1992 Wentworth Lecture

Marcia Langton

In the Wentworth Lecture this year, I have chosen to discuss relations between Aborigines and police and to highlight some of the attempts at solutions which have been initiated by Aboriginal people. The aims and often the outcomes of these Aboriginal-initiated community policing and justice mechanisms have been to achieve law and order within the Aboriginal community and to improve the generally poor relationship between Aboriginal communities and Australian institutions.

In 1983, I examined Aboriginal and police relations in parts of New South Wales (Langton 1983). I wrote then, and submitted to the Australian Law Reform Commission, in respect of forms of Aboriginal swearing and fighting as customary law practices, that there is an urgent need to bring a sense of larger rationality to the problem of Aboriginal dispute processing styles in conflict with the dominant and conflicting Anglo-Australian legal system. The possibilities for this suggested by the discussion papers of the Australian Law Reform Commission seem the most likely to succeed in reducing the Aboriginal arrest and imprisonment rate. In this respect anthropological inquiry may assist in refining the specific kinds of knowledge required by legislators and Aboriginal people to establish legal structures and guidelines to deal properly with this problem (Langton 1983, p. 81).

I wrote then, in relation to the way in which the Aboriginal population is treated in the Australian criminal justice system:

> The question remains: should Aboriginal people be penalised by the Anglo-Australian legal system for responding in adverse conditions to two different forms of cultural knowledge and consequent action in order to achieve favourable outcomes for themselves and their own? The

> answer from an anthropological point of view is that the legal penalties are not only irrational in their own terms, but as well misinformed and ethnocentric habits or codes which the police and judiciary impose for the ostensible purpose of maintaining 'law and order', defined in white terms, with little or no regard for Aboriginal notions of legality and appropriate social behaviour. (Langton 1983, pp. 88–9)

Since that time, Aboriginal communities in the Northern Territory have experimented with various ways of overcoming their problems in the criminal justice system. Most of these have been successful. I should point out, however, that with the exception of the Galiwin'ku Community Justice Program, under review by the Northern Territory government, and some Aboriginal fostering and adoption principles, none of the recommendations of the Australian Law Reform Commission under its terms of reference dealing with the recognition of Aboriginal customary law have been addressed by the federal or Northern Territory Government. From 1989 to 1994, I carried out research for the Royal commission into Aboriginal Deaths in Custody as Head of the Aboriginal Issues Unit in the Northern Territory. What I found in 1983 was confirmed in 1990: cultural and social imperatives shape Aboriginal and police relationships as much as do the impact of history and the legacy of racism and inequity which Aboriginal people endure more than 200 years after the first fatal impact of British settlement.

The Royal Commission into Aboriginal Deaths in Custody was the most thorough inquiry in the history of Australia into the nature of the treatment of Aboriginal people in the Australian criminal justice system and in other Australian institutions. In 1992, almost a year after Commissioner Elliott Johnston QC presented the five-volume national report and the regional reports (Australia 1991), government representatives, leaders, media and other commentators continue to debate Aboriginal and police relations largely within the terms of the traditional Australian racist discourse. For example, recently in the *Sydney Morning Herald* a retired New South Wales magistrate attributed the problem largely to what he perceives as Aboriginal requests for handouts. He clearly had not read the Commission's report, or if he had, had not comprehended its message. A respected current affairs presenter on an Australian Broadcasting Corporation television program asked the Prime Minister of Australia what he would feel if he had to walk with his family through a park full of drunken Aborigines. Likewise, it was clear to me that this representative of the media had not read the report, or if so, had not comprehended it.

There have been many ill-founded complaints about the Royal Commission, probably more vociferous and more frequent than about any other royal commission. On the question of the cost of its operations, it has become clear to me that, if there were ever a question of waste of public resources, the real waste is that which has occurred a year after its national report was tabled. That is, the recurring evidence is that few, if any, of those people who have commented on Aboriginal police relations in the recent controversies, widely reported in the media, have read the five volumes of the national report. This would also appear to be the case in Western Australia, where amending legislation that will mostly affect Aboriginal youth offenders has been passed in that legislature. According to various reports, the legislation contravenes standards of human rights set out in United Nations conventions which Australia has ratified. Since the national report was presented to governments almost a year ago, it is also the case that, in at least some jurisdictions, Aboriginal arrest and imprisonment rates continue to increase above the already alarming rates.

In 1990, I reported to Commissioner Elliott Johnston under the terms of reference provided to the Aboriginal Issues Units established as part of the Royal Commission into Aboriginal Deaths in Custody (Langton et al. 1990). My report stated, among other things, that Aboriginal community policing and justice mechanisms have been successful, and that they are examples of measures which can be taken to rectify the situation of Aboriginal people as the Australians most represented in police cells, before courts and in prisons, despite being a minority of 2 per cent of the population. One important outcome of such projects in the Northern Territory has been to improve relationships between Aboriginal society and the Australian criminal justice system. Because of the continuing racist discourse in which the Aboriginal position in the Australian criminal justice system is discussed, and because of the extent of misinformation, or disinformation, in the current debates on these questions, it is important that the solutions which Aboriginal people have devised become a central part of any discussion which purports to lead to improvements. Thoughtful, experienced police are as anxious to find solutions as Aboriginal people.

The examples of Aboriginal policing and dispute processing discussed here are from the Northern Territory. There are, or have been, Aboriginal police and court systems imposed by state governments in Western Australia and Queensland. Until the amendment of the relevant legislation in Queensland in 1984, the Aboriginal courts on the then Aboriginal reserves in Queensland were considered by members of the International Commission of Jurists to be in contravention of international human rights standards in respect of courts and related matters. The powers of the Aboriginal police in Queensland, in 1991 still not part of the Queensland Police Force, require attention in respect of their training and the extent of their powers. Like the Northern Territory, there is in parts of Western Australia an Aboriginal police aide scheme. However, I confine my comments here to the Northern Territory system, with which I am familiar.

It is important to understand how bad the situation is for Aboriginal people in relation to the Australian criminal justice system, or how bad it was at the time that the Royal Commission presented its national report in 1991. In some respects, since then, the situation has worsened. The major findings of the Criminology Research Unit of the Royal Commission showed that, when allowance is made for age and the relative representation of Aborigines in the Australian population, Aboriginal people died in police custody at a rate more than 40 times the rate of non-Aboriginal people. The alarming Aboriginal death rate is explained, almost entirely, by the over-representation of Aboriginal people in police custody. Other findings showed that substantial differences exist between the states and territories regarding rates of deaths in custody, with the Northern Territory having the highest ratio of deaths to population. Suicide and other self-inflicted injuries were the most common cause of death reported, with deaths by hanging accounting for 95 per cent of all reported suicides. The average length of time that people had been held in police custody, up to the time of death, was 15 hours. In 1987 a dramatic increase occurred in the number of deaths among both Aboriginal and non-Aboriginal people (Biles, McDonald & Fleming 1989b, p. 33).

In contrast to the rates of deaths in police cells, it was found, when allowance is made for age and the relative representation of Aboriginal people in the Australian population, that Aboriginal people died in prison custody at a rate nearly 20 times the rate of non-Aboriginal people. Other findings showed that the average age was 35 years, with the age of death for Aboriginal people being lower (Biles, McDonald & Fleming 1989b, p. 32). Another finding shows that the death rate for Aboriginal people over 15 years in non-custodial corrections was, for 1987 and 1988, 22.6 per 100,000 compared to 3.0 per 140,000 for the same age group in the community (Fleming, McDonald & Biles 1990).

In 1988, Aboriginal people made up 29 per cent of police custodies with substantial differences existing between the jurisdictions in the Aboriginal custody rates. Aboriginal women were heavily over-represented, comprising nearly 50 per cent of the female custodies but less than 1.1 per cent of the national adult female population. The mean age of people held in custody was 28 years. Drunkenness, break, enter and steal, fraud and theft were the most common offences leading to arrests, with Aboriginal people being over-represented in good order (including drunkenness) and assault offences only. Aboriginal people were in custody significantly longer than non-Aboriginal people (McDonald, 1990).

For the years 1980–89, the mortality rates for Aboriginal people in police custody are far higher than those of Aboriginal people in the community, whereas the rates for Aboriginal people in prison custody are somewhat lower than those of Aboriginal people in the community. In other words, a protective factor exists with regard to prison custody, but not with regard to police custody (Thomson & McDonald 1991).

As at 30 June 1989, the Australian adult Aboriginal imprisonment rate was 1464.9 per 100,000 compared with the equivalent rate for non-Aboriginal adults of 97.2 per 100,000. The Aboriginal rate was thus shown to be 15.1 times higher. As at 30 June 1987, it was found that Aboriginal people were over-represented in non-custodial corrections by a factor of 8.3, considerably lower than the level for prisons. It has been speculated that this difference may be due to a belief by some judges, magistrates and parole authorities that Aboriginal people are either less able or less willing to comply with the requirements of non-custodial correctional orders than are non-Aboriginal people (Biles 1990).

The question which must be asked, knowing what these figures tell us, is: how do we stop the police in the various jurisdictions of Australia from arresting Aboriginal people at these extraordinary rates?

The governments are currently preparing to respond to the reports of the Royal Commission into Aboriginal Deaths in Custody, and if the government responses ignore Aboriginal solutions which are working, there is a real possibility that the present alarming situation will get worse.

Finding solutions to the problem of arrest rates is only part of the answer, of course. Urgent improvements are required to lower the ill health and mortality rates of Aboriginal people, and especially the levels of alcohol misuse among a minority of the Aboriginal population. There must be improvements in the levels of inequity in employment, housing and education, as well as in other areas. The recommendations of the various regional reports and the national report address these problems and make hundreds of recommendations. They emphasise the role of Aboriginal decision making and service delivery in solving these problems.

Aboriginal initiatives in community policing, education and crime reduction

What has been the response of Aboriginal people to their experience with police? Throughout Australia, Aboriginal people have become severely disenchanted with the police systems and practices. To overcome the problems perceived in a range of Aboriginal communities in the Northern Territory, Aboriginal leaders and community workers have established and proposed a range of community-based schemes. These include community policing and justice mechanisms; curricula in schools to educate Aboriginal children about the police and court systems; and strategies for crime reduction, especially through alcohol reduction and education.

In the past, non-Aboriginal society and its institutions, in this case the police, have failed Aboriginal people in their attempts to solve problems of alcohol abuse, anomie, alienation and the resultant crime, vandalism, domestic violence, rape, assault, homicide and affray. Aboriginal people have perceived that the political expectation of the police in relation to the exercise of their duties among the Aboriginal population has not been to achieve law and order in Aboriginal communities but to achieve a range of vaguely understood and probably impossible aims, to satisfy the demands of the white population. These demands can be seen to be the legacy of over 200 years of history, throughout much of which the police were an army of occupation. Terms such as 'dispersal' and 'pacification' arise repeatedly in Australian history. They are euphemisms for the physical destruction of Aboriginal people and control in various periods and in various regions in the history of white colonisation. In many parts of Australia still today, it appears to Aboriginal people that the expectations of the police in relation to Aboriginal people have changed only in respect of the extent of force used and the tactics used. In 1989, for example, an Alice Springs alderman publicly suggested that the police should use police dogs against Aboriginal people camping in the Todd River.

Aboriginal people in the Northern Territory have consistently raised the problems created for them and their communities through the interaction and conflict of Aboriginal customary laws with the Australian law. The issues have been recognised and aired repeatedly for well over a decade by Aboriginal people, representatives of their organisations, the Australian Law Reform Commission and more recently by the reports of the Royal Commission into Aboriginal Deaths in Custody. The unavoidable conclusion is that constructive changes in the interactions of Aboriginal people with the criminal justice system throughout much of Aboriginal Australia will occur when there are legislative and other kinds of recognition of Aboriginal Law and indigenous dispute-processing mechanisms from police officers, magistrates, legal counsel and others.

At least one measure taken by Aboriginal people against the unilateral intervention by police in community affairs began back in the 1970s. I turn now to the community justice project at Yirrkala, one example of Aboriginal action to improve the situation with the police.

The community justice project at Yirrkala

Over a number of years Yolngu leaders as members of the community council at Yirrkala developed a system for dealing with police and magistrates. Their most vital concern was 'the unilateral intervention of police in Yolngu disputes' (Williams 1987, p. 233). By 1976, the council of Yirrkala, the Dhanbul Association, had incorporated as a business and trading association. When this became the Community Council, the annual election of officers and members became a problem for the traditional leaders of the Yolngu clans. The clan leaders used a number of constitutional devices to ensure that membership and representation accorded with Yolngu principles of authority and decision-making. When disputes arose, they were dealt with by traditional Yolngu means, and only involved members of the Council in terms of their responsibilities (or liabilities) as kin in any particular case. The leaders also met to consider matters of social control which had been put to them by members of parliamentary committees and the Law Reform Commission.

Dr Nugget Coombs wrote a proposal to the Australian Law Reform Commission when it was investigating the recognition of Aboriginal customary law. His proposal formalised the system developed by the Yolngu clan leaders as a community justice mechanism. Dr Nancy Williams wrote:

> The leaders attempted to maintain their authority by asserting their jurisdiction over 'little trouble' and by proposing a number of procedures for acting jointly with the police. The Council's aim was to have the police function as adjunct to their own authority, rather than to create mutually exclusive jurisdictions. When trouble arose they wanted police to attend their meetings at their invitation, and they wished to remain involved in any matter that concerned a Yolngu person as prisoner, defendant or witness. These aims were consistently expressed through the succession of council structures that came into existence during the ensuing fifteen years. (Williams 1987, p. 233)

Dr Williams lists the essential criteria of community justice mechanisms that are met by Dr Coombs' proposal:

> The viability of Aboriginal community justice mechanisms depends on Aboriginal autonomy. At the most basic level this means that police and other Australian law enforcement agencies will not intervene unilaterally in offences involving Aborigines, but will intervene at the invitation of Aboriginal community leaders. They will keep the leaders involved at all stages of dealing with a community member charged with an offence if the matter is dealt with outside the community, and within the community will act to support the authority of community leaders. Where Aboriginal communities suggest mechanisms of articulation of joint operation with Australian law enforcement agencies, these must be seen as means of providing support for Aboriginal authority, not of superseding it. (Williams 1987, p. 237)

During the work of the staff of the Aboriginal Issues Unit of the Royal Commission from 1989–90, it became clear that other communities had been experimenting, relatively successfully, with similar community-based projects to resolve the problems of over-policing and inappropriate policing. At Tennant Creek and Elliott, two small towns in the Northern Territory, Aboriginal elders had begun voluntary community policing in Aboriginal residential areas on special purpose leases within the town boundaries.

Tennant Creek: The Julalikari Council Patrols: Community policing by Aboriginal people

The Aboriginal community at Tennant Creek had attempted to overcome a number of problems with police and policing by establishing Council patrols, which attended disturbances in the camps at night and attempted to resolve conflicts at morning meetings in the camps. The Julalikari Council insisted that people should bring their complaints to the councillors on patrol, rather than the police, and that the police should not attend disturbances without the presence of councillors to explain the problem to them.

The initiatives of Aboriginal people in providing their own policing, whether at Tennant Creek or Elliott, where police cooperate with the Aboriginal councillors, or in other communities, where less formal and often traditional policing and dispute-processing takes place, are evidence of the extent to which Aboriginal people are dissatisfied with the conventional police system and its practices. (In particular, the involvement of Aboriginal councillors in voluntary policing of their communities, and their preparedness to use their own vehicles and money to patrol the streets and camps every night, points to their dissatisfaction with the policing in these communities.)

The councillors stated that the main factors in Aboriginal offending included alcohol, disrespect by Aboriginal youth and the white community of Aboriginal law, and the inadequacy of essential services, alcohol rehabilitation services and general standards of living in the community. People were concerned that white police did not understand the social and cultural circumstances with which they were dealing when they intervened in disturbances on Aboriginal town leases. They were particularly troubled that the police were used by protagonists on one side of a dispute against the other family or faction in the dispute.

The Julalikari councillors were attempting to resolve conflicts in an Aboriginal way, rather than having the police simply arrest a person or persons, sometimes the wrong person, without solving the problem(s) that had contributed to an open dispute which apparently required police attendance. The Julalikari councillors, most of whom are elders, were able to speak to Aboriginal people and reprimand them with success. Police reprimands may not be successful in some situations, especially those involving domestic violence. The use of Aboriginal languages in these patrols made an enormous contribution to their success.

Councillors worked with their constituents on their night patrols to diffuse arguments and prevent disturbances. Town camp residents did not call police themselves. They called the Council to attend a dispute and, if residents felt that police were required, councillors would call the police on their behalf. This meant that heavy-handed police surveillance was minimised, and that police attending complaints were met by councillors who explained the problem.

The following morning, when intoxicated people had sobered up, meetings were convened in the town camps by the Julalikari Council to resolve conflict between those causing disturbances during the night. Calling offenders to account before a meeting of residents by the Julalikari councillors was a much more effective way of dealing with minor law and order problems than the rotation of intoxicated people through the 'drunk tanks' under protective custody or on minor charges through the police cells and courts.

This program is a clear demonstration, in relation to minor offences, that police practices, particularly their readiness with Aboriginal people to proceed by arrest and protective custody detention rather than cautioning or summons, can be replaced by Aboriginal community policing. The program demonstrates how to achieve law and order in Aboriginal communities where police action has failed. For example, in one case, an argument between two young men on the main road was successfully diffused by the councillors, as explained by one woman elder on the Julalikari Council: 'The old get sometimes hit by their sons and daughters ... old hit young too ... but police is only called for the young offenders, the old sort their problems out within the family' (Langton et al. 1990, p. 440).

Alcohol misuse and intoxication, however, require the Council to call the police sometimes, even though it would prefer not to, as explained by a woman elder in another case: 'One old man who annoyed several neighbours during the night at Marla Marla was taken to the Dry Out Shelter [or Sobering Up Shelter] by police whom the Councillors had called upon the request of Marla Marla residents' (Langton et al. 1990, p. 440.

In 1989, the Inspector of Police at Tennant Creek formed a Domestic Violence Committee and attempted to involve representatives on the Committee in working together with the police with new legislation on domestic violence, which enabled police to remove offenders from homes and detain them for four hours. He had invited the Julalikari Council, the Central Australian Aboriginal Legal Service, Anyinginyi Congress, the women's shelter, the Tennant Creek hospital and other bodies to send representatives to the committee. He reported, at a meeting in 1990 that, in the previous two months, of the 162 disturbances reported to the police, over 50 per cent concerned incidents of domestic violence and 95 per cent of them were alcohol-related. Many of the reports were generated by Julalikari patrols, he said, and their contribution had considerably increased the number of disturbances reported to police.

This increased reportage of domestic violence cases to the police by the Council patrol demonstrates that the law and order problem with which Aboriginal people of Tennant Creek are concerned is not the array of minor offences for which most Aboriginal people are arrested, but the domestic violence in the town camps, which is dangerously exacerbated by alcohol misuse. Fortunately, the Inspector of Police responded by recognising the real law and order problems of the Tennant Creek communities. It seems hardly necessary to say that domestic violence is rife in the non-Aboriginal community as well.

In 1990, it was a high priority of the Julalikari Council that their night patrols meet with success. In 1992, the Julalikari Council patrols continue to achieve success in confining arrests to situations perceived by Aboriginal residents of the town to be the real law and order problems.

Community policing by the Gurungu Council at Elliott

Gurungu Council at Elliott, a two-hour drive north of Tennant Creek, followed the lead taken by Julalikari Council and also instituted Council night patrols. Furthermore, the Council had been working toward establishing rules or laws for camp residents to fill the vacuum left by the partial displacement of traditional laws by the largely irrelevant body of law enforced by the police.

Gurungu councillors explained it in this way to their constituents, their fellow community members and kinsfolk:

> We'll have meeting on Friday to make council rules — if you don't like rules — you say so. We not flash — we trying to keep this place going good. You all have to obey Council rules. You have to tell us if rule is no more good one. At the moment. If you agree with that rule you got to obey it — you can't say it no more good one afterward. If you mob fight at night — at next day you gotta finish it up next day. No good going to pub fighting in public area — it's dangerous. That's one of the rules. When they drunk one person fight — no good. You gotta fight sober. You gotta learn to drink properly like kardiya (white people). Say it to our face — don't say it behind our back. We gotta make it hard. That's the only way we can help our people. What if you killin that man dead — what you gonna do then?
>
> *Punishment is gonna be Aboriginal way in camps — not police.*
>
> We gotta rubbish in camp. They can clean up camp. Aboriginal way so strong. When they go to court and get punishment they have to work in town — not in camp. We want them to work in camp — in Aboriginal way. (Langton et al. 1990, p. 441)

The elders made it clear to their constituents that they were to bring their problems to the Council first, not to the police: 'If people make trouble they have to see Council, not go to police. Council goes to police. People to complain to councillors, not police. Council patrols at night' (Langton et al. 1990, p. 441).

The drain of already limited personal resources among the elders was one of the problems they faced, explained by one eider: 'One bloke was using his car to run around, using his own money for petrol. Other people should help. [The council president] should be using council truck, not his own vehicle'. (Langton et al. 1990, p. 441). This personal generosity and contribution to the project demonstrates the elders' commitment and perception of need to improve the lot of their fellows with the police. When a Commonwealth funding body indicated that it would not be able to fund this scheme, the senior police officer in Tennant Creek with responsibility for this area wrote supporting their need for funding.

Community policing extends to Alice Springs and Yuendumu

Inevitably, when other Aboriginal communities heard of the community policing at Tennant Creek and Elliott, they rapidly initiated their own schemes. In Alice Springs, the major township in Central Australia, Aboriginal town people largely reside in Aboriginal special-purpose leases governed by an Aboriginal local council, called Tangentyere. A scheme was established in December 1990 to involve male and female Aborigines in the night patrol. At the present time, the scheme is enormously successful from the point of view of the town-camp residents. Senior police in Alice Springs seem to be pleased with the outcome. Government funding covers one coordinator position, some administration costs, T-shirts, CB radios and jackets, first aid, and running costs for vehicles for patrollers. Most patrollers are not paid for their work. A minority is paid from Community Development Employment Project funds. Increasingly, youth have become involved in the project, leading to an increase in their self-image and self-esteem, and community cohesion. Aboriginal leaders continue to set an example and provide inspiration to the program. The Aboriginal 'Beat the Grog' program in Alice Springs has also provided strength and inspiration to the community policing project.

At Yuendumu, a group of women elders initiated the Yuendumu Night Patrol in April 1991. In September, when I discussed it with them, they told me that they had dramatically reduced domestic violence and vandalism. They had bought uniforms out of their own pension incomes and had the words 'Night patrol' embroidered onto the pockets. They carry their traditional fighting sticks, as a symbol of their customary authority, which is held in high respect.

Community involvement of the police at Gunbalanya

Innovative use of the Northern Territory Police Force by a small community in western Arnhem Land in controlling alcohol misuse is yet another example to the rest of Australia of how Aboriginal people are prepared to solve, not just the problems which Australian policing presents, but the problem of alcohol misuse as well. At Gunbalanya, formerly called Oenpelli, the location of one of the former Anglican missions to Arnhem Land, the community established a canteen, licensed to sell alcohol, but with strict controls. The police have been involved in the punitive measures used to prevent alcohol-related breaches of club rules and community law and order.

In the 1970s, the sale of alcohol at 'Border Store', situated on the Arnhem Land border, and subsequent dangerously high consumption levels by some Aboriginal people, led to a successful challenge to the store's licence by the then Oenpelli Community and the establishment of the Gunbalanya Sports and Social Club. A woman elder at Gunbalanya told me:

> We used to get grog before social club from Border Store. It was unlimited. The drinking was bad then. [A] few of them drowned. The Council had a meeting about the Border Store. We went to court in Darwin to get its licence taken away from it. We got funding from Aboriginal Development Commission for club in 1978 or 1979. The club had its ups and downs, but the Council has mastered it now. Bringing it here from Border Store, the real main reason was so we could control it and look after our drunken mob and sober mob. (Langton et al. 1990, p. 324)

Importation of alcohol into the community is now prohibited, with alcohol available only through the club, with takeaway alcohol available only to those with permits. At the invitation of the club, the police at Gunbalanya work with the Gunbalanya Social Club to ensure that the club rules are enforced. The club bans people who commit misdemeanours for various periods of time. The club workers write offenders' names on a public blackboard and the dates of their ban periods. The police independently write offenders' names on the blackboard if they have committed alcohol-related breaches outside the club after it closes. This arrangement is supported by the community. However, arrangements for enforcing club rules are not entirely successful in preventing domestic violence and in 1990 women appealed to the police for more action in relation to this major law and order problem.

The Gunbalanya Club has been visited by groups from as far away as Alice Springs to find out how its model might be adapted for other circumstances.

In Alice Springs, the Tyweretye Social Club, an organisation formed to implement a canteen proposal similar to the Gunbalanya one, has not been able to get a licence from the Northern Territory Commission. Yet, as of December 1989, the Commission had granted licences to 72 outlets in Alice Springs. In 1989, Alice Springs had 39.5 per cent more outlets per 100,000 population than the rest of the Northern Territory and 163.6 per cent more than Western Australia (Lyon 1990, p. 5).

The Tangentyere Social Behaviour Project

Another initiative from the Alice Springs Aboriginal community, desperate to overcome the law and order problems within their own settlements, is the proposal by Tangentyere for a Social Behaviour Project. In May 1998, the Tangentyere Council submitted a detailed proposal for what it called 'the social behaviour project' to the then Northern Territory Attorney-General, Mr Darryl Manzie. The Council requested that his officers meet with the acting general manager to discuss funding and other matters, including the priority which the project ought to be accorded to ensure that it commenced operation.

The submission set out the need for a new approach to the question of Indigenous law, especially where this law had been weakened by such problems as the migration of remote Aboriginal people to the township of Alice Springs, alcohol abuse and attendant social problems. It proposed a process of re-establishing the law of the traditional inhabitants of Alice Springs and integrating the rules of the Australian institutions in Alice Springs by ensuring that all Aboriginal visitors to the Alice Springs area know and understand the rules for social behaviour that the traditional owners have devised.

The scheme envisaged joint cooperation with Aboriginal police aides in the Northern Territory Police Force, Aboriginal corrections officers and the mainstream Australian law enforcement agencies. Importantly, it proposed retaining Aboriginal autonomy and authority in decision making and policy making. A holistic approach to social control was taken, with specific regard to disorder arising from alcohol misuse in the town. Recommendations were made on social and environmental problems that had to be addressed in order that Aboriginal people could take some control over problems of law and order in their daily lives.

Barbara Shaw, then acting general manager of Tangentyere, explained the proposal on Aboriginal Law in the following way:

> I believe that many of these problems occur because the visitors are 'outside the law'. They are away from the laws and restrictions of their own communities and do not understand the 'whitefella' law that applies in Alice Springs. Nor do they understand the rules of life on town camps.
>
> Tangentyere is proposing to assist in the creation of awareness of the rules and laws of Alice Springs among these people and also to assist in the application of these. We are calling this our Social Behaviour Project.
>
> We believe that this can best be done by fostering a widespread identification with and commitment to the rules and laws by elders, family leaders and ordinary people in the bush. For this to happen successfully, there needs to be a process whereby the bush people can learn about 'town law', work out their own approach to understanding, teaching and applying that law, and place it in the context of their own laws and customs. Hopefully this could lead to a maximum integration of the two sets of rules, at least in the Alice Springs situation. It is hoped that the bush people could come up with some suggestions for changes or adaptation of either town or bush law in the process, and this could assist the government in its own legal planning.
>
> This project is not meant to be all-encompassing, but to be firmly focussed on areas of day to day life in town. (Langton et al. 1990, p. 391)

The National Campaign Against Drug and Alcohol Abuse funded the project with the assistance of the Federal Minister for Housing, Health and Community Services and the Minister Assisting. The project has been operating since early February 1992, although it was begun in 1991 using private resources. Visits were made by Tangentyere staff to a number of remote communities to commence the project. Particularly, they've examined what constitutes good leadership and how best to pass those skills on in Aboriginal communities. They have looked at styles of Aboriginal drinking and at how to disconnect these styles from popular Aboriginal justifications, particularly of group 'binge' drinking as being part of Aboriginal culture. An anthropologist has given advice on the operations of the project.

Projects such as this one have the potential to solve many of the conflicts between Aboriginal law and the Australian criminal justice system, strengthening the Indigenous system of law and order. For various reasons, police are unable to provide for law and order in Aboriginal communities by themselves. By working in conjunction with such Aboriginal programs, real progress would be made.

Recommendations of the Royal Commission into Aboriginal Deaths in Custody

The national report of the Royal Commission into Aboriginal Deaths in Custody acknowledges the importance of programs like these and makes two important recommendations that are relevant to my talk:

> 220. That organizations such as Julalikari Council in Tennant Creek in the Northern Territory and the Community Justice Panels at Echuca and elsewhere in Victoria, and others which are actively involved in providing voluntary support for community policing and community justice programs, be provided with adequate and ongoing funding by governments to ensure the success of such programs. Although regional and local factors may dictate different approaches, these schemes should be examined with a view to introducing similar schemes into Aboriginal communities that are willing to operate them because they have the potential to improve policing and to improve relations between police and Aboriginal people rapidly and to substantially lower crime rates. (4:108)

> 221. That Aboriginal people who are involved in community and police initiated schemes such as those referred to in Recommendation 220 should receive adequate remuneration in keeping with their important contribution to the administration of justice. Funding for the payment of these people should be from allocations to expenditure on justice matters, not from the Aboriginal Affairs budget. (4:109) (Johnston 1991, p. 118)

It is a salutary lesson in Australian politics that, following the tabling in 1986 of the Australian Law Reform Commission reports on the recognition of Aboriginal Customary Law (Australian Law Reform Commission 1986), it has been left to Aboriginal people to implement the intent of its recommendations. One hopes that this will not be the case with the 339 recommendations of the Royal Commission into Aboriginal Deaths in Custody.

Another project is aimed at educating Aboriginal people to live under two conflicting legal systems. The Barunga School Action Group proposed a community-based curriculum on police and courts. The group, consisting of Aboriginal teachers, teachers' aides, parents and traditional owners, meets regularly at the Barunga School. They want such a curriculum taught from primary school through to high school so that their children would be educated about the Australian legal system, especially the role of police and courts and how to deal with them. This curriculum would be an essential part of the education, they argue, because of the serious difficulties which their children will face.

The criminal justice system and Aboriginal Law in conflict

In discussions with the Aboriginal Issues Unit, Aboriginal people in the Northern Territory offered diverse explanations for the reasons leading to offences committed by their people. Sometimes the cause of offences by youth is one simply of hunger and deprivation in an already impoverished community undergoing further stress. The provision of services to youth, especially recreation facilities, and assistance to families to enable them to cope with the stresses of rapidly changing life, would solve some of these problems. Most communities demanded more appropriate housing, and employment, particularly with respect to the Community Development Employment Project.

Explanations often referred to the specific problems of young men and juveniles: problems created through a lack of knowledge of Australian law and the ways it is implemented, and the trivial nature of many of the breaches committed. Because those that are not punishable under Aboriginal Law are dealt with by police and courts under the Australian system, Aboriginal people perceive the operation of Australian law as extremely heavy-handed in relation to trivial matters.

Many people felt that there is a need for young offenders to be made aware of the consequences of their actions, especially in relation to how harshly the Australian law treats matters considered minor by Aboriginal standards. It was acknowledged that there are mitigating circumstances involved in offences. Some offenders were oblivious to or unaware of the consequences of their actions because of the effects of alcohol consumption and, in some communities, of petrol sniffing.

A real distinction is drawn by Aboriginal people between minor offences and serious offences. Most offences for which Aboriginal people are arrested and imprisoned are considered under Aboriginal Law to be trivial and would probably not constitute an offence, so much as a nuisance. Motor cars and other Western technology do, in fact, come under Aboriginal Law now, for instance as highly-prized gifts in ritual exchange. Most motor car offences for which Aboriginal people are arrested, particularly on Aboriginal land, would not be considered serious under, or even breaches of, Aboriginal Law, and would certainly not warrant imprisonment. Over a quarter of the people in Northern Territory prisons in 1988 were serving sentences for a range of mostly minor motor vehicle offences. Swearing is also another example of an act that would not constitute an offence unless it were the kind of swearing which is specifically forbidden by Aboriginal Law (for example, swearing at certain kinds of in-laws, or a sister swearing in front of a brother). Aboriginal people made it very clear to the Aboriginal Issues Unit that people should not be sent to jail for these trivial offences.

It was further explained that arrest and jail are not deterrents because they do not teach anything to young people to prevent them from behaving antisocially. Aboriginal people are adamant that their own Law and the pressure of families would be a far better deterrent and would work to prevent minor crime, if there were considerably more assistance from Australian institutions in preventing alcohol and substance abuse and in providing better education and more recreational facilities. Some elders have spoken out about the need to set the terms under which both laws operate alongside each other. They evidently feel that Aboriginal offenders would respond better to the dictates of their own Law and culture than to those of an alien one. Aboriginal people argued that Australian laws would work better if there was an attempt to work with the support of traditional Aboriginal Law. After all, why should Aboriginal people accept that a strange system of law, instituted by strangers, is better than their own and deserves the respect and compliance which they accord their own Law implemented by kinsfolk? In some communities there is the ludicrous situation in which two or three white policemen, with one or two police aides, attempt to enforce what is to the community an almost completely irrelevant and alien law, while Aboriginal law and order breaks down because the Aboriginal system, and elders, are not accorded the authority which they once had. In north-east Arnhem Land, an elder explained:

> Yolngu Law and Balanda [white] law come together. We can say, 'leave this matter to us. We can deal with it, if it gets serious, we'll call you in. Your law and my Law can work together to fix it.' We have to be fair dinkum.
>
> Why can't Balanda law recognise Yolngu law. Like police, why can't they recognise us and yet we recognise their law. We recognise them you know, [for instance] court…You know, if [there is] spear and fight, it has to go to Balanda law all the time you know. Because we are Australian citizens, as you mob call it eh, and yet they don't recognise our law. That's the question that always comes up with me. It should be on both ends, both sides. They should recognise our law and we should recognise their law. (Langton et al. 1990, pp. 353–54)

Yet when the Australian system is too lenient in respect of serious crimes, justice is not seen by Aboriginal people to be done. Statistics show, and at least one criminologist agrees (Walker 1989), that the courts are lenient in sentencing Aboriginal people and that serious crimes committed by Aboriginal people are often ignored or overlooked in criminological analyses.

Crimes against women, including assault, especially assault arising from domestic violence, and rape, are ignored by the criminal justice system. Aboriginal women requested that there be many women employed as Aboriginal police aides, and that communities urgently require women's shelters.

Police were seen to sometimes intervene in matters in ways which obstructed the course of traditional law. For members of the families so offended, this only resulted in more tension.

It should be no surprise that the highest rates of Aboriginal arrests and imprisonment are in those areas where there are police or many police. At Groote Eylandt in 1989 there were 11 police, and, for the previous year, the highest recorded imprisonment rate in Australia, 2,274 per 100,000. At Galiwin'ku (or Elcho Island) there was one police aide and no other police; the offence rate on Elcho Island has been falling dramatically since 1983, partly, according to one report, because of the operations over a number of years of a Community Justice Project. The Aboriginal experience of police in smaller communities and remote areas is somewhat different from that in the towns. In small remote communities, police experience the situation of being outnumbered by Aboriginal people and surrounded by Aboriginal culture and lifestyle. Also, outstations provide a haven not only from alcohol and the pressures of living on large communities but also from police interference and sometimes harassment.

Where police have not developed good relations, community elders have some simple, practical suggestions to make to the police:

> If there's a big problem, the police fly or drive in and out. [We want] only the President [to] call the police, and that's better. We want that here. Only the President call the police for serious trouble. When there's warrants they should come in and ask the President.

> I laid some charges with the police. The police didn't notify President through 2-way radio — didn't notify old people and young people. He just came in. Everyone got a surprise ... These police don't do their duty like coming to [community name] every week to see if everything is alright. This settlement is an incorporated community. (Langton et al. 1990, p. 419)

Those remote communities and places where there are as yet no police stations, such as Kintore, Cobourg Peninsula, Minjilang and others, rely almost completely on the mechanisms and rituals provided by Aboriginal culture to deal with disputes and maintain social order. People sort out problems themselves.

From time to time, this is a dangerous exercise, and some people want a police presence in their communities, if only for the duration of a particular crisis. In some of the very remote areas, people often demanded more police or more policing on a more frequent or more permanent basis.

People want police assistance which is in sympathy with the problems which the communities face. They want policing in conjunction with the elders' authority, not mass arrest and incarceration. They want appropriate police intervention which prevents and reduces crime, not intervention that creates criminals, as the present system is perceived to do. The following ideas were provided by Aboriginal people for better policing and better Aboriginal–police relations: Aboriginal people want police to respond flexibly and innovatively in situations involving Aboriginal people, especially in situations which potentially lead to apprehension and arrest. They want police to proceed by summons rather than arrest, but preferably to caution and act to diffuse situations rather than arresting a person or persons. Where practicable, Aboriginal people want apprehension and arrest to be replaced by warnings, directives to leave a public place and assistance to go home.

In more specific terms, Aboriginal people want changes to policing practices in the following ways:

1. An end to intrusive surveillance, spotlighting camps at night and breaches of privacy and peace;
2. An end to unnecessary arrest and violence;
3. Notice of intention to arrive at communities with warrants or to arrest people. This means a working relationship with police as is enjoyed with other government departments, including reporting to council offices, properly arranged meetings and courteous behaviour;
4. The stationing of older, experienced [and preferably married] police in communities;
5. Police with whom communities have developed good relationships to remain rather than being transferred after two years;
6. Negotiation and counselling to replace resorting to force;
7. Fairness and impartiality in policing rather than doing the bidding of powerful factions in the community;
8. Better training for police in Aboriginal culture and community life;
9. Police to have respect for Aboriginal rights, including land rights, and to understand and respect positive features of Aboriginal culture and social life;
10. Aboriginal leaders to be able to open channels of communication with senior police. This would enable complaints about unacceptable police behaviour to be dealt with promptly and solutions to unsatisfactory policing practices to be found quickly. (Langton et al 1990, pp. 426–27)

In relation to the health problems which Aboriginal people face, there were specific recommendations from Aboriginal people and organisations to improve the conditions and care of detainees in police cells. They were:

1. Police need training not only to recognise illness, but to seek medical assistance and to refer prisoners to medical assistance when necessary. Formal procedures need to be developed to ensure that detainees who require medical assistance are promptly referred to the appropriate agency.
2. There is an urgent need for medical alert bracelets to be issued to Aboriginal people with a range of medical conditions requiring treatment and monitoring, and police must be trained to respect such bracelets and the care they indicate is necessary.
3. There is an urgent need for police to be trained by specialists to recognise particular health problems, such as head injuries and mental and behavioural disturbance.
4. There is an urgent need for residential and treatment facilities in Central Australia for the behaviourally disturbed to which police can take detainees with such problems.
5. There is a great need for trained liaison officers at police stations and prisons.
6. Particularly urgent is the need for police to attend cross-cultural workshops with Aboriginal people.
7. There is a need for the Police Department to recognise the valuable work that Aboriginal police aides perform, by improving staffing levels, salaries, career structures and training, and by employing many more women as police aides. (Langton et al. 1990, pp. 427–32)

Despite the fears of the 1950s and 1960s (justifiable in those times, and which no doubt motivated the founders of the Australian Institute of Aboriginal Studies), Aboriginal culture remains a strong force throughout much of Australia, despite high levels of ill health and mortality. There is nothing to gain in the white resistance to Aboriginal culture, and too often the police are seen as the front-line of that resistance. Better community relations will come about, as is happening now in parts of the Territory, as police and Aboriginal people work together in meaningful and constructive ways on projects which are largely designed by Aboriginal people, who say: force doesn't help.

References

Australian Law Reform Commission 1986, *The recognition of Aboriginal customary laws*, AGPS, Canberra.

Biles, D 1990, *Aborigines in prisons and non-custodial corrections*, Royal Commission into Aboriginal Deaths in Custody, Research Paper No. 19, Criminology Research Unit, Canberra.

Biles D, McDonald D & Fleming J 1989a, *Australian deaths in police custody 1980–1988: An analysis of Aboriginal and non-Aboriginal deaths*, Royal Commission into Aboriginal Deaths in Custody, Research Paper No. 10, Criminology Research Unit, Canberra.

Biles D, McDonald, D & Fleming, J 1989b, *Australian deaths in prisons 1980–1988: An analysis of Aboriginal and non-Aboriginal deaths*, Royal Commission into Aboriginal Deaths in Custody, Research Paper No. 11, Criminology Research Unit, Canberra.

Fleming, J, McDonald, D & Biles, D 1990, *Deaths in non-custodial corrections Australia and New Zealand, 1987 and 1988*, Royal Commission into Aboriginal Deaths in Custody, Research Paper No. 12, Criminology Research Unit, Canberra.

Johnston, E 1991, *National report: final report of the Royal Commission into Aboriginal Deaths in Custody*, vols. 1–5, AGPS, Canberra.

Langton, M 1983, 'Medicine Square' for the recognition of Aboriginal swearing and fighting as customary law, BA (Hons) thesis, Australian National University, Canberra.

Langton, M, Ah Matt, L, Moss, B, Schaber, E, Mackinolty, C, Thomas, M, Tilton E & Spencer, L 1990, 'Too much sorry business', Report of the Aboriginal Issues Unit of the Northern Territory. In vol. 5, Appendix D(i) *Royal Commission into Aboriginal Deaths in Custody National Report*, AGPS, Canberra.

Lyon, P 1990, *What everybody knows about Alice: A report on the impact of alcohol abuse on the town of Alice Springs*, Tangentyere Council Incorporated, Alice Springs.

McDonald, D 1990, *National Police Custody Survey August 1988*, RCIADIC, Research Paper No. 13, Criminology Research Unit, Canberra.

Thomson, N & McDonald, D 1991, *Australian deaths in custody 1980–1989: An epidemiological analysis of the relative risks of death for Aborigines and non-Aborigines*, RCIADIC, Research Paper No. 20, Criminology Research Unit, Canberra.

Walker, J 1989, 'Prison sentences in Australia', *Trends and Issues in Crime and Criminal Justice* 20, Australian Institute of Criminology, Canberra.

Williams, N 1987, 'Local autonomy and the viability of community justice mechanisms', in KM Hazlehurst (ed.), *Ivory scales: Black Australia and the law*, UNSW Press (in association with the Australian Institute of Criminology), Sydney.

Original lecture available at:
<http://aiatsis.gov.au/publications/presentations/aborigines-and-policing-aboriginal-solutions-northern-territory-communities>

8

*The end in the beginning:
Re(de)finding Aboriginality*

1994 Wentworth Lecture

Michael Dodson

An old man said: 'I don't care how hard it is. You build Aboriginality or you get nothing. There's no choice about it. If our Aboriginal people cannot change how it is among themselves, then the Aboriginal people will never climb back out of hell' (Gilbert 1977, pp. 304–05).

But this takes us too far ahead in the story, towards the end, 'although the end is in the beginning' (Ellison 1952, p. 9). Since first contact with the colonisers of this country, Aboriginal and Torres Strait Islander peoples have been the object of a continual flow of commentary and classification. I would like to begin by taking you through just a sample of what they saw as Aboriginality.

To the early visitors we varied from the 'noble savage' to the 'prehistoric beast'. For example: 'The natives of New Holland ... may appear to some to be the most wretched people of earth, but in reality they are far more happier than we Europeans ... They live in a tranquillity which is not disturb'd by the inequality of condition' (Cook cited in Smith 1960, p. 126); 'The poorest objects on the habitable globe' (Clark 1825, p. 100); 'Blood thirsty, cunning, ferocious, and marked by black ingratitude and base treachery' (Boyd 1882, pp. 218–21); 'The Australian nigger is the lowest type of human creature about ... But having one splendid point in which he is far ahead of the chinkie. He'll die out and the chinkie won't' (Inson & Ward 1887).

In the law we were defined systematically, though variably, according to proportions of black blood. For example: 'An Aboriginal native of Australia or of any of the islands adjacent or belonging thereto'[1]; 'Any person of Aboriginal descent whose moral intellectual and physical welfare the board was to promote with a view to their assimilation into the general community' (*Aborigines Act 1957*); And then, depending on the year, variously: 'A half-caste child whose age does not apparently exceed eighteen years' (*Aboriginal Ordinance Act 1918* [NT]); 'A half-caste male child whose age does not apparently exceed 21 years' (*Native Administration Ordinance* 1940); 'Every half-caste aged 34 habitually associating and living with an Aboriginal' (*Aborigines Protection Act 1886*); Excluding 'A person less than quadroon blood who was born prior to the thirty first day of December, 1936'(*Aborigines Amendment Act 1936*);

Aboriginal 'half-castes', in particular, came under the scrutiny of the ethnologists. They wrote for example: 'There is no biological reason for the rejection of people with a dilute strain of Aboriginal blood. A low percentage will not introduce any aberrant characteristics and there need be no fear of reversions to the dark Aboriginal type' (Tindale 1941, p. 67); classifiable into various hybrid types: 'first crosses of two types, second generation crosses of three types, 1/8, 3/8, F3, FX, 5/8, quadroon, octoroon' (Tindale 1941, pp. 38–86), and so it went on.

Their men of religion were also concerned to define us. They saw us as: 'Degraded as to divine things, almost on a level with a brute … In a state of moral unfitness for heaven … and as incapable of enjoying its pleasures as darkness is incapable of dwelling with light' (Harper cited in Woolmington 1973); 'Without god in the world, entirely lost to all oral and spiritual perception' (Dredge 1845, p. 11).

Similarly, their hopeful educators assessed our capacity for learning. Alternatively: '[H]aving perfectly infantile in judgements where compass of thought is required' (Harris 1847, p. 386), or 'Materials, which although extremely crude are nevertheless good, the intellect buried in augean filth, yet we may find gems of the first magnitude and brilliance' (Cartwright cited in Woolmington 1973, p. 17).

Their men of science sought to define us through the study of our brains and blood, concluding that 'their Aboriginal blood is remotely the same as that of the majority of the white inhabitants of Australia, for the Australian Aboriginal is recognised as being the forerunner of the caucasian race' (Tindale 1941, p. 67); and 'showing anatomical characters very rare in the white races of mankind, but at the same time normal in ape types (Duckworth 1907, p. 69).

We have been an ever-popular subject for artists who portrayed us in paintings or films. Initially, they portrayed noble, well-built native, heroic, bearded, loin clothed, one-foot-up, vigilant, with boomerang at the ready. Later, after we had fallen from grace, we appeared bent, distorted, overweight, inebriated, with bottle in hand.

We even found our way into poetry: 'Flat as reptiles hutted in the scrub … A band of fierce fantastic savages … Staring like a dream of hell!' (Kendall cited in Elliott & Mitchell 1970, p. 70)

Every one of these statements is drawn directly from the words written about Indigenous peoples in this country. Yes, they have had a lot to say about us. And if you are overwhelmed by this litany of statements, made with a confidence exceeded only by their ignorance, they are but a fragment of what Indigenous peoples have borne in body and spirit since we first came into the view of the colonisers.

Since their first intrusive gaze, colonising cultures have had a preoccupation with observing, analysing, studying, classifying and labelling 'aborigines' and Aboriginality. Under that gaze, Aboriginality changed from being a daily practice to being 'a problem to be solved'. Nor am talking about ancient history. In 1988, at the national congress of the RSL, Victorian state president, Mr Bruce Ruxton, together with the National president, Brigadier Alf Garland, loyal disciples of the geneticists, called on the federal government to 'amend the definition of aborigine to eliminate the part-whites who are making a racket out of being so-called aborigines at enormous cost to taxpayers' (*The Australian* 9 September 1988), and for some kind of genealogical examination to determine whether the applicant for benefits was a 'full blood or a half-caste or a quartercast or whatever' (Slee 1988).

Just last week we once again heard calls from certain members of the National Party in Queensland for the federal government to insist that only people with more than 50 per cent Aboriginal blood be eligible to identify as Aboriginal.[2] Clearly such views have not gone away.

Similarly, the theories of the ethnologists expounding the backward stages of evolution of the Aboriginal race were vividly brought to life once again just last year during the public debate over Native Title when we were all told how Aboriginal people had failed to even invent the wheeled cart.[3]

The obsession with distinctions between the offensively named 'full bloods' and 'hybrids', or 'real' and 'inauthentic' Aborigines continues to be imposed on us today. There would be few urban Aboriginal people who have not been labelled as culturally bereft, 'fake', 'part-aborigines', and then expected to authenticate their Aboriginality in terms of percentages of blood or clichéd 'traditional' experiences.

Constant proclamations that indigenous peoples are remnants of a past doomed to extinction, that 'the old Aboriginal world is now facing its final twilight' (Strehlow 1963, p. 456), and that Aboriginal people are 'powerless to defend themselves against the final onslaught' (Bennett 1978, p. 67), continue to construct us as innately obsolete peoples. In all these representations, all these supposed 'truths' about us, our voices and our visions have been notably absent. There may be an enlightened minority who have been willing to open their eyes and ears to allow the space for Aboriginal people to convey our Aboriginalities. But, as my colleague Marcia Langton so poignantly wrote: the majority of Australians, 'do not know and relate to Aboriginal people. They relate to stories told by former colonists' (Langton 1993, p. 33).

So today, to even begin to speak about Aboriginality is to enter a labyrinth full of obscure passages, ambiguous signs and trap doors. The moment you ask the question, 'who or what is Aboriginal?', you enter a historical landscape full of absolute and timeless truths, which have been set in place by all those self-professed experts and authorities too ready to tell us, and the world, the meaning of Aboriginality.

Nearly suffocated with imposed labels and structures, Aboriginal peoples have had no choice than to insist on our right to speak back: to do as the old man said, and build and represent our own world of meaning and significance.

In the early 1970s, the situation of the world's indigenous peoples began to come to the attention of the international community. In 1972, the United Nations Sub-Commission on Discrimination and the Protection of Minorities commissioned a study on the problem of discrimination against indigenous populations (United Nations 1987), which would examine the situation of indigenous peoples throughout the world. The study explicitly took up the question of definition, detailing all the criteria which governments have used to define indigenous peoples.

The most frequent were the so-called 'objective criteria'. These were 'race or ancestry' and 'culture'. The latter included religion, living under a tribal system, membership of an indigenous community, dress, language, residence in certain parts of the country, and livelihood, the latter often classified in terms of development or backwardness. Also noted were subjective criteria: group consciousness or self-identification, and acceptance by the indigenous community.

Before providing any critique of the so-called 'objective criteria', I give just a few examples reported in the UN study.

In Indonesia, criteria for being classified as indigenous have included 'not matching up to the standards of development required by the government in accordance with the ideals of organisation and development of Indonesian society' or 'having less ability to perform their social functions' (United Nations 1987, ch V, par. 168).

In Paraguay, one of the criteria used for classifying a person as indigenous was that he/she was 'marginalised', 'backward' or 'outside of the economic realities of the country' United Nations 1978, ch. V, par 170).

In Guatemala, where self-identification was in doubt, questions of indigenous dress, use of indigenous language and non-use of footwear were used to assist identification (United Nations 1978, ch. V, par 220).

The Bolivian census classified people according to race, the available categories being: 'white', 'cholo' ('half-caste') and 'indian'. The cholos would include those persons of an indian-white mixture plus the more or less 'racially pure' indians who have learned to speak Spanish well, mastered a skilled trade and abandoned indigenous dress. The indian was identified as 'usually being dark-skinned, illiterate, speaking only a native tongue and providing the unskilled labour in the economy' (United Nations 1978, ch. V, par 57).

You could hardly call such clearly ideological definitions objective. They would better be described as the state's tools for indigenous domination and assimilation.

The study itself recognised how value-laden the definitions were. The defining characteristics of 'indigenous' were frequently described in unambiguously loaded language. Indigenous people were generally identified not in terms of our positive attributes, but in terms of what we lack: we were 'under-developed', 'primitive', unable to speak the language of the non-indigenous population, uneducated in the ways of the non-indigenous population, 'backward'.

Even where the criteria were not so obviously biased, the study rejected any definition which relied exclusively on either descent or cultural characteristics. With respect to classifications based on blood percentages, the study stated unambiguously that the scientific theory which holds that there is an objective biological or genetic basis for race had been widely discredited (United Nations 1978, ch. V, pars 30–6); in other words, that the RSL's dream of a genetic or blood test which would offer some true indication and distinction was a fallacy.

With respect to classification on the basis of cultural characteristics, it recognised the inappropriateness of defining indigenous peoples entirely in terms of a culture free from the influence of non-indigenous societies. Pervasive infiltration as a result of colonisation meant that cultural borrowings and transformations were always present. Thus, it concluded that while cultural considerations were important, they could not be considered absolute.

The study considered the enormous body of evidence it had gathered in the light of the framework of internationally recognised human rights, and concluded that:

> the fundamental assertion (concerning any definition) must be that indigenous populations must be recognised according to their own perception and conception of themselves in relation to other groups. There must be no attempt to define them according to the perception of others through the values of foreign societies or of the dominant sectors in such societies ... [and] artificial, arbitrary or manipulatory definitions must, in any event, be rejected. (United Nations 1978)

The experience of a history of description, ascription, prescription and suppression would provide more than sufficient reason for insisting that definitions of Aboriginality must be generated by Indigenous peoples ourselves. Yet what is so powerful about the UN study is that it goes still further, referring not merely to a just response to oppression, but to fundamental human rights:

The (indigenous) community has the *sovereign right* and power to decide who belongs to it, without external interference. No state must take, by legislation, regulations or other means, measures that interfere with the power of indigenous nations or groups to define who are their members. (United Nations 1983, pp. 49–51)

The definition provided by the study remains the major reference point for the international community. It states that:

> Indigenous communities, peoples and nations are those which, having historical continuity with pre-invasion and pre-colonial societies that developed on their territories, consider themselves distinct from other sectors of the societies now prevailing on those territories, or parts of them. They form at present non-dominant sectors of society and are determined to preserve, develop and transmit to future generations their ancestral territories, and their ethnic identity, as the basis of their continued existence as peoples, in accordance with their own cultural patterns, social institutions and legal systems. (United Nations 1983, p. 50, par. 379)

Continuation was defined to include a number of options including ancestry and culture in general or in specific, which appeared common to indigenous peoples.

These findings have extremely important implications in terms of the recognition of indigenous rights. This is not because the definition captures the truth of our identity but, rather, because it recognises that identity must be self-identity, and rejects all forms of imposed definition. While it provides characteristics which may be present, it does not seek to establish an exhaustive or closed definition of 'Aboriginality'; but rather to establish the process whereby definitions must be reached.

This right to control one's own identity is part of the broader right to self-determination: the right of a people to determine its political status and to pursue its own economic, social and cultural development.[4] It is a right guaranteed to all peoples in international law, and stands at the forefront of international indigenous struggles.

Indigenous peoples throughout the world recognise that at the core of the violation of our rights as peoples lies the desecration of our sovereign right to control our lives — to live according to our own laws and determine our futures. And at the heart of the violation has been the denial of our control over our identity and the symbols through which we make and remake our cultures and ourselves (Broome 1991, p. 45).[5]

Recognition of a people's fundamental right to self-determination must include the right to self-definition and to be free from the control and manipulation of an alien people. It must include the right to inherit the collective identity of one's people and to transform that identity creatively according to the self-defined aspirations of one's people and one's own generation. It must include the freedom to live outside the cage created by other peoples' images and projections.

The question of identity has been taken up explicitly by the United Nations Working Group on Indigenous Populations, where, despite significant opposition from certain of the world's governments, indigenous representatives have consistently asserted that there can be no closed definition of 'indigenous peoples'. The relevant provision in the current draft declaration provides no objective criteria whatsoever. It simply provides that:

> Indigenous peoples have the collective and individual right to maintain and develop their distinct identities and characteristics, including the right to identify themselves as indigenous and be recognised as such. (United Nations 1984, Article 8)

Similarly, the International Labour Organization Convention 169, the only existing international instrument explicitly dealing with the rights of indigenous peoples, provides by way of definition that: 'Self identification as indigenous or tribal shall be regarded as a fundamental criterion for determining the groups to which the provisions of the convention apply' (International Labour Organization 1989, Article 1(2)).

As I outlined earlier, historically, we the Indigenous peoples of this country have been legally defined in terms of proportions of blood. Fortunately, in the last 30 years, virtually all such definitions have been removed from the legislation. In the early 1980s, largely thanks to the work of WC Wentworth, the federal government adopted the following working definition: An Aboriginal or Torres Strait Islander is a person of Aboriginal or Torres Strait Islander descent who identifies as an Aboriginal or Torres Strait Islander and is accepted as such by the community in which he or she lives (Commonwealth of Australia 1981).

This is now the working definition used for establishing eligibility for Aboriginal and Torres Strait Islander specific programs, and is used in Commonwealth legislation. It has also been accepted by the High Court as the interpretation of the expression 'Aboriginal race' in the Constitution (*Commonwealth of Australia Constitution Act*, 1900, Section 51(xxvi)).

For indigenous peoples, there is no doubt that self-determination and self-identification are our inherent and inalienable rights; and in both this country and internationally the principle of self-identification has been enshrined in the law. We need to acknowledge the important work of all those who have brought us this far; it has been a significant achievement when you reflect on the starting position, and even where we were just 30 years ago.

However, in the world of *realpolitik*, neither the existence nor even the legal recognition of a right is sufficient to guarantee its enjoyment. This does not mean that we should not vigorously assert the right, or that we cannot use all available means to exercise it right now. There is nevertheless ample evidence that Aboriginality will continue to be defined and constructed for Aboriginal peoples, regardless of the declarations of international human rights instruments or the Australian law. Neither moral righteousness nor legal guarantee is sufficient to prevent the actions and expressions of a system of bigotry and oppression that continues to serve the agendas of the world's power brokers.

Representations of Aboriginality are not an isolated phenomenon which we can eliminate: they are both weapons and symptoms of the oppressive relationship existing between indigenous peoples and colonising states. In addition, we must acknowledge for ourselves that today the 'enemy' cannot be neatly placed on the outside, nor simply eliminated by censoring those representations clearly imposed on indigenous peoples. As my colleague, Marcia Langton, notes, 'both Aboriginal and non Aboriginal people create Aboriginalities' (1993, p. 34). These constructions, however much we may wish to reject them, are the context in which we live. They inform not only the way others think about and react to us but also the lived experience that we have of ourselves and of each other.

They have also become the enemy within. Thus I see indigenous peoples as having twin projects: at one level we must understand the motivation behind the historical constructions of Aboriginality and understand why they have had such a grip over colonising populations. Simultaneously, we must continuously subvert the hegemony with our own representations, and allow our visions to create the world of meaning in which we relate to ourselves, to each other, and to non-indigenous peoples.

Turning to the first project, the question we are asking is: If Aboriginality is neither a type of blood nor a set of cultural characteristics, why have these definitions been so internationally pervasive? How is it that in one instance Aboriginal includes 'half-caste children whose age does not apparently exceed eighteen years' and in another 'half-caste male children whose age does not apparently exceed 21 years' and in yet another 'every half-caste aged 34 habitually associating and living with aborigines'? How is it that 'Aboriginal' is in one historical period noble and worthy and in another ignoble and corrupt?

Evidently, no one could contend that the definitions are objective. The most definitive statement that one could make about them is that they are infinitely elastic. The question I would therefore ask is: Why are particular types of definitions created, reproduced and embraced by states and non-indigenous peoples at particular times? If the images of Aboriginality do not actually reflect us, and are not actually about us, what purpose have they served for those who constructed and adopted them? The short answer is that they have served to meet the various and changing interests and aspirations of the colonising or 'modern' state. Whether there is a need to create a boundary between 'primitive' and 'modern' man; to legitimise 'progress'; to justify particular economic and political developments; to promote a national identity for the colonial nation; or, more specifically, to control, manage, or assimilate indigenous cultures, 'Aboriginality' has been made to fit the bill.

In other words, 'Aboriginality' becomes part of the ideology that legitimises and supports the policies and practices of the state. At the most immediate level, constructions of Aboriginality are directly linked to the policies of the 'management' and control of indigenous peoples. They form part of an ideology which creates the framework in which the state can act upon, and justify its treatment of, indigenous peoples, however disrespectful or abusive of our rights it may be.

Many of the popular images I referred to earlier were a central tool in the policy of 'de-Aboriginalising' Australia to establish a new nation with a European base. Take, for example, the image of Aboriginal culture as timeless and unchanging: pristine, exotic, a relic of an ancient past. This 'true, pure blooded, traditional aborigine' is at once posited as the arbiter of authentic Aboriginality, and as a member of doomed race. Hence those of us whose mothers were raped by white men, or who were forced, or chose, to incorporate other elements into our Aboriginality are 'not real aborigines'. By defining Aboriginality in terms of purity of blood or purity of culture, the assimilation of those who do not fall within the narrow ambit of the definition cannot even be considered cultural genocide because they were seen as not actually belonging to the culture from which they were being taken.

Where descendants of the original inhabitants could not be 'disappeared' and remained a continual threat to the purity-and- white Australia, ethnologists provided reassurance to society with scientific evidence and elaborate theories about 'the half-caste' and the 'hybrid', allegedly proving that such people had a genetic leaning towards their white parentage, and thus that their assimilation even had a biological basis. For example, one social scientist observed that:

> The aborigines not of the full blood have been all along associates of the white man rather than the black, the patrilineal affinity superseding the matrilineal, even though fatherhood has so frequently been unacknowledged. Regarding his white associates as following a superior way of life to that of his Aboriginal kin, the coloured man has clung to the outskirts of the white community, while the Aboriginal has ostracised him. (Neville 1951, p. 275)

Similarly, representing indigenous peoples as a backward remnant, the prehistory of European man frozen in a distant continent while progress transformed and refined humanity elsewhere, and accepting that Aboriginality would naturally die out, were simply a matter of acknowledging the inevitable. Thus extermination was not a criminal act, but simply the expediting of natural processes. Policies designed to destroy or 'phase out' indigenous cultures were not cultural genocide, but the generous endowment of 'improvement'.

By extension, by representing indigenous peoples as peoples without a social order, without a law, with no system of ownership, the doctrine of *terra nullius* became a logical conclusion. Since a people incapable of ownership cannot be party to a contractual transfer or negotiation, to take possession of the country is not theft, but merely the acquisition of available goods.

A particularly poignant example of the manipulation of authentic Aboriginality is the mythology of Trucannini as the 'last Tasmanian Aborigine'. Having declared the very last Aboriginal person in Tasmania dead, her descendants could not, by definition, be Aboriginal. Aboriginality was extinct, the past, a closed book. To all those who experience themselves as Aboriginal peoples of Tasmania, the official word was: you simply cannot exist.

Yet another example of the ideological power of the definition is the exemption certificate. The *Aborigines Protection Act* 1909–1943 placed all Aboriginal Peoples under the 'protection' of the Welfare Board, in effect, depriving them of the basic, civil, political and economic rights that were the birthright of all other Australians. They could not enter public places such as government institutions or pubs, they could not marry or move freely without permission, and in many cases they could not vote.

In order to enjoy those rights, Aboriginal people could, however, apply for an exemption certificate. Such certificates would be issued if 'in the opinion of the board they ought no longer be subject to the provisions of the Act' (*Aborigines Protection Act*, Section 18). This required that they satisfy certain undefined criteria of the board and that they declare that: (a) they had not been convicted of drunkenness in the last two years; or (b) had not committed any offence against the *Aborigines Protection Act*, the *Police Offences Act*, or the *Crimes Act* in the two years prior.

In other words, the basic assumption was that Aboriginal people were neither competent to look after their own affairs nor to fulfil their status as social subjects, degenerates, drunks and criminals. To be otherwise was to be an exception, and in effect to have moved away from 'Aboriginality'. By loading the definitions with fixed and value-laden characteristics, and then attaching certain privileges or penalties to being Indigenous or non-Indigenous, any Indigenous person wishing to go outside the limited bounds of the definition (not to be classified as a degenerate drunk and not to be deprived of their basic economic, social, civil, and political rights) had to effectively give up his or her public Aboriginality.

The United Nations study similarly observed how in various countries basic policies of assimilation have been facilitated by systems of classification. For example, in Indonesia, a person considered a member of an indigenous community could come to be considered a member of mainstream Indonesian society by conversion to Christianity or Islam, attainment of minimal literacy, or by the extent to which a person's economic activities were capable of producing acceptable levels of cash surplus (United Nations 1983, para 328).

More broadly, these definitions and constructions have not simply been for the control and management of indigenous peoples. Our constructed identities have served a broader purpose of reflecting back to the colonising culture what it wanted or needed to see in itself. The constructions of Aboriginality, in all their variations, have marked the boundaries which define and evaluate the so-called modern world. Whether indigenous peoples have been portrayed as 'noble' or 'ignoble', 'heroic' or 'wretched', has depended on what the colonising culture wanted to say or think about itself.

At times, we are used to affirm their superiority, to provide confirmation of the value of progress. By extension, the destruction or assimilation of the indigenous cultures becomes a necessary and even morally correct part of the battle to overcome 'the primitive', and thereby to save both us and them from a life that is 'nasty, brutish and short'. By our lack we provided proof of their abundance and the achievements of 'progress'; by our inferiority we proved their superiority; by our moral and intellectual poverty we proved that they were indeed the paragon of humanity, the product of millennia of development.

At other times, we are used to create a counterpoint against which the dominant society can critique itself; we become living embodiments of the romantic ideal which offers a desolate society the hope of redemption and of recapturing what it feels it has lost in its march forward. Those who wish to present a critique of individualism point out that Aboriginality is about community; those who wish to highlight the detrimental effects of industrialisation on the environment point to us as the original conservationists. We present a persisting, though strategically distant, image of what has been lost, and what could be regained.

Again, my point is not about whether the content of these images is true or false, though they do contain elements of accurate representation. The critical point here is that they have been selected not because they were true but, rather, because the colonising culture needed to think they were true. In the construction of 'Aboriginality' we have been objects. Objects to be manipulated and used to further the aspirations of other peoples. We are constantly defined as 'other', but we are never permitted to be genuinely independent, genuinely different. In fact, far from being recognised in our difference, in our own terms, we are always defined in terms of the colonising or defining culture.

One could well ask, what is it about genuine difference which is so threatening that it must always be translated and sanitised into more of the same? One answer may be that to allow our difference and our independence would threaten the boundaries of identity, knowledge and absolute truth which give the subject a sense of power and control. If we are reclassified into the established categories we are brought back into check. We may be seen as the opposite, the under-developed version, or even the unspoiled version. Yet in all cases Aboriginality is defined in terms of how it compares with the dominant culture. Because Aboriginality has been defined as a relation, indigenous peoples have rarely come into a genuine **relationship** with non-indigenous peoples. This is because a relationship requires two, not just one and its mirror.

Our subjectivities, aspirations, ways of seeing and our languages have largely been excluded from the equation, as the colonising culture 'plays with itself'. It is as if we have been ushered onto a stage to play in a drama where the parts have already been written. Choose the role of the ancient noble spirit, the lost soul estranged from her true nature, or the aggressive drunk alternatively bucking and living off the system. No other parts available for 'real Aborigines'.

I will now read you some words of other peoples describing their experience of the processes I have described. Vine Deloria, a native American Indian, wrote:

> In 1969, non-Indians began to rediscover Indians. Everyone hailed us as their natural allies in the ancient struggle they were waging against the 'bad guys'. Conservatives embraced us because we didn't act uppity, refused to move into their neighbourhoods, and didn't march in their streets. Liberals loved us because we were the most oppressed of all peoples who had been oppressed ... Blacks loved us because we objected to the policies of the department of the interior ... which indicated that we were another group they could count on in coming to the revolution...Conservationists sought out Indians for their mystical knowledge of the land ... It has been an exciting year. (Deloria 1974, pp. 14–15)

And somewhat more tragically, Ralph Ellison, an African-American wrote:

> I am an invisible man ... I am invisible, understand, simply because people refuse to see me ... It is as though I have been surrounded by mirrors of hard, distorting glass. When they approach me they see only my surroundings, themselves, or figments of their imagination — indeed everything and anything except me. Nor is my invisibility exactly a matter of bio-chemical accident to my epidermis. That invisibility to which I refer occurs because of a peculiar disposition of the eyes of those with whom I come in contact. A matter of the construction of their inner eyes. (Ellison 1952, p. 7)

Ellison's excruciating discovery of his invisibility is the tragedy of all who have been deprived of the right to be seen as full independent human beings. However, at the end of his novel, he has a crucial realisation which provides his, and our, way out of 'hell'. He says quite simply: 'I'm invisible, not blind' (1952, p. 464). None of us have escaped the effect of false representation and invisibility. We feel it every day when we come into contact with the dominant society. We even feel it when we look into the mirror. Our experience of ourselves and of our Aboriginality has been transformed by the representations.

Yet to say that Aboriginality has rarely been more than a relation for non-indigenous peoples does not mean that it has never been more than a relation for us. We may have been forced to feel the gaze of the other almost everywhere we went, we may have even internalised that gaze, but we have never totally lost ourselves within the other's reality. We have never fallen into the hypnosis to believe that those representations were our essence. We have never forgotten that we have an identity which cannot be reduced to a relation, and cannot be destroyed by misconception. Recalling Ellison, we may be invisible, but we are not blind. As a woman of the Quiche people of Guatemala said:

> In our communities, we never sat down to study or discuss issues like 'look, this is our tradition, this is our language'. We have maintained our culture not so much due to conscious effort as to daily practice ... However, there is a moment in our personal lives, in our community ... when we find it necessary to become conscious about who we are. (del Rosario 1992)

In the sanitised history of 'settlement', it was always written that indigenous peoples of this country did not resist. Similarly, to say that Aboriginality is nothing more than a relation to non-Aboriginality is to create another representation of us as peoples who accepted and submitted to the imposed structures.

Alongside the colonial discourses, we have always had our own Aboriginal discourses in which we have continued to create our own representations, and to recreate identities that escaped the policing of the authorised versions. They are Aboriginalities which arise from our experience of ourselves and our communities. Although they draw creatively from the past, including the experience of colonisation and false representation, they are embedded in our entire history, one that goes back a long time before colonisation was even an issue.

These Aboriginalities have been, and continue to be, a private source of spiritual sustenance in the face of the attempts by other to control us. And they are also a political project designed to challenge and subvert the authorised versions of who and what we are. Self-representations of Aboriginality are always also acts of freedom. The Aboriginal writer, Mudrooroo Narogin, wrote of the power of our Aboriginalities to heal the 'rape of the Aboriginal soul' and the wound of being removed from one's mother tongue. Aboriginality would become the emergence of an Aboriginal voice to 'sing of the sad wounds of the whole people, hundreds of mouths forced into shaping the harsh sounds of an alien speech' (Narogin 1990, pp. 50–1).

In making our self-representations public, we are aware that our different voices may be heard once again only in the language of the alien tongue. We are also aware that we risk their appropriation and abuse and of the danger that a selection of our representations will be used to once again fix Aboriginality in absolute and inflexible terms. That one character or one painting will be picked out as the authoritative archetype of Aboriginality is now the 'real Aboriginality' because it came from an Aboriginal person. Without our own voices, however, Aboriginality will continue to be a creation for and about us.

This is of course all the more reason to insist that we have control over both the form and content of representations of our Aboriginalities. All the more reason that the voices speak our languages. In fact, the insistence on speaking back and retaining control are highly political acts. They are assertions of our right to be different and to practise our difference. They refuse the reduction of Aboriginality as an object, and they resist translation into the languages and categories of the dominant culture. They are at times ancient, at times subversive, at times oppositional, at times secret, at times essentialist, at times shifting. It is for this very reason that, even as an Aboriginal person, I cannot say what Aboriginality is. To do so would be a violation of the right to self-determination and the right of peoples to establish their own identity. It would also be to fall into the trap of allowing Aboriginality to be another fixed category. More than enough 'fixing' has already occurred.

This does not therefore mean that Aboriginalities are without content: nor does it suggest that we are not intimately connected with our past. What we need to resist is an essentialism which confines us to fixed, unchangeable and necessary characteristics, and refuses to allow for transformation or variation (Cowlishaw 1993, p. 187).[6] Yet resistance to imposed categories is very different from forbidding us from representing our cultures and peoples in terms of our past, or our distinct ways of being and seeing the world. The recent trend to charge self-representations by indigenous peoples with the politically incorrect crime of 'essentialism' is little more than a modern extension of the politics of control over knowledge that has been going on since colonisation: black people being told what they can say and how they can say it: Redfern come to academia. It is just another form of over-policing.

The right to self-representation includes our right to draw on all aspects of our sense of our Aboriginality, be that our blood, our descent, our history, our ways of living and relating, or any element of our cultures. Certainly, the practice of fixing us to our blood or our romanticised traditions has been a cornerstone of racist practices. Yet depriving us of our experienced connection with the past is another racist practice.

The relationship we draw with our past is not to be confused with the relationships with the past which have been imposed on us. One is an act of resistance, the other is a tool in the politics of domination and oppression. When we talk about an Aboriginality based on the past of our peoples, we are not talking about fabricating an identity based on a past that we have re-discovered or dug up. Rather, we, the Aboriginal peoples are already the retelling of the past.[7] Our memories are not chemicals in our heads but our flesh and our voices and our ways of seeing.

The past and the present and the future do not fall into distinct linear categories. The past cannot be limiting because we are always transforming it. In all expressions of our Aboriginality we repossess our past, and ourselves. It cannot be dead because it is built into the beings and bodies of the living. We do not need to re-find the past, because our subjectivities are inseparable from the past. Aboriginalities of today are regenerations and transformations of the spirit of the past, not literal duplications of the past. We recreate Aboriginality in the context of all our experiences, including our pre-colonial practices, our oppression, and our political struggles. It is only a narrowness of vision, or a misconception of culture as a frozen state, that leads people to limit expressions of essential Aboriginality to the stereotyped pristine.

The same Guatemalan woman I quoted above said of her people's identity:

One can still be a Quiche although one lives in a better house or has a video, or even goes to university ... I get very disturbed when we ourselves promote an image of the indigenous peoples as something very poetic, very romantic, as something ideal. No! Rather, it is something real ... There is a part which is folkloric ... But it is not the base of the culture ... It's an element of our lives. It's an element which has determined moments ... Rather, it's the daily life which you can't see here, the daily life which isn't represented here, which makes us indigenous.

Many things are changing in this time but we remain indigenous ... Although certain things have changed in our thoughts, in our statements, in our traditions ... We did not quit being what we are; there are always these roots that make you who you are that make you different from the others.' (del Rosario 1992)

The roots which make us what we are are the connections between the past and present. Far from being dead, passive, or conservative, the past is dynamic, active and potentially revolutionary. It has been, and continues to be, a powerful reality in which we can root our autonomy, our sense of ownership of ourselves and our resistance against assimilation.

To paraphrase the philosopher Marcuse, there is a liberating power in remembrance.[8] What we are really rediscovering is that our past, far from being a source of constriction, can be a source of freedom.

In this sense, the Australian Institute of Aboriginal and Torres Strait Islander Studies is a resource for freedom. It holds many of the memories and stories from which the contemporary and future voices of Aboriginality will emerge. It has also itself been a site at which the politics and power of knowledge have been challenged and revolutionised.

There was a time when the collection of information about Aboriginal peoples was doubtlessly part of the politics of colonial control: when it served to fix Aboriginality as a pristine culture rooted in a distant time and place, inaccessible to and disconnected from the majority of living Aboriginal peoples. Collecting material on Aboriginal peoples was a project designed to preserve the dead past and to provide future generations with the opportunity to look back at prehistory safely bound in books and sealed behind glass. We could be pacified by being transformed from living peoples into blocks of intellectual real estate: reams of classifications and ethnographic curiosities. Their knowledge gave them a feeling of ownership and allayed the fears that we could not actually be controlled. This knowledge ensured that the past was something that was over and that with it had gone authentic Aboriginality. This 'past Aboriginality' was never more than a memory or a story for living people, but separate from their lived reality.

Yet if the past was once used as a trap for Aboriginality, we have seen a transformation, whereby Aboriginal peoples have reclaimed the key to the trap and have found the 'liberating power of remembrance'. The control which Aboriginal and Torres Strait Islander peoples now have over the institute is both a symbol and an expression of the shift in the politics of knowledge which we have achieved over the last 30 years.

In 1971, WC Wentworth gave a speech entitled, 'Aboriginal identity, government and the law'. In it, he examined the relationship which Aboriginal peoples have to their own identity, and the pride or shame which was associated with being an indigenous person in a historically racist society. He looked forward optimistically to a time when all Indigenous and non-Indigenous Australians would value and respect Aboriginality. He noted that a significant factor in our attitude to our Aboriginality was our relationship with the past, and that pride in our past was a key to pride in ourselves. The repossession of our past is the repossession of ourselves.

WC Wentworth himself is a man who has both possessed and transformed his past. He is of the stock of a people that colonised this country and its Indigenous peoples. Bill is a direct descendant of one of the founders of the Australian constitution, a document in which Aboriginal peoples were invisible. It was Bill's capacity to transform the past that allowed him to become a source of liberation for the future. What we have achieved today owes much to his courage and willingness to challenge and transcend the stereotypes that dominated his generation.

Unfortunately, progress and enlightenment do not always occur in a linear manner, as indicated by the recent election of the current incumbent of WC Wentworth's former seat of Mackellar, the Honourable Mrs Bishop. Nevertheless, the past and present work of the likes of WC Wentworth, and many others, has built a ground concentrated with the resources that will allow Indigenous peoples of the future to exercise our right to define and create ourselves and our lives — to write and sing and paint and tell ourselves from the past into the future.

Our peoples have left us deep roots, which empowered us to endure the violence of oppression. They are the roots of survival but not of constriction. They are roots from which all growth is possible. They are the roots which protected our end from the beginning.

Notes

1   This definition appeared in various acts of the states and territories from early legislation through to the 1960s, for example, the *Aboriginals Ordinance Act 1918* (NT).

2   A resolution was put up by the National Party Council in the electorate of Maryborough Queensland, stating that: 'a claim to be Aboriginal cannot be made unless the claimant has 50 per cent Aboriginal blood'.
3   Comment made by Tim Fisher, leader of the National Party, 1993.
4   The right to self determination is guaranteed by the International Covenant of Civil and Political Rights, Article 1.
5   See Richard Broome: 'The most sacred right of humanity is to be ourselves and be in control of the making of ourselves. Our group identity and control over our lives is symbolised by the name we associate with ourselves' (1991, p. 45).
6   Cowlishaw defines essentialism as: 'the error of imputing essences, fixed and necessary characteristics to a category of people' (Cowlishaw 1993, p. 187).
7   Hall makes this point when he says: 'not an identity grounded in archaeology, but in the re-telling of the past' (Hall 1990, p. 224).
8   Marcuse's actual phrase was 'the liberating power of remembrance' (quoted in Jay 1988).

References

Bennett, G, Royal Anthropological Institute of Great Britain and Ireland & Survival International 1978, *Aboriginal rights in international law*, Anthropological Institute for Survival International, London.

Boyd, A 1882, *Old Colonials*, Gordon and Gotch, London.

Broome, R 1991, 'Shall We Call a Koori a "Koori"?', *Australian Historical Association Bulletin*, vol. 68, September 1991.

Clark, G 1825, Missionary Register, Church Mission Society, London.

Commonwealth of Australia, Department of Aboriginal Affairs 1981, *Report on a review of the administration of the working definition of Aboriginal and Torres Strait Islanders*, AGPS, Canberra.

Cowlishaw, G 1993, 'Introduction: Representing racial issues', *Oceania*, vol. 63, no. 3.

del Rosario, M & Moksnes, H 1992, 'Culture is how we survive', in International Work Group for Indigenous Affairs *Newsletter*, no. 3, July–September.

Delorio Jn, V 1974, *We talk, you listen*, Macmillan, New York.

Dredge, J 1845, *Brief notices of the aborigines of New South Wales, including Port Phillip, in reference to their past history and present condition*, James Harrison, Geelong Vic.

Duckworth, WLH 1907, 'On the brains of Aboriginal natives of Australia in the anatomy school, Cambridge University', *Journal of Anatomy*, vol. 42.

Ellison, R 1952, *Invisible Man*, Penguin Books, Harmondsworth UK.

Gilbert K 1977, *Living Black: Blacks talk to Kevin Gilbert*, Allen Lane; Ringwood Vic.

Hall, S 1990, 'Cultural identity and diaspora', in J Rutherford (ed.), *Identity, community, culture, difference*, Lawrence & Wishart, London.

Harris, A 1847, *Settlers and convicts*, C Cox, London

Inson, G & Ward, R 1887, 'The Glorious Years', *Boomerang*, 17 December.

International Labour Organization 1989, 'Indigenous and tribal peoples convention, 169', viewed http://www.ilo.org/dyn/normlex/en/f?p=NORMLEXPUB:12100:0::NO::P12100_ILO_CODE:C169

Jay, M 1988, 'Reflections on Marcuse's theory of remembrance,' in RB Pippin, A Feenberg & CP Webel (eds), *Marcuse: Critical theory and the promise of utopia*, Macmillan, London.

Kendall, H 1970, 'The Glen of Arrawatta', in B Elliott & A Mitchell (eds), *Bards in the wilderness: Australian colonial poetry to 1920*, Nelson, Melbourne.

Langton, M & Australian Film Commission 1993, 'Well, I heard it on the radio and I saw it on the television…', Australian Film Commission, North Sydney.

Narogin, M 1990, *Writing from the fringe*, Highland House, Melbourne.
Neville, AO 1951, 'The half-caste in Australia', in *Mankind*, vol. 4, no. 7.
Slee, J 1988, 'Definition of an Aboriginal', *The Sydney Morning Herald*, 16 September.
Smith, B 1960, *European vision and the South Pacific 1768–1850*, Clarendon Press, Oxford.
Strehlow, TGH 1963, 'Anthropological and ethnological research', in H. Sheils (ed.), *Australian Aboriginal Studies: A symposium of papers presented at 1961 research conference*, Oxford University Press, Melbourne, pp. 452–8.
Tindale, NB 1941, 'Survey of the half-caste problem in South Australia', from *Proceedings of the Royal Geographical Society of Australasia*, XLII, Session 1940–41.
United Nations 1983, 'Study of the problem of discrimination against indigenous populations: Final Report submitted by Special Rapporteur JR Martínez Cobo', Doc.E/CN.4/Sub.2/1983/21/Add.8, viewed http://www.un.org/esa/socdev/unpfii/documents/MCS_xxi_xxii_e.pdf
United Nations, Sub-commission on Prevention of Discrimination and Protection of Minorities & Martínez Cobo, JR 1978, 'Study of the problem of discrimination against indigenous populations', United Nations, New York.
United Nations Working Group on Indigenous Populations 11th session, 1994, 'Draft declaration on the rights of indigenous peoples', United Nations, New York.
Woolmington, J 1973, *Aboriginals in colonial society, 1788–1850: From 'noble savage' to 'rural pest'*, Cassell, Melbourne.

Legislation

Aborigines Act 1957
Aborigines Amendment Act 1936
Aboriginal Ordinance Act 1918 (NT)
Aborigines Protection Act 1886
Aborigines Protection Act 1909–1943 (NSW)
Commonwealth of Australia Constitution Act 1901
Native Administration Ordinance 1940

Original lecture available at:
<http://aiatsis.gov.au/publications/presentations/end-beginning-redefining-aboriginality>

9

Native title: The beginning or the end of justice?

1996 Wentworth Lecture

RS French

To deliver a public lecture named after William Charles Wentworth is no easy task. It must do justice to an extraordinary Australian and do so in a way that reflects some of his special attributes. Wentworth was born in 1907. Before achieving political office, he was an active advocate of Aboriginal advancement. It was his initiative, as a member of the House of Representatives in 1960, that led to the passage of legislation establishing the Australian Institute of Aboriginal Studies [since 1989, the Australian Institute of Aboriginal and Torres Strait Islander Studies]. This Institute has become a leading national resource in developing an Australian understanding of Indigenous peoples and their culture and history and some appreciation of the lethal effects of colonisation on their societies over the last two centuries. Wentworth was the first person to be appointed as a federal minister with sole responsibility for Aboriginal Affairs, being appointed to that portfolio in February 1968. He held that office until May 1971 and the office of Minister for Social Services until December 1972. During that time he was responsible for the Council for Aboriginal Affairs, which provided government with advice on Aboriginal issues. He was also responsible for the Office of Aboriginal Affairs, an administrative unit which evolved into a separate department. It is a matter of record that Wentworth's passions and interests went well beyond Aboriginal advancement. In what he believed, and how he spoke of it, he represented some of the most open and endearing elements of Australian political discourse.

It is a privilege to deliver this lecture, both because of the great Australian it honours and because of the Institute that sponsors it. My subject is native title and justice. It is framed as a question — Native Title: The beginning or the end of justice? The question so posed refers both to the decision of the High Court in *Mabo v The State of Queensland [No 2]* (1992) and to the enactment and application of the *Native Title Act 1993*. It raises the general issues: what is the context and content of the search for justice for Australia's indigenous people;

how is that justice advanced, if at all, by what the High Court said in 1992 and by what the Commonwealth parliament said in 1993; and what are its future directions?

Discussion of these issues involves exposition and exhortation. In this area it is not possible to say anything that does not involve the recognition of a need for further action. In this area each of us is confronted with the concept of personal responsibility, once explained by Jewish theologian Martin Buber as the answer we give to the questions which our time in history and our place in the world pose for us.

Justice: An empty vessel

One does not have to have read Plato's *Republic* to accept the proposition that opinions about justice vary. Casual scanning of daily newspapers will demonstrate it amply. The contents of those opinions in their applications to Aboriginal and Torres Strait Islander people are defined by individual life experiences and the wider culture and sub-cultures in which they have been formed and developed. The views of Indigenous Australia about what constitutes justice for Aboriginal and Torres Strait Islander people will also vary. As expressed by their leading proponents, they develop out of perspectives about their relationship with the land and the colonial and postcolonial history of this country that are largely inaccessible to non-Indigenous Australians. There appears to be scope for a more developed theoretical framework from which a concept of land rights as an expression of social justice can be derived. Moral, pragmatic and natural law or human rights elements can be detected in various approaches to this question. Each may lead to different responses. Proponents of the recognition of land rights may appeal to concepts of fairness by reference to a history of gross unfairness in the treatment of Indigenous people and their dispossession from their country. Sometimes, however, the appeal is to pragmatic considerations of social order and sometimes to inherent or fundamental human rights, a kind of underlying natural law argument.

The Woodward Royal Commission, which led to the enactment of the *Land Rights (Northern Territory) Act 1976* (Cth), identified a mixture of bases for recognising land rights, including justice to people who had been dispossessed without consent or compensation, the promotion of social harmony and stability, the provision of an economic base, the preservation of the spiritual link giving each Aboriginal person his or her sense of identity, and the maintenance and improvement of Australia's international standing. The practical implications of land rights were emphatically stated by HC Coombs in 1983: 'Quite simply, if Aborigines are going to benefit from health, welfare, education or any other programs, then they need the mental, spiritual and physical sustenance and support of being on their own land' (Coombs et al. 1983).

In 'Letter from Black to White', Galarrwuy Yunupingu wrote:

> The land is my backbone. I only stand straight, happy, proud and not ashamed about my black colour because I still have land. The land is the art. I can paint, dance, create and sing as my ancestors did before me. My people recorded these things about our land this way, so that I and all others like me may do the same. I think of the land as the history of my nation. It tells us how we came into being and what system we must now live [under] ... My land is my foundation ... Without land I am nothing. (1976, p. 9)

The distinctions between justice as fairness, as pragmatism, and as natural law or inherent human rights are not bright-line distinctions. All of these modes of expression have persuasive power according to their setting, their proponents, and their audiences. Guilt is somewhat unfashionable as a foundation for a response to the wrongs of the past. Australians generally cannot, however, fail to be struck by the immense damage that the colonising process of their forebears has inflicted on Aboriginal societies, and the equanimity with which some fellow Australians will accept it as part of the price of progress. It may be, in the end, that the search for any coherent theory to give content to the concept of justice for Indigenous people will give way to the more immediate need to make real gains. Campaigns in that direction may be informed by a harsh pragmatism of the kind referred to by Noel Pearson:

> People in situations like ours must make do with the tools which are on hand. We must be adept and quick footed, indeed schizophrenic, in the employment of strategies. White guilt, pity, their sense of injustice may be tools which may be used, may be co-opted and used by us to secure results ... But as much as these tools may make us want to spew sometimes, the utilisation of white post-colonial guilt and sense of injustice, which may not be as real and as profound as we would like it to be, is most fruitfully tapped sometimes by moderate strategies. (1994, p. 157)

Whatever approach is adopted, no search for just objectives by and for Indigenous people, or resort to justice arguments as a tool of political action, can fail to take account of the historical context in which wider community attitudes have been formed and developed.

The historical perspective

The historical attitudes of colonial Australia to Indigenous people have their resonances in contemporary discourse and in the range of views about what justice for Indigenous people demands of us today. There is ample evidence of those historical attitudes in parliamentary debates, newspaper articles, writings and texts of colonial, post-federation and modern Australia. A militant paternalism which denied autonomy and human dignity to Aboriginal people came out of the nineteenth century, stretched well into this century and still informs some strands of contemporary opinion.

A succinct characterisation of white Australia's attitudes to Aboriginal people at the end of the First World War was set out by Manning Clark, who wrote: 'Extinction was their destiny. The Aborigines were a dying race. The only thing that could be done for them was to make their passing easier' (1987, p. 157). His references were taken from Arthur Mee's *Children's Encyclopedia* (Clark 1987, fn 66). Protective legislation in five of the Australian states and the Commonwealth then provided that no Aborigine could work for wages, or marry or live with a non-Aboriginal person, without the permission of the state. Any person other than an Aborigine who cohabited with Aborigines, or cohabited with a female Aborigine, was liable to prosecution. Any person who supplied, or caused or permitted to be supplied, to an Aborigine any fermented or spirituous liquors or opium could be prosecuted.

As Clark (1987, p. 158) observed, the Aborigine was regarded as a permanent child. He should be civilised, because his own practices and beliefs were barbarous, but, paradoxically, he could not be civilised. The Aborigines must be trained to become persons of 'economic utility' in the white man's society. They could be given opportunities to rise to the top in the professions, the business world, entertainment and sport. But the white man must decide. The missionaries, scientists and secular humanists had not conceded to the Aborigines the right to decide for themselves how they would live and what they would think. Children had no such rights. Under the *Native Administration Act* 1936 (WA), which remained in force until 1954, the Commissioner of Native Affairs was the legal guardian of every Aboriginal child until such child attained the age of 21, notwithstanding that the child had a parent or relative living. The property of Aboriginal people was not their own. The Act empowered the Commissioner to undertake 'the general care, protection and management of the property of any native' and to 'expend or apply any money in possession of any native for his maintenance, education, advancement or benefit'. It has been suggested that there were many instances, particularly in the south-west of Western Australia, where the farming properties owned by Aboriginal people were taken away and sold (Lee 1994, pp. 17–18).

Alongside these paternalistic and protective attitudes, there is evidence of hostility and, indeed, murderously punitive attitudes on the part of some settlers and commentators of the nineteenth and early twentieth centuries. In May Vivienne's book, *Travels in Western Australia*, published in 1901, she tells the story of a posse of settlers from the Bunbury area seeking an Aboriginal man who had killed a White settler after a dispute over damper. This genteel middle-class lady's account of the incident, which occurred in the 1840s, and her comments on it make chilling reading. The settlers attempted to track the suspect but found many difficulties on the way as none of the Aboriginal people would lead them to his tracks. She observed: 'They however tracked him as well as they could and to frighten the tribe they shot down every native they came across'. She commented:

> The shooting of blacks, although it seems cruel, was the means of showing them that the white man was their master and after this no more trouble arose with the various tribes. Had it not been done the tables would have been turned and all the white settlers may have been murdered. (1901, p. 114)

Battye's history of Western Australia, published in 1924, refers to an incident in 1872 in which a settler, Burges, was convicted of the manslaughter of an Aboriginal person and sentenced to five years' imprisonment, later reduced to one year by direction of the Colonial Secretary. Governor Weld had suspended the magistrate who initially heard the case, because of partiality to the accused who came from an influential family. The magistrate had reduced the charge of murder to shooting with intent to kill. Weld sent the settler for trial at the Supreme Court, where alternative verdicts of murder or manslaughter were left to the jury by Judge Burt. Of particular interest is the comment made by Battye, an indication of the attitudes of a leading Western Australian historian in the 1920s:

> The wisdom of punishing Burges at all may be doubted. Although in the settled districts little trouble was caused by the natives, they were still hostile in the North-West, and murders of white settlers caught napping were not infrequent. Men who undertook the burdens of pioneering and went out into unknown districts carried their lives in their hands, and to shoot quickly was often their only safe guard. Such men may have been technically guilty of murder, but even that was preferable to being stalked like game and treacherously slain. (1924, pp. 304–5)

The visibility of punitive and floridly paternalistic strands of thought is greatly attenuated in contemporary Australia, although disturbing reflections of some of these attitudes are still to be encountered in particular locations. There is no doubt, however, that Indigenous action, and advocacy by Indigenous leaders of the need to redress injustices of the past, have led to a general shift away from some of the more primitive concepts of that past. Punitive attitudes may have been inspired in part by the resistance of Aboriginal people to dispossession from their traditional country. Conflict over country started from the early days of the British annexation of New South Wales. There are many recorded accounts of the ways in which Aboriginal people resisted the taking of their land. These included armed conflicts, the spearing of livestock, squatting on small areas of traditional country and employment on pastoral leases which enabled access to country. Some Native Title applications at present before the National Native Title Tribunal are part of an ongoing history of assertion of rights to country which can be traced back to early periods of contact.

Physical resistance evolved into political action. Non-violent political action included passive resistance, public protests, occupation of country, political lobbying and the formation of representative organisations to promote the recognition of Indigenous people's rights. Public demonstrations and protests against policies and practices of dispossession have been heightened, particularly in the second half of the twentieth century. Notable examples include such events as the Yirrkala Bark Petition (1963), the Gurindji walk-off at Wave Hill (1967), the homeland/outstation movement, the Gove Peninsula land rights dispute (1971), the Tent Embassy (1972) and the Barunga Statement (1988), all of which attracted national attention. As Berndt observed:

> public protest is one way through which much can be achieved — if negotiations between the relevant parties break down, or overriding injustices are ignored or sidetracked by those who could do something about them. Public protest, in such circumstances, represents the only forum of the expression of free speech, for the presentation of a case. And, as we have seen, it can bring positive results. (1977, p. 42)

Other modes of action have included the use of land rights and heritage legislation, the acquisition of country through purchase and lease arrangements, the use of common law action, the pursuit of negotiated management and commercial agreements with government agencies and private developers, and other strategies aimed at cultural revival and the celebration of Aboriginal identity. Significant changes in community and political attitudes were evidenced by the development of statutory land rights regimes that predated the *Mabo* decision.

The evolution of statutory land rights

Statutory provision for the granting of land rights to Indigenous people in the Northern Territory and various of the Australian states has involved a recognition of the injustice of non-consensual and uncompensated dispossession. The Woodward Royal Commission that led to the enactment of the *Land Rights (Northern Territory) Act 1976* set out the aims underlying the recognition of land rights in the Territory as follows:

1. The doing of simple justice to a people who have been deprived of their land without their consent and without compensation.
2. The promotion of social harmony and stability within the wider Australian community by removing, so far as possible, the legitimate cases of complaint of an important minority group within that community.
3. The provision of land holdings as a first essential for people who are economically depressed and who have at present no real opportunity of achieving a normal Australian standard of living.

4. The preservation, where possible, of the spiritual link with his own land which gives each Aboriginal his sense of identity and which lies at the heart of his spiritual beliefs.
5. The maintenance and, perhaps, improvement of Australia's standing among the nations of the world by demonstrably fair treatment of an ethnic minority.

In 1979 in New South Wales, a joint parliamentary committee of inquiry was established by the Wran government. It examined various aspects of Aboriginal conditions but agreed to make land the priority area of concern. In 1981 it recommended that land rights legislation be implemented in New South Wales. The government did not accept all the recommendations of the report; however, the *Aboriginal Land Rights Act 1984* was enacted. It was primarily concerned with providing Aboriginal communities with access to an economic land base.

In 1983 Mr Paul Seaman, subsequently to become a judge of the Supreme Court of Western Australia and now a member of the National Native Title Tribunal, was commissioned to consider means of implementing land rights legislation in that state. His report recommended the transfer of reserve and mission lands to Aboriginal ownership, pastoral excisions, and a scheme for acquiring and returning pastoral leases to local Aboriginal communities, as well as a land-claim process. Land rights legislation was introduced into the parliament in 1985 but was defeated in the Legislative Council. In Queensland, the *Land Act (Aboriginal and Islander Land Grants) Amendment Act 1982* established a Deed of Grant in Trust land-holding scheme for Aboriginal communities. The *Aboriginal Land Act 1991* and the *Torres Strait Islander Land Act 1991* transferred all existing Deeds of Grant in Trust reserve lands and the Aurukun and Mornington Island shire leases to Aboriginal trust ownership. Under these Acts, vacant Crown land can be claimed on the basis of traditional association, historical association, or on an economic or cultural viability needs basis. Land granted is to be held and administered by land trusts as community title in non-saleable fee simple. There is no acquisition fund provided for in these Acts.

Specific-purpose, as distinct from general, land rights legislation was enacted in South Australia, being the *Pitjantjatjara Land Rights Act 1981,* under which 100,000 square kilometres of freehold title were returned to traditional owners, and the *Maralinga Tjarutja Land Rights Act 1984*, under which 76,420 square kilometres of freehold title were returned to Traditional Owners.

Specific Commonwealth land rights legislation includes the *Aboriginal Land Grant (Jervis Bay Territory) Act 1986,* which provided for the Jervis Bay territory to become Aboriginal land vested in the Wreck Bay Aboriginal Community, together with some vacant Crown land surrounding it. The community council has freehold title to the land. The *Aboriginal Land (Lake Condah and*

Framlingham Forest) Act 1987 was passed by the Commonwealth government on the request of the Victorian government to grant freehold title to a corporation of elders who had proven their clan's traditional relationship to the land. There is, however, no provision for ongoing Aboriginal land claims in Victoria. There is no land rights legislation in Western Australia or Tasmania.

The impact of land rights legislation in the various states can be seen by reference to the percentages of the area of each state or territory converted to Aboriginal freehold. In the Northern Territory, this figure in 1993 was 33.7 per cent against an Aboriginal population representing 22.6 per cent of the population of the Territory. In South Australia, 1.2 per cent of the population was Aboriginal and held some 18.8 per cent of the state under the land rights legislation. In Queensland, Aboriginal people comprised 2.4 per cent of the population in 1993 and had 2.1 per cent of the land under inalienable freehold. In Western Australia, where there is no land rights legislation, Aboriginal people comprise 2.6 per cent of the population and hold less than 0.1 per cent of the land area (Altman 1994, p. 64).

Contemporary attitudes to land rights and native title

Although gains made by Indigenous people in the enactment of land rights legislation and other areas represented a significant political shift, they could lead to community backlash. Special measures for Indigenous advancement were construed by various groups as equivalent to apartheid or as undermining democracy or the Australian concept of a 'fair go'.

Rowley has observed that:

> it would indeed be naive to assume that the gains by Aboriginal groups over the last two decades have not reinforced the prejudices of a general public that is well meaning but seriously ill informed about both the plight and the opportunities of Aborigines. To be fair, one must take into account that for nearly two centuries certain systems and principles of land ownership and government land management not only became firmly established but were developed free from any real understanding of or influence by the dispossessed Aboriginal owners. Self interest is a firm basis for beliefs and mores in us all, and one can at least understand the shocked disbelief turning to wrath as miners and pastoralists now hear what they claim as their legal rights questioned, or see them restricted. (1986, p. 84)

The general validity of that observation is supported by reaction to the *Mabo* decision and the passage of the *Native Title Act 1993*.[1]

Negative attitudes to Indigenous Australia today often seem to be informed by a notion of fairness or justice which sees Aboriginal and Torres Strait Islander people as the recipients of benefits not available to other sections of the community. There is a degree of cynicism about the uses to which such benefits are put. For some white Australians, the availability of four-wheel drive vehicles to Aboriginal communities has become a symbol of unjust enrichment to which they attach the metaphoric designation 'Toyotas'. In this setting, Native Title is regarded by some as just another unearned benefit conferred upon people who have done nothing more than other sections of the community to deserve it. When Native Title claims are seen as impacting upon property values, pastoral and mining activities, and economic opportunities for the wider community, negative attitudes can quickly escalate to outright hostility. For people bearing these attitudes, justice is enunciated as formal equality of opportunity which discounts the legacies of history to which it is applied.

A somewhat more encouraging, but nevertheless in some respects troubling, picture was painted by the results of a survey of public attitudes to Aboriginal issues published by the Institute in 1994. The public attitudes which were surveyed prior to the *Mabo* decision indicated high popular support for the general proposition that Aboriginal aspirations should be recognised. This support, however, diminished significantly when specific issues were addressed. And, at the time of the survey, the partisan divide, particularly on issues of land rights, was quite marked. Professor Brian Galligan, who wrote a report on the outcome of the survey, observed that popular attitudes are not cast in stone but are very much tied up with symbolic issues. Perhaps more set was the sharp divide between political attitudes. It was necessary, in his view, for Aboriginal people to confront negative political views where they existed and to make their case: 'Any proposals for constitutional change clearly need bipartisan support, as does the continuation of settled policies such as land rights.' (Galligan 1994, p. 101)

While his message was not one of pessimism, Professor Galligan pointed out that the political opinion of Australians was not running in favour of Aboriginal people on some of the key issues. Since then, of course, there has been acute debate both about the *Mabo* decision and the *Native Title Act* and its application and operation. In some segments of the community there will have been a firming or shift to negative attitudes on the land rights question. In other areas, the process of Native Title claims and the dialogue which they mandate have a positive effect. The survival of some of these negative attitudes was reflected in limited aspects of the federal election, particularly in North Queensland.

It is fair to say, however, that at the political level there appears to be bipartisan recognition of the impact that the history of dispossession and social and cultural dislocation has had upon the Aboriginal people of Australia. And now there is no shortage of articulate, well-informed and politically sophisticated exponents of new visions of justice for Indigenous people in this country. In their various ways they are contributing, and have contributed, to a greater community understanding of the special relationship between Aboriginal and

Torres Strait Islander people and their land, the path that that relationship plays in their culture, their sense of identity and the development of the Indigenous communal supports necessary to enable pressing issues of health, mortality, education, housing and employment to be addressed properly.

The *Mabo* decision

The decision of the High Court in *Mabo [No 2]* marked a significant development in the relationship between Australia and its Indigenous people. For the first time the common law of Australia recognised Indigenous relationships to land and derived from them legal rights which could be enforced by Australian courts. This was not an Act of executive grace and favour. Nor was it an *ex gratia* legislative bounty. It did not involve the creation of new rights but the recognition of rights which, according to the legal doctrine underpinning the majority judgments, had existed all along.

The common law of Australia prior to *Mabo* had rejected the concept of Indigenous ownership of traditional country. The recognition of that ownership was a dramatic interaction between two systems of law and culture. One was first brought to the colonies from the United Kingdom 200 years ago. The other has developed over at least 40,000 years of human habitation of the Australian continent. The decision was not only a judicial landmark but a singular point in the history of the relationship between Australia and its Indigenous people. It has been the catalyst for political and legislative action and the reordering of the place of Indigenous people in our society. From that process, for all its difficulties, as well as its promise, there can be no turning back. Indigenous people can assert legal rights on country as a matter of right, and not as a matter of grace and favour. There are uncertainties about the new doctrine and its application to the Australian mainland, but there is undeniably a new psychology affecting discussions which centre on rights rather than applications for executive grants.

The principles enunciated by the High Court in the *Mabo* decision define the general nature of Native Title. Native Title will be recognised where a community has maintained its connection with land and where that connection can be traced back to a time prior to colonisation. The content of Native Title in any particular case is determined by the traditional laws and customs of the community asserting it. The title is inalienable, although it can be surrendered to the Crown. Native Title may be transmitted in accordance with Indigenous laws and custom, but the range of cases in which that transmission can occur and its operation in modern times are open questions. Laws and customs which define the relationship of a people to their society and to their land are not static. A living culture is a dynamic thing which responds to external influences. Law and custom may have changed in response to the impact of colonisation and rural settlement, but that does not mean that the connection with country, necessary to sustain Native Title, is abandoned. The *Mabo* case involved a clear physical connection to the country, but the essence of that connection is seen from the Indigenous perspective as spiritual. It is said that the removal of people from their country does not of itself involve a loss of that spiritual connection. The contention that a spiritual connection can sustain common law Native Title is therefore open. That is not to say that it has been established.

The *Mabo* decision also involved the proposition that sovereignty resides in the Crown — sovereignty, in this context, meaning the authority to deal with the land. Pursuant to that authority, the Crown can extinguish common law Native Title by legislative action and, as it seems, by lawful executive action. Before extinguishment is to be inferred, there must be found or imputed a clear intent to destroy indigenous property rights. A test for that intent seems to be the existence of a clear inconsistency between the way in which the Crown has dealt with the land in question and the survival of Native Title rights. Revival of Native Title once it has been extinguished is not contemplated by the common law.[2]

The doctrine does, however, appear to be consistent with a notion of partial extinguishment or impairment of Native Title in some cases, and it may be that this will extend to temporary impairment, for example, by virtue of a short-term lease or licence. Again, these are open questions. From an Aboriginal perspective, the justice achievable through the *Mabo* decision may be seen to end with the doctrine of extinguishment. It is seen as a theory that ratifies the dispossession and loss of property rights over the past 200 years. From an Aboriginal perspective, it makes no sense and has no meaning. A community's country remains its country irrespective of the common law. To demonstrate the extinguishment of Native Title is not to dispense with the just claims of Indigenous ownership, the demands for recognition and respect, and the need to respond to them. Some of the history of Indigenous assertions of ownership over country that predated *Mabo* demonstrate the point. The doctrine of extinguishment has been legislatively fettered since 1975 by the *Racial Discrimination Act 1975* (Cth). Destruction of Indigenous property rights in ways which would not apply to non-Indigenous rights can constitute discrimination on the grounds of race.[3] Legislative acts of states or territories and executive acts transgressing the *Racial Discrimination Act* may be invalid for that reason by virtue of s109 of the Commonwealth Constitution. Unless the Commonwealth were to pass a law expressly or by implication amending the *Racial Discrimination Act*, Indigenous property rights, even without the *Native Title Act*, are unlikely to be destroyed or injured in the future, as they have been in the past, without regard to procedural justice or entitlement to compensation. Any attempt to amend the *Racial Discrimination Act* to create an exemption for laws or executive acts that would otherwise be unlawful would have significant domestic and international consequences.

The proposition, coming out of the *Mabo* litigation, that the *Racial Discrimination Act* supported the protection of Native Title raised a question about the validity of laws and Acts that may have adversely affected Native Title. This pointed to a new political imperative. Australia, at long last, had to do business with its Indigenous people as the possessors of legal rights. The *Mabo* decision has been criticised by Indigenous commentators as limited in its scope, involving a political compromise and protective of vested non-Indigenous interests at the expense of Indigenous concerns. The doctrine of extinguishment, as presently enunciated, limits the scope of the outcomes achievable under the common law. Nevertheless, the decision opened up a new direction in the search for justice for Australia's Indigenous people. However, the practical sequelae of the decision and the legislative response to it indicate that it is wrong to characterise it as defining the end point of justice for Indigenous people.

The Native Title Act

The *Native Title Act 1993* provides for the recognition and protection of Native Title, the validation of past Acts which may have been invalid because of their impact on Native Title, compensation in respect of those Acts, a regime to govern future grants and Acts affecting Native Title, and tribunal and court processes for determining claims to Native Title and for negotiation and decisions on proposed grants over Native Title land.

The legislative progenitors of the Act seem to have considered that it would have a limited area of application and would deliver only limited benefits, hence the Indigenous Land Fund and the Social Justice Package. Criteria for acceptance of claims in the original Bill authorised the Registrar of Native Title to reject an application if she considered that Native Title in relation to any part of the area under claim had been extinguished or if the application did not contain 'sufficient information' about any physical connection that might be required by the common law concept of Native Title to exist or to have existed between the applicant and any of the applicant's ancestors and the land or waters covered by the application. The reference in the Second Reading Speech to rigorous, specialised and accessible tribunal and court processes for determining claims to Native Title, and for negotiation and decisions on proposed grants over Native Title land, contemplated a different process from that which has turned out to be the fact.

The original vision evidently encompassed a substantial preparation for the lodgement of claims, a screening process applied by the National Native Title Tribunal, a conference to see whether agreement could be reached about the application, determinations of unopposed or agreed applications by the tribunal, and referral of contested claims to the Federal Court. Despite drafting inconsistencies, the scheme of the Act was also consistent with the proposition that registration of a claim and the right to negotiate and arbitrate mining grants and acquisitions were tied to the acceptance of applications. As for intra-Indigenous conflict, that was a matter to be resolved by representative bodies of Aboriginal people, designated as such by the Minister. Amendments to the Act in the Senate and subsequent decisions of the High Court and Federal Court have led to different outcomes.[4]

The lodgement of applications gives rise immediately to the right to be placed on the Register of Native Title Claims and to invoke the compulsory negotiation and arbitration provisions of the Act in relation to the grant of mining tenements and compulsory acquisitions. There is virtually no substantive assessment of applications in deciding whether to accept them. The tribunal's power to make effective determinations has been seriously compromised by the High Court's *Brandy* decision. Mediations are longer, more complex processes than originally thought. All of them involve an interface between Aboriginal people and their state or territory government in an area where governments are as yet developing their policies about Native Title, where governments change and new governments formulate new policies.

The demands placed upon Indigenous groups to come to grips with the issues, to marshal resources and expertise, to develop community consultation processes, to manage internal conflict, to effectively negotiate and to deal with the pressures of non-Indigenous agendas are huge. There are also significant pressures, albeit on a narrower base, placed on many other parties to respond to the process in the face of legal uncertainty and Indigenous agendas which are evolving in the course of mediation. The existence of these pressures and the difficulties posed by the unexpected directions in which the process has been taken will be addressed in time by the precedent guidance of negotiated agreements, the resolution of legal issues by the courts and by amendments to the legislation.

In the meantime, Australia has experienced, on the part of its Indigenous peoples in the space of two short years, an extraordinary flowering of cultural identity accompanied by a drive to take control of Indigenous history and a drive to justice informed by many visions. Some applications will be found to have been misconceived. They will eventually falter and fall away. But whatever the success rate in terms of Native Title outcomes, the assertion of rights over country is itself a consciousness-raising exercise which is, for the most part, irreversible.

An indication of what is happening is given by the figures for applications lodged with the National Native Title Tribunal. At the end of the first six months of its existence, there were 14 applications; after twelve months, there were 43. Eighteen months into the life of the tribunal, there were 82 and, at 31 December 1995, two years after its inception, there were 168. By 10 April 1996, there were 232.

Native title mediation

A significant number of cases are now in the process, or about to commence the process, of mediation. For the Tribunal, as for the parties, mediation of Native Title claims poses unique challenges. And while there are some voices in favour of earlier referral of matters to the Federal Court, the time and expense involved in judicial proceedings are such that, while parties are prepared to negotiate in a way that may lead to a narrowing of issues or a reduction in the number of parties, the Tribunal is reluctant to force them into court on the demand of one party or sub-group of parties. So far, four applications have been referred to the Court. One was referred in February 1995; it seems unlikely that it will come to trial before March 1997. The administrative cost to the Court, and therefore to the taxpayer, of conducting such proceedings may run as high as $200,000 without taking account of the cost of judicial and staff salaries.

A number of the claims which have been made will not be funded because they lack the support of the relevant representative body. If these matters are unable to be resolved consensually, there will be real difficulties for other parties and for the Court in dealing with them adequately. Excessive faith should not be placed in the power of the Court to decide threshold questions of law or fact on strike-out motions or by preliminary hearings. Courts are generally reluctant to deny litigants their day in court. The success rate of strike-out motions is low. In one case where the Court has been asked to determine issues of pastoral lease extinguishment as a preliminary question, it has declined to do so.[5]

These difficulties cannot readily be legislated away. So long as the common law of Native Title stands, the choice of response to Native Title claims will lie between litigation and negotiation. Mediation about Indigenous land ownership is a process that has few, if any, parallels in other areas of dispute resolutions. We are developing unique approaches in that regard. The processes and outcomes have been described in more detail elsewhere (French 1996). It is useful when considering the Native Title mediation process in Australia to have in mind international experience in dealing with Indigenous land claims. The Treaty Commission process for negotiating agreements with First Nations in British Columbia commenced in 1993. By 1995, 43 First Nations had entered the preliminary stages of the process but none had reached a final agreement. This remains the case nearly three years after the Commission first opened its doors.

The Waitangi Tribunal in New Zealand was established under the *Treaty of Waitangi Act 1975*. It has the power to make recommendations to the Crown but lacks the power to make binding decisions. Describing the role of that tribunal, its Chief Judge has said:

The Tribunal arranges its workload according to historic claims, resource claims and claims in respect of current Crown policy. The current policy claims cover diverse areas from education to issues of intellectual property. The Tribunal is assisted by a combination of legal, lay, Maori and Pakeha members. Where a case is well founded the Tribunal recommends to Government the action needed to remove or alleviate the prejudice complained of, and the steps necessary to prevent that prejudice from arising again. In the case of historic claims however, the Tribunal has the additional power to make 'binding recommendations' to transfer substantial former Crown properties to Maori ownership, these ranging from commercial buildings to farms and State forests. The name 'binding recommendations' is, of course, a contradiction in terms but effectively it amounts to an order. (Durie 1994, p. 25)

To date, 571 claims have been registered with the Waitangi Tribunal; 58 have either been settled or are the subject of report to government. These references are not made for the purpose of drawing direct comparisons, as the operating systems differ both in British Columbia and in New Zealand from that which has been established in Australia. They do, however, indicate the difficulty and time-consuming nature of identifying indigenous land rights and related issues everywhere.

Native title and country

The issues raised by Native Title applications extend well beyond the existence or non-existence of common law Native Title. Underlying most, if not all, applications is the demand for recognition and respect for the first owners of this country. The particular visions of the ways that recognition and respect can be given practical effect are various. They may involve recognition of Native Title which is exclusive or non-exclusive. They may involve other forms of land interest being transferred to applicant groups. They may involve compensation. They may involve joint management of publicly owned land and provision for visible symbols of Indigenous connection to the country. The range of responses is limited only by the creativity of those who negotiate with each other. What the map of Australia today tells us is just how much of this process is going on now. And the message is clear: Native Title may come or go, but country is here to stay.

Conclusion

The history of Indigenous agitation about country and related human rights that has been discussed in this lecture illustrates that the *Mabo* decision and the Native Title Act take their place as landmarks in the broad sweep of an evolving relationship between Indigenous and non-Indigenous Australia. An understanding by all Australians that *Mabo* and the Act are part of a much larger process has important practical implications. For then there can be an understanding that, even if Native Title is swept aside by the law, country and its concerns remain. And then, too, there can be an understanding that Native Title represents neither the beginning nor the end of justice.

Notes

1 For an account of contemporary responses to *Mabo*, see Meyers and Muller (1995).
2 *Yuin Council of Elders Corporation v State of New South Wales* (1995) 60 FCR 501, 508.
3 *Mabo v State of Queensland [No 1]* (1988) 166 CLR 186.
4 *Brandy v Human Rights and Equal Opportunity Commission* (1995) 183 CLR 245; *Northern Territory v Lane* (1995) 59 FCR 332; *Kanak v National Native Title Tribunal* (1995) 132 ALR 329; *North Ganalanja Aboriginal Corporation v State of Queensland* (1996) 185 CLR 595.
5 *Ben Ward & Others v State of Western Australia* [1995] FCA 1780.

References

Altman, JC 1994, 'Economic implications of Native Title: Dead end or way forward', in W Sanders (ed.), *Mabo and Native Title: Origins and institutional implications*, Research Monograph No 7, Centre for Aboriginal Economic Policy Research, Australian National University, Canberra, pp. 61–77.
Battye, JS 1924, *Western Australia, a history: From its discovery to the inauguration of the Commonwealth*, Clarendon Press, Oxford.
Berndt, RM 1977, 'The concept of protest within an Australian Aboriginal context', in RM Berndt (ed.), *A question of choice: An Australian Aboriginal dilemma*, University of Western Australia Press, Perth, pp. 25–43.
Clark, CMH 1987, *A history of Australia*, vol. 6, Melbourne University Press, Melbourne.
Coombs, HC, Brandl, MM & Snowden, WE 1983, *A certain heritage*, Centre for Resource and Environmental Studies, Australian National University, Canberra.
Durie, E 1994, 'Native Title re-established', paper delivered at *Native Title: Its extent and limitations, International Bar Association Biennial Conference*, Melbourne, 13 October.
French, RS 1996, 'Native Title: Promise, pain and progress', paper delivered at *AIC Doing Business with Aboriginal Communities Conference*, Darwin, 27–29 February.
Galligan, B 1994, 'Public attitudes to Aboriginal issues', in C Fletcher (ed.), *Aboriginal self-determination in Australia*, Aboriginal Studies Press, Canberra, pp. 99–105.
Lee, A 1994, 'Yeah, but you're different', in F McKeown (ed.), *Native Title: An opportunity for understanding*, National Native Title Tribunal, Perth, pp. 17–18.
Meyers, G & Muller, S 1995, *Through the eyes of the media: A brief history of the political and social responses to Mabo v Queensland*, Murdoch University Environmental Law and Policy Centre, Perth.
Pearson, N 1994, 'Aboriginal law and colonial law since Mabo,' in C Fletcher (ed.), *Aboriginal self-determination in Australia*, Aboriginal Studies Press, Canberra, pp. 155–9.
Rowley, CD 1986, *Recovery: The politics of Aboriginal reform*, Penguin, Ringwood.
Vivienne, M 1901, *Travels in Western Australia*, Heinemann, London.
Yunupingu, G 1976, 'Letter from Black to White', *Land Rights News*, vol. 2, no. 6, p. 9.

Cases

Ben Ward & Others v State of Western Australia (unrep. Federal Court, Lee J, 14/12/95)
Brandy v Human Rights and Equal Opportunity Commission (1995) 127 ALR 1
Kanak v National Native Title Tribunal (1995) 132 ALR 329
Mabo v State of Queensland [No 1] (1988) 166 CLR 186
Mabo v The State of Queensland [No 2] (1992)
North Ganalanja Aboriginal Corporation v State of Queensland (High Court, 21/3/96)
Northern Territory v Lane (unrep. Federal Court, O'Loughlin J, 24/8/95)
Yuin Council of Elders Corporation v State of New South Wales (unrep. Federal Court, Lockhart J, 23/10/95)

Legislation

Aboriginal Land Act 1991 (Qld)
Aboriginal Land (Lake Condah and Framlingham Forest) Act 1987 (Cth)
Aboriginal Land Grant (Jervis Bay Territory) Act 1986 (Cth)
Aboriginal Land Rights Act 1984 (NSW)
Land Act (Aboriginal and Islander Land Grants) Amendment Act 1982 (Qld)
Land Rights (Northern Territory) Act 1976 (Cth)
Maralinga Tjarutja Land Rights Act 1984 (SA)
Native Administration Act 1936 (WA)
Native Title Act 1993
Pitjantjatjara Land Rights Act 1981 (SA)
Racial Discrimination Act 1975 (Cth)
Torres Strait Islander Land Act 1991 (Qld)
Treaty of Waitangi Act 1975 (NZ)

Original lecture available at:
<http://aiatsis.gov.au/publications/presentations/native-title-beginning-or-end-justice>

10

An Arnhem Land story
1998 Wentworth Lecture

Dr Marika

I would like to dedicate the 1998 Wentworth Lecture to the late HC Coombs. I will begin with my story, first in my own language and then in an English translation.

> *Yäkum ngaya Raymattja. Likan yäkum ngaya*
> *Marika. Waripum ngaya yäku likan djinawam'*
> *Gunutjpirr Gunuwanga.*
> *Djinawam'yum likandhu nhänha yaka*
> *mam'thuman nyäkuru ngayili, ngalanguru ngaya ga*
> *nhä nyäku dhäruk. Djinaku mathawu ga romgu*
> *ngaya marnggiyin dhäwu'wu, ngaya ngarrungan*
> *marnggiyin nhänharayu, kjinaku romgu yolnguwu*
> *ngaya marnggiyin, bili ngaya yakan nhängal*
> *nyäkuway bapa'miguny. Ga bulu waripuny*
> *gulku'warrany ngalapalminy banha dhanal gungan*
> *yakan rom yolnguwu warrawu, ga nhalpiyan*
> *ngalma ngarru nyena djinal yutunga romnga.*
> *Banha ngalmaliny ngarrung dhä-munygum*
> *mulkuruyu romdhu, banha yaka ngalmalingu.*
> *Yolnguwum rom yakan dhäyan bewakthuwan, nuku*
> *yolnuwu, djalkiri rom yakan marnggiyin*
> *yolnguwarra be ngätjil baman, ga dhangu wapthun.*
> *Dilakthu rom yaka mayan ga gungan ngunha bala*
> *galinga ngärra'nga dhanalinggum dirramumuwum*
> *ga bulu warrangul rom.*
> *Banhayam rom dhanal yakan marnggiyin,*
> *ngätjilingu rom ga dhäruk dhanal yaka bäki,*
> *ngätjilingu dharukmurru, manikaymurru,*
> *ga ganurumurru, miny'tjimurru, ga ngayimurru.*

My name is [Dr Marika]. [This] name links me to my land, to my religious connections to the land. It defines where I come from, who I am, and with this language, the *rom* that the elders taught over many years and centuries, this is continuing in our community.

Yolngu people have learnt this *rom* for years, through *dilak*, the elders who teach them, and we have been learning this through our fathers and through our elders. Those rules and the language that they have been teaching us are our own language, teaching through songs, *manikay*, through *wänga*, land, and through singing, or songs that women use for crying.

Even though we live in a new world in which foreign law engulfs us, a law that is not ours, Yolngu law has existed from long before and our Yolngu foundation has sustained us — our sacred law and our secular law. My first real learning was about the land, *wänga*, the environment, and my relationship to my community. My grandmothers and my mothers were influential in helping me identify different foods and vegetables from the bush. Hunting and gathering for *borum*, bush fruits, and food and bush honey, *guku*, shellfish. I also learnt the value of work, *djäma*, as everybody was expected to do something — to carry wood for cooking, to cut wood for carving, to polish the wood until it was smooth for painting and for sale to keep food in our bellies.

I looked forward to the oral histories that my grandmother, my *märi*, my mother's mother, told us around the campfire. I loved the hunting trips to Wirrwawuy Lagoon, where we would hunt for water chestnuts, *räkay*, the bulbs and turtle, long-necked tortoise. On other hunting trips that I loved we went in the boat with my father. This was the only boat that our family had and the children used to go with their fathers after school.

I did my schooling at the Yirrkala mission school. The mission had established a kindergarten and a primary school. All I remember about the kindergarten is that we had a Balanda school teacher and we had Balanda stories read to us and did Balanda activities — European activities. A lot of it did not mean much to me but riding the tricycle did. All through my early years of school I read a lot of English literature.

After school we went out in the bush for the fruits we loved to pick: that was my favourite activity, picking fruits and going to Yamuna for the bush apples and figs and other fruits. Weekends were used to go honey-hunting, learning to use our eyes to look for the tiny bees as they went in and out of the tree. We also learnt how to hunt for yams, *gan.guri* and *yukuwa*. We learnt how to get different fruits, *wäyin*, animals and shellfish throughout the seasons. We learnt what we would get during the *midawarr* season and what was available through the *rarranhdharr*. As I got older I learnt to read and write at school in English. Books became my favourite items at school. As a young adult I started to read and write in Yolngu *matha*. We were writing stories in Gumatj for the younger children, primers for the new bilingual program.

In 1976 I went to work at the school, typing stories that the old people had made and translating them. I was exposed to a high level of Yolngu knowledge but I didn't know it at that time. My language was Dhuwaya, a new language that had been developed by children at the mission as their lingua franca. I was a woman with a child but I was still immature.

In fact, there are many young Balanda who go through quality education, through high school then university, but still remain immature. I was like that. I was ignorant of the fact that here was my own knowledge tradition, so rich, though I did not realise it was so powerful until the 1980s. It was not until I spoke in my own language, Rirratjingu, that my view of the Yolngu world would become more meaningful.

It was formal Yolngu education. I was learning to understand the hard language, the esoteric language I was working on at the school. This level of language is similar to the use of old Latin in English. The most significant book I worked on at this time was called *Balngana Mawurrku*, with one of my *bäapa*, my father. This book gave me a new understanding about my place, my *wänga*. It gave me a fresh new understanding of the world from a Yolngu perspective. It was more like a formal Yolngu education through attending ceremonies, *manikay*. Attending these ceremonies and listening to the language of *manikay*, to songlines helped me to grow in my own thinking about the complexities of the content and the context of the Yolngu worldview. I found that this can happen through demonstrating yourself in public, in front of a critical audience. I see it all the time with my brothers and my family. These events are part of continuing learning stages that Yolngu go through. Yolngu have to demonstrate that we have continued to hold on to our values, otherwise we lose ourselves in this ever-changing world and are accused of being a Balanda.

I will now talk about some of the histories that have occurred around Yirrkala. Some of the stories I have heard came from my *märi*, Wandjuk Marika. He told me the Macassan traders called our land, Australia, 'Buthamarrigi'. We call them Manggatharra or Batharripa. They had established *gundirr* or *marngarr* trepang processing ovens. We use these places, which are known as *marngarr*. The Macassans came each year during the wet season to collect *dharripa*, trepang or bêche-de-mer. People from many Yolngu clans around the East Arnhem coast collected trepang with the Macassans and established an extensive network of trade with them for a period of more than 300 years. Rice, songs, tobacco, calico, metal, and knives were some of the items of trade.

Although there were some disputes it was generally a good working relationship, until it was terminated by the South Australian government in 1907. Some Yolngu went for trips to Macassar and back, and some Macassans stayed between seasons. Children from both cultures were born, raised and educated together. Yolngu learnt Macassan words, songs and cultural traditions. The Macassans joined with us in our ceremonial life and Yolngu shared their language. There are many Macassan loan words in our language, such as *rrupiya*, money; *lipalipa*, canoe; and *berratha*, rice. Tamarind trees, rock designs, pottery remains and old trepan-processing sites provide testimony to the rich cultural exchange that occurred. Yolngu possess a wealth of songs and stories about these events, of which only a few have been written down.

An important ceremonial leader, Dula Ngurruwutthun, told me there were Macassans south of Yirrkala at Gän.gan and at Biranybirany and Gurka'wuy, another community. At Gän.gan, Gawarrin's homeland, White men killed almost an entire clan. Then they rode on horseback to Biranybirany, where they nearly wiped out my husband's clan, the Yarrwidi clan, the saltwater people of the Gumatj Nation or language group. Then they rode to Gurkawuy, further to the south, where they nearly wiped out the Marrakulu clan, the mother clan of the Yarrwidi clan, which included the family of the famous artist Old Man Wanambi. We have many stories that have been passed on to us about expeditions like these in southern and north-east Arnhem Land, specifically to wipe out Yolngu and to gather their skulls, which we believe were then sent on to museums overseas. As a result of these atrocities, our Yolngu elders resolved to organise themselves to defend their estates and to protect their families in the face of unwanted intrusion into their land.

The Japanese came into our area to harvest trepang, bêche-de-mer, after the Macassans were stopped at Caledon Bay, Garrthalala. At Caledon Bay they insulted a Yolngu man of the area by throwing trepang guts into his face. The Yolngu retaliated. Five Japanese were killed and one escaped. While investigating these killings, Police Constable McColl held some Yolngu women, one of whom was married to Dhakiyarr, of the Dhudi-Djapu clan, which is my father's grandmother's clan. For this he was killed by Dhakiyarr. Fred Grey, a trepanger who had made friends with my mother's father, escorted Dhakiyarr in his boat into Darwin. Dhakiyarr was tried in court and sentenced to death. His conviction was later overturned in a subsequent trial, but following his release from gaol he was never seen again.

Donald Thomson, an anthropologist, was appointed by the Commonwealth government to investigate the circumstances surrounding the cause of these killings. During these investigations, in the mid-1930s, he learnt about Yolngu culture and subsequently wrote a series of reports and other documents which constituted the first serious studies of our culture after Lloyd Warner, who had been at Milingimbi in the 1920s. Thomson talked about the *rom*, the beliefs and the laws of the Yolngu, and about the social structure and other features of our society. He was a friend and adviser of the Djapu elder Wonggu, who was the grandfather of Gatjil Djerrkura, the current Chairperson of ATSIC (Aboriginal and Torres Strait Islander Commission).

Donald Thomson later established a reconnaissance unit, which provided a defence of the northern coastline during the Second World War against the

Japanese. He was stationed at Bayapula, near Caledon Bay, near the site of the earlier Japanese killings. He taught the Yolngu about machine-guns and defence tactics, and also how to write their names. Some of our elders were justifiably confused about all this change of heart about killing Japanese. Some concluded the Balanda were quite mad.

I will now talk about the mission. The Methodist missionaries came to Yirrkala in 1935, intending to create a buffer zone between Yolngu and Balanda, to stop the tribal warfare and to bring the good news of Christianity. The missionaries set up a school in 1939. They used a bark shelter made from traditional materials by Yolngu men. The shelter was located near where the women's resource centre is now located. Some early missionaries prevented our people from performing Yolngu ceremonies on Sundays and were responsible for the loss of some ceremonies. They also banned the use of our languages in the mission school. The church included a pre-school, which I attended. I remember the building. Its roof was thatched with palm leaves and the floor was made of ant-bed, which we had to collect in an old tractor from the peanut farm. I was just a little girl, a *yothu*. I learnt to read and write by going to church and Sunday schools; I read the hymnbooks in one of the Yolngu languages, Gumatj.

The Reverend Wells was the minister at that time. He is the author of the book *Reward and Punishment in Arnhem Land*. He was sent away by the Methodist Church for helping the Yolngu with the Bark Petition in 1963. Some missionaries were helpful to the Yolngu; some were not. They built the existing church in the 1960s in front of the present offices of the Dhanbul Association, which from the 1970s took on the responsibilities of local government. The church is still being used for Sunday services. The missionaries and some Yolngu built the old mission school, near where the museum is now located. In 1969, the school was transferred to the Commonwealth and was called the Welfare School. It became a government school when the Northern Territory obtained self-government in 1978.

In 1963 leases for mining bauxite on the Gove Peninsula were issued by the Commonwealth government on land which came right to the doorstep of the mission settlement. In protest, the Yolngu clan leaders *ngalapal* prepared a bark petition, which they sent to Canberra. It was a picture of their traditional clan estates and told the story of our law, our language and our identity. They sent a second bark petition two weeks later. They are still on display in the new Parliament House.

The elders feared they would become like the Larakia people, whose land was taken from them to build the city of Darwin. They feared that they would become landless and lose their language and their culture. They would be *wängamirriw*, without language, *dhärukmirriw*, a dominated and marginalised people.

Our elders made history by taking out a writ against Nabalco and the Commonwealth government in 1968, over the establishment of the bauxite mine at Gove, and in doing so challenged the domination and legitimacy of the Balanda legal system. In 1968, they got together to have a *galtha* ceremony for the Supreme Court case. There are *galtha* areas situated all over north-east Arnhem Land, where people have come together over many hundreds of years for hunting, trading, peace-making, politics, marriage exchange and ceremonies.

Galtha in this sense is the place where people assemble, arriving from their different territories to sit for some time with related groups of people, but *galtha* is more than this. It is a place at which important negotiations are carried out, agreements made and plans formulated. More importantly, it refers to the whole process of meeting, discussion, negotiation, planning, agreement and action. *Galtha* marks the nexus between plan and action, between theory and practice.

Thus, the Supreme Court process started with a *galtha*, and a second petition to protest against the desecration of Nhulun, Mt Saunders, where Nabalco had constructed a water tank. The elders performed a *bunggul*, a ceremony to try to explain to the Balanda that the site was sacred. They also sent a petition to parliament to make sure the name Nhulunbuy was kept. Years later we developed a curriculum called *galtha*.

In his judgment in *Milirrpum v. Nabalco Pty Ltd*, in 1971, Mr Justice Blackburn found evidence that Aborigines belong to the land but the land does not belong to the Aborigines. This finding was the beginning of the land rights struggle in Arnhem Land and led eventually to the *Aboriginal Land Rights (Northern Territory) Act 1976*. When our elders returned to Yirrkala from the court hearings in Darwin and Canberra, they realised that the younger generations needed to be competent to a very high level within their own language to be able to translate the principles of Yolngu worldviews and Yolngu law for Australian institutions founded on the foreign, British system of law. They realised that the younger generations would be required to mount complicated and difficult arguments concerning the rights of Yolngu people on the land, sea and resources of their traditional estate. They would need to be able to explain clearly the principles of all aspects of Yolngu society in order to change Balanda views about the legitimacy of the Yolngu way of life.

The administration of Aboriginal affairs in the Northern Territory was a Commonwealth matter from 1911 to 1978. During that time various Commonwealth administrative agencies were responsible for Commonwealth policies dealing with the Aboriginal population in the Northern Territory. Our elders were subject to the assimilation policies of that time. They lived under colonial regimes which were first referred to as 'Native Affairs' and then later as 'Welfare', and were administered by the mission. I too lived under that policy until I was 14 years old.

My elders resisted these policies through the Bark Petition that they presented to the Federal Parliament in 1963 to express their opposition to the mining which led to the litigation by the clan elders to prevent the mine in the *Milirrpum* case.

In the early 1960s, a report was commissioned by the ministers of the states and territories to investigate the curriculum and teaching methods used in the Northern Territory. In her thesis, *Dhangum Djorra'wuy Dhäwu*, Mary-Anne Gale (1992: np) explains:

> The report incorporated an official acknowledgment of the diversity of Aboriginal languages represented in the NT schools. As well as the large cultural differences that existed between Aboriginal and non-Aboriginal pupils, it isolated a number of factors contributing to the lack of academic achievement by Aboriginal children in the current school system and made many comprehensive recommendations for its subsequent improvement. Obviously influenced by the 1953 UNESCO statement, the report acknowledged the advantages to be gained through the use of the vernacular in Aboriginal schools, but it fell short of recommending the implementation of vernacular programs. It wasn't until December, 1972, that the newly elected Labor government, under Gough Whitlam, introduced a program involving teaching in Aboriginal languages.

Bilingual education started in 1974, when the Northern Territory was still a territory administered from Canberra. It was in 1978 that the Commonwealth granted self-government to the Northern Territory. After that, a Northern Territory Education Department was established. During Gough Whitlam's time as Prime Minister, from 1974 to 1975, the Commonwealth Department of Education established and supported the bilingual education needs of Aboriginal communities in the Northern Territory. In a report prepared by the Minister for Education, Kim Beazley Sr, a working definition was prepared and adopted by the Northern Territory Government. It read:

> Bilingual education is the use of two languages, one of which is English, as the medium of instruction for the same pupil population in a well-organised program which encompasses part or all of the curriculum and includes the study of history and culture associated with the mother tongue. A complete program develops and maintains the children's self-esteem and a legitimate pride in both cultures. (quoted in Buckley 1996: np)

The Commonwealth continued its control over Aboriginal education until 1978–79 when self-government was achieved. [Dr M. Yunupingu] in a speech he gave last year at the Language Learning and Culture: Unsettling Certainties conference, outlined some of the major processes we had to go through to gain control of curriculum development in the mid to late 1980s (Language learning and culture 1997). The control of curriculum, teaching, learning and literacy is all about power. We wanted the school to be a place which put together Balanda and Yolngu learning to strengthen our culture. To do this at Yirrkala school, we had to invent a governance structure that would allow us to explore alternative visions of what it means to be educated and literate. We needed to create the space for us to express ourselves. We had to overcome the structural organisational barriers which had been up until then a feature of Western education. This became a collaborative project between community and clans.

We have developed a vision and a five-year plan, called an Aboriginalisation plan, which was accepted by the Northern Territory government in 1986. We worked with the elders, writing down their ideas, then we negotiated the elders' ideas into a form that the Western education system could understand. To negotiate what we wanted, we had to be able to put our ideas in their way. The basis of the plan is the Nambarra School Council, which is the school's governing body and an action group. The action group is made up of all the Yolngu *matha*-speaking members of staff. Managing the day-to-day running of the school, this group, of which the Principal is a member, makes decisions in consultation with and on behalf of the school council. In this way the community becomes more directly involved in the running of the school. This same model still operates today.

A system of mentor training was introduced, with Aboriginal teachers working side by side with Balanda, with equal pay. The relationship is one of partnership. This mentor system continues today as well. The curriculum became more Aboriginal. Our language became a valued part of teaching and learning. Classroom practice and management became more Aboriginal and an Aboriginal-oriented curriculum was introduced. For example, students spent a lot of time out of the classroom on visits to important cultural sites.

Out of this work came what we called our Yolngu curriculum. I want to share with you some of the important esoteric Yolngu words which have informed our curriculum development at Yirrkala.

What is *garma*? In the 1980s the Yirrkala school introduced a program of Aboriginalisation. Yolngu community elders were asked to come to the school to help develop a 'both ways' curriculum for Nambarra School, in maths. The community elders came to meetings to tell the Yolngu teachers what their school curriculum should be like. These elders gave us several words to guide the developmental maths curriculum. These words or metaphors reflect the knowledge of the Yolngu elders about how maths in the Yolngu world and maths in the Balanda world can be taught side by side, so that one does not devalue the other. Several Yolngu metaphors were used to understand Yolngu mathematical ideas. Some of these words are *ganma*, *milngurr*, *garma* and galtha.

Some of the ideas for our practice come from theory related to the Ganma Lagoon. *Ganma* is firstly a place; it is an area within the mangroves where the salt water coming in from the sea meets the stream of fresh water coming down from the land. *Ganma* is a still lagoon. The water circulates silently underneath, and there are lines of foam circulating across the surface. The swelling and retreating of the tides and the wet season floods can be seen in the two bodies of the water. Water is often taken to represent knowledge in Yolngu philosophy. What we see happening in the school is a process of knowledge production where we have two different cultures, Balanda and Yolngu, working together. Both cultures need to be presented in a way where each one is preserved and respected. This theory is Yirritja.

I will now talk about *milngurr*, which is Dhuwa, the opposite theory. *Milngurr* is a name of sacred spring water. It is created by the *mawalan*, the walking sticks of the Djangkawu ancestral being — my ancestor. This is a metaphor that my father used to help me to understand about teaching and learning. *Milngurr* represents the ebb and flow of water. We use this to represent the way we learn.

When the tide is high, we are full of new knowledge, new ideas, new thinking. When it ebbs, we are looking for new things. We hope to produce a dynamic like this at Yirrkala, a continuous striving for a balanced environment.

Garma is also a place. It is an open ceremonial area that everyone can participate in and enjoy. If a ceremony is negotiated and produced in full view of everybody, it will be performed in the *garma* ceremonial area. Yolngu can sit and watch a *garma* ceremony and read from it the network of connections between people, places, songs and totems that make up these particular ceremonies at a certain time. *Garma* also means an open forum where people can share ideas and everyone can work hard to reach agreement. The old people told us the school should be like a *garma* setting.

Galtha is also a place. We talked about it earlier: the *galtha* ceremony which started the Supreme Court case. In a school context, a *galtha* curriculum relates to how children are related to the land and to their *djalkiri*, to their foundations.

We used these ideas as a driving force to help inform our direction and future. In the late 1980s we began a process of incorporating *garma* into the school program, side by side with the Northern Territory maths curriculum and documents. While the notion of *garma* began to be implemented in the 1980s, we are now ready to create a working document that enables all staff, regardless of their experience and cultural backgrounds, to work with the school-based 'both ways' maths curriculum document which is informed by *garma*.

There are four strands to the *garma* maths curriculum. There is *gurrutu*, which is Yolngu, and 'number', which is English; and *djalkiri*, which is Yolngu, and 'location', which is English. But they relate to one another. Number relates to *gurrutu* and *djalkiri* relates to location. In *gurrutu* we have pattern, in the same way as numbers have patterns and names. In *gurrutu* we have individual relationships, as in numbers there are numeration, measurement and money, time, length. And in *djalkiri* the kids learn about area — the area where they come from and their homelands — as in location there is space, mapping. In the same way there is mapping in *djalkiri* too: mapping in the Yolngu way, tracking, *dhin'thun*.

Part of our *garma* curriculum are workshops driven by *galtha*. These workshops can run over one week or a few days. In them students look at Yolngu worldviews, including land tenure systems, kinships, *gurrutu* systems, social structures — like in *djalkiri*, such as clans, land ownerships, place names, mappings of the country. Yolngu art, traditions, *djalkiri*, *dhulang* and *mint'tji* are taught by elders. Dhäruk languages and clan languages are taught. Songs, dances and *manikay*, traditional dance, are also taught in the *galtha* curriculum workshops.

[*Editor's note:* at this point in the lecture, there were several brief audiovisual presentations, illustrating students' work and the descriptions of Yolngu and Balanda understandings in this work, which have not been transcribed.]

Working parties have been established at the school, which are developing outcomes for the different maths strands, linking the *garma* strands of *gurrutu*, number, *djalkiri*, quantifying, location, with departmental curriculum strands of working mathematically: number, space, measurement and algebra. In so doing we have established a new *galtha* area for maths. The process of developing our *garma* maths policy has begun and will continue producing knowledge in the Yirrkala language curriculum.

Another exciting example of bringing the two knowledge systems together is the development and recent revision of the Yirrkala school-based language curriculum. What is important with the school-based working documents is that staff are using the curriculum side by side with other departmental curriculum documents to inform their collaborative planning, teaching and learning practice, assessment, profiling and benchmarking: whose knowledge, whose language, whose priorities?

The Northern Territory Department of Education assesses all territory schools in English only. Every year, children from all Northern Territory schools take part in the multi-level assessment program at Level 5 in primary school. This includes all bilingual schools, which actually are set up to teach literacy in Aboriginal languages in the first years of school, with an emphasis on oral English development. I believe that bilingual schools should have curriculum support, including funding, to develop their own way of assessing children that is appropriate to those schools. Bilingual schools undergo bilingual appraisals every three years and there should be funding allocated to support bilingual schools, particularly in the area of curriculum development, assessment procedures and evaluation of programs. Research is needed in the area of Indigenous languages, as we are still in relatively uncharted waters as far as Indigenous curriculum development goes.

Profiling is a relatively new assessment tool in the Northern Territory. The development of English profiles and other curriculum areas has been an extensive process. We were disappointed to realise that the process was very much geared to mainstream curriculum areas. Language profiling entails teachers preparing a profile on each child and assessing each child's reading, writing, speaking and listening skills.

Unfortunately, these profiles have been developed for children who speak English as a first language. For English we can use the English-as-a-second-language profile, but the bicultural nature of our school program is not acknowledged. The national benchmarking process also wants to know the answer to the question: do Yirrkala children achieve the same learning outcomes at the same time as any other child in Australia? There is no consideration given to the fact that our children are learning in and through two languages, and learning about two knowledge systems or traditions.

The premise from the Northern Territory's view of profiling and the national benchmark is that only the Balanda knowledge system, transmitted in English, is important. They are making a value judgment which is assimilationist and unfair to our children, because of our bilingual approach. At a school level we do assess the level of competency among the children for the Yolngu *garma* curriculum. As the teacher-linguist I collaborated with the teachers to plan the overview of learning outcomes for each term. At the end of each term we use the learning outcomes as a checklist against the performance of each child. A report card and a checklist on the learning outcome are sent to the family of each child. We used the language curriculum documents to plan the outcome for the topics that the children are taught at each level. This assessment is starting to work well, but we are new on this path. We need assistance to develop our assessment procedures, to write our own Yolngu maths profiles as well as using the English as a Second Language profiles to map our children's progress in their second language.

In conclusion I would like to ask this question. Is the government fair dinkum about bilingual education? We believe that our children have a right to know and understand their own cultural beliefs within the model bilingual program. Learning literacy in the children's first language takes precedence in the first primary schooling years from Transition to Level 3. The focus of the English learning during this period is very much an oral one, helping the children to become confident speakers of English before they have to grapple with English literacy and concepts. Once children have mastered literacy skills in their first language they can then transfer them to English literacy.

The task ahead is to convince the Department of Education and the Commonwealth government that Yolngu assessment and evaluation methods can and should be developed. These methods will have to involve our elders and our languages and our knowledge systems. Bilingual schools in the Northern Territory are not adequately resourced, when you consider the enormous task ahead of us.

We are not opposed to profiling or to the national benchmarking process. It is just that the current evaluation systems do not take into account Yolngu curriculum, which is taught in our schools and other Indigenous systems. The current system does not take into account our Yolngu *garma* curriculum or Yolngu 'both ways' pedagogy and curriculum.

Our job as educators is to convince the people who control mainstream education that we wish to be included. Until this happens, reconciliation is an empty word and an intellectual *terra nullius*.

References

Buckley, P 1996, 'What entitles a school to legitimately call itself an Aboriginal school?', *Australian Journal of Indigenous Education*, vol. 24, no. 1, pp. 10–16.

Gale, M-A 1992, '*Dhangum Djorra'wuy Dhäwu*: The development of writing in Aboriginal languages in SA and the NT since colonisation', MEd thesis, Northern Territory University, Darwin.

Language learning and culture: Unsettling certainties: First Joint National Conference of the Australian Association for the Teaching of English (AATE), the Australian Literacy Educator's Association (ALEA) and the Australian School Library Association (ASLA) 1997, proceedings, 8–11 July, Department of Education, Darwin.

Marika, D 1989, *Ngayi Balngana Mawurrku: The song of Yirrkala*, Yirrkala Literature Production Centre, Nhulunbuy NT.

Wells, E 1982, *Reward and punishment in Arnhem Land 1962–1963*, Australian Institute of Aboriginal Studies, Canberra.

Case

Milirrpum v Nabalco Pty Ltd (1971) 17 FLR 141

Legislation

Aboriginal Land Rights (Northern Territory) Act 1976

Original lecture available at:
<http://aiatsis.gov.au/publications/presentations/raymattja-marika>

11

Beyond the mourning gate: Dealing with unfinished business

2000 Wentworth Lecture

Patrick Dodson

Let me first acknowledge the Ngunnawal, the traditional owners of this part of the country, and I pay my respects to all their ancestors. Greetings to the Honourable Bill Wentworth, who is present here today and in whose honour this lecture is given. I pay my respects to him as a leader in the whitefellas' tribe. Thanks to the Institute for the opportunity to deliver this lecture.

In 1938, Australia was sitting at the tail end of the Great Depression, a calamity that created enormous suffering across large sections of the Australian community. Those Australians who survived the Great War and the Depression would soon hear the ominous sounds of another human disaster being cranked up in Europe and northern Asia. Little wonder, then, that the prospect of a party in Sydney to celebrate the 150th anniversary of the arrival of the First Fleet was seen as a welcome diversion from the threat of another world war and the difficulties of life that continued to weigh upon them.

A program of festivities was planned to celebrate the foundations laid in the Colony along British lines, its glorious achievements and its triumphs over the alien environment and the original owners of the land. The highlight was to be a re-enactment of the arrival of Governor Phillip and a party of his sailors at Port Jackson. It was planned that a replica of the ship, HMS Supply, would anchor at Farm Cove and a rowing boat would bring a group of actors, led by Frank Harvey, playing the part of Captain Phillip, to the western side of the point at Lady Macquarie's Chair.

The official program for the event reported that, 'The first boat to land will carry a party of men who will put the aborigines to flight'. Captain Phillip was to arrive in the second boat. Twenty-five Aboriginal people from Menindee had been brought to Sydney by the Aborigines Protection Board to play the part of the fleeing Sydney natives. They were billeted at the Redfern Police Barracks. The police were under strict instructions from the Board to deny them any contact with disruptive influences from outside the timber barracks of the Redfern Police Compound.

No doubt the organisers of the gala re-enactment felt that using Menindee people was a safer option than using local Sydney Aboriginal people. The Menindee group would need no encouragement to head for home. The Sydney mob, however, had declined to flee in 1778 and would have stayed put again in 1938. While the rest of Australia was either preoccupied with the pleasures of the summer break, or those who were in Sydney planned how they might participate in the upcoming Australia Day celebrations, a group of Aboriginal people with a belief in the need for justice and equality were hard at work with some plans of their own.

The Aborigines Progressive Association, with leaders like Jack Patten, Bill Ferguson, Pearl Gibbs, Jack Kinchela and Helen Grosvenor, were planning an Australian Aborigines conference. The event was to be called a Day of Mourning and Protest. It was to be held on Australia Day, Wednesday 26 January. They circulated a motion for debate at the meeting:

> WE, representing THE ABORIGINES OF AUSTRALIA, assembled in Conference at the Australian Hall, Sydney, on the 26th day of January, 1938, this being the 150th Anniversary of the white men's seizure of our country, HEREBY MAKE PROTEST against the callous treatment of our people by the white men during the past 150 years, AND WE APPEAL to the Australian Nation of today to make new laws for the education and care of Aborigines, and we ask for a new policy which will raise our people to FULL CITIZEN STATUS and EQUALITY WITHIN THE COMMUNITY. (Patten et al. 1938)

They met at the Australian Hall at number 148 Elizabeth Street, now a site of significance to all Australian people, thanks to the efforts of Jenny Munro and others.

The Day of Mourning and Protest conference was attended by Aboriginal people from up and down the eastern seaboard. All Australian Aborigines were invited. The views expressed and the arguments put forward were diverse, reflecting the backgrounds and histories of the people involved. The issues, though, were agreed and clear: equality and recognition — the right to be Aboriginal people along with the right to enjoy the equality, responsibility and quality of being an Australian citizen.

It was not a trade off: one set of rights for another. It was about improving the living conditions of Aboriginal people so that they might survive as human beings and break the domination of government regulations and prescription. In the minds of the leaders at that time, both realities could co-exist and be enjoyed. There was no need to extinguish what remained of the Aboriginal uniqueness and heritage after 150 years of the white man's dominance of the land and lives of the Aboriginal people.

The architects of the assimilation policies of the time had a different view. They had their own ideas about what would be best for the Aboriginal peoples. The future for Aborigines would be in their hands and constructed towards their goals. It would not require our consent, so our consent was never sought. Maybe some of today's Aboriginal leaders believe that we have moved on since the Day of Mourning and Protest. Maybe they no longer see any point in remembering the stories and deeds of those who came before. Perhaps some Aboriginal leaders of today have a way of accommodating and remaining at one with their traditions while neglecting their own history.

For many Aboriginal people, however, storytelling, remembering and paying respect to those who led the way in the past are part of our traditions. It is part of intergenerational accountability and responsibility for our traditions, customs and values. If we lose our sense of value and meaning in the Aboriginal world, then we become a successful clone of what the assimilation policies and strategies sought to achieve. If we become no more than what the white man has tried to make us into since he took control of this land and our affairs, then what value do we add to the nation in our assertion as the first peoples of this land?

What right do we have to call upon governments for respect and recognition? The call for recognition of 'full citizen status' and 'equality within the community' by the leaders in 1938 recurs in the numerous reports that we have seen from the Human Rights Commission, the Social Justice Commissioner, ATSIC and the Council for Aboriginal Reconciliation. Gradually, others outside of the Aboriginal organisational structures are also taking interest in how we are being managed. Some are seeking an understanding of the use of the public purse to address the lack of formal equality. Some are seeking to get their hands on that public purse. Some, even many, of us are concerned at how that public purse is allocated and used. We appear, however, to be a long way from stronger, broader community support or informed debate on the key issues of fundamental equality.

The question of rights asked in 1938 still echoes in the halls, unanswered by governments. It has echoed in the Yirrkala Bark Petition, the Barunga Statement, the Eva Valley Statement and the Boomanulla Oval Statement. The Redfern Speech by Prime Minister Keating and the agreement by Prime Minister Hawke to a treaty process at Barunga were visions of what might be shared and realised for all Australians. They were prepared to lead so that a majority of the citizens might be inspired to follow. Why was it so hard to seize those moments and deliver real and lasting change? Will we again fail as a nation to grasp this opportunity to change the political architecture of the country? Will we again fail to rise above the mediocrity that ties us to seeking incremental change through short-term stopgap bureaucratic solutions? Or can we work towards realigning the relationship between us?

The Aboriginal leaders who were involved in the Day of Mourning and Protest events took the conference outcomes to Prime Minister Lyons. They called on him to respond to the motion that was carried at the Day of Mourning and Protest conference and to deliver on a petition (organised by Bill Cooper), which had been directed to Cabinet. Mr Cooper's petition sought from the government 'some political representation' by providing for a seat in the federal parliament so that 'an Aborigine might represent their interest'. The prime minister had written to Cooper offering to meet a delegation on 31 January 1938, to discuss the petition and other matters. [In September 2014, 80 years after the petition was given to Lyons, William Cooper's grandson was able to see it reached the Queen. Governor-General Peter Cosgrove attended a ceremony in Aberdeenshire, Scotland, where Sir Peter finally relayed the document to the Queen.]

Why has it been so hard for the larger questions of justice to be answered by governments in good time so that Aborigines can achieve some freedom and dignity in their own lifetime? This same fundamental question is at the heart of the current reconciliation dynamic today.

I am fairly sure that the prime minister does not want my advice. However, if he wishes to retrieve the current situation, he needs to state clearly that he is fully prepared to interact with Aboriginal people. After an extensive public consultation process, the Council drew up two documents of reconciliation: the *Australian Declaration Towards Reconciliation* and the *Roadmap for Reconciliation*. At Corroboree 2000, held on 27 May 2000, it presented these to the prime minister, other national leaders, and the nation as a whole. The Council had earlier advised the prime minister that these documents represented its formal recommendations to him as minister in relation to the 'nature and content' of documents of reconciliation under paragraph 6(1)(h) of the Act.

Others have different reasons for attending and I encourage them to do so and wish the council well on the day.

The leaders of the Day of Mourning and Protest in 1938 confronted the legacy of the past and they paved the way for the later successful 1967 referendum. These campaigns have a history for us all, and the people involved have my greatest admiration. We should remember that the process of achieving the referendum was not always supported. The people themselves were often subjected to ridicule and obstruction. Their persistence in the face of this adversity has achieved results that are still significant today.

The referendum changes to the Constitution are symbolically important but they have not measured up to the high hopes that our leaders of the day wished for: to end the discrimination and allow the Aborigines proper enjoyment of citizenship and Aboriginality, the dignity to be Aborigines in their own country.

The reality was that we became slaves to a series of government programs and policies that continued to determine our political and social lives, a sort of 'assimilation with consultation'. The same bureaucracies that supplied the Native Protectors provided us with policy mandarins and with field officers. Many Aboriginal leaders of the time believed that the head of power achieved through the 1967 referendum would be used by the federal government to make things right between us; that they would override the states if the states proposed policies and practices detrimental to our rights as Aboriginal people and as citizens. Alas, a forlorn hope.

We have the legacy of the 1967 referendum, the common law recognition of Native Title, and the findings of the *Bringing Them Home* report. There are other legacies that relate to the way Aboriginal people have been dealt with by governments, its institutions and the broad community as well. These dynamics were brought to the fore in the Aboriginal Deaths in Custody Royal Commission report in 1991. It outlined the underlying issues and explained the impact of the criminal justice regime on the lives of Aboriginal people, especially when in custody.

It is hard to be optimistic when such reports and their recommendations rely upon governments hearing them, adopting them and driving forward to achieve the intended outcomes.

It is one thing for the Council for Aboriginal Reconciliation to make the strongest possible statements and recommendations, but quite another matter as to what the government and the parliament commit to doing about them. This is the aspect of the current reconciliation process with which I am most concerned. This is the relevant period of the process of reconciliation when outcomes have to be focused upon and made real.

We should not be distracted by political posturing but argue for an effective government response. The fact that there is a people's movement associated with the formal process of reconciliation at the present time may add to the optimism but is no guarantee that their goodwill and resolve will be any more rewarded than that of the council itself. The prime minister has successfully convinced the nation and the council that the deadline of 1 January 2000 was not appropriate and has offered little to pick up the momentum and address the seriousness of the moment. His emphasis on practical reconciliation involving health, housing, education and employment are matters government should be concerned to address in its normal responsibilities to its citizens. All Australians want to see an improvement in the social conditions we experience as Aborigines and hope for improved outcomes from public expenditure. Yet there is more to consider.

Reconciliation involves beneficial resolution of our status as the first peoples of this country and restitution for the way our inheritance as owners and custodians of the land have been taken from us. It also requires us meeting our obligations and responsibilities in the changed world of contemporary Australian society.

What will governments say? How will they respond to these issues? Who knows now what the role of the prime minister should be? How will he respond to the document, 'Towards a Document of Reconciliation',[1] when he and the governor-general receive it from the Council for Aboriginal Reconciliation and the people of Australia? Justice requires that the efforts of all involved in the reconciliation process and over the past two hundred years or so have some reward. The reconciliation dynamic involves truths in both fields of practical and spiritual domains in order for the ongoing cause of discord and division between us to be resolved. The council's May events will highlight what is still required to be done before there is a proper reconciliation between us. The council could not possibly present the total Indigenous position, and by its nature is not required to do so.

I am hopeful that its references to a treaty and self-determination will give these matters some credibility with those who will march in favour of reconciliation. What matters is whether there is a way for the Aboriginal people to advance these matters with the government. There has been nothing from government that indicates its preparedness to respond in any innovative manner to the issues of reconciliation beyond its concern with practical reconciliation. Such a response requires a commitment from the prime minister that he will enter into the spirit of this direction and negotiate their meaning and application with the Aboriginal people. To date he has not given any such commitment.

The council cannot deliver the results on the issues that it highlights, so it does a service to all of us to bring them to the forefront of the nation's consciousness. It is for government to commit to finding the path of lasting reconciliation. Its hour has come. Will we again see, as so often in the past, when Aborigines protested and mourned, that there is no action? Will government simply revert to its traditions of superiority rather than face a new spirit of reconciliation and lead the nation to the healing and unity it requires?

In the main, our intertwined history since 1788 can be put into four divisions. The first is the British instruction to 'take possession of the continent with the consent of the natives' — an instruction that was never followed! Instead, there was a penal colony established at Sydney Cove. The legal fiction of *terra nullius* provided the basis for the ongoing justification of reducing the Aboriginal people to a disinherited and destabilised people in our own land.

The second was made up of 'the darkest deed of colonial Australia and the incremental dispossession' that accompanied it (Parson 1899). This allowed for the murder, poisoning, rape, and enslavement of the Aboriginal people in the name of expansion and development of the colonies. There has never been any redress, except those pieces of land rights legislation that today are seen as maybe having given too much to the Aborigines, and that therefore the rights that they enjoy under these laws should be removed or taken away now, so that others might again 'peacock' the land and its resources. The third set of the activities involves those with good intentions who were motivated by assimilation and salvation in their relationship with the Aboriginal people. They bowed to government authority and participated in the process of eliminating Indigenous belief and thinking. The land had been taken from the people so now the battle was between the rival Christians, governments and other groups for the mind and hearts of the Aboriginal people. Their roles played a major part in destabilising and traumatising the Aboriginal peoples. The dynamic to control our hearts and minds resides in this context.

In the last decade there has been a fourth dynamic, that of reconciliation. For the first time as a nation, the parliament allowed us a formal process over ten years to make right our relationship by addressing the legacies that cause and sustain discord and division and to found a new basis for our future, one that expresses the truthfulness of the reconciliation upon which we might mutually agree.

Throughout these phases of our intertwined history there is good and bad, enlightenment and ignorance, joy and great sadness, pride and shame. However, woven through all these periods is an alarming virulent dynamic that has persisted on the non-Aboriginal side, enabling it to reject the legitimate status of who and what the Aboriginal people are, what we represent and what rights and interests we might enjoy.

For successive Australian governments, whether colonial, federal, territory or state the four divisions of our intertwined histories have been about their solutions to us as the problem: the problem of our being here, the problem of our disposal, the problem of our assimilation, and the problem of having us appreciative of all that governments have done 'for our own good'.

For Aboriginal Australians, the hope has always been for governments to enter into serious dialogue about our position in the nation and for the Constitution to recognise us as the first Australians, with our Indigenous rights, obligations and responsibilities respected and recognised. There has never been any agreement about how we might progress this fundamental dilemma. They have been met with obstruction and deferral. The reasons often given have been that the electorate will not support them to do so.

The Day of Mourning and Protest, like many other gatherings held by Aborigines since, has always been about rights. Most, if not all, have had little success in achieving lasting security and protection of the rights that we have sought. The priority on the government's side of the equation has been about securing the non-Aboriginal voters. For the people's movement for reconciliation to count, this is where it will have to make a difference. Our interests and rights simply just do not count in the context of government ideology and political pragmatism. Only on very rare occasions have governments led the community against the contrary view of the polls.

The demands and petitions may have varied in language but never in content and intent. The Harris delegation that met the Western Australian State government in 1928 sought the same rights as the Day of Mourning campaigners. The people of Noonkanbah and the Pilbara Strikers sought only to protect the rights and responsibilities that they had in the law and the land.

The history has not been told of all the occasions that Aboriginal people throughout Australia have protested or mourned for their stories. Most of these occasions appear to have fallen upon half-hearted or empty responses. Their comfort has come from their fellow Australians who have shared in our pain and disappointment.

No more or no less, the Aboriginal people who have survived the theft of their lands, the removal of their children and the destruction of their law and languages are seeking the guarantee of their rights to live within our law and culture: to have recognition and respect in the Australian law that has assumed its power over our ancient rights and people; and to be able to carry out our laws, customs and traditions through a formal accord recognising our equal status alongside the Australian law.

The government wishes to drive a wedge not only between the concepts of rights and welfare but also between those who advocate a rights agenda and those who seek relief from the appalling poverty. This is an attempt at a new spin on a very old wicket of divide and rule. If it were a matter of rice-bowl politics, it might not be so bad, but it is far more sinister than that. It is about removing the centrality of community as the life centre and models on the individual as the essential unit of society. This is not our way. With all our social problems the answer is not to attack the foundations of our community by putting the individual before the community.

Aborigines have never wanted to be the same as the White man. What we have sought is to have substantial equality so that as human beings there might be a quality of life that we can enjoy in keeping with our own values and societal ways. Lives for our peoples, similar to those of the majority in Australia, but lives uniquely ours, not ones that governments wished to impose upon us; lives where we meet our obligations as citizens but where we are accommodated also as Aborigines; lives where our human and cultural rights are respected by the governments that have told the world they would respect them.

We have been an affront to the foundational thinking and perceptions that underpin the British mould of Australian institutional principles of society. The confidence of the nation to celebrate its achievements with some pride is always tempered with the concern that the issues of unfinished business between us would surface and detract from the moment. This inevitably sends the message to those who observe us, as a nation divided in the one country. It further highlights the inability of a modern democracy to come to grips fairly and respectfully with its Indigenous peoples.

From a cultural position, the only way that the mourning period can be ended is when the proper protocols and practical arrangements have been carried out, when the people who have had a wrong or an injustice done to them have been accommodated by the action of those responsible. Then we can come together as friends and mates.

What are the protocols to provide the relief to the causes of the mourning and trauma flowing from the intertwined history? There is no easy cultural match up. This is not about a fresh event, it is about a continuing state of being for the government and the society. If this were a matter of a singular recent event in everyday life, then the cultural leaders amongst us would know what to do. Yet this is beyond that relatively simple situation. We have offered on occasions the deepest secrets of our societies to those in highest authority who claimed to be seeking empathy and understanding, only to have that encounter and the gift be diminished, as of no account.

Cross-cultural learning has not happened. Everything about us has to be subject and subordinate to the rules, practices and values of the dominant society. Customary law details of the initiation business are not immune to the Native Title processes of our courts. Lawmen are forced to violate their own law to the superior demands of the Australian court proceedings and rules to highlight connection and continuity for the benefit of the other parties, including the government, without necessarily securing the title to their lands.

At the Day of Mourning ceremony after the meeting in 1938, flowers were thrown into the sea as a sign of respect for and remembrance of all the Aboriginal people who died since the White man's arrival. It was also an expression of the pain, hurt and frustration that the people had witnessed and experienced in their time and before that. It was also about their underlying fear for their future.

Those leaders of 1938 saw the loss and destruction of their peoples over the 150-year period as a sad and painful episode. The prospects of this past continuing required the leaders to look with hope to the future. They would give up their sons and daughters to the god of war in a matter of months in defence of a nation that had rejected them. They would go on into the life of the nation with great contributions of citizenship when they had none of the rights that go with being a citizen. One went on to become a State Governor, but only after being forced to sleep in the sheds of country pubs in towns where he had gone to compete in athletic events.

Yet more than this, these leaders, who had the temerity to challenge those who would seek to prolong the suppression of their cultural, political and human rights, have demonstrated that we have survived — no matter how the impacts of policies of assimilation, cultural genocide and exclusion have affected our people. The need to defend our rights for our children (and out of obligations to our people and the land) remains.

What then is the focus of this year's Reconciliation Week? It has to do with the culmination of the ten-year process of reconciliation provided by the parliament through the *Council for Reconciliation Act 1991*. This Act gave to the nation the first serious opportunity for us to make a fundamental appraisal of the relationship between us and to establish a new foundation to the way the relationship in the future would be expressed and acknowledged in the law, societal practice and Constitution of this country. The Council for Aboriginal Reconciliation will present to the Australian people the fruits of its labour of reconciliation over the past nine or so years. What it presents will no doubt be what it has been able to agree about, on a cross-party and cross-cultural basis, the best way forward for the nation to advance reconciliation. That in itself will be no mean feat, because consensus will have guided the content of their recommendations as well as the thrust of those recommendations and not just numbers. It delivers an Australian agenda for reconciliation, not an exclusive Aboriginal one.

We will have to wait and see the nature of the council's recommendations to the Minister. Some of you might know them already. However, to the majority it is not clear what, if at all, the council is recommending in terms of its capacity under the functions set out in sections 6g and 6h of its Act: the sections that deal with a document or documents of reconciliation and the nature and content of the documents, as well as the manner by which such documents need to be given effect. Getting a set of words right is a difficult task but achieving their adoption and implementation is the real issue here. With all due respect to the celebratory events the council has planned for 27 and 28 May, we do not know what government will do with its endeavours, nor do we know how government will progress matters with the Aboriginal peoples.

Let there be no misunderstanding. The anger and disappointment that many Indigenous Australians evince with the way the content of the 'Towards a Document of Reconciliation' proposal is being handled is not directed at the Council for Aboriginal Reconciliation. We are angry and disappointed at the cynical manipulation of the process that has been employed by the federal government and, in particular, the leader of that government. This manipulation is an affront to the millions of Australians of goodwill who have sought a genuine reconciliation between our peoples, one based on equity and justice for all.

On other occasions I have endeavoured to outline to people of this country what I believe are the key principles that must be addressed in any legislated framework agreement or treaty between our two peoples. Core principals, the extent of which must be negotiated between us, come under these main headings: political representation, reparations and compensation, regional agreements, Indigenous regional self-government, cultural and intellectual property rights, recognition of customary law, and an economic base. In common with all other Australians we must have the right to maintain our unique cultural identity without having our entitlements as Australian citizens held hostage to the social imperatives of governments, whose leaders are unable to comprehend the value of the contribution that we bring to this country as first Australians.

It may well be beyond the imagination of this current government to grasp the consequences of what the continued denial of the rights of the first Australians will be. It may be beyond their imagination to grasp the importance in the same way that so many Australians have come to terms with the truth of our past and are seeking to provide a shared future of justice for all our children. However, one thing the leaders of 1938 taught us is that unless we have the courage to persevere and confront the denial and prejudices placed before us, a just future for our children will not be secured.

For us to pass through the mourning gate, I am proposing today, with the completion of the work of the Council for Aboriginal Reconciliation only seven months away, is that they place before the parliament of this country the following proposal:

First, before the council's 27 and 28 May event, the prime minister needs to make it clear that he will accept what the council has put forward and that he will commit to a process with the Aboriginal peoples of finding practical, legal and political ways of advancing all aspects of the council's recommendations.

Second, council has recommended that forty distinguished Australians — twenty from each side — be commissioned with drafting a treaty between the Australian Government and Aboriginal peoples. The treaty is to be based on the matters raised by the council's recommendations and those other matters relayed to it during the course of its life as the ongoing causes for discord and division between us. The government is to nominate half the dignitaries and ATSIC will nominate the Aboriginal dignitaries. The government's response to this proposal needs to be made clear.

Third, that the Aboriginal people and the government nominate their respective representatives to negotiate the draft treaty. This process of negotiation should be overseen by all past prime ministers, High Court judges and former heads of state and an equivalent number of senior Aboriginal representatives.

An independent treaty commission should be established, independent of the government and the bureaucracy. It should be resourced appropriately.

If no agreement is reached between the government and Aboriginal negotiators, the government should put the question of a treaty with Aboriginal people to a referendum. If there is a positive result from the negotiations or the referendum, the government should adopt the treaty as part of our modus operandi and legislate for its adoption.

Just the other day, I received a lovely letter from a 73-year-old non-Aboriginal Tasmanian woman, full of kindness but also with a vision. Her kindness was in seeking advice on changing her will to fund a scholarship for future Aboriginal legal students. Her vision was one of reconciliation. She lives next to a conservation zone. She said in a postscript to her letter:

> Hope the pelicans helped to ease your heart. I witnessed a riotous event one day. A pelican paddled in with a seagull on its back. The seagull hopped off at one stage and the pelican continued on its way. Realising he was alone, the pelican turned and paddled back to the gull. I could almost hear him saying, 'Hey are you coming or not?' The gull hopped back on and the twosome continued on their navigation of the area.

In my home country, an event witnessed in the natural world such as this can be read as a vision of spirit, or *rai*. The pelican gliding across the water is like the spirit of reconciliation, black and white together moving forward. The seagull is in some ways like the governments of the day, forever changing, coming on and off the process, flying off to scream loudly before one day returning and joining the voyage, navigating towards a new future. This future is our future, if we have the courage and will. Otherwise, as the Irish saying goes, 'bigots and begrudgers will never bid the past farewell', and we will be trapped in our history.

Thank you once more to the Australian Institute of Aboriginal and Torres Strait Islander Studies for the opportunity to speak to you today, and thank you for hearing my views.

Kulia!

Note

1 The final document, *Australian Declaration Towards Reconciliation*, can be found at <http://www.austlii.edu.au/au/other/IndigLRes/car/2000/12/pg3.htm>.

References

Parson JG 1899, 'Dark deeds in a sunny land', *The West Australian Sunday Times*, 12 February, p. 1.
Patten, JT, Ferguson, W & Aborigines Progressive Association 1938, 'Australian Aborigines Conference: sesqui-centenary Day of Mourning and Protest', Aboriginal Progressive Association, Sydney.

Legislation

Council for Reconciliation Act 1991

Original lecture available at:
<http://aiatsis.gov.au/publications/presentations/beyond-mourning-gate-dealing-unfinished-business>

12

Unusual couples:
Relationships and research on the knowledge frontier

2002 Wentworth Lecture

Peter Sutton

In this lecture I make some observations about various pairs of research collaborators who have figured in the history of Indigenous studies in this country. This is in no way meant to be a 'who's who' of that history, and the people I want to talk about are not a rigorously defined sample, more an intuitive one. Today I concentrate on just four: Biraban and Lancelot Threlkeld, Mahkarolla and Lloyd Warner, Billy Mammus and Ursula McConnel, and Smiler Durmugam and William Stanner. My main purpose here is to pay tribute to these and other similar intellectual partnerships, in the positive spirit associated with the occasion – not uncritically, but in recognition of the fact that the development of similar relationships is an object lesson in the futility of forever racialising, demonising, romanticising and in other ways rendering the rough grain of the personal into the smoothness of the collective, when considering the history of the last 200 years in Australia. It is of practical importance, I argue, that the future of relationships between us achieves a better balance between the collective and the personal than we have achieved in recent decades. We are struggling badly with the relationship between the corporate and the individual on many fronts.

AIATSIS itself, and the field of Indigenous studies in this country generally, are primarily built on the intersection of two originally very different traditions of knowledge. I say 'intersection' because the role of those imparting knowledge in these cases is not on the whole revealed to us as that of passive subjects of research. Researchers frequently make it clear how dependent their own work has been on the engagement, intelligence and commitment of the key people from whom they learned, and also, at times, on the systematising capacity of their teachers.

My focus here is not on these individuals as representatives of large collectivities such as coloniser and colonised, or black and white, but as pairs of individuals whose relationships were usually complex, may have been at times emotionally intense, and often had an impact on both individuals over a long period. In recent decades, the old division of labour between Indigenous subject and non-Indigenous investigator has begun to fade. Nevertheless, it is more or less inevitable that differences of power, of culture and, at times, of gender are woven into these stories in ways that will become apparent, and relevant perhaps to any social research situation between individuals.

Lancelot Threlkeld (1788–1859) was a Congregational missionary at Lake Macquarie in New South Wales in the early nineteenth century. He is remembered partly for his courageous opposition to the colonial 'war of extirpation' then being carried on against the original inhabitants of his region (Harris 1994, p. 57). As early as 1824, he began learning the Awabakal language of the Lake Macquarie area, principally with Biraban, also known as John McGill (born c.1800, died before 1850).[1] Threlkeld's aim was to use a local translation of the Gospels and other literature, and his own ability to speak the local language, as a means to converting the people to Christianity. This piece of research, as it was in part, resulted in the first biblical translation into any Australian indigenous language (Harris 1994, p. 806). It also left us with an early example of what appears to have been an enthusiastic intellectual partnership.

Biraban or 'Eaglehawk', as his name translates (Threlkeld 1892, p. 88), was in a number of ways like many of the Indigenous people I discuss here. He had control of both of the main languages used in the research, having been at least partly brought up in the Military Barracks in Sydney, where he was an officer's servant (Threlkeld 1892, p. 88; Gunson 1974, p. 317). That he was more bicultural than culturally 'assimilated' to European ways is emphasised by Threlkeld in an affectionate memoir that appeared in print alongside a portrait of Biraban (Threlkeld 1892). He was an exceptional person, with an exceptional intellect.

Biraban and Threlkeld had been 'almost daily companion[s] for many years', said Threlkeld, who wrote in admiration of Biraban's intelligence, his knowledge, his language teaching skills, his leadership role in ceremonies and other assemblies, his attachment to the customs of his own people, and also the fact that 'he was much attached to us, and faithful to a chivalrous extreme' although he first mostly wrote in admiration of what he considered Biraban's good looks (Threlkeld 1892, p. 88). This mention of Biraban's 'faithfulness' mirrors observations made at many points during frontier times, not just among anthropologists, that once a strong one-on-one relationship had developed between them, the Aboriginal person's devotion to looking after the needs and wellbeing of the newcomer often followed (Gunson 1974, p. 317). This protective and, as Threlkeld says, 'chivalrous' response, which I and many others have enjoyed, is utterly at odds with the opposite kind of reportage from the frontier, which could tediously repeat stereotypical descriptions of

Aboriginal people as 'treacherous'. That the same people could engage in sneak attacks during guerrilla-type conflicts and also manifest the devoted loyalty of a Wylie or a Jacky Jacky should not be surprising. These opposites are measures of relationship.

Biraban is one of the first cases, historically, of the so-called 'main informant' also being a person of local or regional political eminence. Perhaps, as in some other cases, this eminence was a particular kind of frontier-generated eminence, the sort of high profile conferred not only by having traditional forms of standing but by combining older kinds of eminence with expertise in dealing with outsiders, in particular the Europeans. Biraban was, after all, honoured by Governor Darling as the king of the tribe at Lake Macquarie, and Thomas Chester referred to him as 'chief of the Black Tribe at Newcastle' in 1838 (Gunson 1974, p. 317).[2] We shall find this pattern repeated a number of times, but by no means consistently, through the other examples. In some cases it is likely that a person's eminence was not only reflected in their teaching role but also something pursued through it.

Mahkarolla and W Lloyd Warner (1920s)

Mahkarolla (Makarrwala, c.1881–c. 1957)[3] was born in north-east Arnhem Land. In 1926, when he was about 45, he appears to have been selected by a group of senior men to act as primary mentor to anthropologist Lloyd Warner (1898–1970). Warner, then aged 28, carried out PhD research in the Milingimbi area and elsewhere (1926–29). The title of his resulting ethnography, *A Black Civilization*, provides an indication, one designed to shock perhaps, as to Warner's attitude of deep admiration for the people with whom he worked. He acknowledged that his deepest obligation in producing the book (which has long been regarded as an excellent example of the anthropology of its time) was to the Murngin (now Yolngu) people who gave him 'a fine, whole-hearted hospitality'. He particularly thanked Makarrwala, of whom he said that he was 'one of the finest men I have had the good luck to count among my friends. I sometimes wonder at the futility of so-called progress when I think of him' (Warner 1958, p. xi).

Warner is one of the earliest of the social researchers in Indigenous Australia to publicly espouse a sentiment that combines admiration for an Aboriginal society, and especially for its High Culture manifestations, with self-doubting or even plainly critical comments about the author's own Western society. In the period from after the First World War to the 1950s, we see this strain of thinking appear in variable ways in the writings of Donald Thomson, Ursula McConnel, CP Mountford, and Olive Pink, perhaps among others. I doubt it would be easy to fully disentangle their kind of love affair with Aboriginal culture from their at times uneasy relationship with the world in which they had grown up. That two world wars and a Great Depression occurred in the first half of the twentieth century may have formed some of the background to the role of repulsion in creating the conditions of attraction towards the people and cultures studied by anthropologists and others in that era. Naturally, not all of these scholars were attracted to Indigenous societies for the same reasons.

The second edition of Warner's book, published over twenty years later than the first, contained a new section, 'Mahkarolla and Murngin Society'. This is another first, as far as I know, being the earliest even reasonably intimate written portrait of the life and character of an individual Aboriginal person. In it Warner assumes two voices, first that of the anthropologist reporting on other people, then he writes as if he were Makarrwala himself, and then he reverts to being himself as author.[4]

Warner tells us how his relationship with Makarrwala came about.

> When I arrived in the Murngin country the men who had been on board the sailing vessel with me quickly spread the news of my arrival among all the people. A number of the older men came to see me. Among them was a man who, I discovered, could speak a fair amount of English ... although he spoke English his thinking was native; and he considered himself, and was looked upon, as a person of consequence and authority among the people. (Warner 1958, p. 567)

Here, as in so many similar moments in the first fieldwork experiences of other researchers, it is clear that the local people regarded the forthcoming relationship as of such importance as to warrant involvement of elders, and the emergence of a person of consequence to act as the one who would mostly work with the newcomer. Makarrwala remained a man of consequence in the region till his death.

> Magarawala was not just any man. He was the Nurudawalangu, the headman of the whole area. In his time Magarawala had been treated as an equal by white scientists and educated men, and had been mentioned in books both learned and unlearned. His was a personality that could have met princes with courtesy and dignity and without servility, for though he could neither read nor write his knowledge of his people was far-reaching and his understanding of human nature was profound. (Wells 1963, p. 45)

The role of social broker and teacher of cultural knowledge to a long-term researcher has in many cases in the past been considered of real political significance within the community concerned, but there has also been recognition of the fact that ultimately there will be a duo of significance, not a many-to-one relationship, at the core of the researcher's links to the wider population or host community. In some cases, there has even been overt conflict between local people of prominence, who have competed either on their own behalves or on those of others, to control the role of so-called 'main informant' to a researcher. On one occasion I recall personally, spears were brought out. I am also reminded of the territorial contests and sensitivities carried on between some researchers, such as when Olive Pink and TGH Strehlow in the 1930s were both trying to secure the services of Mick Dow Dow in Central Australia, at about the time that Ursula McConnel was almost tiptoeing around groups with whom Donald Thomson had already established some research relationship in Cape York Peninsula (Marcus 2001, p. 71; McConnel 1926).

The researcher who was the object of competition had to be seen as, among other things, at least a potential source of something highly desired. What was desired, it seems to me, could be to do with a range of things, from prospects of rations or wages to prestige or even tapping into a new form of political 'go-betweening' with the wider polity — all of these have played roles at times. Yet another additional if not central factor, at least in the remoter frontier cases, was a desire for a 'boss'. Makarrwala addressed Warner as *bunggawa*, a Macassarese and Buginese word glossed as 'boss' and long absorbed into languages of northern Arnhem Land (Warner 1958, p. 588, and see Zorc 1986, p. 41; Urry & Walsh 1981; Walker & Zorc 1981). WEH Stanner similarly was addressed as *marluka* by his much admired and also considerably older collaborator Durmugam (Stanner 1979 (1959), p. 76).[5] Again, *marluka* was not a local word but one borne into the Daly River area on the tide of colonisation. When I worked in the Daly Waters area fifty years later some local people, including senior men a generation older than me, called me *marluka* also, again using an imported word for a kind of relationship that had some strong classical roots and a strong dose of innovation as well.

This experience had by then long become familiar from my years in Cape York Peninsula since 1970. The defining moment of reaching a significant degree of integration with the people one had come to learn from was typically being taken as a junior close kinsperson (mostly as a son of a man, in my own experience) by a prominent person. These people are now usually much more occupied with the political and bureaucratic conduct of Aboriginal affairs, and even formerly quiet remote settlements have in many cases entered the revolving door of consultations, inquiries, surveys and meetings, and so many communities have now experienced having a researcher in their midst. So it may be less likely that proposals to carry out long-term research projects with Indigenous people, mediated by these intensive partnerships, will in future be met with the same keenness of the past. What does have rising importance for many Indigenous people is the status of records created by such partnerships in the past. These play an increasing role in research carried out by Indigenous scholars on their own people.

When I began work in the Wik region of Cape York Peninsula in 1976, the senior Cape Keerweer people had more or less worked out who would play which roles in their planned outstation once it was firmly established. They would move out, but they overruled my plan to remain in the mission and visit them on bush trips, and so I and my family moved to Watha-nhiin. My main brother-in-law told me that his wife, whose father had taken me as a son, would be 'boss' of the outstation, one man would be in charge of the cattle, one in charge of fencing, another the carpentry, and another the church services. These were all clan brothers of his wife and me, of one country, language and Story. The occupations these men had learned, I was told, were part of a deliberate mission policy to engender a wide spread of different kinds of skills of the kind relevant to their time and place.

Anxious to see where I might belong, I asked, 'where do I fit in?' 'You [will] be our boss-help-us', he replied — saying it twice. They wanted me to stay, he added, 'forever' (11/8/1976, field book 20, pp. 64–5). For some time thereafter I resisted being called the boss, because I had failed to see how the people themselves understood the relationship. I was initially taken aback to be greeted each morning at Watha-nhiin outstation by all the senior men, usually in a bright mood at least at the start, who assembled before me to find out what 'we' were doing that day. I was, as a sound left-leaning baby boomer, in fact repeatedly embarrassed at having what I saw as this kind of Somerset Maugham rubber-plantation plot thrown upon me.

However, I needed to grasp hold of the fact that no ethnographic visitor was viewed as a 'boss' in the ordinary or cruder English senses. Although the term implies seniority, which can be a structural seniority that disregards actual age and knowledgeability, it has overtones more of nurturance than of coercion. In the literature on Aboriginal Australia much has been written about the relationship between authority and looking after others, and between autonomy and dependency. I was having to learn that my own naïve idea that I could unilaterally determine the nature of my relationships with Wik people was inevitably going to be a failure. Perhaps more so than most Aboriginal people I have known, Wik traditions have long placed considerable emphasis on bosses. But not all bosses are equal.

The anthropologist Jeff Collmann was told by some Aboriginal men in Central Australia in the 1970s that a good cattle station boss was one who looked after his workers and left them to do their work unsupervised. A bad boss was one who only paid the minimum wage and supervised the work at all times (Collmann 1988. p 144). Yet, as he once told me himself, the same term 'boss' was also applied to Collmann himself by the fringe-dwelling Aboriginal people with whom he worked in Alice Springs, thus suggesting another dimension existed for their range of meanings of 'boss' — or did it? If nurturance combined with the taking of some responsibility for collective affairs is the common factor, the anthropological 'boss' is not perhaps too far from the pastoral 'boss'. But this kind of nurturance usually has to envisage being responsive to requests as much as being open-handed or taking the initiative in providing for others. It is not a role one can take to oneself unilaterally so much as a requirement generated by the way Aboriginal societies in this country have, especially in the past, dealt with the opening up of what were formerly extremely localised perspectives to a new and largely independent and dominant other society.

The long-term researcher, more than any other kind of outsider, has played a critical role in destroying older false and damaging stereotypes about Indigenous people, and in providing the positive factual base on which significant degrees of recognition have been accorded to Indigenous cultural achievements and rights, especially land rights. Most motivations for integrating anthropologists, linguists and others into Indigenous social fields have probably been largely local ones. But the job of being ambassador, agent, personal patron, badge of group superiority, etc., worked also in relation to the 'other' world of power and economics that lay behind the individuals who were sent by it to carry out research. Relationships with the 'outside', as the wider world was still sometimes described during the 1970s at Aurukun, were typically mediated by elite pairs of individuals who felt they could trust each other. This can be read as people looking outward, but seeming to prefer to do so via a proxy on whom one could be somewhat dependent; that is, someone both dependable and supportive. The reciprocity of this conception becomes more apparent when considering the typical dependency of the researcher on the local person for their safety and wellbeing in field conditions, and on local knowledge alone for the main rationale of their being present at all.

These positive relationships with the researchers have at times been strangely at odds with relationships to other Europeans, most of whom have not been regarded as kin unless 'married in'. It is understandable that the researcher may be proud to belong, when so many other outsiders don't, won't or can't, in the same way. Yet this belonging, which can be a lot more than merely tolerated social integration, never removes the outsider origins of the person who has been taken in.

We are sometimes still reminded that the fight against racial stereotyping is for everyone, not just those who historically had the power to impose theirs on the conquered. Makarrwala, to return to Arnhem Land in the 1920s, told Warner that when he was a teenager the Macassans had told his people, at Elcho Island, that the White men were getting very dangerous and were going to bring the annual Macassan visits to an end. The White men were portrayed to the Arnhem Landers as being just like animals, big and hairy, and very fierce. They 'killed people just because they liked to kill', and always stole the women of people they visited. Makarrwala's old men believed the Macassans, he told Warner, and were afraid.

Later, though, Makarrwala came to the view that white men had 'fathers and mothers and wives just as much as black men', here stressing the cultural universal of kin relatedness as evidence of a common condition. Makarrwala then joined his brother in braving contact with a boat that carried a European man, an Aboriginal man, and some Malays. He even stayed behind to work as a cabin boy for its Malay crew. On being reunited with his people, they were enraged and wanted to kill this European boat person. According to Makarrwala's account reported by Warner, 'I said no, that it was no good. The white men talk very hard and sometimes they swear at you, but inside they are all right. Sometimes when they swear, they mean good' (Warner 1958, pp. 573–8).

Here we see the so-called illiterate informant, coming from a tradition in which out-group enmities could be vigorously naturalised, rather than the anthropologist from a liberal-democratic political tradition, advancing himself as a destroyer of negative racial stereotypes. But unlike several anthropologists of the same era, Makarrwala seems to have been rather more generous in looking past the stereotype of the European as a foul-mouthed frontier oaf, the kind of colonial bumpkin figure who received such a bad press from Stanner, Thomson, Mountford and others of high aesthetic sensibility who found themselves living among the farthest outposts of poor Whites during the Great Depression. Some shared even a certain vocabulary for their revulsion, words like 'foul' and 'oaf' being typical. It is not surprising that the refinement of manners, dignity and grace of their Aboriginal hosts made them stand out as attractive people on a rough frontier.

But in the ordinary sense of the word we would not say that the couples I discuss here have also been lovers. Nevertheless, some of their relationships have been of such intensity as to bring out at least expressions of platonic love, as when Lloyd Warner told us that his friendship with Makarrwala was as strong and enduring as any he had experienced with his own people. Close to the end of his life Warner considered he knew Makarrwala as well as he had known anyone, and hoped the last section of the 1958 memoir would express Warner's 'love, respect, and admiration for him' (Warner 1958, p. 566).[6] It is the openness of the account, not its glowing terms, that marks it as modern.

That Makarrwala also felt deeply and strongly about their relationship is suggested by his tears of fear for Warner's safety during a dangerous sea journey by canoe, and the fact that he was also crying during his final parting from Warner on Darwin pier in 1929. Unlike many more recent pairs of this kind, who have been able to maintain lifetime contact, the two never saw each other again (Warner 1958, pp. 588–9).

Billy Mammus and Ursula McConnel (1920s and 1930s)

Bambegan,[7] known in English as Billy Mammus, was in 1927 the most senior man of the Bonefish clan whose country is in the Small Archer River area of western Cape York Peninsula, part of the area now known as Wik country.[8] People of this group played an important role in relations with the new authority structures of church and state from at least the 1920s to the recent present. These included Billy's brother Arthur Pambegan Sr, the latter's daughter Geraldine, and Athur's son Arthur Pambegan Jr. It was their language, Wik-Mungkan, that McConnel studied most thoroughly, and which evolved into the mission lingua franca. It was primarily through the personal link forged between Billy Mammus and Ursula McConnel that the idea of Wik-Mungkan as a people — misleading as it is — became reified in the global anthropological literature.

After Ursula McConnel arrived at Aurukun in 1927 she camped a while with people who were mainly from north of Aurukun (McConnel to Radcliffe-Brown 12/5/27, Aurukun; Elkin Papers, University of Sydney Archives). She wanted to work with bush people outside the mission, both to reduce the effects of culture contact and, it seems clear, to get away from her nemesis, the mission superintendent William MacKenzie. She was warned off travelling up the Archer because an 'outlaw', said to have been a rapist who had murdered his wife and supposedly eaten his mother, was at large in the area. Her plan was to go south and work with people whose language was Wik-Ngatharr, but no one, as she put it, 'seemed free' to go with her. The fact that the wider area was in a state of tension and conflict may have been responsible. She told her supervisor: 'There have been a lot of rows here, very serious & several districts are impossible to go into in which certain outlaws are hiding from the police' (McConnel to Radcliffe-Brown 12/5/27).

> My first step was to try and find a reliable man who could use my gun, would act as interpreter, and take care of me generally, and whose wife could look after me personally.
>
> It was whilst watching [a mission corroboree] that my problem was happily solved for me. I found a woman with a shy but winning smile sitting beside me, determined to make friends. (McConnel (1928d)

The woman who was so determined, and in that sense took the first step, was Jinny, one of two wives of Billy Mammus. The three of them made their first hunting trip together the next morning. Writing to Radcliffe-Brown she said:

> I began to pick up new threads at the mission & found Billy (& Jinny) who not being a mission working man is free to come about with me. Also he was intelligent & ready to help. He therefore drew me inevitably into the Wik munkän group & I got onto the kinship system & language with him. (McConnel to Radcliffe-Brown 12/5/27)

Billy had worked on Thursday Island and elsewhere, and was therefore conversant with the "white man's" ways.

> He had refused to go to school as a small boy, preferring to remain an unlettered bushman. He retained an interest in his native lore, which, coupled with a certain aloofness from it, made him a valuable go-between and interpreter (McConnel 1928d).

Here once again we encounter a familiar combination of qualities: local political eminence; an ability to move at some level between the two cultures and act as an interpreter, and an interest in his own traditions. The 'aloofness' McConnel describes may be an attempt to convey his capacity for objectifying his own cultural practices, for which there is evidence elsewhere.

Billy Mammus was probably also something of a risk-taker. His mission card read in part: 'Gentleman with a hectic past by all accounts. Now a very dependable person. Guide to Miss McConnel, ethnologist, April to Nov. 1927. Has been known to spear a bullock.'[9] There is probably a certain amount of code here. Being 'known to spear a bullock' in those days could bring the attention of the police and years of exile to far-distant Palm Island. Earlier it could have been far worse. A 'hectic past' probably refers to spear fighting.

In June 1927 McConnel wrote to her supervisor, AR Radcliffe-Brown:

> I have been out camping for 3 weeks with Billy Mammus, his two wives & son [and a number of other relations]. These people were mostly from the bush, just come in to see the family… (McConnel to Radcliffe-Brown 10/6/27)

Billy took her to see what she called 'his bonefish spot', the main totemic centre of his estate, after which she said 'I think I will stick to Billy for a while & try to get up to the Archer River (McConnel to Radcliffe-Brown 10/6/27). Stick to him she did, and he and his family were her close companions for months. Discovering Billy had a second wife Rosie, McConnel said she 'set about making her acquaintance, and found her a stalwart ally'. She wrote, 'To these three friends I owe any success I may have achieved whilst working among the bush people' (McConnel 1928d.

This statement may sound extravagant, but Billy Mammus himself, with or without his wives, dominates McConnel's references to individual Aboriginal people both in her published and unpublished material (see e.g. McConnel 1930, p. 193; 1936, p. 472; 1957, pp. 39–43, 48–9, 74, 119–24). His is one of the few Wik genealogies recorded by McConnel that remains available. It is the only one to survive in manuscript form, copied into a letter to Radcliffe-Brown (McConnel to Radcliffe-Brown 12/5/27).[10] Tragically most of her field notes appear lost. [Since the lecture, her papers have been discovered, but only one field notebook was in the tin trunk.] She also published his photograph in one of her first publications, although without providing his name (McConnel 1930, plate V(A)).

The apparent reason why Billy did not accompany her on her ground-breaking packhorse trip to Kendall River in 1928 was that he was either unable or unwilling, more likely unwilling in my view, to join her. It was, after all, well to the south of Billy's country, on the coast, and even though he had a grandmother from the area he may have had good reason to want to avoid it.

McConnel's focus was not entirely on Billy Mammus or indeed on men generally, but she was shown aspects of ceremonies normally privy to men only, and collected sacred sculptures which were highly restricted to men at the time. Of Billy's wives Jinny and Rosie, McConnel said early in her field experience that she was 'trying to get at Jinny's & Rosie's minds — & thru' theirs to the other womens'. But McConnel, unlike her near contemporary Phyllis Kaberry, was not aiming specifically at a study focused on women. Her pursuit of gender equality as an anthropologist was not framed in terms of concentrating her work on women, but in terms of tackling most of the same topics normally covered by the men who dominated the professional scene of her day. These were principally social and local organisation, and religion. Less conventionally, she also took a considerable interest in the interpretation of dreams.

I would not go so far as to say this was a case of today's progressivism being tomorrow's lost opportunity, because the evidence is not clear that McConnel was actually a progressive in regard to gender roles generally.[11] Anne O'Gorman even noted that, '[l]ike Olive Pink, [McConnel] had a tendency to elevate men' (O'Gorman 1993, p. 94). Pink's biographer Julie Marcus did say that Pink wanted equality with men: she 'wanted to study precisely what the men studied and did not want to be caught up in work which everyone else thought was of minor significance'. Unlike McConnel, Marcus tells us that Pink saw women's lives as trivial compared with the men's, on top of which 'she liked very few women at all, whether Aboriginal or European' (Marcus 2001, pp. 77–8, 115). Pink said the men with whom she worked in Central Australia 'treated me as sexless as far as their secret life is concerned (or like "an old man")' (Marcus 2001, p. 203). This neutralisation is akin to what happens partially, at least, when Aboriginal women and men become so senior in 'the Law' that gender recedes as a factor in determining who may know what. Relevantly, perhaps, in the Wik languages it has been customary to refer to Europeans of any age, including infants, by the local words for 'old woman' and 'old man'.

McConnel seemed somewhat surprised that at the second stage male initiations of the area, which were 'very much more prolonged, secretive & drastic' than the first stage, 'nothing really takes place which the women might not see, with one exception as far as I could fathom from Mr MacKenzie [the Superintendent]' (McConnel to Radcliffe-Brown 1/7/27 Aurukun; Elkin Papers, University of Sydney Archives). According to McConnel Billy Mammus once asked her: '"What about this flour, Mum, *torri* (totem) bin make him?"[12] & then he told me that yams were plentiful at Yonke [Cape Keerweer] because there was a yam *torri* there = "*torri* bin make'im".'[13] Actually Billy addressed Ursula not only as 'Mum' but also as 'Sir', and 'sometimes with a non-committal and puzzled air, as "Mum-Sir"'. McConnel tells us this after observing that 'Billy was amused at the idea of a woman boss' (McConnel 1928d).

Billy Mammus died in April 1937 (Aurukun Mission card for Billy Mammus).

Durmugam (Smiler) and WEH Stanner (1930s–1950s)

WEH Stanner acknowledged long-term relationships with a number of Aboriginal people, including Pandak of what was then Port Keats, whom he described as 'close friend' for over forty years between the 1930s and 1970s (Stanner 1979 (1959), p. 26). The relationship of which he has left us the most detailed published record, however, and one that is justly famous, is that between himself and Durmugam, or Smiler as he was also known.

In 1932 at Daly River, after seeing Durmugam perform superbly as a combatant in a major spear-fight involving more than a hundred men and over a hundred onlookers, Stanner was 'much taken with him' on meeting him personally. He was also immediately invited by Durmugam to make his camp near his own, at the Daly River crossing. Once again the forces at play in the two being drawn together were in some ways shared, but it was probably Durmugam who in a sense claimed Stanner first. This impression is compounded when we learn that, at a circumcision ceremony some time later, Stanner was joined by Durmugam who sat with him.

> I soon began to feel that we could become friends. I could not fault his manner and found him to be quick to see the drift of questions. When he pointed out some of the ceremony's features which I had missed, I began to see him as a new main informant, always one of the most exciting moments of fieldwork. (Stanner 1979 (1959), p. 71)

The two men were to work together intensively in 1935, and also spent time together in 1952, 1954 and 1958, the year before Durmugam passed away. As is usually the case, we have only the researcher's record of the relationship, so that when the author said that he did not believe Durmugam 'ever formed a deep attachment to any European, myself included', (Stanner 1979 (1959), p. 98) we have to remind ourselves that this comes from only half, though perhaps more than half, of an ideally dual picture of the relationship. We also need to recall that from around the age of thirty Durmugam met an 'energetic, vital European, who gave him work at a variety of jobs ... At the end of the [1920s] this man went to the Daly River to try his fortune as a farmer. Durmugam joined forces with him and, apart from a few interruptions, remained in permanent association with him' (Stanner 1979 (1959), pp. 82–3).

Stanner's account of Durmugam has elements we see elsewhere in records of such relationships, though probably none of these is present in each account: at the outset Durmugam chose Stanner as his anthropologist more than Stanner chose him as 'main informant'; Durmugam showed enormous solicitude, courtesy, loyalty and generosity towards Stanner, shepherding him through the bush, breaking off or holding back foliage that might impede Stanner, even plunging into crocodile-infested waters to retrieve wildfowl; Durmugam took Stanner as a 'boss' (*marluka*); Durmugam had great mental stamina and had a gift for explaining things by the use of visual demonstrations; he had a constant temper, and was prudent and judicious about making observations.

Perhaps above all, Stanner praises Durmugam for his truthfulness. That is not to say anything about the truth in an objectified sense, but merely to address the extent to which Stanner felt confident that Durmugam was being straight with him. This is a difficult subject to discuss when the focus is on the meeting of two so profoundly foreign approaches to the problem of knowledge, with their odd mixture of commonalities — such as the appeal to empirical observation as evidence for propositions, and a basically identical approach to deductive logic — alongside some deep differences such as the role of publication and secrecy, the acceptability of questioning, and the nexus between religious power and the privilege of being right. Like all field workers Stanner wanted knowledge, and like all who have proceeded broadly within the Western scientific tradition he needed to feel that the person mainly giving him so much instruction was 'reliable'.

In the essay, Stanner actually draws two contrasting portraits, one of the truthful Durmugam, the other of another man called Tjimari or Wagin (probably 'wagon').[14] Of Durmugam he said: 'I never proved that he misled me, and found him correct on innumerable occasions. He had a feeling for the truth, whereas Tjimari had none. Durmugam would be very open if he made mistakes and offer the correction candidly (1979 (1959), p. 90).

The two men 'made an interesting comparison', part of which included the following:

> Tjimari was at least Durmugam's equal with fighting weapons, though only half his size ... I found [Tjimari] to be a fascinating mixture — a liar, a thief, an inveterate trickster, a tireless intriguer, an artist of high ability, and a man of much if inaccurate knowledge ... I thought him an arch-manipulator, with wit and charm but no principles, and ready for any villainy that paid. (1979 (1959), pp. 72, 74)

Stanner was clearly not interested in homogenising or idealising personality along lines marked out by race or culture. He was critical of Roland Robinson for, while greatly admiring Tjimari's 'intelligence, knowledge, and imaginative gifts', at the same time taking 'a somewhat sentimental view of other aspects of his character' (1979 (1959), pp. 72, 74). Stanner also took what in more recent times, at least, would be regarded as considerable political risks by pursuing his own truthfulness and capacity for self-questioning. Even where the language of these passages remains crafted with poise, they can also be quite raw. What is remarkable is the broadly high esteem in which Stanner has continued to be held, and rightly so, in spite of his often brutal honesty, over the decades.

But truthfulness is not necessarily a good uniter of people. Fictions, or mere simplicitudes, so often better bind us — at least for a time. The end of political consensus on Australian Indigenous policy, which has been taking place over the last several years, has been a casualty less of the standard Left-Right tensions of 'race politics' than of a battle to get vested interests to acknowledge and deal squarely with the various profound failures of policy and practice rather than to re-emphasise alleged solutions that will magically materialise after further changes in stratospheric rights. Even people who support a treaty, formal reconciliation and reparations, for example, can no longer be counted on to believe the myth that these things will put food in the bellies of toddlers in the bush. Some of them, who might be identified as the southern urban soft Left, have now become targets of criticism and rejection even by those for whom they have long formed a key supportive audience (Langton 2002; Manne 2002).

There is a sense around that the old political alignments have been thrown up in the air. No one yet knows where the pieces will fall. Are we in an interregnum between illusions? I hope not. My feeling is that the current wave of unusual honesty and self-examination in Indigenous affairs needs to proceed a while longer before the future becomes any clearer.

What anthropologist of the last three decades has written so freely and openly, as Stanner did in this single memoir dedicated to an admired friend, of things such as the details of Durmugam's 'record of blood' — his admitted killings of four other men in the region. While all could be interpreted as being in accordance with customary law, in one case Stanner did comment: 'If [his] duty coincided too neatly with his personal interest, the same might be said of many honoured men in history' (Stanner 1979 (1959), p. 88). The absence of moral judgement here by Stanner is, I think, genuine.

Stanner also wrote in this essay of the 'endless, bloody fights between the river and the back-country tribes, and numbers of drink-sodden Aborigines lying out in the rain' (Stanner 1979 (1959), p. 82) recalled from Durmugam's youth. He described the eagerness of local women for associations with Europeans and Chinese men in the 1930s, their own men 'often push[ing] them to such service'. He put forward his view that what was left of the religious tradition of the area 'amounted to a Low Culture', as opposed to the High Culture then still extant in some other regions (Stanner 1979 (1959), pp. 83–84). He said that the people's economic condition 'bound them to parasitism on a settlement where the farmers themselves barely had enough to eat' (Stanner 1979 (1959), p. 85). He reported that 'what the women thought' about Sunday Business 'did not matter' from the men's point of view (Stanner 1979 (1959), p. 85). And so on. All this in the midst of a passionate admiration not only for Aboriginal High Culture and for the society's high elaboration of social rules, forms and norms (Stanner 1979 (1959), pp. 83–84, 101), but also in the midst of a celebration of Durmugam's apparently resolved, mature and vigorous reflection of traditional Daly River ideas about what it was to be a fully initiated and accomplished man. The fire in his belly was not characterised as a 'social problem', but as a dimension of his manliness (Stanner 1979 (1959), p. 101).

One of the things Stanner most seems to have liked about Durmugam was his rock-like commitment to his own people's view of the world. He had a self-contained dignity in the midst of the lower Daly peanut croppers of the time who were consistently portrayed by Stanner as a kind of bad-joke version of Saltbush Bill.[15] Durmugam had, he tells us, 'found a way of living with duality, an oafish Europeanism and an Aboriginal idealism' (Stanner 1979 (1959), p. 101), not by allowing the fact that in some sense both occupied a common space, or dwelt in an intersection of social fields or domains, but because psychologically he was able to dissociate the two realms. While he preferred one, he could live with two (Stanner 1979 (1959), pp. 101–2). Durmugam switched between these two incommensurate worlds rather than attempting any integration of them.[16] Stanner's portrait here, as at many points, is decidedly modern, with its searching of individual personality and character.

I wonder if the decline of such sharp dualisms of individual thinking, resting on a decline in the necessity to alternate between one clearly marked domain and the other, which in turn has been attendant on advancing cultural convergence and social integration over much of Australia, has itself influenced social models which may now seek to account for inter-ethnic relations in terms of a single shared domain.

John von Sturmer has recently written to me:

> I'm working towards a point – which I suspect you yourself are considering: namely, that such relationships do develop in particular contexts, that they are counter-relationships to what is otherwise on offer (seen clearest here in relation to McConnel and the mission regime), and that, far from supported, they may be seen as actively threatening. What is crucial to these relationships is that they create their own order — in which blackness/ [versus] whiteness and the rest of the categorical baggage simply go out the window. It is this possibility which is so fiercely resisted by people on both sides of the black/white divide — which they so busily re-create and insist on in order to maintain the sorts of interests which arise only in [those] circumstances in which the divide may be maintained. (pers comm.)

Conclusion

Why my title, 'Unusual Couples'? I meant it in two ways. Yes, it has been historically unusual for two people to commit themselves in such a demanding way to the creation of knowledge and understanding across what has often been a vast cultural divide, and over such long periods. There have been other such pairs than those created by research, but it is those associated with research and publication that arguably have had the widest impact on the rest of us.

Not only have these relationships been rather unusual in Australia's history, they have also had few consistent parallels anywhere outside the geographic spread of European colonialism, or in any earlier time than the nineteenth century. As a model of how to 'grow up' an ignorant newcomer to one's place, and of how to be 'grown up' as an anthropologist, linguist or other researcher whose job is to, in turn, educate a wider audience, the 'unusual couple' in the mode I have discussed here should not be assumed to be a permanent fixture. Its short and interesting past, however, has arguably underpinned many milestones in the overcoming of ignorance and prejudice. These milestones tend to be written works, widely available in a largely open globally spread society, one that has many secrets but also a cultural commitment to freedom of information, one whose people would, if they thought about it, probably see things like medical, technological, political and economic advances as dependent on the free circulation of publicly testable knowledge.

For members of a relatively closed society restrictions on knowledge may not lead to impoverishment but to the reverse, a retaining of things of highest value, a guarding of the sacred. After much thought I remain puzzled as to the generosity with which Aboriginal people have told so much, revealed so much, to anthropologists and others in the past, not only to make an urgent record of almost forgotten traditions, but even in cases where the religious systems have remained vigorous.

The ease with which female scholars have been made privy to the male secret religious life, at least in the past, remains a related puzzle. In some areas there are signs that the welcome mat for visiting scholars has been worn thin by regrettable experiences, and it has become generally unacceptable for researchers of one gender to seek out restricted knowledge belonging to the other. The days of female anthropologists being treated as honorary males may be over, although we now have a recent inversion of this: Aboriginal women being prepared to reveal secret business to male judges during land claim hearings, under appropriate restrictions.

The final puzzle I will mention here is that of our ability to connect across what in many cases seems a deep gulf, a gulf not just of manners and grammars but of understandings about what it means to be a person, a friend, a stranger, a relative, a 'boss', an 'informant', and so on. 'Friends', 'kin', 'colleagues' – why are all these one-off tags for these particular kinds of relationships so inadequate, masking as they do the complexity of the phenomena? Relationships may be emotionally or intellectually close or distant in quite different ways, depending on which of the pair of people one is thinking of. The visiting researcher has generally arrived 'in the field' with the baggage of a modern Western conception of an emotionally positive, voluntary relationship of an already known kind, namely friendship. It is one that has parallels but no precise equivalent in classical Aboriginal thinking. Nor has the cultural relativism that has so often informed the mood of openness and acceptance among researchers any classical Indigenous parallel.

Warner, McConnel, Thomson and Pink were among the strongest advocates of cultural relativism in the inter-war years, a point on which the last three, at least, clashed with mission authorities. But relativism's embracing of difference does not necessarily extend to conversion. Aboriginal people have often tested me by asking if I believed what they had told me about the creation of the landscape or about sorcery accusations, for example, or have asked if I too had seen a spirit-image of a recently deceased person during the ceremony for sending it home to its country. Like a church-going non-believer, I have given 'when in Rome' kinds of answers, and answers based on fellow feeling rather than unity of cosmology. This testing, I suspect, must almost always lead to disappointment. It reveals one of the irreducible differences between the people in the relationships I discuss here. McConnel may have been 'tested' on her visit to the Bonefish Story Place on Small Archer River in 1927: 'As we passed by in a canoe I was asked if I had heard the heart of the bone-fish beating' (1930, p. 193). She did not tell us what her answer was.

But both kinship and friendship can survive cultural difference. Thirty years ago when carrying out linguistic survey work in far north Queensland, and many times later, I was struck by the translations people offered for the English word 'friend'. The literal meanings of the answers ranged from cross-cousin, to lover (often in the sense of *bandji*),[17] to fellow initiation novice, to a term for 'company' (as in keeping a visitor company by sleeping at the same fire) – there were probably others — but the common factor was generally that no one-to-one equivalence was there. I am aware that in some languages there may be closer equivalents.[18] But one dimension of the asymmetry in the way these relationships were conceived of by the two parties is a cleavage between understandings of closeness. In particular, the scholars have tended to report their experiences in terms of a European tradition of 'friendship' without telling us much about how their opposite number experienced the encounter with the other party.

Typically, a relation of fictive or adoptive kinship is established between the two people, because of an Aboriginal initiative to do so. Not just any kind of relationship will do. People have generally structured the relationship in only a few of all possible ways. At the point of incorporation, the researcher is typically made a son, a daughter or a sibling of the person first 'claiming' them as kin.[19] There are other kinds of genealogical links established, and there are cases where no kin incorporation takes place, or a person is assigned a kin status on the basis of their relationship to another person, even to another non-Indigenous person.

Kin incorporation can be of prime importance in granting members of the host community knowledge of how to behave towards the new kinsperson, given that familiarity, restraint, food-giving, joking and swearing, for example, are widely subject to customary rules about how to behave with which particular kin. More importantly, perhaps, kin incorporation renders the researcher socially real, or at least socially present, in a way otherwise not very attainable, where people have maintained a system of classificatory kinship. Just as 'friendship' naturalises the newcomer's experience of their hosts, 'kinship' does something similar for the hosts' capacity to treat the researcher in a positive and realistic way. Both kinds of relationship impose their own forms of mutual demand. But their demands overlap, rather than coincide. For this reason, when one party experiences the relationship primarily in terms of 'friendship' and the other primarily in terms of 'kinship', each is likely to notice that the other sometimes fails to meet expectations.

One also has to consider the possibility that one or both halves of the equation experiences the other person through a mixture of knowledge and illusion, insight and fantasy. Of itself this would hardly be exceptional in the field of human relationships. But where deep cultural differences are involved, it can be a tribute to the humanity of both parties that their efforts to connect can actually work, and so often have worked, to contribute to the rich fabric of understanding and appreciation of Australia's cultures that we enjoy today.

Notes

1   In early life he was known as We-pohng, and probably assumed the name Biraban upon going through the higher male initiation ceremonies (Gunson 1974, p. 317).
2   Biraban was also chief guide to at least one exploration party. Biraban's name has been conferred on a Canberra street, in the suburb of Aranda.
3   Warner spelled the name Mahkarolla. For name respelling in current orthography, see Zorc (1986, p. 167); for dates, see Warner (1958, pp. 566–7).
4   Here he all too unsettlingly reminds us of those many books written by non-Indigenous authors and which employ pronouns of the 'first person Aboriginal' kind in their titles: *I, the Aboriginal* and *We, the Aborigines* by D Lockwood; *Your Land is our land* by K Maddock; *But now we want the land back: a history of the Australian Aboriginal people* by H Middleton; *Our Place, Our Music* by M Brunton & M Breen; *That's my country belonging to me* by ID Clark; *Ngurra walytja: Country of my spirit* by J Downing & M Smith; *Dingo makes us human: life and land in an Australian Aboriginal culture* by DB Rose; and there are many more.
5   Durmugam was about ten years older than Stanner (Stanner 1979 (1959), pp. vi, 81), and Makarrwala about seventeen years older than Warner (Warner 1958, pp. xi, 567; Barnard & Spencer 1996, p. 592).
6   In rather different vein and lighter mood, Marie Reay in 1970 published a rare account of the passionate infatuation of a Borroloola woman for herself in 1959–60. One gets the impression that Reay was glad to escape her attentions at the end of her fieldwork (1970, pp. 169–70, 172).
7   Also spelled Bambeigan by McConnel, which I would render *Pam-piikenh*: *Pam* = man, *piikenh* = hits, beats.
8   'I am indebted to Bambeigan, the leading man of the Bonefish clan for the myth and ritual of the bonefish and the *moiya* and *pakapaka* [bullroarer] totems which belong to his clan' (McConnel 1935, p. 68).

9   Mission card for Billy Mammus, which appears to have been filled in during January 1929. This part of the card also noted: 'Hookworm [treatments given]: 22/6/29, 13/8/29, 4/11/29, 18/8/30, 20/10/32. Blankets: 18/6/27, 2.'
10 The relevant letter page was reproduced in O'Gorman 1993, p. 97.
11 Like several of her anthropological contemporaries she enjoyed her upper-class connections.
12 *Torri* is the English word 'story', which is the common Cape York Peninsula translation for what are more widely known as Dreamings, totems or Ancestral Beings.
13 I comment here only on the fact that Billy called Ursula 'mum', although much could be said also about Billy's question, which suggests the kind of inquiry into European culture that every now and then belies the often repeated generalisation that Aboriginal people of remote places have shown little interest in the workings, as opposed to the products, of the West.
14 Tjimari was the first Aboriginal person Stanner met (1979 (1959), p. 72).
15 Contrast this with the 'European of sensibility' who knew Durmugam in his later life and who remarked on his 'dignity, patience, courtesy to Europeans and readiness to meet any requests for help' (Stanner 1979 (1959), p. 102).
16 Of John Mathew's Kabi Kabi informant Kagariu (Johnny Campbell, 1846–1880), Mathew's biographer has written: 'Mathew was clearly fascinated by Campbell. He did not fit an Aboriginal stereotype. After all, Mathew did not come to anthropology via the study of 'scientific specimens', but through the accidents of personal acquaintance. It is easy enough to see Johnny Campbell as an incomprehensible victim. It is also easy to paint him as a black Robin Hood. He was typical and not typical, a black man who welcomed much of the white world without leaving his kin, traditional life and skills behind. He was in, not between two cultures, impatient with one, unhappy in the other ... He had personal demons, not just racial ones. His relationships with women were generally short and unstable. He lost his father as an infant. There was no general crusade against all Europeans: he was used well by some whites and badly by others, and reacted accordingly. He was a bushranger like other bushrangers, but his use of bushcraft and kinship links to remain at large were also Aboriginal. He was an individualist, though one who used kinship when he needed to' (Prentis 1998, pp. 66–7).
17 Sometimes regarded as an Indigenous word, *bandji* is in my opinion short for *bandjiman*, a formerly more common version, which is an Aboriginal pronunciation of the English term 'fancy-man' or male lover, a man who fancies, and, one presumes, is fancied.
18 It is likely, as one would expect on various grounds, that the higher the negotiability of genealogical distance in an Aboriginal subculture, the higher the salience of 'friendships' would be. I am thinking here of the Western Desert, where relationships described as *marlpa*, usually translated as 'company', 'companion', 'friend', 'similar species', 'mates', 'boyfriend/girlfriend' etc., seem to play a stronger role than similar kinds of relationships in north Australia in the places with which I have some familiarity. See, for example, *malpa* or *marlpa* in Goddard (1996, p. 67), Valiquette (1993, p. 77), Marsh (1992, p. 171; it can refer to a weapon as well as a human being), and *yamatji* (Douglas 1988, p. 113).
19 McConnel's status as 'mother' for Billy Mammus may have been derived from an earlier incorporation as kin to someone else. It is worth noting, however, that the mission superintendent and his wife were 'father' and 'mother' to everybody at Aurukun and McConnel's role may have been identified to an extent with that of Geraldine MacKenzie (wife of the superintendent).

References

Berndt, RM & Berndt, CH 1970, *Man, land and myth in North Australia: The Gunwinggu people*, Ure Smith, Sydney.

Brunton, M, & Breen, M 1989, *Our Place, Our Music*, Aboriginal Studies Press, Canberra.

Clark, ID 1998, *That's my country belonging to me: Aboriginal land tenure and dispossession in nineteenth century Western Victoria*, Heritage Matters, Melbourne.

Collmann, J 1988, *Fringe-dwellers and welfare: The Aboriginal response to bureaucracy*, University of Queensland Press, Brisbane.

Douglas, WH 1988, *An introductory dictionary of the Western Desert language*, Institute of Applied Language Studies, Western Australian College of Advanced Education, Perth.

Downing, J & Smith, M 1988, *Ngurra walytja: Country of my spirit*, Australian National University, North Australia Research Unit, Darwin.

Goddard, C 1996, *Pitjantjatjara/Yankunytjatjara to English Dictionary*. Alice Springs: IAD Press.

Gunson, N (ed.) 1974, *Australian reminiscences and papers of LE Threlkeld, missionary to the Aborigines, 1824–1859*, 2 vols, Australian Institute of Aboriginal Studies, Canberra.

Harris, JW 1994, *One blood: 200 years of Aboriginal encounter with Christianity: A story of hope*, Albatross Books, Sydney.

Langton, M 2002, 'Senses of place', *Overland*, vol. 166, pp. 75–87.

Lockward, D 1962, *I, the Aboriginal*, Rigby, Adelaide.

—— 1963, *We, the Aborigines*, Cassell, Melbourne.

Maddock, K 1983, *Your land is our land*, Penguin, Ringwood.

Manne, R 2002, '*Mabo*: a moral crisis festers', *The Age*, 27 May, viewed 24 May 2014 at <http://www.theage.com.au/articles/2002/05/26/1022243289534.html>.

Marcus, Julie 2001, *The indomitable Miss Pink: A life in anthropology*, UNSW Press, Sydney.

Marsh, J 1992, *Martu Wangka–English dictionary*. Summer Institute of Linguistics, Darwin.

McConnel, UH 1926, McConnel to Radcliffe-Brown, Coen, 3 July 1928; Elkin Papers, University of Sydney Archives.

—— 1928a, '"Belong Archer": Where black man still holds sway. Woman's amazing trip, penetrates, alone, to heart of York Peninsula', *The Sun* [Sydney], 2 May.

—— 1928b, 'Among blacks: Woman's adventures in Gulf, sea-snakes and sharks, Thursday Is to Archer River', *The Sun* [Sydney], 3 May.

—— 1928c, 'Gulf nights: Woman's adventures among blacks', *The Sun* [Sydney], 4 May.

—— 1928d, 'Black magic" Native hunting grounds of north, mysteries of cook-pot. Australian girl befriended by wild tribes', *The Sun* [Sydney], 5 May.

—— 1928e, 'Wikmunkans: White woman among Gulf blacks. "Goannas" as food', *The Sun* [Sydney], 7 May.

—— 1928f, 'Mystic rites. Ceremonial among Gulf blacks: "Modern" influences. Australian woman's unique experiences', *The Sun* [Sydney], 8 May.

—— 1928g, '"Plenty alligator"! Braving infested Gulf rivers. Black man's law. Australian woman faces many perils', *The Sun* [Sydney], 9 May.

—— 1928h, '"Big snake"! Sacred home of spirits, Aborigines' belief. Woman penetrates secret', *The Sun* [Sydney], 11 May.

—— 1928i, 'Totem mysteries: White woman among Gulf blacks. Crocodile egg diet. Hundred mile trip up Archer River', *The Sun* [Sydney], 12 May.

—— 1930, 'Wik-munkan tribe of Cape York Peninsula,' *Oceania*, vol. 1, nos 1–2, np.

—— 1936, 'Illustration of the myth of Shiveri and Nyunggu', *Oceania*, vol. 7, no. 2, np.

—— 1957, *Myths of the Mungkan*, Melbourne University Press, Melbourne.

Middleton, H 1977, *But now we want the land back: A history of the Australian Aboriginal people*, New Age, Sydney.

O'Gorman, A 1993, 'The snake, the serpent and the rainbow: Ursula McConnel and Aboriginal Australians', in J Marcus (ed.), *First in their field: Women and Australian anthropology*, Melbourne University Press, Melbourne, pp. 84–109, 169–70.

Prentis, MD 1998, *Science, race and faith: A life of John Mathew, 1849–1929*, Centre for the Study of Australian Christianity, Sydney.

Reay, M 1970, 'A decision as narrative,' in RM Berndt (ed.), *Australian Aboriginal anthropology*, Australian Institute of Aboriginal Studies, University of Western Australia Press, Perth, pp. 164–73.

Rose, DB 1992, *Dingo makes us human: Life and land in an Australian Aboriginal culture*, Cambridge University Press, Melbourne.

Stanner, WEH 1979 (1959), 'Durmugam: A Nangiomeri', in *White man got no Dreaming: Essays 1938–1973*, ANU Press, Canberra, pp. 67–105.

Threlkeld, LE 1892, *An Australian language as spoken by the Awabakal, the people of Awaka or Lake Macquarie (near Newcastle, New South Wales): Being an account of their language, traditions, and customs*, re-arranged, condensed and edited, with an appendix by John Fraser, Charles Potter Government Printer, Sydney.

Urry, J & Walsh, M 1981, 'The lost "Macassar language" of Northern Australia', *Aboriginal History*, vol. 5, pp. 90–108.

Valiquette, H 1993, *A Basic Kukatja to English Dictionary*, Balgo, WA: Luumpa Catholic School.

Walker, A & Zorc, D 1981, 'Austronesian loanwords in Yolngu-Matha of Northeast Arnhem Land', *Aboriginal History*, vol. 5, pp. 109–34.

Warner, WL 1958, *A black civilization: A study of an Australian tribe*, Harper & Brothers, Chicago.

Wells, AE 1963, *Milingimbi: Ten years in the Crocodile Islands of Arnhem Land*, Angus & Robertson, Sydney.

Zorc, RD 1986, *Yolngu-Matha dictionary*, School of Australian Linguistics, Charles Darwin University, Darwin.

Original lecture available at:
<http://aiatsis.gov.au/publications/presentations/unusual-couples-relationships-and-research-knowledge-frontier>

13

Indigenous Australian Studies and higher education
2004 Wentworth Lecture

Martin Nakata

In 1959, Mr Bill Wentworth presented his original proposal for a national Institute of Aboriginal Studies (Wentworth 1959). He was motivated, in part, by a concern that anthropology departments in Australian universities were not doing enough to document Aboriginal societies that were undergoing rapid transformation (Peterson 1990). Forty-five years later, Indigenous Studies, the current inclusive, though somewhat contentious, term that encapsulates Aboriginal Studies and/or Torres Strait Islander Studies, and more recently also includes comparisons from the international indigenous context, is a discrete and much expanded field of academic study and inquiry in universities across this nation.

It would seem timely to examine where we are currently at with 'Indigenous Studies' in Australian universities, with a view to considering future directions. It is not my intention today to present an audit of Indigenous Studies, or discuss its structural organisation within universities, or offer an historical assessment or critique. Rather, I talk about the way we, the Indigenous academic community, approach Indigenous Studies as scholarly and intellectual activity. My aim is to stimulate some thinking within the Indigenous academic community about the way we approach Indigenous issues in universities.

To speak broadly about scholarly and intellectual practice in the field of Indigenous Studies from an Indigenous perspective is to speak about it quite differently from non-Indigenous academics, who speak from within the disciplinary intersections where their knowledge production and practices take up issues about us, our historical experience, and our contemporary position.

For us, the field of Indigenous Studies is part of a broader landscape that includes not just Indigenous Studies but also higher education for Indigenous students (see Bennett 1998), and the rebuilding of Indigenous communities and futures. These are not entirely separable, which complicates discussion of Indigenous Studies for Indigenous academics whose scholarly interests are diverse and scattered across the disciplines. Our work in universities addresses many concerns beyond scholarly ones, and must always remain articulated to community concerns and sensibilities.

Yet the theoretical and methodological issues of knowledge production and representation emerging in Indigenous Studies are fundamental to understanding both the broader landscape in which we educate Indigenous students and the way we think about Indigenous relationships to the Australian community (Nakata 1993a; 1993b). Furthermore, understanding theoretical and methodological issues is critical to producing new and more effective approaches to negotiating the intersections of different knowledge systems as they converge, circumscribe and condition the possibilities for understanding the past and its legacies, and improving Indigenous futures.

Underpinning Indigenous academic involvement in Indigenous Studies is first and foremost a definitive commitment to Indigenous people, not to intellectual or academic issues alone. Generating new ideas and lines of inquiry and experimenting with practice forged in the intersections of Western knowledge and our own help us to theorise people's lives and attempt to reshape opportunities for their futures in the same way that others have, no matter how we bring our perspectives and interpretations to bear on it.

For Indigenous academics, therefore, the tension existing between the expectations of academic and Indigenous communities both informs and constrains the development of an Indigenous intellectual community. So when we stray into perceived intellectualisms or activity that does not appear to have a direct relation to community interests, our communities may question us as to the relevance of our work and whether or not we are leaving community interests behind and becoming too immersed in the ways and thinking of the 'White world'.

These are confronting issues that seek to regulate not just our thinking and intellectual activity but also our identity, according to the perceived application of our work to community interests. They question our allegiance to the Indigenous community: are we members of the Indigenous or the academic community? The choice is sometimes this stark, making us as Indigenous intellectuals an object of suspicion from both sides. The irony of course is that entry to the academic community is activated not merely by our presence and work in the institution. Academia has its own gatekeepers, with whom we must also negotiate. Thick skin and secure identities are essential job requirements.

Unless Indigenous academics begin to focus more sharply on the intellectual issues associated with our co-option into the academic disciplines as a 'knowable' subject of study, we may not meet our commitment to Indigenous people and futures. Two imperatives for the twenty-first century are that we develop an Indigenous intellectual community and that there is mutual understanding as to the function and purpose of both bodies.

My focus in this lecture is on disciplinary and scholarly issues within Indigenous Studies and how these might be approached in ways that retain the necessary cohesion and solidarity so important to the Indigenous struggle, while allowing enough space for Indigenous scholars to pursue different avenues of inquiry aimed at generating new and more productive knowledge and practice for Indigenous communities. This freedom to explore is critical, and without it Indigenous knowledge production in the academy will be stifled, impoverished or fractured by different schools of thought and their associated politics. I discuss the broader framework of Indigenous Studies in two ways: first, in terms of how we approach the intersections of different knowledge systems in Indigenous Studies; and second, in terms of the overarching narrative through which we frame and connect our struggle to shape the content and teaching of Indigenous Studies and the education of Indigenous students.

First, though, I need to sketch briefly the trajectory we have been on so far.

When the Australian Institute of Aboriginal Studies was established, Aboriginal Studies was defined in clear and unambiguous terms and everyone knew where it belonged. The 1964 *Australian Institute of Aboriginal Studies Act* defined Aboriginal Studies as:

> anthropological research and study in relation to the aboriginal [sic] people of Australia (including research and study in respect of culture and languages). (cited in Bennett 1998, p. 2)

At that time, there were three anthropology departments in Australian universities and the work of the Institute helped develop the disciplines of archaeology and linguistics in universities (Peterson 1990). This triad of subjects that once dominated Aboriginal Studies now forms a much smaller portion in a greatly expanded field. These subjects have themselves undergone change in their direction and practices. The early study of Indigenous societies had little interest in Indigenous peoples beyond how we, as living evidence of the human past, could contribute to knowledge of human social evolution (Berndt 1982; Hiatt 1984; Jones 1978; Mulvaney 1986; Attwood 1996). The value of such study was to capture knowledge of us and our 'primitive social organisation' before it was 'lost' or we were 'transformed' (Peterson 1990).

This early knowledge production was therefore all about us and yet had nothing to do with us either — it was quite external to our society and concerns (Nakata 1998). The purpose of study about Indigenous Australians changed in the decade leading up to the 1967 referendum, and scholarly output accelerated in the following three decades. In a context of public policy reform, academic research began constructing new ways of understanding Indigenous people in order to develop effective reform measures (Sherwood 1982).

Knowledge production in the early period of reform was largely external to us, underlain by the application of theories and methodologies of the relevant disciplines, including the pervasive use of statistics. In this period, explanations of educational failure, cultural deprivation, cultural differences, poverty and disadvantage emerged in a renewed consideration of who we were and what we needed in terms of reform measures. In other words, we were no longer dying out, but pathetically transformed and in need of reform.

At a steady pace, from the beginning of the 1970s, Aboriginal Studies came to include topics in a revised history and literature that uncovered a silence about frontier violence (e.g. Loos 1982), theft of land (e.g. Reynolds 1989) and children (e.g. Wilson 1997), racism (e.g. Cowlishaw & Morris 1997; McConnochie, Hollinsworth & Pettman 1988), and the effects and practices of colonisation (e.g. Beckett 1987) and native administration (e.g. Kidd 1997).

We became subjects of the social sciences through sociological theory about minorities, analyses of race relations, the politics of identity, and so forth. We also became subjects in the emerging cross-disciplinary areas of Cultural Studies, Australian Studies, and Post-colonial Studies. We have also become subjects within the disciplines of Law, Education, the Health Sciences, the Environmental Sciences, and the Fine Arts, among others (Bennett 1998).

The definition put forward by the Commonwealth Aboriginal Studies Working Group report to the Australian Education Council in 1982 reflected a changing agenda in relation to understanding Indigenous Australia:

> Aboriginal Studies is the study of the history, cultures, languages and life styles of Aboriginal and Torres Strait Islander peoples, both prior to and following European colonization in a context which places emphasis on understanding of issues central to Aboriginal and Torres Strait Islander contemporary society and on their relevance to the total Australian community. Its contents are the descriptions, insights and explanations of human experience derived both from Aboriginal and from non-Aboriginal sources. (Hill 1986, p.1)

This definition signalled an expanded purpose, that of understanding contemporary Aboriginal and Torres Strait society, which reflected not just the goals of reform but our inclusion in the national story. The definition also includes an important addition to the corpus: descriptions, insights and explanations of human experience from Aboriginal sources. This is an important change. Indigenous Studies, though still about us, would now include insights from within Indigenous society. This definition of Indigenous Studies informs most Indigenous Studies courses today.

This change was in part due to the other major influence on Indigenous Studies during this period: the political activism and presence of Indigenous people in Indigenous affairs, including higher education. Early activism has evolved into an entrenched and recognised presence of Indigenous interests within universities, though in many places it is not an entirely secure one. Early political activism pursued both equitable access to higher education and education for self-determination, especially for Indigenous people who worked in communities and emerging Indigenous organisations, and who needed to develop specific sets of skills to assist community development and provide leadership (Bin-Sallik 1990).

With various beginnings and continuing developments, Indigenous people have been involved in two major arenas: developing both academic and cultural support centres and specially designed programs, which now cross seven gradations of qualifications from preparatory to postgraduate levels. Although initially dependent on and supported by non-Indigenous academics, most of these programs are now Indigenously run, managed and taught. Special programs exist to meet an ongoing demand for skills in urban, regional and remote Indigenous communities and organisations that standard academic programs do not fulfil adequately or appropriately. They include Indigenous Studies content from the disciplines, but often develop content for their own particular needs and purposes. Increasingly, Indigenous students have also entered unchanged programs across the faculties, and may or may not take Indigenous Studies subjects. Indeed, in many places non-Indigenous students constitute the major student cohort in these subjects.

As I stated earlier, Indigenous academics have grown as a community over this period as graduates have advanced through the system. Once largely confined to support activities, increasing numbers of qualified Indigenous academics teach Indigenous Studies, some within the disciplines, but most from the Indigenous centres or in special programs. Indigenous Studies is increasingly under the nominal authority or management of Indigenous academics, even when it continues to be taught by non-Indigenous academics. The growing cohort of Indigenous scholars that has emerged is making an important contribution to Indigenous Studies.

We are speaking back to, and challenging, the disciplines, by critiquing, interrogating, asking different questions and producing alternative, sometimes disruptive, accounts aimed at achieving better understanding on the part of others (e.g. Anderson 2003; Behrendt 2003; Birch 2003; Cronin 2003; Davis 2003; Dodson 1994; Heiss 2003; Langton 1992, 1998, 2003; Moreton-Robinson 2003; Morrissey 2003; Quiggin & Janke 2003).

In the twenty-first century, Indigenous Studies is now cross-disciplinary. It draws concepts, analysis, theories and methodologies from other disciplines and also from Maori Studies, Native American Studies and other international Indigenous Studies contexts. It also inserts knowledge about Indigenous people and their realities into a range of disciplines, for example, anthropological knowledge on culture goes into education, health, and law. Indigenous Studies is now a cross-discipline, circulating an ever-expanding corpus of knowledge about Indigenous people that it collects and redistributes.

The time has come for Indigenous academics to redefine Indigenous Studies in order to reflect our concerns. We have had content-based definitions emerging from the concerns of others, but we now need to consider definitions that also pursue a renewed purpose for Indigenous Studies at the tertiary level, in ways more reflective of Indigenous intentions and goals. This is particularly important as we grapple with the effects of our construction within and by the Western disciplines and work to renegotiate the meanings of these understandings at the intersections of our own understandings of our traditions, historical experiences, contemporary positions and possible futures. Defining Indigenous Studies in these terms implies that questions of concepts, theories, methodologies, underlying principles and boundaries are relevant; and they open up Indigenous Studies for consideration as a discipline rather than simply a collection of subjects garnered from across the disciplines.

In the academy, Indigenous Studies is clearly the study of and about Indigenous people. What does it mean then for an Indigenous academic to participate, from within the academy, in the continuing production of knowledge about Indigenous people, when our goals and commitment are to serve our own people, to rebuild communities and futures? What does it mean for our participation in the continuing production of knowledge in Indigenous Studies if our Indigenous perspectives, knowledge and analyses are inscribed in and through the Western ontological world and circulate back to shape practice in Indigenous contexts?

These questions, which are prominent in the minds of Indigenous academics here and abroad, lie at the heart of the Indigenous dilemma in Western education, which demands an ongoing denial or exclusion of our own knowledge, epistemologies, and traditions. We are also further co-opted by a system quite different from our own: one deeply implicated in our historical treatment and continuing position, but unable adequately to comprehend or give representation to our own histories, knowledge, experience and expression of our reality. Also, through its discursive complexities, it always circumscribes our own representations and understandings in its re-presentations.

Different approaches to this problem that reflect this central contradiction have emerged, but the various Indigenous approaches have one aspect in common. When Indigenous Studies in higher education is discussed from concerns internal to Indigenous society, it is invariably not separated from what it means for the education of Indigenous people or for re-establishing continuities with former traditions and knowledge.

There has been much more discussion of the broader issues associated with Indigenous Studies as a discipline in the North American, Hawaiian and Aotearoan contexts. Although Indigenous Australian academics are in conversation with international indigenous scholars, this has not tended to result in similar conversations within our milieu. Instead, the issues are taken up by individuals in their scholarly work or by networks in particular places, yet neither produces much conversation in the literature about the forward movement of Indigenous scholarly production or practice in Indigenous Studies. Although Indigenous Studies in international contexts share intellectual and scholarly issues similar to ours, they tend to be discussed at length and more robustly.

As early as 1970, there was a view amongst American Indian scholars that Native American Studies was about 'defense of the land and indigenous rights' (Cook-Lynn 1997, p. 9). The discipline was envisioned as 'the endogenous study of First Nation cultures and history' (1997, p. 10); that is, to be studied from within these cultures, and refute 'exogenous' knowledge of indigenous people constructed by the methodologies of Western knowledge systems. Inherent in this view was a great desire by Native American scholars to assert themselves not merely as 'the inheritors of trauma but [as] heirs to vast legacies of knowledge about [their] continent and the universe that had been ignored' since colonisation (Cook-Lynn 1997, p. 9).

This view of Indigenous Studies (as a discipline that can be developed from within Indigenous epistemologies to continue tribal knowledge traditions) is a strong ongoing strand in the international literature (e.g. Battiste, Bell, & Findlay 2002; Ermine 1995; Forbes 1998; Grande 2000; Smith 2000; Walker 2000; Wildcat & Pierotti 2000). Very few scholars in these international contexts discuss Indigenous Studies in their home context without reference to the underlying philosophy of tribal knowledge systems and how they differ from Western knowledge.

From a perspective foregrounding the role that Western education plays in supporting colonial goals, a major position expressed in this literature concerns developing Indigenous Studies as a discipline that assists an ongoing decolonising education process (Walker 2000). Thus the purpose of Indigenous Studies is not simply to decolonise through revival of Indigenous Knowledge but also to defend it by re-instating Indigenous ontologies and epistemologies. It would achieve this by developing new frameworks to redress the submergence of Indigenous peoples' knowledge in colonial regimes (Battiste et al. 2002; Cook-Lynn 1997; Meyer 1998; Smith 1999; Smith 2000; Thaman 2003; Wildcat & Pierotti 2000).

This position recognises that Western paradigms cannot adequately portray Indigenous realities, and asserts that developing more adequate representations requires the privileging of Indigenous realities via Indigenous ways of knowing — which, in turn, involves rediscovering, developing and applying 'Indigenous' paradigms (Swisher 1998). This literature contains a deepening exposition of the characteristics and concepts of Indigenous systems of knowledge. It also discusses how to employ these as principles informing the discipline of Indigenous Studies. Some scholarship in this area attends to Indigenous concepts and formations of knowledge that have been 'unknowable' from the Western epistemological standpoint: knowledge that was and is deemed 'unscientific', 'irrational' and 'primitive' from the Western standpoint, but in particular aspects that are 'beyond belief', as Cherryl Smith (2000, p. 47) puts it.

An extreme aspect of this position, however, is continuity with Indigenous knowledge traditions through rejection of much of what Western society has to offer. In which case, disciplinary development of these principles faces the inevitable question: 'How does it fit in' to the academy (Cook-Lynn 1997, p. 25)? Less extreme positions discuss this continuity in terms of transformation of the representations within the disciplines and via the education process (Battiste et al. 2002). Others (e.g. Champagne 1996) view the academy as an unsuitable place for transmitting tribal knowledge. This view argues that Native Americans should receive a cultural education from elders in a tribal context, and should attend university to learn the history of their relationship to the nation–state and understand what influence this may have on their current position.

The challenge of 'mainstream' education for Indigenous peoples is thus to understand that mainstream, develop skills for operating in it, and maintain tribal standpoints through knowledge gained via tribal relations in tribal contexts. These positions are not mutually exclusive, except in their extremes, and what is being acknowledged in a range of the literature is that, to defend indigenous peoples, indigenous students require understanding concepts and methodologies drawn from both systems of knowledge. To do battle with Western systems of thought demands a strong understanding of them. Likewise, the inconsistencies inherent in those systems cannot be replaced by an indigenous perspective without a rigorous understanding of indigenous concepts (Battiste et al. 2000; Champagne 1996; Deloria 1998; Smith 2000).

Despite this theorising, in practice and in these contexts Indigenous Studies has emerged as a cross-disciplinary specialisation in much the same way as it has evolved in Australia — a field expanded across the disciplines as they have taken up Indigenous issues. However, there are major structural differences between North America's strong community-controlled tribal college systems (or the dual system of education in Aotearoa), which perform similar roles to our special programs in Indigenous enclaves within Australian universities. Here, issues surrounding the theoretical underpinnings that might guide the progression of Indigenous Studies as a discipline are not discussed. Arguments for Indigenous-controlled schools of Indigenous Studies (e.g. NIHEN 2002) or Indigenous-controlled universities (e.g. Bourke & Bourke 2002; West 1999) may be advanced. What remains unresolved, though, is the central dilemma regarding the corpus of knowledge that inscribes how we are understood as Indigenous people.

In Australia, our primary approach to resolving this contradiction of working and studying in the very institution that has constructed ways of thinking about us that have not historically served our interests, and have played a role in the injustices perpetrated against us, is that of 'Indigenisation'. In simple terms, Indigenisation has been about making a space within universities that is recognisably Indigenous: one formed by inserting and asserting content, practices and processes that culturally affirm Indigenous people, students, community and perspectives.

This process has ranged from employment of Indigenous people in different roles, recognition of cultural ways that require different policies concerning special leave, cultural celebrations, support services, and so on to issues of academic content. At both personal and structural levels, the process has worked well because it defines boundaries and unambiguously separates Indigenous from non-Indigenous interests. At the academic level, Indigenisation has achieved a measure of success. With the exception of anthropology, Indigenous people were, not so long ago, invisible in the disciplines of the academy.

Early efforts to 'Indigenise' curricula were necessary and important because content and knowledge about Indigenous people had to be brought in and extended across the disciplines if Indigenous issues and realities were to be understood and responded to. Likewise, inclusion of 'insights from Indigenous sources' depended on bringing in accounts from Indigenous people. These accounts, both oral and written, have enriched the understanding of others about who and what we were and are, and have contributed to a growing Indigenous corpus. However, as the decades roll by, Indigenous academics have become more deeply concerned about the difficulties of cross-cultural aspects of the education task. These include the tasks of educating Indigenous students without further erosion of culture or assimilation into Western ways of thinking, and of bringing non-Indigenous students to a fuller understanding of Indigenous world views.

As a result of this concern, inclusion via the concept of 'Indigenisation' is being extended and discussed at deeper levels. Now, some of us are not content to talk of superficially descriptive course content, which has been constructed in the Western disciplines, but want deeper acknowledgment of Indigenous knowledge, epistemologies and pedagogies. We are looking for recognition and representation of our own systems of knowledge and thought within the academy.

Increasingly, there is an assumption that inclusion of Indigenous knowledge and pedagogy into tertiary curricula will provide an alternative to the Western corpus, or allow the development of an ongoing Indigenous intellectual tradition, or contribute to Indigenous problem-solving. However, there are problems with this view that are not being discussed in the literature. It is right to argue that the complexities of knowledge and epistemological intersection are critical in understanding the difficulties we are having in developing deeper understanding of the cross-cultural space where Indigenous knowledge, cultural practices and histories intersect non-Indigenous ones.

In this space we are indeed in crisis, yet we are taking up these considerations before we have thought enough about the cross-cultural space in which we all operate. 'Indigenisation' is a strategy that seeks to define a space that is recognisably Indigenous. At the level of knowledge, it works on a premise that if we just keep adding more and more 'authentically' Indigenous content in, we will build up a knowledge context that is more representatively 'Indigenous', and from this place will somehow generate 'Indigenous' solutions to our problems that are couched in Indigenous meanings.

This, however, is flawed thinking. In the academy, any Indigenous space is always circumscribed by non-Indigenous systems of thought. To 'study' Indigenous knowledge in a Western institution is a very different enterprise from 'learning' the deeply embedded cultural and social meanings of them in their own context. 'Study' of it distorts and reduces its meanings to fit with Western knowledge and disciplines (Eyzaguirre 2001). The practice of carving up Indigenous knowledge, the meanings of which are embedded in local and oral contexts, into a myriad of subsets across the academic disciplines has already been well critiqued (see Nakata, 2002). We need to be clear on the purpose and the limits of what can be achieved.

Indigenous knowledge can be studied so as to discern its differences from Western epistemologies of knowledge and illustrate just how complex the cross-cultural space is. Yet the general application of simple comparisons to understanding and/or practice risks the reduction and simplification of complex, highly nuanced meanings through a different language and a process of superficial application of the meanings of the differences. This practice also reifies the 'us–them' opposition and carries it through as a necessary condition of learning, which it is not.

There is a danger that, in the rush to engineer a quick resolution of the intersection of these different knowledge systems, we will bring in, for example, some impoverished, corrupted and misapplied version of 'Aboriginal pedagogy' to some equally impoverished, corrupted or misunderstood version of Indigenous knowledge — both of which are already circumscribed by Western understandings of them and by the Western knowledge also being conveyed. It is evident in the literature that some problematic work is going on in this area. While traditional knowledge does need to be documented and preserved and may have a place in the academy as a subject of study, this is a separate endeavour from mixing it into formal education systems and teaching practices in order to make these systems somehow more representatively 'Indigenous'. A whole range of issues arises that should ring alarm bells: whose knowledge, which parts of knowledge systems, whose language, who is in charge of them, what can be written about them, who owns the intellectual property, for what purposes can they be taught, who decides, what survives in the translation (Agrawal 1995a, 1995b; Forrest 2002; Nakata 2002).

As Indigenous academics, we need to ask ourselves whether we are more intent on authorising ourselves within institutions or in seeking fuller understanding of our position. In the strong and long arguments we have made to gain some measure of authority on Indigenous matters in Australian universities, Indigenous academics have taken on roles, on behalf of the broader Indigenous community, as custodians, authorities, and points of references for Indigenous perspectives in the curricula. However, I would argue that we must not let the political argument delude us in relation to the knowledge reality.

To be clear about this: in universities, the great mediator between Indigenous and non-Indigenous understanding is not us, is not Indigenous people or academics, but *the ontological world of Western knowledge systems*. It is the disciplines and their knowledge and practices that mediate meaning and interpret the Indigenous world to both Indigenous and non-Indigenous students.

When we talk of cultural traditions, we talk of them as constructed through anthropology; when we study Indigenous life stories, we study them as an addition to the Western literary or history tradition; when we speak of Native Title, it is via another system of land ownership; and when we talk of traditional language revitalisation, we talk of language as described by linguistics and disembodied from its community of speakers. All knowledge that is produced about us and all knowledge that we produce ourselves are added to the Western corpus, where it is reorganised and studied via the disciplines of Western knowledge.

It is important not only to accept this reality but also to think about the space that the academy provides for bringing in Indigenous knowledge, histories, experiences and perspectives and making something of it for our own purposes. In educating ourselves and our children, we may want to deploy a traditional form of education that is often forgotten in our anxiety about assimilation through education; that is, we might teach ourselves and our children about our 'locatedness' or 'situatedness' in relation to what is around us, in this case not environmental elements but knowledge systems. This is already familiar to us in the ways we know ourselves in relation to country and people and is a useful way to consider our relationship to the corpus of knowledge circumscribed by Western systems of thought. What does this corpus of knowledge mean for us and what do I have to know about it to understand where I am situated in relation to it, how it positions me and how I might position myself to engage with it in my interests or on my own terms? (Nakata 1993a). In simple terms, it is about knowing where you are, where you stand in relation to a big knowledge map, the distinct features, the quicksand that might swallow you, the difficult areas that slow you down, the features that obscure what is beyond, the blurred boundaries, the paths that one has to negotiate.

With an awareness of our 'locatedness', we then might develop knowledge positions embedded from our 'standpoint'; that is, not traditionally Indigenous or Indigenous per se, but embedded from the particular historical and knowledge location from which we read and understand the disciplinary constructions of us — a way, if you like, of authorising the position from which we speak back to the disciplines, but not so arrogantly as to suggest that a singular Indigenous intellectual position is *the* Indigenous intellectual position. Any Indigenous standpoint must respond to diversity, namely older traditions, historical experience that shapes contemporary positions, and the possibilities open to us. To be understood by others, our construction as subjects of the Western disciplines should be revealed to others as well. There are myriad conversations to be had at these conjunctures between ourselves, with our communities, and with non-Indigenous academics, which will necessarily be quite varied but which over time may identify a clearer, recognisably and referenced Indigenous position.

If we consider the intersections of knowledge not just as a simple Indigenous/non-Indigenous intersection but as an interface that is complex and layered by many, many historical and discursive intersections, then the difficulties of representing ourselves within or outside of this corpus become apparent. Explorations at this interface where two different sets of knowledge and historical understanding meet, reveal not simple oppositions of black and white, us and them, but a tangled web in which we are caught, with boundaries that are perhaps both clear and very blurred. This is much more representative of our position than the constant reduction of complexity to simple oppositions, which posit us in ways that confine us to either/or options.

Explorations of this kind that reveal and accept the complexity of knowledge intersections are also more likely to allow a better theorisation of this cultural interface as a place of contradiction and tension, a site of constant negotiation, which is the everyday life-world of many Indigenous people. We may learn to accept ambiguity and contradiction as part of being Indigenous, instead of self-regulating ourselves as the subjugated Other. Such a stance also allows for a different view of Western knowledge. While there is much of value in the Western disciplines that benefits us and which we need to master, the point at which this knowledge circumscribes the ways that Indigenous people, interests and issues can be understood is where we should be: exploring, investigating, interrogating, unsettling, responding to, re-interpreting, constructing alternative opinions and theories, and reshaping the knowledge of those disciplines in relation to their Indigenous circumscription.

From this view, Indigenous Studies in the academy is not the study of Indigenous societies, histories, cultures or contemporary issues alone but necessarily, given historical circumstances, *the study of how we have been studied, circumscribed, and represented*, and how this knowledge of us is limited in its ability to understand us. What Indigenous Studies needs to attend to is the great difficulty in understanding and knowing Indigenous people and their issues, owing to the mediation of our histories, knowledge, experiences and social realities by the Western corpus and its disciplines. We need to reconsider a different conceptualisation of the cross-cultural space, not as a clash of opposites and differences but as a layered and very complex entanglement of concepts, theories and sets of meanings of a knowledge system.

If this were to be our starting point, then the deeply cross-cultural encounters between different knowledge intersections emerging daily in communities, in health, in education, in governance and so on, could be approached — not ambivalently as heralding further cultural loss, but more robustly as the source of new sets of negotiated meanings. These may or may not look distinctly Indigenous but connect with older traditions in ways that, rather than disrupting and alienating people from those traditions, continue them by enriching practices aimed at producing much better outcomes.

In formal education contexts, then, the consideration of Indigenous knowledge, standpoints or perspectives, at whatever level we want to consider them, should be primarily about bringing them into conversation with knowledge in the traditional disciplines in order to negotiate a new set of meanings and reinterpretation of meanings. Neither set of understandings is set in stone: they are constantly shifting and intersecting, and drawing concepts and meanings from everywhere. The quest is always for fuller understanding, both in a micro-sense and in the interest of producing bigger pictures and better explanatory narratives.

An example of this emerges in Indigenous health worker education, a deeply cross-cultural encounter (see Clapham, Digregorio, Dawson & Hughes 1997). Consider the complexity involved in finding ways to educate the Indigenous professionals in remote communities who need to interpret concepts of health and medical practice across two deeply different systems of knowledge, each with its own concepts and practices: Western medicine and traditional healing and medicine.

In this context, negotiated notions of 'community pedagogy', described by Clapham et al. (1997) in the health-worker education literature, are far more useful than simple applications of 'Aboriginal pedagogy' or the imposition of Western paradigms. This is because they represent a negotiation of meanings and purposes between Indigenous and non-Indigenous contexts, thus clarifying goals, needs, strategies and roles in the education process. The notions of Clapham et al. are far from unproblematic, yet they represent what has to occur: the negotiation of meanings attached to the social practices surrounding different systems of knowledge and the weaving of them into something quite different from both Western and Indigenous traditional contexts of education and health practice in a way that allows both elements to work together harmoniously.

We need to gain a much clearer understanding of the theories and concepts being brought to any analysis. What this requires is much more sophisticated analysis and development of higher order skills amongst our students. It also needs much more Indigenous scholarship that engages with and takes on the disciplines for a range of purposes, as well as much better understanding and more complicated analyses of the diversity and complexity of Indigenous knowledge contexts than currently being produced in the Australian context.

This type of engagement with the disciplines is difficult, challenging work and risky because it implies the generation of new knowledge that may discontinue or transform some aspects of Indigenous knowledge and understanding. This anxiety might be allayed to some degree if Indigenous academia could adopt a more positive position in its approach to Indigenous Studies as a field of inquiry. We still see ourselves as reflected in a portrait of us, painted by early anthropologists, as a dying race, and preoccupy ourselves with knowledge production that affirms first and foremost notions of cultural maintenance. We have adopted a 'narrative of cultural loss' (Bauman 2002) to underpin our political arguments for cultural affirmation and a definable cultural space, a position of defence against further loss.

Well, we are still here, we have survived, and we might ask ourselves and our community, if now, after thirty years of activity in higher education, a more positive *narrative of survival* might not take us further than the narrative of cultural loss. It is not enough to protect and defend our past; we must protect our future interests by understanding much more fully what sort of knowledge landscape we are currently traversing — one that grows more complex by the day as information increases exponentially. We particularly need a positive thesis that will hold us all together in the struggle for better futures and which will encourage risk and exploration rather than passive acceptance of the status quo.

In conclusion, I note that, forty-five years ago, Mr Wentworth recognised the changing circumstances of Indigenous Australians and did something very positive to assist in the documentation of knowledge about us — knowledge that we now can access and use. It is time we brought a new purpose to Indigenous Studies, one that generates knowledge for us. While Indigenous Studies in the academy will always be study *about us,* we must shape it to ensure it is also study and inquiry *for us.*

We as Indigenous academics need to think long and deeply about our position at the intersection between Indigenous and Western systems of knowledge, about the intersection itself as it is constituted in the academy, and as it emerges in conditions on the ground in communities. There is much hard work ahead to conceptualise the intersections differently, to re-theorise them in all their complexity, and to find better methodological approaches for negotiating them. A narrative of survival may be more conducive to this sort of exploration and should be an important part of the future work of Indigenous Studies in the higher education sector.

References

Agrawal, A 1995a, 'Dismantling the divide between Indigenous and Western knowledge', *Development and Change*, vol. 26, no. 3, pp. 413–39.

—— 1995b, 'Indigenous and scientific knowledge: Some critical comments', *Indigenous knowledge and development monitor* [electronic journal], vol. 3, no. 3, pp. 3–4, viewed 25 July 2002 at < http://app.iss.nl/ikdm/ikdm/ikdm/3-3/articles/agrawal.html>.

Anderson, I 2003, 'Black bit, white bit', in M Grossman (ed.), *Blacklines: Contemporary critical writing by Indigenous Australians*, Melbourne University Press, Melbourne.

Attwood, B 1996, 'The past as future: Aborigines, Australia and the (dis)course of history', in B Attwood (ed.), *The age of Mabo: Histories, Aborigines and Australia*, Allen & Unwin, Sydney.

Battiste, M, Bell, L & Findlay, L 2002, 'Decolonising education in Canadian universities: An inter-disciplinary international, Indigenous research project', *Canadian Journal of Native Education*, vol. 26, no. 2, pp. 82–95.

Bauman, T 2002, '"Test 'im blood": Subsections and shame in Katherine', *Anthropological Forum*, vol. 12, no. 2, pp. 205–20.

Beckett, J 1987, *Torres Strait Islanders: Custom and colonialism*, Cambridge University Press, New York.

Behrendt, L 2003, *Achieving social justice: Indigenous rights and Australia's future*, The Federation Press, Sydney.

Bennett, D 1998, 'Aboriginal and Torres Strait Islander Studies', in *Knowing ourselves and others: The Humanities in Australia into the 21st century*, Vol. 2 Discipline Surveys, prepared by a Reference Group for the Australian Academy of the Humanities for the Australian Research Council.

Berndt, R 1982, 'Looking ahead through the past', The Wentworth Lectures, viewed 20 November 2003 at <http://aiatsis.gov.au/publications/presentations/looking-ahead-through-past>.

Bin-Sallik, M 1990, *Aboriginal tertiary education in Australia*, Aboriginal Studies Key Centre, Underdale, South Australia.

Birch, T 2003, '"Nothing has changed": The making and unmaking of Koori culture', in M Grossman (ed.) *Blacklines: Contemporary critical writing by Indigenous Australians*, Melbourne University Press, Melbourne.

Bourke, C & Bourke, E 2002, 'Indigenous studies: New pathways to development', *Journal of Australian Studies*, pp. 181–201.

Champagne, D 1996, 'American Indian Studies is for everyone', *American Indian Quarterly*, vol. 20, no. 1, pp. 77–83.

Clapham, K, Digregorio, K, Dawson, A & Hughes, I 1997, 'The community as pedagogy: Innovations in Indigenous health worker education', *Journal of Higher Education Policy and Management*, vol. 19, no. 1, pp. 35–43.

Cook-Lynn, E 1997, 'Who stole Native American Studies? *Wicazo SA Review*, vol. 12, no. 1, pp. 9–28.

Cowlishaw, G & Morris, B (eds) 1997, *Race matters*, Aboriginal Studies Press, Canberra.

Cronin, D 2003, 'Indigenous disadvantage, Indigenous governance and the notion of a Treaty in Australia: An Indigenous perspective', in *Treaty: Let's get it right*, a collection of essays from ATSIC's treaty think tank and authors commissioned by AIATSIS on Treaty issues, Aboriginal Studies Press, Canberra.

Davis, M 2003, 'International human rights law and the domestic treaty process', in *Treaty: Let's get it right*, a collection of essays from ATSIC's treaty think tank and authors commissioned by AIATSIS on Treaty issues, Aboriginal Studies Press, Canberra.

Deloria, V 1998, 'Intellectual self-determination and sovereignty: Looking at the windmills in our minds', *Wicazo SA Review*, vol. 13, no. 1, pp. 25–31.

Dodson, M 1994, 'The end in the beginning: Re(de)finding Aboriginality', The Wentworth Lectures, viewed 15 June 2015 at <http://aiatsis.gov.au/publications/presentations/end-beginning-redefinding-aboriginality>.

Ermine, W 1995, 'Aboriginal epistemology', in M Battiste & J Barman (eds), *First nations education in Canada: The circle unfolds*, UBC Press, Vancouver.

Eyzaguirre, P (2001), 'Global recognition of Indigenous knowledge: Is this the latest phase of globalisation?' *Indigenous knowledge and development monitor* [electronic journal], vol. 9, no. 2, pp. 1–2, viewed 11 June 2014 at <http://app.iss.nl/ikdm/ikdm/ikdm/9-2/column.html>.

Forbes, J 1998, 'Intellectual self-determination and sovereignty: Implications for Native Studies and for Native Intellectuals', *Wicazo SA Review*, vol. 13, no. 1, pp. 11–23.

Forrest, S 2000, *Indigenous knowledge and its representation within Western Australia's new curriculum framework*, online paper viewed 20 February 2004 at <www.kk.ecu.edu.au/sub/schoola/research/confs/aiec/papers/sforrest01.htm>.

Grande, S 2000, 'American Indian identity and intellectualism: The quest for a new red pedagogy', *International Journal of Qualitative Studies in Education*, vol. 13, no. 4, pp. 343–60.

Heiss, A 2003, *Dhuuluu-Yala: To talk straight*, Aboriginal Studies Press, Canberra.

Hiatt, L 1984, 'Aboriginal political life', The Wentworth Lectures, viewed 15 June 2015 at <http://aiatsis.gov.au/publications/presentations/aboriginal-political-life>.

Hill, M 1986, *Aboriginal Studies in tertiary education: Project report*, Committee to Review Australian Studies in Tertiary Education, Canberra.

Jones, R 1978, 'Calories and bytes: Towards a history of the Australian islands', The Wentworth Lectures, viewed 15 June 2015 at <http://aiatsis.gov.au/publications/presentations/calories-and-bytes-towards-history-australian-islands>.

Kidd, R 1997, *The way we civilise: Aboriginal affairs — the untold story*, University of Queensland Press, Brisbane.

Langton, M 1992, 'Aborigines and policing: Aboriginal solutions from Northern Territory communities', The Wentworth Lectures, viewed 15 June 2015 at <http://aiatsis.gov.au/publications/presentations/aborigines-and-policing-aboriginal-solutions-northern-territory-communities>.

—— 1998, *Burning questions: Emerging environmental issue for Indigenous peoples in Northern Australia*, Centre for Indigenous Natural and Cultural Resources Management, NTU, Darwin.

—— 2003, 'Aboriginal art and film: The politics of representation', in M Grossman (ed.), *Blacklines: Contemporary critical writing by Indigenous Australians*, Melbourne University Press, Melbourne.

Loos, N 1982, *Invasion and resistance: Aboriginal-European relations on the North Queensland frontier 1861–1897*, Australian National University Press, Canberra.

McConnochie, K, Hollinsworth, D & Pettman, J 1988, *Race and racism in Australia*, Social Science Press, Wentworth Falls.

Meyer, M 1998, 'Native Hawaiian epistemology: Exploring Hawaiian views of knowledge', *Cultural Survival Quarterly*, pp. 38–40.

Moreton-Robinson, A 2003, 'Tiddas talkin' up to the white woman: When Huggins et al. took on Bell', in M Grossman (ed.), *Blacklines: contemporary critical writing by Indigenous Australians*, Melbourne University Press, Melbourne.

Morrisey, P 2003, 'Aboriginality and corporatism', in M Grossman (ed.), *Blacklines: contemporary critical writing by Indigenous Australians*, Melbourne: Melbourne University Press.

Mulvaney, J 1986, '"A sense of making history": Australian Aboriginal Studies 1961–1985', The Wentworth Lectures — 1986, viewed 15 June 2015 at <http://aiatsis.gov.au/publications/presentations/sense-making-history-australian-aboriginal-studies-1961-1985>.

Nakata, M 1993a, 'An Islander's story of a struggle for a "better" education', *Ngoonjook*, vol. 9, pp. 52–66.

—— 1993b, 'Culture in education: For us or for them?' in N Loos & T Osanai (eds), *Indigenous minorities and education: Australian and Japanese perspectives of their Indigenous peoples, the Ainu, Aborigines and Torres Strait Islanders*, San-You-Sha, Tokyo, pp. 334–49.

—— 1998, 'Anthropological texts and Indigenous standpoints', *Journal of Aboriginal Studies*, vol. 2, pp. 3–15.

—— 2002, 'Indigenous knowledge and the cultural interface: Underlying issues at the intersection of knowledge and information systems', *IFLA Journal*, vol. 28, no. 5/6, pp. 281–91.

National Indigenous Higher Education Network (NIHEN) 2002, *Achieving equitable and appropriate outcomes: Indigenous Australians in higher education*, online paper viewed 11 June 2014 at <https://www.acu.edu.au/__data/assets/pdf_file/0004/7897/equitable_approp_outcomes.pdf>.

Peterson, N (1990), '"Studying man and man's nature": The history of the institutionalisation of Aboriginal anthropology', The Wentworth Lectures, viewed 15 June 2015 at <http://aiatsis.gov.au/publications/presentations/studying-man-and-mans-nature-history-institutionalisation-aboriginal-anthropology>.

Quiggin, R & Janke, T 2003, 'How do we treat our treasures? Indigenous heritage rights in a Treaty', in *Treaty: Let's get it right*, a collection of essays from ATSIC's treaty think tank and authors commissioned by AIATSIS on Treaty issues, Aboriginal Studies Press, Canberra.

Reynolds, H 1989, *Dispossession: Black Australian and white invaders*, Allen & Unwin, Sydney.

Sherwood, J 1982, 'Aboriginal education in the 1970s: What of the 1980s?', in J Sherwood (ed.), *Aboriginal education: Issues and Innovations*, Creative Research, Perth.

Smith, C 2000, 'Straying beyond the boundaries of belief: Maori epistemologies inside curriculum', *Educational Philosophy and Theory*, vol. 32, no. 1, pp. 43–51.

Smith, L T 1999, *Decolonising methodologies: Research and Indigenous people*, University of Otago Press, Dunedin.

Swisher, K 1998, 'Why Indian people should be the ones to write about Indian education', in D A Mihesuah (ed.), *Natives and academics: Researching and writing about American Indians*, University of Nebraska Press, Lincoln & London.

Thaman, K 2003, 'Decolonising Pacific Studies: Indigenous perspectives, knowledge and wisdom in higher education', *The Contemporary Pacific*, vol. 15, no. 1, pp. 1–7.

Walker, P 2000, 'Native approaches to decolonising education in institutions of higher learning,' *The Australian Journal of Indigenous Education*, vol. 28, no. 2, pp. 28–34.

Wentworth, WC 1959, 'An Australian Institute for Aboriginal Studies', unpublished paper, Australian Institute of Aboriginal and Torres Strait Islander Studies, Canberra, pp. 1–9.

West, E 1999, 'What should be the role of Aboriginal Studies at any of the three tiered systems of Australian education', in R Craven (ed.), *Aboriginal Studies: Educating for the future. Collected papers of the 9th annual ASA Conference*. Self-concept Enhancement and Learning Facilitation Research Centre, University of Western Sydney.

Wildcat, D & Pierotti, R 2000, 'Finding the Indigenous in Indigenous Studies', *Indigenous Nations Studies Journal*, vol. 1, no. 1, pp. 61–70.

Wilson, R 1997, *Bringing them home: Report of the national inquiry into the separation of Aboriginal and Torres Strait Islander children from their families*, Sterling Press, Sydney.

Original lecture available at:
<http://aiatsis.gov.au/publications/presentations/indigenous-australian-studies-and-higher-education>

14

'Difference' and 'autonomy' then and now: Four decades of change in a Western Desert society

2006 Wentworth Lecture

Robert Tonkinson

I begin by acknowledging the Ngunnawal people on whose ancestral lands we meet today. I also sincerely thank the Institute for honouring me with its invitation to be this year's Wentworth Lecturer. Bill Wentworth deserves to be long remembered as a great Australian, and especially as the statesman whose determination and persistence brought to fruition the idea of a national Australian institute for the promotion of Aboriginal studies. It was a long and tough struggle, one that you will eventually be able to learn much more about when Jacquie Lambert completes her current research.

My talk revolves around two interrelated themes: the status of cultural difference and the exercise of autonomy, with particular reference to the Martu, a Western Desert people of the East Pilbara region of Western Australia. It covers the period since 1963, when I first began working among them as a University of Western Australia Master's student in anthropology (under the supervision of Ron and Catherine Berndt, whose unfailing support to me, and enormous contribution to Australian Aboriginal Studies, and to the Institute, I would like to acknowledge today). Like many other Aboriginal people living in remote regions, the Martu still see, between themselves and other Australians, many significant differences that they appear to have no wish to transcend. A Martu expression, 'whitefellas do that', neatly conveys their recognition of certain fundamental differences. They note the contrast, generally without value judgment and without acting on it.

I should say at the outset that, as themes, 'autonomy' and 'difference' have no analytical force per se in that neither exists apart from more pressing issues in community life, such as power relations, social cohesion and social control. Difference is a two-edged concept, which has been employed by whites both to exclude Aboriginal people and to justify their assimilation. For their part, Martu use it to validate their uniqueness and to label those things about Whites and their ways that mystify them or do not attract their interest or conformity. 'Autonomy' is a slippery notion: Martu value it very highly, but within limits, because there are things that they would really rather leave to others. For many politicians, bureaucrats and commentators, autonomy means taking responsibility for actions and outcomes and becoming self-reliant, whereas for Martu it spells not only freedom from paternalistic and authoritarian strictures but also access to resources that extend their ability to forage for cash and other necessities while at the same time abdicating the hard yakka that Whites used to demand as quid pro quo, and that local 'leaders' now cannot or will not impose.

From an outsider's view, though, the autonomy exercised by the Martu is minimal or even illusory, since they mostly lack the wherewithal to exercise it, either as individuals or communities, because of their quite limited access to power, knowledge, money and even good health. I will come back to these issues later, in relation to current trends in government policies concerning Indigenous Australia, and the present situation of the Martu. But I begin by offering a roughly chronological overview of what has gone on among the Martu since Europeans first made their presence felt in the desert.

The settlement of Jigalong is about 1200 kilometres north-east of Perth, near the western edge of the Gibson Desert. Established as a camel-breeding station on the rabbit-proof fence, the settlement later functioned also as a ration depot for an increasing influx of Martu from the desert, who eventually settled there. Following the depot's closure shortly after the Second World War, a Christian mission was established. The ensuing struggle for the hearts and minds of the Martu was the subject of my 1974 community study, *The Jigalong mob: Aboriginal victors of the desert crusade*, the central theme of which was Indigenous adaptive strategies. It described the forging of new, non-traditional social entities (such as 'the Mob' of my title), successful resistance, and ultimate victory, as signalled by the withdrawal of the missionaries in 1969. In a situation of chronically unstable accommodation between two antagonistic parties, the Martu reacted to their reduced autonomy by what David Martin (2005) aptly terms 'strategic engagement': they pragmatically acquiesced to an imbalance in power favouring the missionaries as local agents of the nation-state, while selectively accepting, modifying, contesting or rejecting things and ideas Western.

The Martu are but one of the Western Desert peoples who once occupied a culturally homogeneous region comprising about a sixth of our continent. Ensconced in their arid environment and insulated by its forbidding marginality, they had for many millennia enjoyed maximal autonomy and flexibility of movement in their small and scattered bands. At the same time, though, everyone was firmly anchored by multiple attachments to a home estate or heartland, bound to many others by ties of kinship and ritual, and shared a worldview based solidly on the primacy of the spiritual realm. This was Australia's last frontier, which ended in the 1960s when the few remaining nomadic groups either walked or were transported out of their heartlands to settlements on the fringes of the desert.

Much earlier than this, though, rumours of intruders would have reached into every corner of the desert vastness, along with the arrival of artifacts and animals totally foreign to their prior experience. As I came to construe it from my fieldwork, the Europeans represented a scale of difference so drastic and unassimilable that the Martu consigned them to a completely separate category, one that lay beyond the bounds of the Dreaming. The strong denial of human agency at the heart of their worldview was most probably what motivated this reaction. My attempts to interpret what has happened since stem in some part from this sudden expansion of a 'cosmic order' dominated by the ancestral creative beings of the Dreaming into two contrasting arenas or, more aptly, domains (cf. Trigger 1992). This dichotomisation was soon given linguistic reality through the words *ngurra*, meaning 'camp', 'hearth', or 'home', and *maya*, meaning 'house' or 'settlement' but symbolising the whole European socio-spatial domain.

It was clear that 'coming in' from the desert had demanded a revolution in Martu notions of self and other, and of difference and boundedness. Once in face-to-face coexistence with frontier Europeans, predominantly single male pastoralists, Martu began to categorise peoples: 'whitefella', *matamata* (mixed descent), *martu*, and after the arrival of the mission, '*krijin*' ('Christian'), a negatively evaluated category standing in contrast to 'whitefella'. This dynamic process of differentiation reflected the steepness of the Martu learning curve once their formerly high levels of self-regulation were replaced by the near-constant demands of life 'under the white man's law'.

Coming in from the desert had for many Martu entailed a gradual seduction and ultimate entrapment — perfectly rendered in one man's assertion that 'we were captured by flour and sugar'. This was the initial inducement; and once they had become sedentary it would prise, rather than wrench, more of their cherished autonomy away from them. A growing economic dependence would leach them of their ability, and will, to retreat back into the desert. The second, and equally insidious, entrapment and loss of cultural integrity would come, ironically, in the wake of government policies intended to end paternalism and, specifically, to *increase* Aboriginal autonomy — about which I will soon say more.

Back in the 1960s, the Martu at Jigalong seemed to me to be faring well despite their very poor living standards. True, the dramatic transition from nomadic to settled life entailed a reduced autonomy, manifest in their heavy dependence on rations and the missionaries' strongly paternalistic stance. At the same time, though, they were successfully defending their autonomy in religious matters against those who were intent on the destruction of their entire culture, denigrating it as 'the work of the devil'. On occasion, the male elders were even emboldened to threaten trespassing missionaries with physical harm (a not inconsiderable challenge to authority when you think that, in the early 1960s, older Martu believed the killing of Aborigines by policemen to be as legally permissible as their terrifying dawn raids aimed at shooting camp dogs). I will never forget the palpable fear of the police that obtained back then, well before the advent of Aboriginal Legal Services brought a much needed and more accurate understanding of where the police officer stood in the whitefellas' legal hierarchy.

The Martu sense of what really mattered in life, along with family and their huge, scattered networks of kin, was inescapably bound up with the imperative of following the dictates of 'the Law'. The dormitory kids, for all the surveillance and disciplining they were subjected to by missionaries and teachers, enjoyed daily access to their kin and to the lively milieu of the camp, so their socialisation was still primarily into Martu behaviours and values. Attempts by the missionaries to turn them from the ways of their elders and make Christians of them was having little effect. In economic terms, there was work available — at the mission for the mothers and older men and women, and on pastoral stations for the able–bodied men.

Each year's end brought the 'pinkeye' season, when workers came home from the stations and Martu society was reinvigorated. Neither pastoralists nor missionaries interfered overtly in the 'big meetings', where religious business, centred on male initiation, took place. These meetings were the highlight of the Martu calendar: groups from several settlements would assemble at the chosen location for a few weeks of intense social activity. Throughout the year, though, ritual continued back in the various home communities, and religious matters remained front and centre for the elders, men and women. However, for those younger people not charged with the imperative of acting for the whole society, life at the missions and on stations hinted at possibilities of alternative futures.

Presented with new forms of work and leisure, younger Martu had their horizons widened, though to a limited extent. They were the first generation to face a dilemma as to how far they would conform to their elders' expectations. For their part, the elders carried on their traditional roles but their authority was undermined in a number of ways. Ultimately, the younger generations came to assert increasing autonomy while their elders found their influence diminishing.

In the decades of engagement and flow between the two socio-spatial arenas, the Martu readily accepted those things, mostly material, that posed no obvious threat to their Law. At the same time, they engaged with the Whites mostly in the latter's spatial domain. There was a mutual tendency to segregation, with Martu strongly resisting missionary intrusions and interference in the life of the camp and the missionaries and frontier Whites (in general) enforcing separation, both social and spatial, for their own reasons. Martu men, for example, were rarely permitted to set foot in their boss's quarters on stations, and very rarely did so in missionaries' houses.

When Myrna Tonkinson and I spent almost a year at Jigalong in 1974, we were witnesses to a pronounced rise in the tempo of change in Martu lives. First, there were social problems that had been emerging since the weighty lid of missionary control had been removed just a few years prior, and then out of the blue came enormous and unprecedented adaptive challenges with the implementation of 'self-determination' policies shortly before our arrival.

In just a few decades, the Martu had journeyed from undisputed masters of the desert to the cocky's 'boys' and the missionaries' wards. Now they were catapulted from a situation of complete paternalism to managing their settlement and negotiating their bureaucratic relationships with the nation-state — but without a modicum of training or any meaningful preparation. Jigalong was pronounced theirs, a legal Aboriginal corporation, to be run by their council, assisted by White employees whom, incredibly, they were now expected to boss. (And, I might add, they soon learned to boss, though with a twist: they tended to judge their employees on the basis of sentiment rather than any evaluation of competence).

Not only were the Martu not ready for administrative responsibilities but their coping strategies had been focused on the very opposite: insulating their 'traditional' domain and its religious core from the kinds of 'whitefella business' threatening to invade it. That they would soon be expressing nostalgia for the now-departed missionaries against whom they had struggled for 25 years speaks volumes for their deep-seated reluctance to take on what was thrust upon them in the name of 'self-determination' — much of which was, in their view, really the 'whitefella business' from which they had long been excluded but also sought to avoid. They had already been forced to cope with the progressive loss of work on stations since 1968 and the impact of easier access to alcohol in the late 1960s after the nearby mining town of Newman was established, and from which for many years they were excluded by company fiat. To a large extent, these conditions happened to the Martu rather than being controlled by them, with often catastrophic consequences for their society. Consultation was, and continues to be, expressed as an ideal but inadequately effected, as the goals and schedules of officialdom differ greatly from those of the Martu.

Policies of 'self-management' undoubtedly brought about some positive changes in Martu confidence levels and skills in dealing effectively with Whites, but there is also ample evidence of the conspicuous failure of these policies to significantly ameliorate Aboriginal disadvantage (cf. Sutton 2001, pp. 128–30). Although generally welcomed as offering Aboriginal people the right to make their own decisions (see Tonkinson & Howard 1990, pp. 67–74), the new initiatives soon showed troubling signs of not matching their underlying ideals.

The Whitlam government's term 'self-determination' was later changed to 'self-management'; and though the word 'autonomy' was not used, it suggests much the same idea. Both concepts are variably realised in time and space, and are also constrained, inasmuch as Aboriginal policy is framed within financial and political limits imposed by the dominant society, and subject to the whims of particular governments. In 1985, John von Sturmer (1985, p. 48) presciently warned that the language of 'self-determination' concealed a discourse aimed at drawing Aboriginal people inexorably into the corporate state, either by their direct recruitment into the bureaucracy or more indirectly by the creation of 'Aboriginal organisations' that would be invited, required or compelled to participate in government decision-making. As inimitable former AIATSIS Chairman, Ken Colbung, put it to me at the time, 'Are we talking about Aboriginal-managed organisations or managed Aborigines?'

At Jigalong, this 'capture and encapsulate' element was a significant factor in undermining Martu cultural integrity during the self-management era, and it is easy to see why: it eroded the boundary between the ideational domains that the Martu had erected and maintained with considerable success up to that point. While the Whites assumed that the Martu were incapable of self-regulation, the Martu reinforced the separation of domains to ensure autonomy in those areas they valued most highly. In fact, many senior Martu came to view, and use, the council as a convenient buffer against direct bureaucratic dealings between the camp domain and agents of the dominant society. The separation and paternalism that had freed Martu of much of the day-to-day minutiae of administration also regrettably prevented them from acquiring knowledge and skills necessary for effective self-management. Consequently, when White officials decided it was time for self-management, the Martu were neither willing nor able to put it into effect.

In some of my published work I have highlighted a fascinating aspect of domain separation on the part of the Martu; namely, their refusal to apply the organisational and logistic skills so patently exemplified by their annual 'big meetings' to comparable situations in the White domain. Yet I have heard Whites complain that 'they [the Martu] couldn't organise their way out of a paper bag'. This stems from a quite different leadership style, about which I will say more shortly.

Regardless of how they are perceived by others or of what policy dictates, the Martu, like other remote Aboriginal Australians, have clung to their differences. They want to retain their present distance and level of autonomy, but also the right to participate freely in some aspects of Australian society (cf. Trigger 2004); they self-identify as Martu first, and Australians second, if at all.

The vision of self-management held by many interested parties during and after the 1970s included the notion that Aboriginal people would eventually take control of their communities. However, the Martu were not given the tools to make this a reality, whatever their attitudes towards change may have been at that time. This period has seen a dearth of effective leaders, possibly because leadership in traditional Martu society was highly situational and context-dependent, and always included kin considerations. Kinship systems function relationally and conditionally, so they do not leave room for individuals to make and enforce decisions for what they may see as the common good. This of course begs the question of whether or not there can *be* any notion of 'common good' in a kin-based polity, especially when the matter at hand is categorised as 'whitefella business' (cf. Peterson 2005, Trigger 2005). Today, emergent economic inequalities in desert settlements tend to favour those, predominantly men, who hold leadership positions through a kind of community inertia, and seem to act more often in the interests of self and close kin than as dispassionate community leaders working for the general good.

A dimension of Martu society that has always been kept separate from 'whitefella business' is the religious life, the particular concern of mature men and women who have earned the status of ritual leaders. In recent decades, the erosive forces of Westernisation that conspire to weaken Martu resolve have led to attenuation of the flow of knowledge from elders to the younger adult generations. A youth's journey from first initiation to marriage used to take about fifteen years, but this period is now severely truncated, along with the volume of religious knowledge and traditions being transmitted, and the number of mature men available to conduct the necessary 'Law business'. Gaps have appeared in the ritual hierarchy of their once vibrant and complex religious system. The interdependency that made the system function efficiently is now insufficiently active in other religious contexts. This is most evident in the induction of novices into higher grades, which entails the transmission of vital knowledge and assignment of religious responsibilities, and in the conduct of ritual activities during the bulk of the year when there are no 'big meetings'. The time allotted to Law business has shrunk since the 1960s, even though it is no longer constrained by the demands of the pastoral economy. What still transpires mostly relates to male initiation and remains highly valued, as are the regional ties nourished by these meetings.

Regarding the diminution in ritual activities, elders complain that they are 'too tired' and that the young men are too preoccupied with sex and drinking, while younger men in turn blame the elders for being lazy and failing to pass on vital knowledge. Some elders also complain that they are not being consulted by members of the middle-aged generation to whom they wish to transfer religious knowledge. The current standoffs within the male ritual status hierarchy may yet be resolved, and the Law will undoubtedly persevere, though not as the edifice it was even thirty years ago.

In the mundane realm, expectations since the 1970s that Martu would eventually occupy all the major community roles have not been realised, and today there are more non-local staff than ever before in their settlements, including Aboriginal people from elsewhere and even occasional young European pack-backers who respond to job ads placed in Perth, and are paid CDEP [Community Development Employment Program] wages. This has occurred reportedly in response to a marked reluctance of Martu to work locally. With notable exceptions, those few who have the qualifications or experience to take on such jobs do not consider the top-up to their CDEP wage sufficient to make it worthwhile. Also, working in their own community can be all relatedness and little autonomy, so they will be subjected to 'jealousing' and to criticism. Exposure to the risk of shame and anger, many say, is 'not worth it'; and besides, there is no moral evaluation of work that links it in Martu minds to feelings of self-respect. As Peter Sutton has noted, there is an abiding tendency to forage among resources that are already available rather than producing substance through labour.

Among Martu, strong cultural continuities in sharing practices and obligations to kin, the *bêtes noires* of policy-makers intent on turning every Aboriginal family into a fiscally responsible economic isolate, will ensure that they will not be penniless and hungry, though the weekly feast–famine cycles that plague these communities affect even well-paid Martu. There are conflicts inherent in combining demand-sharing and other kin-based Martu values with the wage economy and the kind of individualism that many policy makers and commentators take to be the ideal. This is part of the dominant society's reluctance to accept difference colliding with the Martu tendency to cling to many of their values no matter the cost — at least to the eyes of observers like us. There is also gambling, the redistributive functions of which are well documented, though the personal costs perhaps less so. In the Martu case, changing conventions (about withdrawal from card games, and hoarding and spending proceeds, for example) may be indicative of pressures towards greater material consumption and increasing individuation. Still, the vast majority of Martu remain equally poor, so no one seems about to become anything beyond a bit more selective in their attitudes to sharing.

On the question of conformity to a work ethic favoured by the dominant society that entails punctuality, sticking to schedules, and so on, Victoria Burbank's (2006) recent account of why Aboriginal people may be reluctant participants in Western institutions is apposite. Her focus on dissonance, along with comments by a doctor who has worked among Aboriginal people for decades, led me to ponder the implications of yet another cultural continuity among desert people: a very high tolerance of discomfort. Martu habitually put up with hardship and huge inconvenience without expressing frustration or reacting against the situation or vowing never to repeat the ordeal. An unpalatable consequence of current government thinking is that the amelioration of pressing community problems in remote Aboriginal Australia can be made to succeed only by deliberately increasing levels of discomfort until they trigger the desired reactive behaviour, and it could be that people like the Martu will simply endure more hardship.

The Martu have done a number of things suggestive of the kind of autonomy they desire. For example, they have increased their mobility as a result of several changes: the lifting of bureaucratic controls, the loss of pastoral employment, the establishment of outstation communities, and, more recently, the retention of access to one's monetary entitlements in the event of visits to other settlements. Increased vehicle ownership, and better road construction and maintenance, have also facilitated a greater tempo and range of Aboriginal movement. While intensifying the ethos of inclusivity among desert people, access to vehicles has many costs: accidents, recurring expenditure on repairs that drain limited resources, and vehicle ownership itself — and sometimes big trouble with hire purchase companies, especially since the debt so often outlives the vehicle. More significantly, a lot of the Martu's current involvement with the justice system concerns motor vehicle offences: unpaid bills and fines, lack of licences, ignored summonses and breached community work orders — testament to a value system that rates obligations to kin as immeasurably more important than accountability to bureaucracies they see as having little or no moral claim over them.

The Martu readiness to travel, on whatever pretext and sometimes with just minutes of forewarning, is a major manifestation of their sense of autonomy today. Core values reinforce the virtues of nomadism, mobility and spontaneity of movement. Temporary absences and time spent visiting kin elsewhere may, amongst other things, function as a kind of pressure valve that eases some of the tensions entailed in staying put in a remote community. Yet mobility can be disruptive for settlements when kids are taken from school at a moment's notice, or attempts to run training programs are foiled by strongly felt obligations to attend funerals, or when leaders use their privileged access to resources to evade their responsibilities by fleeing from community crises instead of attempting to resolve them.

Another major change pertaining to difference and autonomy concerns relativities internal to the Martu social system: the way women and young people have exploited changed circumstances to increase their ability to function as what many refer to as 'free agents', at the expense of the power wielded by mature men. Gender relations favouring greater female autonomy began changing on pastoral stations, continued at the mission when older widows successfully asserted their right to refuse remarriage, and by the 1970s saw young women becoming increasingly successful in ignoring their parents' wishes about arranged marriage and their sexual conduct more generally. These assertions of autonomy, however, entail costs as the girls risk losing the protection of kin, leaving them more susceptible to violence. There has also been an alarming increase in adolescent pregnancy, low birth-weight babies and other problems. Men, too, are now marrying much younger than they used to and parental or community control over youth is minimal, so transgressions that used to result in severe public chastisement and beatings often go unpunished.

It is now more than forty years since my first sojourn in the desert, and I have made countless returns in the intervening decades, so, as a living exemplar of anthropology's extended case method, I am taking this lecture as a good opportunity to tackle some of the questions surrounding policy failures. Increasingly, reports and articles by journalists, academics and various commentators are cataloguing numerous problems and paradoxes in Aboriginal communities across the country. Broadly similar historical responses to oppression, racism, displacement, poverty and marginalisation undoubtedly account for some of these similarities. Also, the onus for coping and surviving has always lain with the small powerless minority, which, as Austin-Broos (2005, p. 6) observes, has had to draw on its existing institutional resources, making an impact on emerging difficulties, for better or worse. Today, both the costs and the benefits of staying remote are palpable and widely observed, so the imperative remains to refine our theorising and analysis to better comprehend the nature of Aboriginal responses. Perhaps we can then offer practical advice to those highly placed non-Aboriginal and Aboriginal people charged with the responsibility for bringing about positive and enduring change.

Over time, a succession of governmental policies has been based on the gulf of difference between Aboriginal and other Australians, and aimed at either overcoming or maintaining it. Despite our nation's avowed multiculturalism, government policies concerning Aboriginal Australians seem to have become more intent on discounting 'difference'. This shift was suggested in the decision to abolish ATSIC in 2004, but also in 'practical reconciliation' strategies and a determination to mainstream service delivery to Aboriginal Australians. Last year, we had what is possibly the clearest indication of federal government thinking about 'difference' when, in a number of speeches, the then Minister Assisting the Prime Minister for Aboriginal Affairs, Amanda Vanstone, heralded a major shift from 'the theoretical and ideological to the real and practical' (quoted in Landers 2005, p. 1). She characterised remote Aboriginal communities as 'living museums' whose inhabitants need to be moved closer to where economic opportunities exist. Senator Vanstone seemed to be implying that the maintenance of 'difference' is debilitating to remote Aboriginal peoples, and that the tyrannies entailed by this kind of distance/difference would at least be minimised, if not removed, by impelling them into a more active economic and social engagement with the dominant society. Few would challenge the notion that cultural differences may impede economic participation, but in this case no indication was given as to how and why. There is a strong tendency on the part of many in government and of commentators to concentrate on cultural difference rather than structural inequalities in seeking to account for a variety of problems.

The preference of most Aboriginal people living in remote locations to stay where they are often leaves them severely disadvantaged by poverty and the lack of access to services and opportunities available elsewhere, and exposed to a range of dysfunctional and damaging behaviours wrought by some of their number, but it can also protect people from adversity. As gleaned from Vanstone's punchy rhetoric, Aboriginal people in remote communities face two choices: to stay with 'culture' along with a lifelong welfare dependency that undermines 'local authority, material well being and social-moral coherence', as Diane Austin-Broos (2005, p. 2) has put it, or else migrate and embrace some ill-defined 'mainstream' culture that foregrounds economic values and urges universal engagement with them. The federal government is also signalling that it is not prepared to support the first of these options indefinitely. There is a not-too-subtle message in much of the recent policy rhetoric that 'difference' in many of its manifestations equates with dysfunction and — unless of course it entails positive economic outputs, as in the case of much Aboriginal art production — will not be supported. This trend would seem to render 'self-management' as little more than assimilation by another name. Perhaps my friend Betty Meehan can again aptly evoke a *bon mot* she attributes to former NT National Park Ranger, Danny Gillespie, about the bureaucratic reading of 'culture change': 'we've got the culture, you've got to change'.

The implicit choice between staying put so as to maximise difference and cultural autonomy while suffering disadvantage, and emigrating to towns, where your difference is on show to an audience of critics, and where disadvantage often persists, raises the question of possible alternatives. From my experience of circular migration in Vanuatu, where I have also been doing research since the 1960s, and from past patterns of Aboriginal seasonal pastoral employment, it seems that both provide possible models for participation in the workforce while retaining a base in one's homeland. Noel Pearson, who has contributed much to debate about alternative strategies, is also prominent among those Aboriginal leaders who are unhappy with ideas about 'cultural autonomy' if their effect precludes solutions to Aboriginal disadvantage and premature death.

How ready, though, are people like the Martu to move away from their heartlands and the autonomy and security associated with that life?

ARC [Australian Research Council] research that Myrna Tonkinson and I have done recently confirms the continuing pull of country and 'home'; everyone we interviewed in remote communities expressed a preference for staying put rather than relocating to towns. Most people want to be able to visit towns or cities and enjoy some of what they offer, but not to abandon their home places.

As things stand, if people like the Martu are either lured or compelled away from the homelands they have often struggled long and hard to win back via successful claims to Native Title, most will be reluctant émigrés – in, but not of, towns. There they are largely segregated by a sense of difference held positively by themselves through their Aboriginal identity, and negatively by entrenched racist attitudes among many of their co-residents. Today, significant numbers of Martu live in Port Hedland, Nullagine, Marble Bar, and Newman, and a few reside in the Perth metropolitan area. Some of this migration has been necessitated by chronic health problems that require people to remain close to services unavailable in home communities, notably dialysis. As reasons for their move, Martu also cite the availability of public housing, Aboriginal reserves, and proximity to a range of services catering to Aboriginal needs.

Town is at once more exciting and dangerous than home, attractive for its shopping, fast-food and liquor outlets, and often the supportive presence of many kinsfolk. But it is also alien, overrun with whitefellas and traumatic when drinking fuels violence and fatal accidents. There are 'shame' factors, especially when inebriated relatives are in the public gaze, and of course there are police, always on the lookout for those being sought for various kinds of infraction or outstanding debt. Deep ambivalence is evident in individual Martu commentaries, where the same factor, for example grog, is cited as both positive and negative. A number of town-dwelling Martu are heavy consumers of alcohol and state this as a, or the, major reason they live there. Many others, however, are non-drinkers who have come to town principally to care both for their alcohol-misusing adult children who are drinking, and/or grandchildren who are being neglected as a direct result.

Our research in Newman indicates that although children growing up in town increasingly identify it as 'home', as do many long-term resident adults, the basis of their identity is still strongly 'Martu'. Apart from a few dwellings on the township Aboriginal Reserve, their housing is dispersed and many have non-Aboriginal neighbours, yet their friendship networks and social world are almost exclusively Martu. They betray no hint of any desire to abandon their cultural heritage, and regularly travel back and forth to the Martu settlements, often to attend funerals, and feel entirely at home among their desert relatives. Their present level of autonomy includes the freedom to return to their old homelands at any time, and they place high value on this — it energises and sustains them. And of course, many others now live out in their homelands, though are frequently on the road.

Understanding that Martu dealt with the shock of the new by locating Europeans entirely outside their Dreaming-ordained cosmic order helps explain why, still today, a striking feature of their outlook is their general lack of curiosity about the nature and workings of the world 'out there'. Our recent ARC research strongly suggests that at all age levels fundamental orientations to the world show remarkable stability; many Martu values, attitudes and behaviours remain firmly anchored by deep emotional attachments to home, kin, country, and sentiments about sharing and compassion.

This cultural conservatism does not sit well with many values prominent in Australian society, such as those relating to property, time management, employment, wealth accumulation, future-orientation and education. Education probably best exemplifies this stark contrast in perspectives, and the distance separating tradition from modernism (cf. Sutton 2001, p. 132). As in other hunter-gatherer societies, formal instruction was mostly absent as a framed activity, and learning took place predominantly via unstructured observation and imitation. Remote area schools today have never been better equipped or (in many cases) staffed, yet among Martu attendance levels and scholastic performance have probably never been worse. The lack of employed locals as suitable role models could be a factor, but schooling as a means to an end has little meaning to Martu children, given their circumscribed horizons.

The strong desire of the Martu to maintain both a measure of distance and key elements of a distinctive identity has long been in tension with an ambivalence and inconsistency on the part of other Australians towards difference, comprising both demands for more responsibility and the wish to limit its expression. There is a lack of fit between what governments and others interpreted 'autonomy' to mean, and how it was understood and used by people like the Martu. What most of us thought and hoped would transpire once paternalism was eradicated by the new policies clearly did not, and the big question for anthropologists, other researchers and policy-makers alike remains, 'Why not?'

Whatever room to manoeuvre was increased for the Martu via 'self-management' has been used by them to amplify and sustain their cultural distinctiveness, but at a certain price that they are apparently willing to continue to pay. The issue of how difference is perceived and dealt with is moot here. The Martu have never expected Whites to behave in the same manner as they do; they simply accept the difference and feel that they and Whites occupy parallel domains, with no need for either comparison or value judgments about which one is better. This is not the case for members of the dominant society, who have always assumed that Aboriginal Australians would embrace what was presented to them as a superior way of life.

A lot therefore depends on how much difference Australia as a nation will tolerate and how long remote peoples like the Martu can continue to resist assimilation. Their difference is likely to remain salient for them and for others, with both positive and negative consequences. Current policy directions strongly suggest that the nation-state is looking to claw back some of the manifestations of Aboriginal autonomy it does not approve of, like allowing children to make their own decision about attending school, or the use of recreational drugs, or spending patterns it considers aberrant. Shared Responsibility Agreements (SRAs), viewed by critics as a carrot and stick approach that is more coercive than collaborative, are about modifying autonomy, reducing difference, and doing things for people's own good. The current prominence of SRAs strongly suggests that the federal government's price for allowing so-called 'living museums' to persist in remote Australia will be a more active coercion of their inhabitants into community-based reciprocal duties aimed at minimising or removing problems, identified via consultation between its agents and community organisations, often under duress. Minister Tony Abbott's call for a 'new paternalism' seems to have supplied an apt label for current policy orientation.

As I noted earlier, the reluctance of the Martu to apply the organising principles that serve them so well in their own domain to what they see as that of the 'whitefella' has denied them effective control over many administrative and development-related matters. While this no doubt has partly satisfied their strong desire for autonomy, their continuing struggle to keep the two domains discrete has been perilous precisely because it renders their Law incapable of dealing with problems that flow from the whitefella arena. This has left Martu autonomy in thrall to grog, cash and motor vehicles, for starters. The wall separating the two domains has certainly become much more permeable to elements of 'whitefella business', so if the Martu *could* somehow succeed in stimulating a flow of knowledge, strategies and power deriving from their Law to the whitefella domain, this should enhance their level of control over circumstances that continually challenge them. The ways they are adapting funerals, for example, hint at the kind of syncretism I have in mind here.

The need for transcendence of what could be termed 'the domain problem' is manifest in the wake of Native Title, in the form of the recently constituted Western Desert Lands Aboriginal Corporation (WDLAC) as the Martu's regional 'prescribed body corporate'. Such bodies are meant to function as the conduit through which Aboriginal Native Title groups will mediate their economic relationships with the wider Australian society, so their potential role must not be underestimated. The success of WDLAC will depend significantly on the extent to which it can also serve and satisfy its constituents. Some Martu have already expressed the hope that this regional forum will respond to pressing matters of Law and tradition in addition to its major economic function, and most particularly that it will bolster their Law. A flow of enabling power out of the Martu domain could well give WDLAC the kinds of strategies and skills necessary to make it a truly effective institution. Models for success are being identified in several communities, as Mick Dodson has pointed out, so there is hope for a positive and enduring outcome.

Forty-odd years on, much has been achieved in the Martu's quest for their version of self-management, and they now deal with the wider world with a higher level of self-confidence, but probably also with more cynicism than optimism. They are still much poorer and unhealthier than the population at large, though materially better off than before. The warmth, humanity, compassion, resilience, and, above all, sense of humour that captured me in the 1960s are still very much in evidence, though today's is certainly a considerably more fraught world — funerals are, after all, by far the commonest contemporary ritual. The biggest challenge facing the Martu, as I see it, will be to maintain sufficient strength and continuity in the workings of their Law, especially in its religious manifestations, that it can continue meaningfully to be the linchpin of their cultural integrity.

I would like to conclude with heartfelt thanks to the Martu for taking me on 43 years ago, convinced that their Law was well worth telling the world about. They were right, of course, and it still is, though considerably more complex in the telling.

References

Austin-Broos, D 2005, 'Culture, economy and governance in Aboriginal Australia,' in D Austin-Broos & G Macdonald (eds), *Proceedings of a workshop held at the University of Sydney, 30 November–1 December 2004*, University of Sydney Press, Sydney.

Burbank, VK 2006, 'From bedtime to on time: Why many Aboriginal people don't especially like participating in Western institutions,' *Anthropological Forum*, vol. 16, no. 1, Mar 2006, pp. 3–20.

Landers, K 2005, 'Vanstone snubbed at reconciliation talks', *The World Today*, ABC Radio, 31 May, viewed 15 June 2015 at <http://www.abc.net.au/worldtoday/content/20005/s1381072.htm

Martin, D 2005, 'Governance, cultural appropriateness and accountability within the context of Indigenous self-determination', in D Austin-Broos & G Macdonald (eds), *Aborigines, culture and economy: The past, present, and future of rural and remote Indigenous lives*, University of Sydney Press, Sydney, pp. 189–202.

Peterson, N 2005, 'Thomson's place in Australian anthropology,' in B Rigsby & N Peterson (eds), *Donald Thomson: The man and scholar*, Academy of the Social Sciences in Australia with support from Museum Victoria, Canberra, pp. 29–44.

Sutton, P 2001, *Aboriginal country groups and the 'community of native title holders'*, National Native Title Tribunal, Perth.

Tonkinson, R. 1966 'Social structure and acculturation of Aborigines in the Wesern Desert', MA thesis, Unviersity of Western Australia.

—— 1974, *The Jigalong mob: Aboriginal victors of the desert crusade*, Cummings, Menlo Park Calif.

—— 1978), 'Aboriginal Community Autonomy: Myth and Reality', in Howard (ed.) Whitefella Business: Aborigines in Australian Politics (Philadelphia: Institute for the Study of Human Issues.

Tonkinson, R & M Howard 1990, 'Aboriginal autonomy in policy and practice: An introduction,' in R Tonkinson & M Howard (eds), Going it alone? Prospects for Aboriginal autonomy, Aboriginal Studies Press, Canberra.

Trigger, D 1992, *Whitefella comin': Aboriginal responses to colonialism in northern Australia*, Cambridge University Press, Cambridge.

—— 2004, *Anthropology in native title court cases: 'Mere pleading, expert opinion, or hearsay'*, Melbourne University Publishing, Melbourne.

—— 2005, 'Mining projects in remote Aboriginal Australia: Sites for the articulation and contesting of economic and cultural futures', in D Austin-Broos (ed.), *Culture, economy and governance in Aboriginal Australia: Proceedings of a Workshop of the Academy of the Social Sciences in Australia held at the University of Sydney, 30 November–1 December 2004*, pp. 41–62.

—— 2006, 'Whales, whitefellas and the ambiguity of 'nativeness': Reflections on the emplacement of Australian identities', *Island*, no. 107, Summer 2006, pp. 25–36.

Von Sturmer, J. 1985, 'On the notion of Aboriginality: A Discussion', Mankind, vol. 15, no. 1, pp. 46–9.

Original lecture available at:
<http://aiatsis.gov.au/publications/presentations/difference-and-autonomy-then-and-now-four-decades-change-western-desert-society>

15

Guarding ground: A vision for a national Indigenous cultural authority

2008 Wentworth Lecture

Terri Janke

Prelude

In the past 20 years, Indigenous Australians have called for greater recognition of Indigenous cultural and intellectual property rights. The intellectual property system does not acknowledge Indigenous communal ownership of cultural expressions and knowledge passed down through the generations, and nurtured by Indigenous cultural practice. Sacred knowledge is also at risk. In a 1999 report, *Our culture: Our future — Report on Australian Indigenous cultural and intellectual property rights*, I made 115 legislative and policy recommendations. Today, Indigenous cultural and intellectual property rights remain largely unprotected in Australia, and are a hotly debated international issue. Now is the time for us to reassess the current framework.

In this lecture, I sketch out the ground covered by Indigenous copyright cases and examine international model laws and draft provisions, arguing for greater infrastructure to support and defend Indigenous cultural and intellectual property rights. My vision is for a national Indigenous cultural authority to facilitate consent and payment of royalties, develop standards of appropriate use to guard cultural integrity, and enforce rights.

Introduction

I acknowledge the Ngunnawal people on whose traditional lands we gather today. I also thank the Chairman, Professor Mick Dodson, and the Australian Institute of Aboriginal and Torres Strait Islander Studies for inviting me to present the 2008 Wentworth Lecture. I am honoured to join the esteemed list of presenters.

This biennial lecture is in honour of Bill Wentworth. I acknowledge his family and thank them for their continuing support of this lecture series. Bill Wentworth was an extraordinary Australian with great passion and persistence who brought the idea of a national Australian institute for the promotion of Aboriginal and Torres Strait Islander studies into fruition. This wonderful institution, and its books, documents, films, photographs, sound recordings, and its knowledgeable staff owe a great debt to Bill Wentworth's energy, determination and influence.

Bill's visionary nature has influenced my lecture today. He was the first Minister of Aboriginal Affairs, appointed after the 1967 Referendum, which delivered powers to the Commonwealth to legislate with respect to Aboriginal people. He was Minister in 1968, for the passing of the current Copyright Act, and remained in office through its subsequent enactment on 1 January 1969. My working career has been focused on Indigenous intellectual property, mostly copyright, and the advancement of Indigenous cultural and intellectual property rights.

I discovered a link between Bill Wentworth's time in office and the focus of my paper when I was reading a book written by a colleague, Michael Davis, entitled *Writing heritage*. In 1969, Bill Wentworth was involved in the early stages of exploring the need for Indigenous traditional cultural property protection. The Chair of the newly established Council of Aboriginal Affairs, Dr Nugget Coombs, outlined a proposal for legislation to protect 'traditional Aboriginal property' and 'establish property rights in certain works of art, designs, areas of religious, ceremonial, ritual, artistic and tribal significance' to Aboriginal people.

The proposed Traditional Aboriginal Property Act would serve to vest traditional Aboriginal property rights in a Trustee and by his (*sic*) delegation to corporate bodies, and to provide for the protection, development and, where appropriate, economic exploitation of these property rights in the interests of Aboriginal people. It further aimed to protect the work of Aboriginal people from 'imitation and unreasonable commercial practice, and to also provide effective marketing of their products' (Davis 2007, p. 283).

This proposal more than likely influenced the moves of the Whitlam Government in the early 1970s to establish a Working Party on the protection of Aboriginal folklore. The Working Party took several years to complete its findings, which were finally released in 1981 (Department of Home Affairs and Environment 1981).[1] Generally, the Working Party recommended the enactment of an Aboriginal Folklore Act which would provide safeguards against certain uses of Aboriginal arts and cultural material that are offensive to Aboriginal people and their traditions, while at the same time encouraging fair and authorised use of Aboriginal arts and cultural material. These proposed Australian laws did not take shape as law, but the fact that such discussions took place in the early stages of Aboriginal affairs highlight the fact that there was a debate about Indigenous cultural and intellectual property rights.

In the last four decades there has been a remarkable growth in the value and demand for Indigenous arts, cultural expression and knowledge. The Aboriginal art market is currently valued at $300 million per annum, and traditional knowledge has applications in industries that range from tourism and entertainment through to the biotechnology industry. The increase in demand also meant the rise of a rip-off industry, where Indigenous arts and knowledge have been taken without consent or acknowledgment. In 40 years of calling for legal protection, most of the measures have been instigated by Indigenous advocates guarding their ground by asserting cultural rights, bringing test cases, devising protocols and enforcing rights under agreement — hence my call for a national Indigenous cultural authority for Indigenous people to continue the advancement of rights.

My paper is in four parts: forty years of Indigenous cultural rights advocacy; *Our culture: Our future* — what happened to that big report?; Proposal for a national Indigenous cultural authority; and Prior informed consent models: learning from international experience.

Forty years of Indigenous cultural rights advocacy

Indigenous arts and cultural expression are interconnected with land and seas, handed down through the generations as part of cultural heritage. Painting, dances, stories, songs, and knowledge come from the land, and are passed on from generation to generation as Indigenous cultural heritage. Culture is not static, it evolves and adapts, and Indigenous people must be recognised as the primary custodians of their culture.

Since the 1970s, Indigenous artists have been calling for recognition of their creative rights on the same level as that of other Australian artists. In Australia, the *Copyright Act 1968* (Cth) provides rights for copyright owners to control the use and dissemination of literary, dramatic, artistic and musical works, and also certain listed subject matter including sound recordings, cinematograph films, television and sound broadcasts, and published editions. There are certain requirements that must be met before protection is granted. Yet if a work, film or sound recording meets these requirements, then the law makes it the subject of copyright, without the need for registration.

This feature of the law has two significant impacts for Indigenous people: first, Indigenous arts and culture are orally and performance based, and therefore do not meet requirements of copyright, at least in the old days of the 1960s and 1970s. Prior to the recent case law, Aboriginal arts was seen as folklore and considered unoriginal in that copying artistic traditions did not amount to innovation and interpretation. Secondly and importantly, copyright was recognised, however, in the written interpretations and recordings made of Indigenous knowledge, arts, dances, music and stories. Copyright protected the films and tapes that recorded Indigenous people and their cultural knowledge. However, that copyright was recognised in the material form created in many cases by non-Indigenous people, and the ownership vested in the recorder as the 'author' of these works. So songs, dances, customs, knowledge about bush foods and medicines have been, and continue to be, recorded — but not by the Indigenous knowledge holders or their communities.

Cases involving appropriation of Indigenous images

In 1966, when Australia switched to decimal currency, the one-dollar note depicted 'ancient Aboriginal art' by artist David Malangi. The selection of this art for the note involved no consultation with the artist. The original bark painting was purchased by an international art collector three years before, and had subsequently been donated to the Paris Museum of Arts of Africa and Oceania. The collector gave a photocopy of the art to an officer of the Reserve Bank of Australia who then gave it to the designer of the one-dollar note. Nugget Coombs, Governor of the Reserve Bank, was deeply embarrassed by the incident, since he was a great advocate for Indigenous artists' rights. The Reserve Bank had not consulted anyone, assuming the design was the work of an 'anonymous and probably long dead artist'. It was, of course, a copyright work. David Malangi was given $1,000, a fishing kit and a silver medallion.

In 1975, Wandjuk Marika, the first Chair of the Aboriginal Arts Board, called for greater protection after seeing his important sacred works reproduced on a tea towel. He said, 'This was one of the stories that my father had given to me and no one else amongst my people would have painted it without permission. I was deeply upset and for many years I have been unable to paint. It was then that I realised that I and my fellow artists needed some sort of protection' (Johnson, 1997, p. 11. He pointed out that copyright did not cover Indigenous arts and craft, which was referred to as 'folklore' and dealt with as if it were in the public domain and, like *terra nullius*, free for all to exploit.

These early cases reflect a *terra nullius* notion of Indigenous arts where much of the artwork was labelled 'artists unknown' and collected for its value as an object of curiosity rather than its cultural significance. Wandjuk Marika's call set the ground for action by Indigenous people over the following years.

Another case involving currency occurred when the ten-dollar note commemorating Australia's bicentennial reproduced a morning star pole, with rights granted under licence by the Aboriginal Artists Agency to the Reserve Bank. Morning star poles are made for the sacred morning star ceremony. This one, by Terry Yumbulul, was made and sold to the Australian Museum. Yumbulul had entered into a licence agreement that had allowed his agent, the

Aboriginal Artists Agency, to license the work to the bank. Yumbulul came under considerable criticism from members of his clan when they found out that the morning star pole had been reproduced on the ten-dollar note. He took action against the Agency and the Bank but was unsuccessful. Justice French recognised that customary and copyright law have divergent interest when he said, 'Australia's copyright law does not provide adequate recognition of Aboriginal community claims to regulate the reproduction and use of works which are essentially communal in origin' (*Yumbulul v. Reserve Bank of Australia* 1991.

In 1989, the Ganalbingu artist John Bulun Bulun commenced action in the Darwin Federal Court against a T-shirt manufacturer who had copied his ceremonial artwork, *Magpie geese and waterlilies at the waterhole*. The clever Melbourne barrister, Colin Golvan, had heard the then Chair of the Aboriginal Arts Board, Lin Onus, on radio, discussing the case, and had then called Lin to offer his services on the case. Thirteen other Aboriginal artists were joined to the proceedings, because other artistic works were copied. The Court granted an interlocutory injunction to stop the manufacture and sale of the T-shirts. Before the trial, the parties settled. The defendant T-shirt company agreed to halt sales, and pay $150,000 in damages to the artists; the money was shared between the artists and their families (for the deceased ones). It became known as the *'Flash T-shirts' Case*, and articles in legal journals began to appear all over the world, speculating on how the case may have been decided.

In 1994, *Milpurrurru v Indofurn* (1993) became the first Federal Court judgment recognising that Indigenous artist's works, which depicted pre-existing clan owned designs, were original copyright works. At that time, I was working for the National Indigenous Arts Advocacy Association as a junior legal information officer. I remember watching the fax machine curl out over 100 pages. The artists had met this requirement because of the skill and interpretation they had expended. In this matter, Justice von Doussa considered a claim that carpets with Indigenous designs amounted to copyright infringement. Justice von Doussa made a collective award to the artists rather than individual awards so that the artists could distribute it according to their custom. The court's finding that the company directors were also liable for copyright infringement was overturned on appeal. Still, the case set an important precedent and one media article likened it to the *Mabo* case.

The judgment of *Bulun Bulun & Anor v R & T Textiles Pty Ltd* was reported in 1998. This case concerned the artist Johnny Bulun Bulun once again. The potential reach of this case in copyright law is, in my opinion, yet to be determined. It builds upon previous cases by making some important statements about the copyright and the relationships between individual Indigenous artists and their community, when the artwork incorporates communally owned ritual knowledge.

By way of background, copyright laws grant exclusive rights to authors to use, adapt and reproduce their works without conditions. This is at odds with the Indigenous cultural heritage material. In many Indigenous clans, there are laws, based on responsibility for cultural heritage, to ensure that it is maintained and protected, and passed on to future generations. An individual or group of individuals may be empowered to act as the caretaker of a particular item of heritage.[2] Traditional custodians are empowered to protect a particular item only to the extent that their actions harmonise with the best interests of the community as a whole.

Johnny Bulun Bulun was the artist and copyright owner of the bark painting, *At the waterhole*. The painting embodied traditional ritual knowledge of the Ganalbingu people. Johnny Bulun Bulun's use of ritual knowledge to produce the artworks was given to him under Ganalbingu customary law, based on the trust and confidence that those granting permission had in the artist. R & T Textiles Ltd had imported and sold within Australia fabric which copied parts of *At the waterhole*. Once issued with the statement of claim, the textile company was quick to negotiate a settlement. However, the case still went to court to consider issues relating to clan interests in the copyright work (*Bulun Bulun v R & T Textiles Pty Ltd* 1998).

Justice von Doussa, the same judge who presided on the *Carpets Case*, found that there was no Native Title right to the painting. He also considered that there was no equitable interest in the work. The court found that there was no evidence that the artist had created the work as part of an implied legal trust that would make his clan equal owners of the copyright. The witnesses and affidavit evidence showed that 'on many occasions paintings which incorporate to a greater or lesser degree parts of ritual knowledge of the Ganalbingu people are reproduced by Ganalbingu artists for commercial sale for the benefit of the artists concerned'. Nor was the copyright in the work jointly owned by the artist and the clan, because there was no evidence that anyone other than Johnny Bulun Bulun had created the bark painting (Brown 2003, p 64).

Justice von Doussa found that there was a fiduciary relationship between the artist and the clan. Customary laws affected the rights of the artist to deal with the work embodying the ritual knowledge in a way that he had to discuss and negotiate use of the traditional knowledge with relevant persons in authority within his clan. In his evidence, Djardie Ashley discussed how the Ganalbingu laws dealt with the consent procedures. Mr Ashley noted that in some circumstances, such as the reproduction of a painting in an art book, the artist might not need to consult with the group widely. In other circumstances, such as its mass-reproduction as merchandise, Mr Bulun Bulun may be required to consult widely. Mr Ashley further noted that:

the question in each case depends on the use and the manner or the mode of production. Yet in the case of a use which is one that requires direct consultation, rather than one for which approval has already been given for a class of uses, all of the traditional owners must agree; there must be total consensus.

Bulun Bulun could not act alone to permit the reproduction of 'At the waterhole' in the manner that it was done. (McCausland 1999, pp. 4–6)

This relationship imposed the obligation on Johnny Bulun Bulun not to

exploit the artistic work in any way that is contrary to the law and customs of the Ganalbingu people, and, in the event of infringement by a third party, to take reasonable and appropriate action to restrain and remedy infringement of the copyright in the artistic work. (McCausland 1999, pp. 4–6)

If the artist had been unable or unwilling to take copyright action, equity would have allowed the clan leader to take action to stop the infringement.

The potential extent of fiduciary duty

This fiduciary obligation, which is imposed on the artist owning the copyright, has much potential for Indigenous people. The potential repercussions of the judgment pertain to whether this type of obligation may extend in certain circumstances where notice of the 'Bulun Bulun equity' is given to outsiders. For example, a third party licensee of an Indigenous artwork who is on notice of a custodian's interest may be open to claims by an Indigenous clan to whom they owe a fiduciary duty to safeguard the integrity of the work when dealing with the copyright work. Perhaps the Bulun Bulun equity applies to other copyright works that incorporate traditional ritual knowledge. A non-Indigenous third party fiduciary duty might arise where traditional custodians allow access to a filmmaker to interview community members. If the filmmaker is given notice of the custodians' interest in traditional ritual knowledge communicated in the interviews, the filmmaker may owe a fiduciary duty to the custodians when dealing with copyright in the filmed interviews. A custodians' interest notice incorporated in the access permit would help to establish this duty.

In other areas, too, where outsiders enter communities to record traditional cultural expression, an Indigenous community could use written agreements to impose the fiduciary obligations of third parties when they access, record and publish traditional ritual knowledge. For example, where a researcher wants access to traditional ritual knowledge for a particular project or film and record it, the community could enter into a written agreement with that person, requiring her to consult on an ongoing basis about the future use of that material. It could also require her to display a custodians' interest notice on any copyright material created. The community could even require copyright in the project to be jointly owned or held on trust for its benefit. This line of thought has implications for scholars, authors, filmmakers, sound recorder, compilers, researchers and other recorders of Indigenous traditional knowledge and cultural expression, where copyright is created. Since the Bulun Bulun case, there has been a growing trend for a traditional custodian's notice to be affixed to reproductions of art, and inside the cover of publications that incorporate Indigenous cultural expression.[3]

Brandl rock art: A case study

In 1997, Riptide Churinga, a Sydney based T-shirt manufacturer, produced a range of T-shirts with Mimi rock art figures. The T-shirts were discovered on sale, to the surprise of a descendant of the Badmardi clan and Dr Vivien Johnson, an Aboriginal art lecturer. The use of the Mimi figures was guarded carefully under customary law, and they are still significant to Indigenous cultural beliefs. Stories, and information surrounding the sites, the sites themselves, and the right to touch up or depict images like those embodied in rock form should, for cultural heritage purposes, belong in theory to the owners of the cultural images therein. The rock art is estimated to be about 4,000 years old and therefore not the subject of copyright (Janke 2003, p. 106). The problem for the Badmardi clan was how to stop the T-shirt maker from transgressing their laws. Some rock art sites can only be painted or depicted by certain people with the relevant ritual knowledge and the right to do so under customary law (Environment Australia 2006).

In the 1970s, Eric Brandl received grant funding from the Australian Institute of Aboriginal Studies (now the Australian Institute of Aboriginal and Torres Strait Islander Studies — AIATSIS) to visit and record rock art sites in the Northern Territory. His methods of recording involved photographing the various rock art sites, which were in very difficult place to get to, in the Deaf Adder Creek region. Back in his office, Brandl projected the images onto a wall on which he had affixed sheets of paper, and then traced the works in Indian ink.

These drawings and photographs of the Mimi Rock Art were published by the Australian Institute of Aboriginal Studies in 1973 (Brandl 1973). There was copyright in the book, the photograph and the drawings. In line with the originality principles of copyright, that such skill and labour applied to the original rock art, would give a copyright interest in the derived sketches. It was obvious that Riptide Churinga had taken designs directly from the book to produce its T-shirts. AIATSIS, the Brandl Estate and the Badmardi clan demanded that the company stop production of the T-shirt. They entered into a settlement in which damage to, and delivery of, unsold items were included. There was also a national public apology posted in *The Australian*, a national newspaper.

The Brandl case illustrates that copyright owners can work with 'cultural owners' to commence action, even though the 'cultural owners' have no copyright. This case, which occurred prior to the Bulun Bulun fiduciary duty, was commenced by AIATSIS in observation of their cultural custodial status as a national keeping place for Indigenous studies. AIATSIS was not legally obliged to do so. But consider if the researcher Brandl had been on notice of the traditional custodian interest in the rock art, and had published a notice at the front of the publication. Then it may be open for speculation that the issue of whether the clan could compel the copyright owner to take action, or if the copyright owner was unwilling or unable to take such action against the copyright infringer, then equity may allow them to commence and seek an appropriate remedy.

In summary, these cases changed the copyright landscape, so that now Indigenous cultural and intellectual property rights are seen as important rights for Indigenous people to be managed and administered. The questions now remain about the shortfalls, the areas that are not protected: namely, communal rights, the longer term protection, and issues for secret–sacred works.

Our culture: Our future – what happened to that big report?

Ten years ago, I worked on a project, coordinated by the Australian Institute of Aboriginal and Torres Strait Islander Studies, for the then ATSIC. It was to review and report on Indigenous cultural and intellectual property (ICIP) rights. In 1994, the government released an issues paper entitled *Stopping the Ripoffs* (Janke & National Indigenous Arts Advocacy Association 1995), which examined shortfalls in the law in protecting Indigenous arts and cultural expression. Significant work was also undertaken as part of the Social Justice Package, which advocated for greater cultural rights.

ICIP rights had been a significant inclusion in the then draft Declaration on the Rights of Indigenous Peoples. These rights still remain in the final draft, passed by the Council of the United Nations last year. Australia was one of the four countries that voted against it. The *United Nations Declaration on the Rights of Indigenous Peoples*, was passed. Article 31 states:

> 1. Indigenous peoples have the right to maintain, control, protect and develop their cultural heritage, traditional knowledge and traditional cultural expressions, as well as the manifestations of their sciences, technologies and cultures, including human and genetic resources, seeds, medicines, knowledge of the properties of fauna and flora, oral traditions, literatures, designs, sports and traditional games and visual and performing arts. They also have the right to maintain, control, protect and develop their intellectual property over such cultural heritage, traditional knowledge, and traditional cultural expressions.
>
> 2. In conjunction with Indigenous peoples, States shall take effective measures to recognise and protect the exercise of these rights. (United Nations 2008)

In 1999, the report *Our culture: Our future* was released, with 115 legislative and policy recommendations (Janke 1999). The Indigenous reference group of some fifteen Indigenous people was clear in setting its priority for *sui generis* legislation. The group wanted legal foundations for the protection of Indigenous cultural and intellectual property rights. The report took a view that such legislation would be long term and recommended a range of potential legal and non-legal measures, including changes to copyright, patent, trademarks and cultural heritage laws. It also introduced practices within government departments such as including an Indigenous advisory committee or unit within IP Australia, the responsible government agency for trademarks, patents and design registration. My favourite recommendation was for the establishment of a national Indigenous cultural authority to act as a leading organisation for the promotion and administration of ICIP rights. The following recommendation appears in the report:

22.1 National Indigenous Cultural Authority
A National Indigenous Cultural Authority should be established as an organisation made up of various Indigenous organisations to:
- Develop policies and protocols with various industries.
- Authorise uses of Indigenous cultural material through a permission system which seeks prior consent from relevant Indigenous groups.
- Monitor exploitation of cultures.
- Undertake public education and awareness strategies.
- Advance Indigenous Cultural and Intellectual Property Rights nationally and internationally.

The National Indigenous Cultural Authority should be the peak advisory body on Indigenous Cultural and Intellectual Property Rights.

Representation on the Authority should aim to cover all areas of Indigenous Cultural and Intellectual Property. The National Indigenous Cultural Authority should be funded by both industry and government. (Janke 1999, p. 237)

Very few of the measures were considered, not even a draft of a *sui generis* law, and nor were there moves to establish a national Indigenous cultural authority. Most of the initiatives have involved the development of protocols, and the use of contracts by Indigenous people and supporting industry organisations. There was, however, a proposal to amend the Copyright Act to include Indigenous communal moral rights.

In 2000, when the moral rights amendments were being discussed in the Senate, the then Senator Aden Ridgeway drew attention to the fact that the moral rights proposals did not take account of Indigenous communal interests. The Howard government said that it would consider this and in 2003 drafted proposed amendments of the *Copyright Act 1968* (Cth) for Indigenous Communal Moral Rights (Copyright Amendment (Indigenous Communal

Moral Rights) Bill 2003). If the draft Bill becomes law, Indigenous communal moral rights (ICMR) will exist alongside an individual author's moral rights.[4] ICMRs will exist in works and films that draw from a traditional base.[5]

Under the ICMR model, an authorised representative of an Indigenous community can take action against infringements of the communal moral rights of attribution and integrity. These are two important rights for custodians of culture: first, the right to be acknowledged as the source of the cultural material, thus identifying the people who are responsible for the cultural continuum of the work; and second, the right of integrity, which addresses cultural obligations to guard against derogatory treatment and the need for Indigenous people to be recognised as the primary guardians and interpreters of their cultures, arts and sciences, whether created in the past or developed by them in the future. The proposed ICMR model has an important limitation. For a work or film to have ICMR, there must be a voluntary agreement between the creator of the work or the film and the Indigenous community that ICMR exists, before the first dealing of the work or film.[6] Another limitation of the proposed Bill is that ICMRs would exist for the term of the copyright period. As discussed above, Indigenous people see ICIP rights as extending much longer, in perpetuity, for continuing cultural practice.

The Bill has never seen the inside of the houses of Parliament and its current status is uncertain. Perhaps this is for best, in light of international advances. I say this because we should be developing a bigger vision in which we need to re-examine some of the recommendations of *Our culture: Our future*. The change in government at the Federal level and developments in international law offer a chance to rethink whether an Indigenous-managed entity, with a clear mandate to promote cultural and intellectual property rights, has a place in the Australian cultural landscape.

Proposal for a National Indigenous Cultural Authority

In April 2008, I was invited to attend the Australia 2020 Summit. For my one big idea, I suggested the establishment of a national Indigenous cultural authority. In the lead-up to the Summit, web pollster 'GetUp' solicited the public for ideas. An on-line submission from the Australian Lawyers for Human Rights (ALHR) stated:

> ALHR is of the opinion that Intellectual Property protections in Australia need to be considered in respect of the unique significance arts and culture holds for Indigenous peoples. In particular, ALHR recognises that there are various protections that could be afforded to Indigenous cultural heritage, including: the protection of the underlying ideas or information that is put into a work; a style or method of art; some performances such as dance and music regardless of whether they have been recorded; and a community's rights in an artwork. (ALHR 2008)

The participants in Options for the Future of Indigenous Australians had many ideas, ranging from education, business, health, constitutional reform, a treaty, a new dialogue to a national representative organisation. Indigenous cultural and intellectual property rights were referred to in the initial report:

> There was a strong sense that Indigenous culture represents a real economic opportunity, and among the suggestions was a formalised structure for promoting Indigenous cultural and intellectual property rights and developing standards for appropriate use, attribution and royalties for such works. (Department Prime Minister and Cabinet 2008)

It was the Creative Arts stream that gave the strongest support for Indigenous culture.[7] The Australia 2020's initial report captured their idea as follows:

> Creativity is central to Australian life and Indigenous culture is the core to this. To measure, document and leverage the strengths of this culture, to articulate our role and improve protection of indigenous culture, language and heritage through a National Indigenous Cultural Authority. (Department Prime Minister and Cabinet 2008, p. 29)

The final Summit report, released in May 2008, expanded the idea in the Indigenous stream to a recommendation under the heading of 'Culture, art, symbols'. Idea 7.40 states: 'Establish a national cultural authority for the protection of Aboriginal and Torres Strait Islander intellectual property'. Also of interest was the idea at 7.43: 'Consideration should be given to whether people with cultural knowledge should be accredited' (Department Prime Minister and Cabinet 2008, p. 229).

The Final Report elaborated further on the Arts Stream's National Indigenous Cultural Authority in Recommendation 8.70:

> Establish a National Indigenous Cultural Authority; measure, document and leverage the strengths of Indigenous culture; and articulate the role and improve protection of Indigenous cultures, languages and heritage. (Department Prime Minister and Cabinet 2008, p. 273)

Since the Australia 2020 Summit, the Aboriginal and Torres Strait Islander Arts Board of the Australia Council articulated an interest in the establishment of a national Indigenous cultural authority. In May 2008, the Aboriginal and Torres Strait Islander Arts Board and the National Indigenous Arts Reference Group discussed the Australia 2020 results. Reporting back from the meetings, the first edition of *Aboriginal and Torres Strait Islander Arts News* stated that there

> was keen interest and much discussion about calls from the Australia 2020 Summit for a national cultural authority for the protection of Aboriginal and Torres Strait Islander intellectual property. (Australia Council, 2008)

This is an indication that national infrastructure is seen as an important consideration in the advance of Indigenous cultural and intellectual property rights.

This option is a self-determining model which could best address the comprehensive nature of Indigenous cultural and intellectual property. It could also be a way to overcome the problems associated with customary laws being enshrined in legislation.

A national Indigenous cultural authority is needed to provide leadership and to administer rights either directly or by establishing a distribution framework, for Indigenous cultural and intellectual property rights. Another important function of the national Indigenous cultural authority is to lobby for these rights holders. Experience has shown that industries have developed through the support of a leader authority. Intellectual property rights themselves are managed collectively internationally because it makes more sense commercially and in time for collection of royalties to be collected and distributed in a structured way.

This deals with the economies of scale but there are also the cultural maintenance reasons — caring for culture. We need to make sure it is appropriately used, properly recompensed, that our Indigenous creators are valued and attributed, and also that our culture is not derogatorily used.

There is no national independent organisation that represents Indigenous artists and creators. Since the demise of the National Indigenous Arts Advocacy Association in 2003, legal advice has been provided by the Arts Law Centre of Australia through its Artists in the Black program (Arts Law Centre 2005). Further, there has been some important work in Indigenous visual arts conducted by the National Association for the Visual Arts (NAVA) including the development of protocols *Valuing Art, Respecting Culture* (Mellor 2001) and *Indigenous Australian Art Commercial Code of Conduct* (Australia Council 2009). These two organisations have done well to advance the rights of Indigenous artists; however, there is a need for an Indigenous managed and controlled agency to take the lead on these important issues, and to provide a collective voice and meaningful representation. A national Indigenous cultural authority will give a collective voice for Indigenous culture that to date has been absent.

I note the Australian government's response to the Senate Standing Committee on the Environment, Communications, Information Technology and the Arts Committee Report — Indigenous art — *Securing the Future,* the report on the Inquiry into Australia's Indigenous visual arts and craft sector (Senate Standing Committee 2007). The Committee recommended that the Indigenous Art Commercial Code of Conduct be developed and that the Commonwealth undertake a project examining and making recommendations regarding further initiatives to enhance the integrity of the Indigenous arts market (Senate Standing Committee 2007, Recommendation 23). The report also recommended resale royalty rights — another administration and management issue for Indigenous artists. Perhaps the national Indigenous cultural authority could perform some of these functions.

The other important role of the national Indigenous cultural authority would be to administer the framework for prior informed consent rights to cultural material. Currently, Indigenous cultural expression and knowledge are supplied and used without a fee. If we charged a royalty on use, as for copyright and other intellectual property, the resulting income could be distributed, through such an authority, to the traditional owners and communities, which in turn would support community development, artistic and cultural development and maintenance.

This body could also monitor Indigenous cultural and intellectual property protection nationally. A national approach to protecting Indigenous people's rights is required. It also has an important networking role. Decision makers in all States and Territories need to be aware of developments in other areas and communities of Australia, as well as internationally.

Under this system, corporations would give back to Indigenous communities what they now take for free. More art and culture would be performed and encouraged. Indigenous people would find employment opportunities in not only arts and culture but in management, business, investment and as professional advisers to these industries including as lawyers and accountants. This system could promote the practice of culture and the business of culture at the same time.

Setting up a National Indigenous Cultural Authority

The Australian Society of Authors (ASA) lobbied government for the establishment of Public Lending Rights (PLR) in 1975 and Educational Lending Rights (ELR) in 2000.[8] These rights are about the number of books writers have in public libraries; authors receive a certain amount of money for the books they have in the libraries because the loan of books reduces their income through the loss of sale of books. What about Indigenous oral recordings that are held in libraries and made available to the public? The national Indigenous cultural authority could lobby for payments like PLR and ELR for Indigenous storytellers, as they are the authors of orally transmitted cultural expressions. Other models to draw on include the statutory licensing schemes set up Copyright Agency Limited (CAL) and Australasian Performing Right Association (APRA). These collective copyright management agencies have developed large industries, and are leading cultural organisations that turn over millions of dollars per annum, which they distribute to their membership of copyright owners. Consider the role played by these collecting societies in developing and enhancing Australian creative industries. The root for this invigoration is prior consent models: copyright exploitation rights and the collection of fees. Surely we could make use of these types of models to develop a culturally appropriate organisation to promote Indigenous arts and cultural expression?

How should the national Indigenous cultural authority be legally structured? Will it be a government agency or statutory authority or should it be independent from government? One option is to establish a statutory authority like the Australian Institute of Aboriginal and Torres Strait Islander Studies. Bodies such as AIATSIS have their own establishing legislation: a statute passed by the Commonwealth Parliament.[9] It could be a government company like the Australian Securities Commission. It could be a company limited by guarantee, a not-for-profit company. It must have the power to raise money and invest. An example of this type of structure is the National Indigenous Television Inc. (NITV) which is funded by government but is an independent legal entity. However, it relies on government funding to operate, and the funding agreement imposes a means for government to monitor the organisation's work, ensuring that it meets important agreed criteria.

For a cultural organisation to thrive, the national Indigenous cultural authority should be underpinned by strong membership that is open to Indigenous cultural practitioners with voting rights to effectively elect a representative board. The membership base should be made up of Indigenous stakeholders, the owners of Indigenous culture. The board could be formed from a range of traditional owner representatives, and industry and legal experts. The national Indigenous cultural authority should be accountable to its membership to continue its charter, and implement good governance. The National Indigenous Arts Advocacy Association, which shut its doors in 2002, failed to do this. According to the NIAAA Review Report, the leadership of the organisation was highly volatile and unstable (Rimmer 2004, p. 161).

In setting up the new agency, there are lessons to be learned from the previous models that, although sometimes classed as 'failures', have some successful aspects. In the 1990s, the National Indigenous Arts Advocacy Association (NIAAA) received funding from the Australia Council's Aboriginal and Torres Strait Islander Arts Board and the Aboriginal and Torres Strait Islander Commission (ATSIC). Its functions included advancing Indigenous artists' rights, which it did quite well in the first five years, through coordinating cases such as the *Carpets Case* (referred to above). Another important function of NIAAA was to develop the National Label of Authenticity project — a certification trade mark to denote authentic Indigenous arts products and to ensure fair returns to Indigenous artists, while also promoting greater understanding of Indigenous heritage and art (NIAAA 1998). The Label of Authenticity project faced many challenges and within two years of its launch, in 2000, the Australia Council suspended funding to NIAAA, and commissioned a review (Rimmer 2004, pp. 139–79). The Final Report of the NIAAA Review (Australia Council, 2002) noted that NIAAA was lacking in governance and structure. Although it was a national body, it did not invite membership generally and did not have representation on its governing committee from states other than NSW.

The members were not elected by their community. NIAAA had failed to win stakeholders' support, and respondents to the reviewer's survey noted that they had lost contact with NIAAA over the two years. Despite the downfall, NIAAA had many positive contributions, including the cases it coordinated and the development of a model for certification. This model inspired the New Zealand Toi Iho trademark, now into its sixth year. Fiji is also considering a model based along the original NIAAA model.

Such an agency would require government funding, at least initially. The board and management should be required to report to government and meet certain threshold performance criteria in the same way that the collecting societies are kept in check by reporting to government and tabling their annual report in Parliament. Collecting societies must also comply with developed codes of conduct.

To undertake its functions, the national Indigenous cultural authority would need to make use of a range of tools which are intellectual property (IP) based, such as trademarks, and copyright licensing agreements. It would also use other measures such as protocols, benchmarking and Indigenous mediation services.

The authority would need to develop a strong trademark and branding system — once developed the trademark should be registered, and should operate to endorse projects, goods and services which are facilitated by the authority processes of prior informed consent. Like the National Heart Foundation mark is applied to goods that meet criteria for healthy food, the authority's trademark would appeal to consumers who are looking for authentic products and services that are made with fair trade through the sharing of benefits with Indigenous custodians of culture.

Keeping track of who owns rights, and who has made use of them, is an important feature of a rights access and management system. A national Indigenous cultural authority could manage rights clearances by keeping a comprehensive database of intangible cultural material and list rights holders, so that those who want to negotiate or seek appropriate use can do so, by contacting the relevant parties. A register would be a fundamental implementation tool for the national authority. It should be made clear, however, that the database is not a rights registration system, which infers rights once registered, like the trademark registration system, but the database would be an identifier of who owns the rights to a particular item of cultural heritage. The United Nations University's report on *The role of registers and databases in the protection of traditional knowledge* will be useful to consider in developing a model for the national Indigenous cultural authority (Alexander & Institute of Advanced Studies 2004). Databases can also be used as a measure to inform other rights based systems and assert Indigenous rights to material by preventing others from registering rights in Indigenous traditional knowledge or cultural expression. Also of note is the Database of Official Insignia of Native American Tribes, which stops others from registering Native American insignia as trademarks in the United States of America (United States Patent and Trademark Officer 2001).

The national Indigenous cultural authority would be responsible for developing standard terms for licence agreements entered into for the use of material, as well as the branding to use the its trademark. Collective organisation models have long known the benefits of using standard agreements to limit administration costs, as well as set appropriate terms of use. See, for example, the Australian Society of Authors Model Contract of publishing agreements (ASA nd).

The national Indigenous cultural authority could develop protocols which set standards for consent procedures, attribution and integrity, but consultation with Indigenous communities will be necessary to develop them. Already a strong protocol framework has developed and although largely ethical in nature, or enforced in funding agreements for projects, protocols provide scope to examine how things might be implemented by a national coordination body such as the national Indigenous cultural authority.

The Australia Council for the Arts has published protocols for the development of Indigenous music. These advise that when performing or recording communally owned musical works, it is important to seek permission from the relevant community owners of the music. Robynne Quiggin, author of the *Music protocols for producing Indigenous Australian music*, states:

> Observing customary law means finding out who can speak for that music, so the right people are asked for permission to use the music. For instance, if a musician wanted to use a rhythm or phrase from music belonging to a Torres Strait Island language group or family, it is essential to locate the correct language group or family group from the particular Island owning that song or music (Quiggin 2007, p. 14).

In this respect, the model can be used to enhance the preservation of traditional knowledge and expression of culture. It acknowledges the role of community ownership and control within that culture.

An authority and rights regime of this nature will almost certainly require thought about how competing interests and overlapping knowledge are dealt with. Mediation is a flexible method to resolve disputes. Although the World Intellectual Property Organization (WIPO) has a dispute resolution program, I am in favour of the use of alternative dispute resolution services in Indigenous disputes generally.[10] However, I consider that the application of alternative dispute resolution, especially mediation, by the national Indigenous cultural authority would be useful. Such a rights administration body would need to develop skills in resolving 'IP disputes' and negotiating rights between Indigenous individuals, and communities (clan groups), Indigenous and non-Indigenous commercial entities, and between Indigenous and non-Indigenous groups.

This approach is used in Native Title and lessons learned in that arena can be shared. Also, see the WIPO mediation of international disputes concerning domain name registration. An approach for Indigenous mediation services is recommended. The Arts Law Centre of Australia has mediation guidelines and convenes a mediation service to deal with arts disputes. In my opinion, there are benefits in this approach.

Prior informed consent models: learning from international experience

I would now like to examine some international prior informed consent models. Since 2000, the World Intellectual Property Organization (WIPO) has convened an Intergovernmental Committee on intellectual property and genetic resources, traditional knowledge and folklore.[11] The WIPO Committee has developed two documents: 'Draft provisions for the protection of traditional cultural expressions', and 'Draft provisions for the protection of traditional knowledge' (WIPO nd).

It is expected that the draft guidelines will shape future laws and policies relating to traditional cultural expressions and traditional knowledge. The 'Draft provisions on traditional cultural expressions' cover 'traditional cultural expressions', which include songs, stories, ceremonies, rituals, dance and art, including rock art, face and body painting, sand sculptures and bark paintings.

WIPO provisions on traditional cultural expressions include compliance with the 'free, prior and informed consent' principle and the 'recognition of customary laws and practices.' Under the WIPO provisions, prior consent of the traditional owners of cultural expressions would be required before recording, publication or communication to the public. There would also be moral rights for communities but these would be automatic and not just voluntary.

The *Pacific Regional Framework for the Protection of Traditional Knowledge and Expression of Culture* establishes 'traditional cultural rights' for traditional owners of traditional knowledge and expression of culture.[12] The prior and informed consent of the traditional owners is required to reproduce, publish, perform, display, make available on line and electronically transmit, traditional knowledge or expressions of culture. The Pacific Model Law for the Protection of Traditional Knowledge and Expressions of Culture recognises the pivotal role of a cultural authority in administering prior informed consent rights. The explanatory memorandum of the Pacific Model law states:

> The model law provides two avenues by which a prospective user of traditional knowledge or expressions of culture for non-customary purposes can seek the prior and informed consent of the traditional owners for the use of the traditional knowledge or expressions of culture. The two avenues are: applying to a 'Cultural Authority' which has functions in relation to

identifying traditional owners and acting as a liaison between prospective users and traditional owners; or dealing directly with the traditional owners.

In both cases, the prior and informed consent of the traditional owners is to be evidenced by an 'authorised user agreement'. And in both cases, the Cultural Authority has a role in providing advice to traditional owners about the terms and conditions of authorised user agreements and maintaining a record of finalised authorised user agreements.[13]

I consider that this model law would be a great reference point for those seeking the introduction of a national Indigenous cultural authority, and such a model may not need legislation but could be established to facilitate negotiated agreements for use of Indigenous cultural and intellectual property, where both parties are willing to recognise I cultural and intellectual property rights, and where there are certain incentive for commercial interest groups to do so, for instance, where use of a branded trade mark or authentication label is given, as part of the licensed user rights.

Using this model as a guide, five Pacific countries are lined up to introduce Traditional Cultural Expression law: Fiji, Palau, Cook Islands, Papua New Guinea and Vanuatu. Palau has drafted a *Bill for the Protection and Promotion of Traditional Knowledge and Expressions of Culture*. The Bill aims to establish a new form of Intellectual property identified as 'traditional knowledge and expressions of culture' and to vest ownership of this new property in the appropriate traditional groups, clans, and communities. 'Ownership' is defined as 'the manner of collective property control recognised in traditional law and does not create or imply non-traditional property interests for individual members of the owner'. The Palau proposed law requires prior and informed consent for all non-customary uses of traditional knowledge and expressions of culture.

In South Africa, an *African Traditional Knowledge* Bill proposes to provide for the recognition and protection of traditional performances having an indigenous origin and a traditional character, and to provide for the recognition and protection of copyright works of a traditional character. In this way, the Bill confers copyright on a traditional work if: (a) the work was created (i) on or after the date of commencement of the Intellectual Property Laws Amendment Act, 2007; or (ii) within a period of fifty years preceding the date contemplated in subparagraph (i); and (b) the community from which the work or a substantial part thereof originated is or was an indigenous community when the work was created.[14]

The drafters of this proposed law have also provided for the establishment of a national council in respect of traditional intellectual property and a national database for the recording to traditional intellectual property. There is the establishment of a national trust fund which indigenous clans can access for cultural purposes. Amendments to the Trademark Laws are also included which provides protection for geographical indications, recognising that art and culture comes from specific areas. The Bill is being reviewed after submissions and public consultation revealed that the majority of stakeholders present thought that amending the current laws may be unworkable. The general feeling is that a new law — a *sui generis* law, would be better to deal with traditional knowledge issues. The South African Department of Trade and Industry plans to redraft the Bill and present it to the Parliament later this year. The SA developments will inform our own framework.

Conclusion

In summary, the establishment of a national Indigenous cultural authority would set up an appropriate structure to advance the rights of Indigenous artists and creators and to allow them to share in the benefits from the appropriate use of the culture. A national Indigenous cultural authority will set a new dialogue that would enrich the artistic, social and economic lives of Indigenous artists.

The national Indigenous cultural authority model aims to be flexible to allow Indigenous Australian communities to implement a practical strategy for protecting and managing their Indigenous cultural and intellectual property.

It is important for the right infrastructure to be in place to manage rights and to provide good sound policy for service delivery. This is where my vision for a national Indigenous cultural authority comes in. This peak Indigenous cultural agency will have multiple functions relating to the promotion and protection of Indigenous arts and culture. It has a role to assist users make contact and identify relevant Indigenous owners. For there to be effective and efficient management of Indigenous cultural and intellectual property rights, there needs to be infrastructure to assist rights holders. I propose the establishment of a national Indigenous cultural authority to promote Indigenous cultural and intellectual property rights and to develop standards for appropriate use including royalties, cultural integrity and attribution.

To conclude, I thank Bill Wentworth for giving me the courage to put the vision of a national Indigenous cultural authority on the table. It needs to be debated and considered at length. I also thank AIATSIS for giving me this opportunity to set the parameters for this debate. I would also like to encourage Indigenous artists and Indigenous people to front up and take action: it's time to guard ground.

Notes

1   The Australian Working Party into the Protection of Aboriginal Folklore defined 'folklore' as the 'body of traditions, observances, customs and beliefs of Aboriginals as expressed in Aboriginal music, dance, craft, sculpture, painting, theatre and literature' (Department of Home Affairs and Environment 1981).

2. Although in some groups, where customary laws are less intact, this may not be the case, owing to the disruption of cultural practices since colonisation.
3. The Arts Law Centre recommends that, following traditional custodian notice in artworks with traditional knowledge: 'The images in this artwork embody traditional ritual knowledge of the (name) community. It was created with the consent of the custodians of the community. Dealing with any part of the images for any purpose that has not been authorised by the custodians is a serious breach of the customary law of the (name) community, and may also breach the *Copyright Act 1968* (Cth). For enquiries about permitted reproduction of these images contact (community name)'. Viewed 21 August 2008 at <http://www.artslaw.com.au>.
4. The *Copyright Act 1968* (Cth) provides creators the unalienable rights: (i) The right of attribution of authorship, (ii) The right not to have authorship falsely attributed, and (iii) The right of integrity of authorship.
5. 'Drawn from a traditional base' means that the work or film must be drawn from the 'particular body of traditions, observances, customs and beliefs held in common by the Indigenous community'.
6. A 'community' is defined loosely and can include an individual, family, clan or community group. (Janke nd, pp. 1, 2, 7 & 8).
7. This stream included Indigenous participants Rachel Perkins, Larissa Behrendt and Wesley Enoch.
8. See Australian Society of Authors website, <https://www.asauthors.org/campaign/lending-rights>. PLR was introduced in 1975 and ELR in 2000.
9. The Australian Institute of Aboriginal and Torres Strait Islander Studies is established under the *Australian Institute of Aboriginal and Torres Strait Islander Studies Act 1989* (Cth) and Tourism Australia is established under the *Tourism Australia Act 2004* (Cth).
10. I also note the recommendation of Toni Bauman, a participant at Australia 2020. Toni is working on the project, Indigenous Facilitation and Mediation Project, at the Australian Institute of Aboriginal and Torres Strait Islander Studies. Her one big idea for Australia 2020 was a recommendation for a National Indigenous Mediation Centre.
11. See the World Intellectual Property Organization's website, viewed 15 June 2015 at <http://www.wipo.int/tk/en/igc>. Our government is represented on that Intergovernmental Committee, but there has been limited input from Indigenous Australians into the government's contribution, and little feedback to Indigenous communities. The Australian Francis Gurry is the nominee for the position of Director General of WIPO. [Editor's note: Gurry was appointed in October 2008, and for a further term in May 2014: viewed 12 May 2015 at <http://www.wipo.int/pressroom/en/articles/2014/article_0006.html>.
12. Secretariat of the Pacific Committee, drafted by legal experts in July 2002, WIPO/UNESCO, Section 6 of the Model Law for the Protection of Traditional Knowledge and Expressions of Culture, South Pacific Community, Noumea, 2002. A copy of this document can be found at <http://www.forumsec.org/resources/uploads/attachments/documents/PacificModelLaw,ProtectionofTKandExprssnsofCulture20021.pdf>, viewed 12 May 2015.
13. Explanatory Memorandum for the Model Law for the Protection of Traditional Knowledge and Expressions of Culture, South Pacific Community with legal expert teams from UNESCO, WIPO, 2003.
14. Republic of South Africa, Department of Trade and Industry, Intellectual Property Laws Amendment Bill, 2007, viewed 12 May 2015 at <http://www.pmg.org.za/bill/20080605-intellectual-property-laws-amendment-bill>.

References

Alexander, M & Institute of Advanced Studies 2004, *The role of registers and databases in the protection of traditional knowledge: A comparative analysis*, United Nations University Institute of Advanced Studies Report, Yokohama, Japan.

Arts Law Centre of Australia 2005, *Artists in the black*, Arts Law Centre of Australia, Sydney.

Australia Council for the Arts 2002, *Final Report of the Review of the National Indigenous Arts Advocacy Association*, Australia Council for the Arts, Sydney.

—— 2008, *Aboriginal and Torres Strait Islander arts news*, Australia Council for the Arts, Sydney.

—— 2009, *Indigenous Australian art commercial code of conduct*, Australia Council for the Arts, Sydney.

Australian Lawyers for Human Rights (ALHR) 2008, 'Submission to GetUp poll on 2020 Summit ideas', viewed 12 April 2008 at <http://www.getup.org.au/2020/idea.php?ideaID=45>.

Australian Society of Authors (ASA) nd, 'Model publishing agreement template, viewed 12 March 2015 at <https://www.asauthors.org/contracts-papers/model-publishing-agreement-template>.

Brandl, EJ 1973, *Australian Aboriginal paintings in western and central Arnhem Land, temporal sequences and elements of style in Cadell and Deaf Adder Creek art*, Aboriginal Studies Press, Canberra.

Brown, MF 2003, *Who owns native culture?*, Harvard University Press, Cambridge MA.

Commonwealth Government 2008, *Australia 2020 Summit final report*, viewed 18 March 2015 at <http://pandora.nla.gov.au/pan/81461/20080610-0000/www.australia2020.gov.au/final_report/index.html>.

Davis, M 2007, *Writing heritage: The depiction of Indigenous heritage in European–Australian writings*, Australian Scholarly Publishing, Melbourne & National Museum of Australia Press, Canberra.

Department of Home Affairs and Environment 1981, *Report of the working party on the protection of Aboriginal folklore*, AGPS, Canberra.

Department of Prime Minister and Cabinet, Australia 2020 Summit Secretariat 2008, *Australia 2020 Summit: Initial summit report*, Department of Prime Minister and Cabinet, Canberra.

Environment Australia, Commonwealth of Australia, 2006, viewed 31 May 2007 at http://www.environment.gov.au/parks/kakadu/artculture/art; updated and viewed 12 June 2014 at <http://www.environment.gov.au/system/files/resources/880173ff-56cc-4a0e-bb4d-7f123f515417/files/gunbim.pdf>.

Janke, T 2003, *Minding culture: Case studies on intellectual property and traditional cultural expressions*, World Intellectual Property Organization, Geneva.

Janke, T 1999, *Our culture: Our future — Report on Australian Indigenous cultural and intellectual property rights*, Michael Frankel & Co. under commission of ATSIC & AIATSIS, Sydney.

Janke, T nd, 'The moral of the story: Indigenous communal moral rights', *Arts Law Centre of Queensland Inc Bulletin*, vol. 3, no. 5, viewed 20 February 2105 at <http://www.terrijanke.com.au/img/publications/pdf/19.ICMR_Article.pdf>.

Janke T & National Indigenous Arts Advocacy Association 1995, *Stopping the ripoffs: Intellectual property protection for Aboriginal and Torres Strait Islander people*, National Indigenous Arts Advocacy Association, Sydney.

Johnson, V 1997, *Copyrites*, Exhibition Catalogue, National Indigenous Arts Advocacy Association, Sydney.

McCausland, S 1999, 'Protecting communal interests in Indigenous artworks after the Bulun Bulun case', *Indigenous Law Bulletin*, vol. 4, no. 22, np.

Mellor, D & Janke, T 2001, *Valuing art, respecting culture: Protocols for working with the Australian Indigenous visual arts and craft sector*, National Association for the Visual Arts, Sydney.

National Indigenous Arts Advocacy Association Inc. (NIAAA) 1998, 'Label of authenticity' viewed 19 August 2008 at <http://www.culture.com.au/exhibition/niaaa/labelqa.htm>.

Quiggin, R 2007, *Protocols for producing Indigenous Australian music*, Australia Council for the Arts, Sydney.

Rimmer M 2004, 'Australian icons: Authenticity marks and identity politics', *Indigenous Law Journal*, vol. 3, pp. 139–79.

Secretariat of the Pacific Committee, drafted by legal experts in July 2002, WIPO/UNESCO, Section 6 of the Model Law for the Protection of Traditional Knowledge and Expressions of Culture, South Pacific Community, Noumea, 2002

Standing Committee on Environment, Communications, Information Technology and the Arts 2007, *Indigenous Art: Securing the Future Australia's Indigenous visual arts and craft sector*, viewed 21 August 2008 at <http://www.aph.gov.au/senate/committee/ecita_ctte/completed_inquiries/2004 -07/indigenous_arts/report/report.pdf; updated and viewed 12 June 2014 at <http://www.aph.gov.au/binaries/senate/committee/ecita_ctte/completed_inquiries/2004-07/indigenous_arts/report/report.pdf>.

United Nations 2008, *Declaration on the rights of Indigenous peoples*, viewed 20 August 2008 at <http://www.un.org/esa/socdev/unpfii/documents/DRIPS_en.pdf>.

United States Patent and Trademark Office 2001, *USPTO Establishes Database of Official Insignia of Native American Tribes*, press release 29 August, viewed 21 August 2008 at <http://www.uspto.gov/web/offices/com/speeches/01-37.htm>.

World Intellectual Property Organization (WIPO) nd, *Draft Provisions/Articles for the Protection of Traditional Knowledge and Traditional Cultural Expressions, and IP & Genetic Resources*, viewed at http://www.wipo.int/tk/en/igc/draft_provisions.html

Cases

Bulun Bulun & Anor v R & T Textiles Pty Ltd [1998] 1082 FCA.
Milpurrurru & Others v Indofurn Pty Ltd & Others [1993] 30 IPR 209.
Yumbulul v Reserve Bank of Australia [1991], 21 IPR 481 FCA.

Legislation

Australian Institute of Aboriginal and Torres Strait Islander Studies Act 1989 (Cth).
Copyright Act 1968 (Cth).
Copyright Amendment (Indigenous Communal Moral Rights) Bill 2003 (Cth).
Tourism Australia Act 2004 (Cth).

Original lecture available at:
<http://aiatsis.gov.au/publications/presentations/guarding-ground-vision-national-indigenous-cultural-authority>

16

First Australians, Law and the High Court of Australia

2010 Wentworth Lecture

Michael Kirby

I, like those who have gone before, offer my respects to the traditional custodians of the land. A genuine respect, one such as we hear given in New Zealand; not perfunctory. A moment of reflection upon the wrongs that have been done to the Indigenous people of our continental land; and a reminder of our obligation, as citizens, to ensure that the wrongs are repaired, not just with words, but with action.

My talk today, like Caesar's Gaul, is divided into three parts. The first will be a tribute to Bill Wentworth, because I do not think we should be attending a named lecture and ignore the person in whose name it is given. The point of this lecture series is for us to remember, and take inspiration from, the life of Bill Wentworth and the lives of similar spirits. Second, I propose to talk about the time I spent in the High Court of Australia, when issues of Aboriginal law came before the court on a number of occasions. This was just across the paddock. There in the great building of the High Court, where I was proud to serve for thirteen years as a judge in this, the final court of our nation. Third, I propose to say a few words on the Northern Territory intervention and a case, *Wurridjal v The Commonwealth* ((2009) 237 CLR 309). The decision came down in the High Court in February 2009, just as I was about to leave office. This was the last case in which I delivered a decision as a Justice of the High Court. It happened on the last day of my service. Subsequently, it attracted little attention from the media or the community generally. Yet it will, I hope, be of interest and of use for me to remind you of it. There is little point in having decisions of great constitutional and legal moment decided in the High Court if no one knows about them. The media of our country are altogether too concerned about infotainment. They seem not sufficiently concerned about matters of justice, of principle, of constitutionality and of law. In this lecture, I intend to help correct that default.

Reflections on the Hon Bill Wentworth

I knew Bill Wentworth because of my service from 1975 to 1984 as the inaugural Chairman of the Australian Law Reform Commission. Drivers of Commonwealth cars used to say that the driveways of our respective Sydney homes, in those years, were the hardest navigational challenges they faced. Bill was certainly famous, or perhaps notorious, amongst Commonwealth drivers. I don't think I'll say anymore about that subject in light of the events that later unfolded in my life. Suffice to say that both Bill Wentworth and I had only the most cordial relationships with those drivers, who were only too happy to assist us up and down our steep driveways at home and in life.

Bill Wentworth was involved in a project of the Law Reform Commission (ALRC) on the recognition of Aboriginal customary laws. It was led by Professor James Crawford, a most distinguished Australian academic scholar who is now Whewell Professor of Law at Cambridge University in the United Kingdom. The resulting report has not been implemented in full, or even in large part. Still, it is the most popular report of the Australian Law Reform Commission, judging by the number of hits on the ALRC website. It still stands before us as a reminder of the unfinished business of working out the precise relationships between Aboriginal customary laws and the general laws of this country.

Bill Wentworth had many ideas on the subject, which he made well known to us. I came to appreciate his quirky, somewhat difficult, informative but insistent personality; it was an unusual one for people in public life. Most such people, as we know, are too tamed and bland because of their desire to 'wedge' their opponents and to avoid anything that might act to their disadvantage. Bill Wentworth did not mind what people thought of him. He was more interested in the ideas that he presented. We need more politicians of this calibre and inclination.

In a decision to which I was a party in 1998, two years after I joined the High Court, namely in the case of *Kartinyeri v The Commonwealth*, ((1998) 195 CLR 337) I referred to Bill Wentworth and to his dedication to the cause of the Aboriginal people. The question in the case was whether or not the amendment to Section 51(26) of the Australian Constitution, to remove the exclusion of people of the Aboriginal 'race' from the provisions whereby the federal parliament was empowered to make laws with respect to ('people of any race for whom it is necessary to make special laws'), was to be interpreted beneficially. That is whether this phrase was to be interpreted as meaning *for the benefit* of them or simply meant 'for', in the sense of "in respect of" them. If the latter was the correct meaning there would be no inference that the laws were only to be laws of a beneficial character. In the end, the majority of the High Court adopted the second interpretation. They held that 'for' meant merely 'in respect of'. It did not carry an inference that the enactment of the laws by the federal parliament had to be 'for the benefit of' people' on the ground of their 'race'.

I took a different view. I did so, in part, by reference to the parliamentary record, but also many other sources. My view was partly agreed in by Justice Gaudron. However, the other Justices did not take the same view. Accordingly, the law of our country is as stated by the majority. Section 51(26) in authorising laws 'for' people of any race, for whom it is deemed necessary to make special laws, can include good or awful laws or beneficial or antagonistic laws. They do not have to *demonstrate* a beneficial character.

In seeking, contrary to that majority opinion of the High Court, to demonstrate that the purpose of the amendment effected by the great constitutional referendum of 1967, was to ensure that the races' power in the Constitution was only to be used beneficially, I drew upon the history of the steps that had been taken in which Bill Wentworth played a significant part. Part of my reasons for judgment included these words:

> In March 1966 Mr WC Wentworth, later the first Australian Minister for Aboriginal Affairs, introduced a private member's bill to amend the Constitution to substitute for the race power in paragraph (xxvi) a new provision, 'The advancement of the Aboriginal natives of the Commonwealth of Australia. (*Kartinyeri v The Commonwealth* (1998) 195 CLR 337 at 405, [141])

I proceeded:

> Mr Wentworth also proposed a new Section 117A of the Constitution. This would forbid the Commonwealth and the States from making or maintaining any law which subjected any person born or naturalised within the Commonwealth 'To any discrimination or disability within the Commonwealth by reason of his racial origin.' The proposal contained a proviso that the Section should not operate 'So as to preclude the making of laws for the specific benefit of the Aboriginal natives of the Commonwealth of Australia.' One of the reasons given by Mr Wentworth for his amendment was his concern that the deletion of the exclusion of people of the Aboriginal race from paragraph (xxvi) could leave them open to 'discrimination adverse or favourable.' He suggested that 'Power for favourable discrimination was needed, but there should not be a power for unfavourable discrimination.' His bill was supported by the opposition Labor Party, but it ultimately lapsed. (*Kartinyeri v The Commonwealth* (1998) 195 CLR 337 at 405, [141])

Remember that at the time Mr Wentworth was a member of the Menzies government. According to the entry about him in the *Australian Encyclopaedia*

(1996, p. 3068), he did not advance far during Mr Menzies' (later Sir Robert Menzies) time as Prime Minister, into the ministry. This was because Sir Robert did not always agree with the somewhat robust and independent-minded attitudes that Bill Wentworth adopted on a large number of controversial subjects, including the subject of Aboriginal and Torres Strait Islander advancement.

I should mention that in this respect Bill Wentworth was not picky and choosy. During the Second World War, when the Labor Party was in government, he lost office in a role he had in the military because he had demonstrated that Sydney in 1942 was extremely vulnerable to foreign invasion. For being so bold as to raise this issue publicly, he was immediately punished by the then Labor Government. So both major parties, Labor and Liberal, found Bill Wentworth difficult to live with. We need more people of this kind in our Commonwealth. They certainly stimulate the democratic process.

As you know, the 1967 referendum subsequently removed the constitutional provisions relating to the exclusion of Aboriginal people from the races power. The races power was then left in its pristine state, applicable equally to the Australian Aboriginal and Torres Strait Islander people. The net result was that the power, historically inserted in the Constitution to allow the new federal parliament to make laws adverse to the interests of 'Chinamen' (as they were labelled during the 1890s), became available for use in respect of the Aboriginal people.

The net result of this change was that the power to make special laws on the basis of race was available to do good and not so good things, beneficial and adverse things. The history of our Commonwealth since 1967 has shown the wisdom of Bill Wentworth's asserting the need to have something in the Australian Constitution which made it clear that (in the light of the history of the terrible wrongs done in racially designated legislation introduced by a civilised country like Germany prior to the Second World War) it was only possible in Australia for 'advancement of people on racial grounds', or 'so that no discrimination or disability could be imposed by reason of racial origin'. In short, that Australians should restrict the powers of law makers because law makers will often do beneficial things under a racist power. Yet as history has shown, they may also do things that are not beneficial either to the people involved and, specifically, on the grounds of their race.

I am very pleased to be here to honour Bill Wentworth. I am particularly glad that Georgina and Mara are here present during this lecture. My tribute to him is sincere and respectful: Bill Wentworth was an early and faithful advocate of Aboriginal advancement.

Reflections on the High Court and Aboriginal law

In the High Court of Australia, when I joined it in 1996, the issue of Aboriginal rights and the then interface with the law was one of the major factors on its agenda at that time. Remember that the *Mabo* decision, *Mabo v Queensland [No. 2]* ((1992) 175 CLR 1), had been reached by the High Court in 1992, four years before my appointment. The *Mabo* decision of the Mason Court was undoubtedly one having the greatest importance for our country. It was crucial for our Indigenous peoples. It was unquestionably a bold decision; a step taken that showed foresight, insight and courage. It was a majority decision of six Justices to one. It had to overrule a series of earlier decisions about the common law of Australia and a decision of the Privy Council which held that, upon the acquisition of sovereignty over the Australian continent by the British Crown, all pre-existing rights to land of the Indigenous people had been expunged and vested in the Crown; and that, therefore, no recognition would be given under Australian common law to the interests in land of the Indigenous people. Legally speaking, Australia was a kind of *terra nullius* so far as the Indigenous people and the laws were concerned.

How to overcome that longstanding series of decisions? How, in particular, to overcome a decision of the Privy Council so holding at a time when the Privy Council in England was the final court of appeal in the Australian judicature? The answer to those questions was provided by Justice Frank Brennan, later Chief Justice of the High Court. In his reasons in *Mabo* ((1992) 175 CLR 1 at 42), Justice Brennan invoked the universal principles of human rights. He said that the earlier decisions of the Privy Council, and of Australian courts, denying recognition to the rights to land on the part of Indigenous Australians was a principle of law which had at its heart racial discrimination; and that, if there was one principle of universal human rights which was accepted by the international community of civilised countries today, it was that a legal system cannot deprive people of basic rights simply on the basis of their race.

This invocation of universal principles of international human rights law in *Mabo* was the key that unlocked the door barring the High Court of Australia from stating a new principle of the common law in terms not infected with racial discrimination. It was decided on that footing by six Justices to one (Justice Dawson dissented). Thus, the High Court set aside the old statement of the common law. It embraced a new principle in which the flaw of racial discrimination was absent. This, of course, set in train a very large public debate, as is natural and proper in a democracy. It also gave rise to many assertions by pastoral and mineral interests that: it would be the end of civilisation as we knew it; it would destroy investment in the country; it would mean that nobody would have any certainty in their land interests; the homes of people throughout the country would be at risk; it would greatly damage Australia's standing in the international community; and, in particular, that the international economic community would lose confidence in Australia because it would render unstable something which every society demands to be absolutely stable, namely legal interests in land.

Nothing of the sort happened, of course. The world accommodated itself to the statement of the new principle of the law in Australia. The economy went on to enjoy a record decade and the Australian community came to appreciate the great injustice that had been done in the earlier statement of the common law. It came to appreciate what a very important decision the *Mabo* decision was – and how proud we could be that the highest court in the land had corrected the errors of insight of earlier judges over more than a century and restated the common law on a basis which was not racially biased.

All this goes to demonstrate, yet again, how important it is to have independent judges in conversation with elected parliaments. For those who say that elected parliaments in Australia will right every wrong ever done to any group (and in particular, wrongs done to minorities, especially wrongs done to sometimes unpopular minorities), it is very important for us to always remember *Mabo*. We had 150 years of elected parliaments in Australia before *Mabo* was decided. This nation has some of the oldest continuously elected parliaments in the world. We nonetheless did not correct in our parliaments the basic injustices. It took a decision of the High Court of Australia, by six Justices to one, to do so (*Mabo v Queensland [No. 2]* (1992) 175 CLR 1). Please keep this in mind when you next hear politicians and the media saying: 'We must never have a Charter of Rights in Australia. We must never give unelected judges power. We must always keep power in parliament, because parliament always does the right thing.' This is not always the case. Parliament often does correct injustices. Usually it does correct injustices. Yet sometimes a parliament needs a little help from its friends. That was what the High Court did in the *Mabo* decision.

I can take neither credit nor blame from the *Mabo* decision, which happened four years before my appointment to the High Court. Indeed, it was a given by the time I joined the High Court. Yet in my initial year, a question arose concerning the application of the *Mabo* principle to pastoral leases. There were particular statutes – federal, state and territory – dealing with Aboriginal land rights. However, none of them questioned or corrected the basic premise of the Australian common law. Were pastoral leases excluded from the *Mabo* principle? By the operation of the *Mabo* principle, were or were not pastoral leases cut out from the application of claims for Native Title? Ultimately, this question, too, was argued before the High Court in a decision published at the end of 1996 in the *Wik Peoples v Queensland* ((1996) 187 CLR 1). This decision upheld, by majority of four to three, the assertion by the Wik Peoples that the *Mabo* principle applied in pastoral leases. The majority comprised Justice Toohey, Justice Gaudron, Justice Gummow and me. The minority were Chief Justice Brennan and Justices Dawson and McHugh.

Had someone other than me been appointed in February, it would have depended on that person to be the deciding vote in *Wik*. However, the fact is that I was there. My deciding vote was in favour of applying the *Mabo* principle.

So important to me was the essential foundation of the *Mabo* principle as explained in *Mabo* by Justice Brennan. Its foundation was a rejection of racial discrimination in our law.

That was my first exposure to the issue of Aboriginal title and Aboriginal law in the High Court. For our pains, the majority Justices were lambasted in and out of parliament and in the media and in many areas of the community. We were called 'a group of basket weavers' by the then Premier of Queensland, Mr Borbidge. We were also described as the 'kings and queens of Canberra'. We were otherwise excoriated for our decision. Yet the decision was a matter of the application of a basic principle of law. It really was simply the application of the *Mabo* principle to new factual circumstances. So it was not a particularly difficult legal decision to make, for me at least.

After the *Mabo* decision, we had a number of other cases concerned with the application of the *Mabo* case, apart from *Wik*. Those cases included that of *Fejo* ((1998) 195 CLR 96) in the Northern Territory, which held, contrary to the assertions in parliament and elsewhere, that the title of property held in freehold (that is to say what we normally conceive of as ownership of land), was at risk, such interests were not diminished by the *Mabo* principle. People's ownership of their homes, whether in the Northern Territory or anywhere else in Australia, was safe. That was so held by unanimous court in *Fejo*.

There was then a decision in a case of *Ward v Western Australia* ((2002) 213 CLR 1) which dealt with many other particular aspects of land law. There followed numerous other cases concerned with land and other rights, rights over water and so on, as the Court, interpreting the *Native Title Act*, gave meaning to that Act and the application of the principles expressed in the earlier decisions. At that time, the end of the twentieth century, much of the work in the High Court concerned Aboriginal title. This was inevitable and natural once one accepted that *Mabo* had changed the direction in which the law had been travelling and laid down a new principle that required several readjustments in the law of Australia.

There were two other important decisions concerning Aboriginal Australians during my time on the High Court. One of them, the *Kartinyeri* case, concerned the meaning of section 51(26) of the Constitution, referred to above. Was the 'races power' by the language and the use of the word 'for' confined to beneficial legislation so characterised? Or was it simply at large, meaning 'in respect of?' This very important decision was decided in 1998: *Kartinyeri v The Commonwealth* ((1998) 195 CLR 337).

Shortly before I left the High Court, a further important constitutional decision was reached in the court in the case of *Roach v Electoral Commissioner* ((2007) 233 CLR 162). Ms Roach was an Aboriginal Australian who had been convicted and imprisoned for a crime of fraud. When she was in prison she decided to do two unusual things: first, she decided to undertake university studies, specifically studies for a doctorate; second, she decided that she did not agree with legislation that had been enacted by the federal parliament in 2006, depriving her of the right to vote in federal elections. She therefore began to look around for someone who would help her to challenge that legislation in the High Court of Australia, asserting that the legislation was constitutionally invalid. The subject legislation changed the longstanding law that had deprived people from voting in federal elections if they were in prison and serving more than a three year sentence. New legislation, in 2006, was enacted through the parliament when the then government gained control of the Senate. It deprived all prisoners of the right to vote.

Material was placed before the High Court showing that very large numbers of people are in prison in Australia for very short periods of time. Often, they are incarcerated because they cannot afford to pay their fines. Therefore, on the face of things, a disqualification from the important right of the franchise for all prisoners seemed to have been a disproportionate response by the parliament to their antisocial conduct. However, the legal question was whether or not this matter had been left by the Constitution to the federal parliament to decide, one way or the other. Ms Roach pointed to the fact that a considerable portion of prisoners, certainly disproportionate to their numbers in the population, were Indigenous Australians. She therefore argued that the legislation was disproportionate in effect and that steps should be taken by the court to uphold the right of electors to vote as central to their rights (and in Australia their duties) to take part in the political process for which the Constitution provided.

Ms Roach also pointed to various other inconsistencies between taking away the rights to vote of other groups of Australians. She argued that, although our Constitution did not contain a bill of rights or a specific statement about fundamental rights, it did contain very detailed provisions about the elections to the federal parliament. Those provisions were written on an assumption that prisoners would take part in the vote, at least prisoners who were not in prison for a lengthy period, and that parliament could not take away the right to vote of all prisoners.

In the end, the High Court upheld Ms Roach's argument. Here I want to pay a tribute to the lawyers who acted on her behalf *pro bono*. When I was a young lawyer I performed a lot of work *pro bono*, which tends to be more interesting and exciting than the high-paying work that lawyers perform, much of which is really glorified debt recovery. The lawyers acting in the case included Mr Ron Merkel QC, who had been a federal judge in Victoria and had been a close friend of Ron Castan QC. Both of them were great friends to Aboriginal causes. Also involved was the venerated and famous old legal firm of Allens, Arthur Robinson Solicitors, acting *pro bono*.

The *Roach* case is also important for the introduction into Australian law of general legal principles derived from international law. In his decision in favour of Ms Roach, Chief Justice Gleeson referred to decision of the European Court of Human Rights in a case called *Hirst v The United Kingdom [No. 2]* ((2006) 42 EHRR 41) and a decision of the Canadian Supreme Court in a case called *Sauvé v The Queen* ((2002) 3 SCR 519 at 585 [119]). In both cases, concerning respectively British legislation and Canadian legislation, the removal of all prisoners from the vote was struck down or disapproved, as it was in the case of Australia. The legislation of 2006 was held to be unconstitutional. It was incompatible with the design and implications of the Constitution as to the right to vote. Subsequently, many of the prisoners in Australia, certainly all of those who were in prison for offences and punishment of less than three years, were given the vote in the federal election of 2007. This is the law of this country as it now stands.

Two Justices, Hayne and Hayden, dissented. Both not only dissented in the result but also strongly dissented over the reference by the majority to principles of international human rights law. They declared that these principles were completely irrelevant to the consideration of the meaning of the Australian Constitution. The slow but certain, inevitable and predictable impact of international law (and in particular, international human rights law) on the understanding of our legal rights in Australia, and in particular of our Constitution, will come, come ever come. It is inevitable. The case of *Roach*, like the earlier decision in *Mabo*, was merely one further step in what I consider to be the right direction.

Reflections on *Wurridjal* and the Northern Territory 'intervention'

I now reach the third part of this lecture, in which I demonstrate the wisdom of Bill Wentworth in his feeling that if our parliament in Australia were to be given a power to make 'racial' laws, it should be limited to racial laws for the *advancement* of the 'race' concerned. Or at least not to *discriminate* against the group concerned. This approach, as proper to racial laws, would seem to be borne out by the terrible wrongs that were done in Germany under the Nuremberg Laws by the Nazi regime, and in South Africa during the apartheid years, following the advent of the government of Dr Verwoerd and the National Party. At that time, laws were enacted to discriminate against black people on the basis of their race and to reduce their dignity and diminish their legal rights.

The case of *Wurridjal v The Commonwealth* ((2009) 237 CLR 309) arose in the High Court of Australia on a very technical legal issue, on a process called 'demurrer'. This process was devised in the English law for the purpose of allowing a party who is sued in a court to respond to the suit by saying, in effect, 'Even if everything you say in your statement of claim is accepted factually, you have no legal foundation for the case. Therefore, I should not be troubled and harassed by your case. It should be stopped'. You will see that it is quite a sensible procedure, designed to stop people being troubled by expensive, time-consuming and sometimes stressful litigation if the other party has no legal leg to stand on. So a demurrer was brought when Mr Wurridjal and his colleagues sought a declaration from the High Court of Australia that the Northern Territory intervention legislation was constitutionally invalid.

The challenge to this legislation was brought before the High Court in 2008. It was defended in the High Court by the Solicitor General, acting on the instructions of the Rudd Commonwealth government. The court, in the usual way of the development of argument in these things, was taken most carefully through the language of the legislation (*Northern Territory National Emergency Response Act* 2007 (Cth)) and through the parliamentary record. It was directed to certain documents that preceded the enactment of the intervention legislation. These included the report of a special committee in the Northern Territory of Australia concerning the protection of children, which had been written by a board of inquiry, co-headed by Mr Rex Wild QC. The Committee had suggested that steps needed to be taken to protect children in Aboriginal communities in the Northern Territory from instances of child abuse and from lack of support, education and nutrition (Northern Territory 2007).

The report produced by Mr Wild and his colleagues insisted, repeatedly, on the crucial importance of consulting the Aboriginal community before remedial steps were taken. It held that such consultation was an absolute prerequisite to the proper introduction of remedial laws and policies. The speed with which the legislation was introduced, some eight weeks before the 2007 federal election, would be enough to make one concerned about the legislation and about its true purposes. It could, of course, reveal a somewhat belated interest of the then government and parliament in responding to the report of the Northern Territory. However, since the advent of self-government in the Northern Territory, it would have been normal – at least in the first instance – for the matter to be considered by the NT government and legislature.

The speed of the federal measures has been described by the President of the Law Council of Australia as 'outrageous and unsettling'. It was a speed to which I referred in my reasons in *Wurridjal* and, in particular, to the fact that the legislation was so hasty, having been drawn up within days of its announcement. It encompassed about 300 pages of printed text. Although a perfunctory inquiry was conducted in the Senate, it was simply impossible, under the impetus of the haste that was demanded by the then government (and in particular by the Prime Minister, Mr John Howard, and the then Minister for Aboriginal Affairs, Mr Mal Brough). It soon became evident that no real attention would, or could, be paid to valid criticisms of the legislation, including by the Aboriginal communities concerned.

As I saw it, the legal point that was ultimately contested in the High Court was whether there was a valid legal argument on the part of Mr Wurridjal and his colleagues concerning their contention that the imposition of five-year compulsory leases upon Aboriginal communities in the Northern Territory failed to accord with the obligations of the Australian Constitution. In this respect, unusually, the Constitution contains a human rights provision, which says that if there is (putting it generally) to be a federal acquisition of property, it can only happen in this country on 'just terms'. Such a provision does not apply to state legislation. An earlier decision of the High Court, in a case called *Teori Tau* (*Teori Tau v Commonwealth* (1969) 119 CLR 564), had held that it did not apply to territory acquisitions by the Commonwealth. Therefore, the first contention of the Commonwealth, in support of its demurrer, was that the demurrer should be upheld because the constitutional requirement of 'just terms' applied neither to the acquisition of Mr Wurridjal's land nor to the land of others in the Northern Territory and their property there. This was because they were in the Territory and were thus not covered by the general constitutional provision (which, it was argued, covered only specifically federal legislation, operating otherwise than solely in the Territory).

Had *Teori Tau*, a decision of the Barwick Court, stood, this would have been a perfectly valid and fatal demurrer point. It would have knocked out the case and revealed, at least so far as to claim based on the failure to accord 'just terms' was concerned, that it was fatal to the case. However, in a number of earlier decisions, doubt had been cast in the High Court about the correctness of the *Teori Tau* decision. In a case called *Newcrest* (*Newcrest Mining (WA) Ltd v The Commonwealth* (1997) 190 CLR 513 at 561, 613–4, 652), decided in 1996, it was said that the principle in *Teori Tau* was now to be seen as dubious (*Wurridjal* (2009) 237 CLR 309 at 344 and 359 [86] per French CJ; 385-8 [179–89] per Gummow and Hayne JJ; 419 [287] per Kirby J). Although four of the judges of the court had cast doubt on it, *Teori Tau* had not been formally overruled.

So this was that the preliminary question to be decided. On it, a majority of the High Court (Chief Justice French, Justice Gummow, Justice Hayne and I) held that *Teori Tau* was wrongly decided. Therefore, the 'just terms' requirement did apply to legislation applicable in the Territory, just as much as to federal legislation applying anywhere else in Australia. So that ruling knocked away the first and primary (and, one might think, chief) argument of the Commonwealth that the legislation for the Northern Territory intervention did not have to give 'just terms'. Therefore, the argument of the Commonwealth about the failure to give 'just terms' was not legally tenable. It was irrelevant.

That ruling drove the parties to the second line of argument, which was that there is a distinction in the Australian Constitution in the requirement for 'just terms.' It was fairly clear that the basic constitutional provision was borrowed from the Fifth Amendment to the United States Constitution. The Fifth Amendment is part of the Bill of Rights of the United States Constitution.

It contains a specific statement in the United States that if your property is taken by the federal government or under the federal legislation, the government must give 'just compensation'.

The distinction between the American requirement to give 'just compensation' and the Australian requirement to give 'just terms' was drawn to notice by that great judge of the High Court of Australia, Justice Dixon, in a case called *Nelungaloo Pty Ltd v The Commonwealth* ((1948) 75 CLR 495 at 569; see *Wurridjal* (2009) 237 CLR 425 at 388 [190]). That was some 40 years ago. He said that, if it had been intended to require only that the federal parliament provide for 'just compensation', it would have been so easy for the Australian founders just to copy the American provision. Instead, a nuance was introduced, with a requirement that a person whose property is taken has to be given 'just terms'.

In this sense, the second question in *Wurridjal* was: what was the requirement of 'just terms' in the type of legislation that was under consideration there for the Northern Territory intervention? Specifically the submission was put that 'just terms' required fairness in dealings. It therefore required not just that the Commonwealth provide money (as would arguably be sufficient to be 'just compensation'), but that the Commonwealth must, in a way appropriate to the case, engage in proper consultation and prior discussion in order to ensure the provision of 'just *terms*'. The Commonwealth contested this argument, saying that 'just terms' and 'just compensation' meant roughly the same. In any case, that 'just terms' had been provided. Certainly, monetary compensation was provided. To me, it was at least legally arguable that the Aboriginal interests could maintain a contention that they had not been given 'just terms' – specifically so, because they had not been consulted at all when such a radical intrusion was authorised by federal law into their peaceful enjoyment of their property rights.

In the course of my reasons I said this:

> If any other Australians selected by reference to their race suffered the imposition on their pre-existing property interests of non consensual five year statutory leases, designed to authorise intensive intrusions into their lives and legal interests. It is difficult to believe that a challenge to such a law would fail as legally unarguable on the ground that no property had been acquired or that just terms had been afforded, although those affected were not consulted about the process and although rights cherished by them might be adversely affected … the Aboriginal parties are entitled to have their trial and day in court. We should not slam the doors of the court in their face. This is a case in which a transparent, public trial of the proceedings has its own justification. (*Wurridjal* (2009) 237 CLR 309 at 337 [14])

I therefore supported the order that the demurrer should be overruled. The majority rejected that contention. They gave effect to the demurrer. So effectively terminated Mr Wurridjal's claim as legally unarguable. In the course of his reasons, Chief Justice French, who had been at the court only a matter of weeks when the *Wurridjal* case was decided, wrote this:

> The conclusion at which I have arrived does not depend on any opinion about the merits of the policy behind the challenged legislation, nor contrary to the gratuitous suggestion in the judgement of Justice Kirby is the outcome of this case based on an approach less favourable to the plaintiffs because of their Aboriginality. (*Wurridjal* (2009) 237 CLR 309 at 337 [14])

I responded to this in my opinion: 'The issue for decision is not whether the approach of the majority is made on a basis less favourable because of Aboriginality' (*Wurridjal* (2009) 237 CLR 309 at 395 [215]), with a footnote as reference to Chief Justice French's reasons:

> It is concerned with the objective fact that the majority rejects the claimant's challenge to the constitutional validity of the federal legislation that is incontestably less favourable to them on the basis of their race and does so in a ruling on a demurrer. Far from being gratuitous, this reasoning is essential and, in truth, self evident. The demurrer should be overruled. (*Wurridjal* (2009) 237 CLR 309 at 395 [215])

Earlier in my reasons I had said this:

> History and not only ancient history teaches that there are many dangers in enacting special laws that target people of a particular race and disadvantage their rights to liberty, property and other entitlements by reference to that criterion. The history of Australian law, including earlier decisions of this court, stands as a warning about how such matters should be decided. Even great judges of the past were not immune from error in such cases. Wrongs to people of a particular race have also accord in other courts and legal systems. In his dissenting opinion, in *Falbo v United States* ((1944) 320 US 549 at 561), Justice Murphy of the Supreme Court of the United States observed in famous words that the 'law knows no finer hour' than when it 'protects individuals from selective discrimination and persecution'. This court should be specially hesitant before declining effective access to the courts to those who enlist assistance in the face of legislation that involves an alleged deprivation of their legal rights on the basis of race. All such cases are deserving of the most transparent and painstaking of legal scrutiny. (*Wurridjal* (2009) 237 CLR 309 at 393 [209])

The reference in my reasons to 'history and not only ancient history teaches' was to the very words of Justice Dixon in the *Communist Party Case*, 1951 (*Australian Communist Party v Commonwealth* (1951) 83 CLR at 193). That was certainly one of the greatest decisions of the High Court of Australia. There the High Court struck down as unconstitutional the legislation of the

Menzies' Government which purported to dissolve the Communist Party of Australia and to impose on Australian communists various disadvantages in their civil liberties. Still, my words were to no effect. The *Wurridjal* case failed. The Northern Territory intervention legislation was upheld. In substance, it still operates.

This is what we said: **Aboriginal voices**

Recently, I was sent a book, *This is what we said* (Concerned Australians 2010), in which Aboriginal people and others give their views on the Northern Territory intervention. At this time, when the legislation is again before the Australian Parliament, we would do well to reflect upon some of the words expressed in that book. Our chair here today, Professor Mick Dodson, Australian of the Year for 2009, said 'The intervention is a bully-boy approach handled with no respect to the Aboriginal people.' In other statements, Mr Malcolm Fraser, former Prime Minister and Liberal leader said:

> It [the intervention] was based on old-fashioned paternalism, an arbitrary process that of course implied no respect for the people that one was trying to help, no partnership and that someone in Canberra knows best. (2010, p. 57)

Professor Larissa Behrendt, a most notable scholar and leader in the Indigenous community, but also in the law generally, said;

> The profound flaw of the intervention package is that the whole approach is predicated on dealing with the symptoms, rather than the causes of dysfunctional Aboriginal community. (2010, p. 57)

Mr Rex Wild QC, who had been co-chair of the Committee into abuse of children and whose report was given as the reason for the exceptional and rushed federal legislation for the 'intervention', wrote:

> Why is it that after all of the reports, it's now necessary to move in a patronising, paternalistic way which is the very same thing that has caused all the difficulties in the last 200 years? (2010, p. 57)

Sir William Deane, a past Governor General said:

> Indeed, in seeking to advance true indigenous reconciliation or to address the awful disadvantage which still afflicts our country, adequate and informed dialogue with full indigenous participation is not only desirable at every stage, it is absolutely essential and let me digress to express the hope that that unfortunate word 'intervention' will disappear from our language, at least as far as government policies affecting indigenous Australians are concerned. (2010, p. 58)

Report of UN Special Rapporteur Anaya

After the change of government in Australia, a Special Rapporteur of the United Nations, Professor James Anaya (who is the Special Rapporteur on the situation of Human Rights and Fundamental Freedoms of Indigenous People) came to Australia. With the assistance of the Australian Government, he conducted his enquiries and made a detailed examination of the situation here. His report, which was released in February 2010, contained what can only be described as an extremely critical review of the enactment of the intervention legislation, and of the haste and lack of consultation that attended its enactment. He also described the serious discrimination that was involved in the detailed provisions of the legislation and the fact that, in order to justify such serious discrimination, warranting such exceptional measures, it was essential that the proponents do so to a very high standard, and establish that it was proportional and necessary to attain a valid objective.

Professor Anaya accepted that it was part of the obligations of the Australian Government, and indeed governments everywhere, to protect people (and in particular women and children) from cases of abuse; and that this was actually part of the obligation of the Australian government to ensure the upholding of the human rights of those Australians who were so affected. However, Professor Anaya said in his report, evaluating the responses of the Australian Government, that, while reiterating the need to purge the legislation of its racially discriminating character, the Australia Government was obliged by international law to conform to the relevant international standards and to do so 'through a process genuinely driven by the voices of the affected indigenous people'.

It is a source of pain for many Australians that, despite reports of this kind and despite views that have been expressed in Australia by many distinguished and thoughtful observers since the Northern Territory intervention legislation, such remedial steps as have been taken have not completely dealt with the paternalistic and discriminating legislation that was enacted by the Australian Parliament in its previous manifestation. One would hope that, even now, the prudent, cautious and balanced words of the United Nations Special Rapporteur will be given very close attention (closer than it has to date) in the final enactment of the laws that remove the discriminatory provisions existing in the legislation. This does not seem to be in the amendments to the intervention legislation now being proposed. This is a matter where our national honour and reputation are at stake. More fundamentally, it is one in which the human rights of our citizens, including our Indigenous citizens, are threatened. If you read *This is what we said*, you will see the sense of disquiet that the Special Rapporteur says is 'growing in its intensity'.

Holding our tongues: Lifting our voices

These issues should concern us today as Australian citizens. They relate to how the members of Indigenous communities are affected; the way that they feel dishonoured by being treated in a second-class manner; and the way that they have been dishonoured by having signs placed outside their communities with explicit statements about sexual offences and the imposition of fines and other offences for bringing alcohol and pornography into the place. The members of the Australian Aboriginal communities in the Northern Territory feel that they have been treated in a way which, if it were ever done to Australians of Irish, Greek, Chinese or other non-Australian ancestry, would be a national outrage.

I commend *This is what we said* for spelling out the reactions that were not sought, or asked for, before the legislation was enacted, and that have still not been sufficiently seen or heard in this land since the legislation was enacted. In it, Australian Aboriginal people and others at last give their views on the Northern Territory intervention. These are words that we should hear and that our parliament and our leaders should hear. These are the words that speak to us, the citizens of Australia. It is essential that our community should listen to those words, attend to them, reflect on them and act on them.

I am sure that, if Bill Wentworth were here at this lecture today – although it was in his nature always to try to find faults, inadequacies and defects in what was said by the lecturer (many of which he would be able to find in these few remarks of mine) – he would nonetheless agree with my central message. People should read the *Wurridjal* case. Not enough Australian people bother. Few know about the case, and not enough Australians know about the working of the court. What do they cover in the media about the High Court of Australia? Generally, it is about matters of infotainment and personality, mostly trivial and little in the way of matters of substance, about which there is silence. Well, I've come here today to talk on substance and to break the silence, though not to unnecessarily re-contest matters decided in the *Wurridjal* case. It is all there in writing and on the Internet. Nothing I can do or say now will add to those words. They are there. Attend to them. Read them. Listen to them. Listen to the debate which divided the High Court on matters of high principle. Think about them. And have your say.

If those words of mine are listened to and if the words of the Aboriginal people of the Northern Territory are attended to, our parliament and our people will surely take action without more delay. This is a great affront by our laws and under our Constitution in Australia. That affront should burn into our consciousness with 'growing intensity'. We should finally right a large constitutional, legal and ethical wrong. So far, I do not see the will to do this in Australia. One day, however, we will see these issues more clearly. Then the *Wurridjal* decision and the intervention legislation will be sources of further shame. And the greatest shame will be upon those who held their tongues when they should have lifted their voices and acted with all the resolution that it was within their power to exercise.

References

Australian Geographic Pty Ltd 1996, *The Australian encyclopaedia*, 6th edn, vol. 8, Australian Geographic, Sydney.

Concerned Australians 2010, *This is what we said: Australian Aboriginal people give their views on the Northern Territory intervention*, Concerned Australians, Melbourne.

Northern Territory, Board Inquiry into the Protection of Aboriginal Children from Sexual Abuse 2007, Ampe akelyernemane meke mekarle: Little children are sacred, NT Government Printer, Darwin.

Cases

Australian Communist Party v Commonwealth (1951) 83 CLR 1
Falbo v United States (1944) 320 US 549
Fejo v Northern Territory of Australia (1998) 195 CLR 96
Hirst v The United Kingdom [No. 2] (2006) 42 EHRR 41
Kartinyeri v The Commonwealth (1998) 195 CLR 337
Mabo v Queensland [No. 2] (1992) 175 CLR 1
Nelungaloo Pty Ltd v The Commonwealth (1948) 75 CLR 495
Newcrest Mining (WA) Ltd v The Commonwealth (1997) 190 CLR 513
Northern Ganalanja Aboriginal Corporation v Queensland (1996) 208 CLR 1
Roach v Electoral Commissioner (2007) 233 CLR 162
Sauvé v The Queen (2002) 3 SCR 519
Teori Tau v Commonwealth (1969) 119 CLR 564
Western Australia v Ward (2002) 213 CLR 1
Wik Peoples v Queensland (1996) 187 CLR 1
Wurridjal v The Commonwealth (2009) 237 CLR 309

Legislation

Northern Territory National Emergency Response Act 2007 (Cth)

Original lecture available at:
<http://aiatsis.gov.au/publications/presentations/first-australians-law-and-high-court>

17

To recognise or not to recognise: The place of Aboriginal and Torres Strait Islander peoples in the Australian Constitution

2012 Wentworth Lecture

Megan Davis

Thank you, Mick, for that generous introduction. I think my career has essentially mimicked Mick's. He was the Director of the Indigenous Law Centre; now I am the Director of the Indigenous Law Centre. Mick was a Professor of Law at the University of New South Wales [UNSW] and I am a Professor of Law at UNSW. Mick was a member of the UN Permanent Forum on Indigenous Issues and I am now a member of the Permanent Forum. Next, I'll be taking over the National Centre for Indigenous Studies.

Professor Mick Dodson, Principal of AIATSIS Russell Taylor, AIATSIS Council members, ladies and gentlemen: my country is Warra. I have connections to the Bunya Mountains in south-west Queensland. I have family in Mackay, Cherbourg, Hervey Bay and Eagleby. As a Cobble Cobble Aboriginal woman from south-east and south-west Queensland, I would like to pay my respects to country, to elders past and present of this country, and to the people of this country who are gathered here today.

I begin by acknowledging in the audience my little brother, John Davis, who has travelled down here today from Brisbane to represent my family. It is nice that my family always sends a representative to support me at such events. It is a special occasion for John because he is the newly appointed inaugural principal of Hymba Yumba, which is a new Indigenous community school in Ipswich, Queensland, which goes from prep to year 12. Hymba Yumba is striving to achieve academic, sporting and creative excellence but also foster in young Murris, young Indigenous kids, respect for self, respect for elders and respect for country, family and community. We are very proud of John. We have five brothers and sisters. When we were growing up, our mum was very strict about our education and our study–work ethic. Mum instilled in us that the only way for children from low socio-economic backgrounds to achieve social mobility in Australia is through the education system.

It is a privilege to be invited to deliver the 2012 Wentworth Lecture. The Australian Institute of Aboriginal and Torres Strait Islander Studies (AIATSIS) has played an important role in my own academic journey. In the early days of my doctoral studies at the Australian National University, I held a Visiting Scholar position for four months at AIATSIS, organised and mentored by Dr Lisa Strelein. She helped me in those early days to develop my initial, confused ideas for a doctoral thesis. In addition, I have benefited enormously from the support and encouragement of Professor Mick Dodson, who is truly passionate about the ideals of AIATSIS and research excellence in Australian Indigenous studies. I am eternally grateful that he was so supportive of my PhD idea, which, in the words of Frank Brennan is radical and critical in examining limitations of the rights to self-determination of Aboriginal women.

Like me, many Aboriginal and Torres Strait Islander scholars, people and communities have benefited from the work of AIATSIS. Bill Wentworth's legacy has been at the forefront of my own work as a member of the Prime Minister's Expert Panel on Constitutional Recognition of Aboriginal and Torres Strait Islander Peoples. Many people we consulted during 2011 referred to Billy Wentworth's 1966 proposal, which was very similar to the expert panel's recommendations, about which I will speak later.

Today, I have chosen to speak about the idea, the discussion, the debate and the momentum toward constitutional recognition. My lecture is in two parts. First, I draw attention to the comprehensive work of the expert panel and provide an explanation of who has been advocating for constitutional reform and why it is a core aspect of unfinished business. I explain the origin and methodology of the panel and outline the recommendations made in our final report to the Prime Minister. This report is an important contribution to a deeper understanding of the exigencies of constitutional change in relation to Aboriginal and Torres Strait Islander peoples in Australia.

Second, I pay tribute to Bill Wentworth by sharing with you my personal observations as a member of the panel travelling the length and breadth of Australia. I will explain why I am optimistic about the future of constitutional recognition of Aboriginal and Torres Strait Islander peoples. Consequently, rather unconventionally, I will speak to Billy Wentworth's legacy in the latter part of my talk rather than at the beginning.

I hope that this lecture, highlighting the recommendations of the expert panel in particular, will not only contribute to an understanding of the technical aspects of constitutional reform but also provoke conversations in our communities about the importance of constitutional recognition.

Part 1

Since the 1970s, there has been advocacy for the alteration of the Australian Constitution to remedy the silence that exists in the text about the existence of First Peoples in Australia. There have been many different and distinct suggestions for the inclusion of Aboriginal and Torres Strait Islanders in the text. These suggestions have included, but have not been limited to, provisions to protect Aboriginal and Torres Strait Islander peoples' culture, heritage and language; suggestions for a treaty or agreement-making power in the Constitution; the provision of designated parliamentary seats; and the contemporary suggestion — arguably a relic of the failed 1999 referendum — that there be recognition of Aboriginal and Torres Strait Islander peoples in the preamble to the Constitution. In any event, the impetus is for the shaping of the Constitution to reflect the unique status of Australia's First Peoples and Australia's respect for Aboriginal and Torres Strait Islander peoples' culture, and the contribution that this culture has made, and continues to make, to the identity of Australia; that is, what it means to be Australian.

The message is that, in general, it is a very well-crafted Constitution and, for the most part, it works. Yet when it comes to Aboriginal and Torres Strait Islander peoples, in terms of fairness it has not delivered. This advocacy for constitutional reform has come from Aboriginal and Torres Strait Islander peoples themselves and can be found in, but is not limited to, the work of the Council for Aboriginal Reconciliation, the Aboriginal and Torres Strait Islander Commission, the social justice package which was negotiated as a consequence of the *Mabo* decision, and by the many, many reports from the Australian Human Rights Commission's Aboriginal and Torres Strait Islander Social Justice Commissioner.

In addition, there have been a number of Senate and House of Representatives Legal and Constitutional Affairs Committee reports that have recommended alteration of the Constitution to include, in a variety of ways, Aboriginal and Torres Strait Islander peoples in the text. This may be through the entrenchment of particular rights such as agreement making and/or through recognition of their unique status as First Peoples of Australia.

Today, political bipartisan agreement exists with respect to recognition in the Constitution. In the 2010 federal election, this was a feature of both the ALP and Liberal Party election platforms. In resolving the hung parliament, the Greens and Independent Rob Oakeshott included in their agreements with Prime Minister Gillard the requirement that she pursue recognition of Aboriginal and Torres Strait Islander peoples in the Constitution during her term of office.

The many reasons why we need constitutional recognition have been canvassed extensively in the report of the expert panel. One of the more compelling arguments is that the utilitarian nature of the Australian polity means that Aboriginal and Torres Strait Islander peoples' political and legal concerns are dwarfed by the principle of the greatest good for the greatest number. Playing out in the majoritarian framework, 2.5 per cent of Australia's population are tasked with the epic struggle of convincing Australian parliaments of the utility of passing legislative measures or adopting policies that benefit Aboriginal and Torres Strait Islander people alone.

In those circumstances where such measures and policies have successfully passed, they have been committed as special measures under the *Racial Discrimination Act* that permit a state to discriminate effectively in favour of Aboriginal people in order to achieve equality. However, special measures are intended only for a temporary period and are supposed to cease once their objectives have been fulfilled. When more permanent measures are put in place — for example, the *Native Title Act* — history demonstrates how easily these rights can be abrogated or repealed. This is because of the principle of parliamentary sovereignty, which means that the legislative agenda of one political party can be easily amended or abolished by the next. With three-year political terms in Australia, Aboriginal rights are insecure and uncertain.

The argument goes that, in order to have sustained attention on, for example, the chronic disadvantage that is suffered in Aboriginal communities across Australia, Aboriginal and Torres Strait Islander issues need to be taken out of the political arena. Indeed, I was struck by the preference of Aboriginal and Torres Strait Islander peoples for constitutional recognition because then the High Court of Australia would become the final arbiter on these rights. This preference is understandable, given the fact that the interests of Aboriginal and Torres Strait Islander peoples are not often served well in parliament, which can enact and repeal without accountability — well, accountability outside the ballot box.

We know that a mere 2.5 per cent of the populace cannot persuade via the ballot box, so what do small groups do in liberal democracies? Indeed, this is the conundrum facing most indigenous peoples living in liberal democracies. The majoritarian nature of our democracy is one main reason constitutional reform remains the central, though not the singular, pursuit of what is labelled unfinished business.

The Current Process

In any event, we are now at this point in our constitutional history because of the agreement between the Greens and the Independents with the Prime Minister in 2010. Some have fixated on this as evidence of a lack of commitment, but both the ALP and the Liberal Party had this issue in their election platforms. Clearly, in the history of constitutional reform, no one remembers how you got there if you get there, with the exception of what happened in 1967.

In 2010, the Prime Minister asked for public nominations and consulted with the Leader of the Opposition, the Greens and the Independents to constitute a panel to consult with the Australian community and with Aboriginal and Torres Strait Islander communities about altering the Constitution to recognise the unique status of Aboriginal and Torres Strait Islander peoples of Australia. In the Prime Minister's press release, she said that this constitutional recognition would be 'a significant step towards building an Australia based on strong relationships and mutual respect between Indigenous and non-Indigenous Australians' (Macklin 2010).

The terms of reference that were given to the expert panel were very specific:

- lead a broad national consultation and community engagement program to seek the views of a wide spectrum of the community, including from those who live in rural and regional areas;
- work closely with organisations such as the Australian Human Rights Commission, the National Congress of Australia's First Peoples and Reconciliation Australia who have existing expertise and engagement in relation to the issue; and
- raise awareness about the important of Indigenous constitutional recognition including by identifying and supporting ambassadors who will generate broad public awareness and discussion. (Recognise nd)

In developing options for constitutional change, the panel considered the range of views. We were asked to propose to the Prime Minister options for change that would have the best chance of success at a referendum. Over the course of 2012, we developed and undertook an extensive consultation program to seek the views of a broad range of Australians. We published a discussion paper (Recognise 2011). We developed a website (http://www.recognise.org.au/). We travelled around Australia, hosting and participating in public discussions. We held a formal public submissions process and we sought advice from Aboriginal and Torres Strait Islander leaders and constitutional law experts. In addition, to test the community responses to our proposed recommendations, the panel adopted a number of strategies, including engaging Newspoll.

Probably the most important thing we did from the outset was to develop a methodology for how we would devise recommendations to the Prime Minister. In March 2011, we agreed on four principles to guide the assessment of proposals for constitutional change; namely, that each proposal must:

- contribute to a more unified and reconciled nation;
- be of benefit to and accord with the wishes of Aboriginal and Torres Strait Islander peoples;
- be capable of being supported by an overwhelming majority of Australians from across the political and social spectrums; and
- be technically and legally sound.

This methodology we took very seriously. The report contains chapters of content drawn from submissions and public consultations that our panel decided were not capable of carrying the support of the nation or attracting multi-party support. That is why issues of sovereignty and treaty were the subjects of individual chapters in the report, but we decided not to carry forth any recommendations in relation to them. They were not capable of carrying support.

Five recommendations were made by our panel. The first was that Section 25 of the Constitution be repealed. Briefly explained, Section 25 is the provision in the Constitution that contemplates the possibility of state laws disqualifying people of a particular race from voting at state elections. It is essentially a section concerned with federalism and the fair apportionment to each state of representation in the House of Representatives. Because Section 25 is a disincentive for the passage by states of discriminatory laws that disenfranchise racial groups, curiously there is a rebound action to reclaim Section 25 as some kind of unequivocal testament to the constitutional framers' belief in racial equality, as a small seed of civil rights. I reject this as being ahistorical. Even so, there is multi-party support for the deletion of Section 25 and there is universal agreement that it is outdated and should be deleted from Australia's Constitution. There is no controversy in relation to the Panel's view of Section 25.

The second recommendation was that Section 51(xxvi) be repealed. Section 51(xxvi) is a provision in the Constitution that many refer to as 'the race power'. In order for the Australian Parliament to make laws on any number of subjects, it requires powers in the Constitution to authorise it to make those laws. Again, this stems from the nature of our federal system, which sees the division of powers between the state and federal parliaments as central to the Constitution's structure.

Many of you would recall that this section was amended in the 1967 referendum to remove the words 'other than the Aboriginal people in any state'. This removal then conferred upon the federal parliament the power to make laws with respect to Aboriginal and Torres Strait Islander peoples. The expert panel, in its extensive consultations with the Australian people, was persuaded by the view that this section as interpreted by the High Court of Australia can authorise or support the enactment of laws that have an adverse application against a people of any race. Overwhelmingly, we found that the judicial opinion was that this power authorised both beneficial laws and adverse discrimination.

To digress for one moment, this reminds me of the 1966 proposal offered by Billy Wentworth when he introduced a private member's bill to repeal section 51(xxvi). His proposal was to confer on the Commonwealth Parliament power to make laws 'for the advancement of the Aboriginal natives of the Commonwealth of Australia' but, in addition, contained a carve-out that the section should not operate so as 'to preclude the making of laws for the special benefit of the Aboriginal natives of the Commonwealth of Australia'. Wentworth worried that deleting the exclusion of Aboriginal people from section 51(xxvi) could leave them open to discrimination, adverse or favourable. Although his bill passed both houses of parliament, it lapsed and did not go to referendum. Nevertheless, his concerns were prescient.

In any event, in the course of our work, discussing and consulting with the broader Australian community, the fact that the race power could support adverse as well as beneficial laws was a source of surprise and shock. However, full repeal of this provision in the absence of a replacement power would result in an unsatisfactory situation where there would be no head of power under which the Commonwealth Parliament could pass laws for Aboriginal and Torres Strait Islander people.

Therefore, while our second recommendation was the deletion of Section 51(xxvi), our third recommendation was the insertion of a new power for the federal parliament to make laws for Aboriginal and Torres Strait Islander peoples. This third recommendation (section 51A) has an innovative structure. It serves two functions: first, it is a head of power replacing section 51(xxvi) to make laws for Aboriginal and Torres Strait Islander peoples; second, it includes, as introductory words to the head of power, a statement of recognition.

Why have an introductory preamble? Why have introductory words to Section 51A? One of the main suggestions for recognition has been recognition in preamble. This is no doubt a hangover from the 1999 referendum, where there was an attempt to insert a new preamble into the Constitution with some form of recognition of Aboriginal and Torres Strait Islander people alongside other groups. We were persuaded by scholarly submissions that you cannot have a preamble to the UK Act. In addition, you cannot simply place a preamble at the beginning of the Australian Constitution because of interpretive challenges.

Also, in our travels around Australia, Aboriginal and Torres Strait Islander communities almost universally did not want a preamble at the beginning of the Constitution, especially if it contained a 'no political effect' clause, viewing such a measure as tokenistic. This is the path that has been taken by Victoria, Queensland and New South Wales. A 'no legal effect' clause was similarly rejected in the consultation with the broader Australian community. They too felt that it would be a meaningless exercise to go to the effort of recognition, yet at the same time say that it has no effect.

We were satisfied, then, that this option met our criteria, including that it must be of benefit to, and accord with, the wishes of Aboriginal and Torres Strait Islander peoples and be legally and technically sound. Our recommendation was for the insertion of a new section 51A. The language that we chose for the introductory words was as follows:

> *Recognising* that the continent and its islands now known as Australia were first occupied by Aboriginal and Torres Strait Islander peoples;
>
> *Acknowledging* the continuing relationship of Aboriginal and Torres Strait Islander peoples with their traditional lands and waters;
>
> *Respecting* the continuing cultures, languages and heritage of Aboriginal and Torres Strait Islander peoples; and
>
> *Acknowledging* the need to secure the advancement of Aboriginal and Torres Strait Islander peoples;
>
> the Parliament shall, subject to this Constitution, have power to make laws for the peace, order and good government of the Commonwealth with respect to Aboriginal and Torres Strait Islander peoples.

The fourth recommendation is for a new section 116A. Section 116A is a non-discrimination or racial equality clause. The submissions to the panel overwhelmingly supported a racial non-discrimination provision and argued in favour of the principle of racial equality. It was our job to reflect what the community was thinking. Australia's commitment to the principle of racial non-discrimination is reflected in the *Racial Discrimination Act* and is accepted in legislation and policy in all Australian jurisdictions. The *Racial Discrimination Act* already binds what the states and territories can do, so they will not be in a position that is very different from the current one.

The significance of this recommendation is that only the Commonwealth Parliament will have an additional burden placed on it. The Australian people we spoke to quite liked that idea. In addition, many argued that there must be allowance for measures to address disadvantage and ameliorate the effects of past discrimination, as a necessary aspect of a racial non-discrimination provision as well as a recognition of the distinct rights of Aboriginal and Torres Strait Islander peoples as a necessary part of ensuring equality.

Some have suggested that this provision, this recommendation to insert Section 116A, is not recognition and that it is outside our terms of reference. I would argue that the panel, given its extensive consultations with Aboriginal and Torres Strait Islander communities, developed an insight into the devastating impact of discriminatory policies upon Aboriginal and Torres Strait Islander communities. The practical need for this section is based on real experiences of Indigenous people of discrimination at the hands of the Commonwealth Parliament. The most commonly cited examples in community consultations were the Northern Territory intervention and the *Native Title Act* Wik amendments (1998).

One panel member, Noel Pearson, Director of the Cape York Institute, argued strongly that section 116A is recognition. He said:

> Elimination of racial discrimination is inherently related to Indigenous recognition because Indigenous people in Australia, more than any other

group, suffered much racial discrimination in the past. So extreme was the discrimination against Indigenous people, it initially even denied that we existed. Hence, Indigenous Australians were not *recognised*. Then, Indigenous people were explicitly excluded in our Constitution. Still today, we are subject to racially targeted laws with no requirement that such laws be beneficial, and no prohibition against adverse discrimination. (Dodson et al. 2012, s. 6.5)

Noel Pearson has also stated that if the race power was removed, which he strongly advocates, but an anti-racial discrimination clause was not included, Indigenous people would go backwards. He said:

Whereas if you had an Aboriginal and Torres Strait Islander power and you prohibited discrimination, that's the best result because all Australians, regardless of race, would be free from discrimination. (cited in Karvelas 2012)

Newspoll conducted national surveys of Australians on the topic of constitutional recognition. The final Newspoll survey on 28 October 2011 confirmed that 80 per cent of respondents — *80 per cent* — were in favour of amending the Constitution so that there is a new guarantee against laws that discriminate on the basis of race, colour or ethnic origin.

The fifth recommendation is that a new Section 127A be inserted, which is a recognition of languages. This particular section responds to the deep concern that we found in the broader Australian community about the loss of Aboriginal languages.

The response to our recommendations has been somewhat predictable. Those for and against 'rights' generally shape opposites or support. This will never change. It will be as it has always been. These matters will be decided in the political and public realm, shaped by well-rehearsed positions on rights, Indigenous rights and judicial activism et cetera.

Generally, though, we should be glad for the restraint shown by our politicians in not engaging on the issue. There appears to be a consensus that in 2012 and 2013 the political environment is too toxic to be able to support a referendum on Aboriginal and Torres Strait Islander peoples. In the meantime, the Minister for Families, Community Services and Indigenous Affairs, Jenny Macklin, has funded a $10 million public awareness campaign on this issue to foster debate and discussion. In funding this program, Minister Macklin has essentially responded to the concerns of the expert panel. We deduced, in many of the Australian people with whom we consulted, a great anxiety about the lack of knowledge of all Australians, including Aboriginal and Torres Strait Islander people, about civics and the need for civics education. There was a deep concern in the community about a lack of knowledge of Australian history and Aboriginal and Torres Strait Islander history.

Part 2

Essentially, they are the recommendations of the expert panel. In the latter part of the lecture, I want to share with you my own experiences and thoughts, having had the privilege of travelling around Australia, meeting people and discussing this issue. Let's face it, the Constitution and constitutional reform is not the most riveting topic to walk into a community to discuss. We really did empty some rooms when we walked in! I travelled to many remote and regional towns, as well as cities, during the consultation period. I was really struck by the generosity and honesty of the Aboriginal and Torres Strait Islander community and the broader community in their participation in our consultations.

Someone warned the expert panel that we would suffer from consultation fatigue, hearing the same things over and over again. I cannot speak for all of the expert panel, but I do not for a second feel that way. First of all, race relations or the relations between Aboriginal and Torres Strait Islander people and the rest of the community in each region, town and state differ. It is a federal system after all, and the impact of state or territory policy upon Indigenous communities revealed itself in a number of ways. There were different attitudes in Aboriginal and Torres Strait Islander communities across the country toward the state government. There was a preference for or a dislike of Native Title. There were differing attitudes towards the police. They were extremely diverse communities.

On a more national and global level, most Aboriginal and Torres Strait Islander communities we visited shared many of the same anxieties as other Australians, including conversations about asylum seekers, terrorism, the introduction of Sharia law, the economy, job security and the mining boom. It is this commonality that, although not unremarkable, I found intriguing in my travels.

There is one story that I want to share with you from my experiences. I recall that, in one regional town we visited for consultations, the mayor was late, and one of his councillors turned up before him. This councillor said, 'I can't wait to get stuck into this', clearly unimpressed with the notion of recognition of Aboriginal and Torres Strait Islander peoples in the Constitution. She came armed with a dossier that never got opened, but I am sure it was stacked full of crime statistics, et cetera. The mayor arrived and took his seat. The first thing that he said was, 'Well, in my experience, this town is racist. It has had troubled race relations.' He did not deny the problems, but he spoke about the enormous contribution that Aboriginal people have made to his town. He went on to describe in great detail his own childhood and adult life interactions and friendships with the Aboriginal people who grew up in his town. What I found fascinating was the reaction of the councillor. When at first he said, 'This town is racist,' she interjected with, 'Do you think it is?' She was genuinely shocked. But as she sat and listened, like the rest of us, to the mayor's speech, her whole body language changed. When her turn came to speak, she talked not of the bad things, such as crime statistics, but of her own contribution to the Aboriginal community through employing them on her property and the contribution made by Aboriginal people to her life as a pastoralist. She spoke of their shared history and the intersections. For me, it was a really pivotal moment.

It made me think back to a poem that my mum loved and used to read to us as children: 'The Orange Tree', by John Shaw Neilson. This poem is about a young girl who sees an orange tree and tries to describe it to an adult:

> The young girl stood beside me. I
> Saw not what her young eyes could see:
> — A light, she said, not of the sky
> Lives somewhere in the Orange Tree. (Neilson 1919, p. 82)

The rational adult questions the young girl. To him, it is just an ordinary tree. He tries to understand what the young girl is describing, but through his own lens. He is unable to understand what she can see. She gets frustrated at his inability to understand what she is describing:

> — Listen! the young girl said. For all
> Your hapless talk you fail to see
> There is a light, a step, a call,
> This evening on the Orange Tree. (1919, p. 82)

I thought of this poem a lot last year because, racism aside, every day Aboriginal and Torres Strait Islanders and the broader Australian community interact in the places where we live. There is a normality, an ordinariness, to these daily interactions. Everyone negotiates their own space through experience — no fanfare, just living. It is layered and it is complex. Yet the relations between us are too often filtered through the lens of pollsters and opinion-keepers, intelligentsia and ideologues and politicians. We are told time and again that we do not trust each other, we do not like each other and we do not like special rights.

There is more to this relationship than quantitative and qualitative analysis, the stale binaries, the bitter disputes over evidence-based research. Most of us do not live in the world of black and white. We do not have the luxury of being inflexible and righteous. On our travels around Australia, so many Aboriginal and Torres Strait Islanders and [other] Australians spoke to us about these stories, about these very Australian stories.

When I was growing up, my mum also used to read a lot of Henry Lawson and Les Murray to us. My mum isn't Aboriginal, but when she left my dad this is what she gave us. She schooled us in a history of Australian politics and literature. She loved Australian poetry and Australian literature, which were the inheritance she passed on to us. I recall one Henry Lawson story in particular that we were fascinated by as children. It is called 'Water Them Geraniums' and it is part of the Joe Wilson stories. In the story, which traverses the solitude, the alienation and the madness of the Australian bush, the only beauty that the main character, Mrs Spicer (who is past caring) finds in her world is geraniums. Before she dies, she says, 'Remember to water those geraniums'.

As a kid I used to obsess over Mrs Spicer. Perhaps 'obsess' is too strong a word, but I remember distinctly, in Grade 6, thinking that it was the saddest thing in the world that someone would be past caring. I also remember reading the following paragraph in the story:

> And I think the saddest and most pathetic sight on the face of God's earth is the children of very poor people made to appear well: the broken worn-out boots polished or greased, the blackened (inked) pieces of string for laces; the clean patched pinafores over the wretched threadbare frocks. Behind the little row of children hand-in-hand — and no matter where they are — I always see the worn face of the mother.

I had that quote on my wall above my desk in Eagleby. One day I realised that this was me. Those children were me. My mum would hate me saying that. I used to get great nourishment out of reading Henry Lawson and Les Murray. I identified with it because I, too, was poor.

When I went to university, I was told by my fellow Aboriginal English students that in fact Henry Lawson and Les Murray were racists. I got the shock of my life. But I do identify with both Henry Lawson and the poetry of Les Murray. That is me. That is my Australia, and it doesn't replace my Aboriginality or my culture. Still people will say to me, 'why do you love Les Murray so much?' — people who haven't read him and people who have forgotten long ago why it is that they are supposed to dislike him.

We have a tendency to reduce each other to caricatures. We become one-dimensional. It is the tendency of all groups to muzzle 'many-sided human beings into one dimension' through the 'ascription of singular identities'. (Sen 2006, p. 8) The problem with the reductionist approach is that it disregards the importance of autonomy in our lives and the decisions that people make throughout their lives: the decision of a radical activist to marry a non-Indigenous woman, the decision of our white mother to marry our Aboriginal father. In fact, the reductionist approach disregards the way that people actually live their lives today in Australia.

I suppose I share these things with you because that is what I saw as a member of the expert panel, travelling around this country: complex and layered identities, relationships that are really sophisticated. Like all relationships they will break down and boil over. They will forgive. But these relationships are textured and nuanced. This thesis is by no means original, of course. If anything, this is what the Wentworth Lecture stands for.

Many Australians have been capturing the complexities of the daily relationships between Aboriginal and Australian people. Les Murray is one. I think of Bill Gammage, whose incredible book just won the Prime Minister's

Literary Award. I think of the beautiful essays of Nicholas Rothwell. I think of Inga Clendinnen, Grace Karskens and the stories of Kim Scott. I think of the many Wentworth Lectures that have gone before me, like Peter Sutton's wonderful lecture on unusual couples or frontier pairings. Peter Sutton wrote:

> [W]here deep cultural differences are involved, it can be a tribute to the humanity of both parties that their efforts to connect can actually work, and so often have worked, to contribute to the rich fabric of understanding and appreciation of Australia's cultures that we enjoy today. This is the kind of reconciliation that matters most. (see Sutton Wentworth Lecture, this volume, pp. xx–xx)

Martin Nakata, in his 2004 Wentworth Lecture (see this volume, pp. xx–xx) said:

> What is needed is a reconsideration of a different conceptualisation of the cross-cultural space, not as a clash of opposites and differences but as a layered and very complex entanglement of concepts, theories, sets of meanings of a knowledge system.
>
> If this were to be our starting point then the deeply cross-cultural encounters between different knowledge intersections that emerge every day in the communities, in health, education, governance and so on, could be approached, not ambivalently as heralding further cultural loss, but more robustly as the source of new sets of negotiated meanings that may or may not look distinctly Indigenous but which connect with older traditions in ways which do not disrupt and alienate people from those traditions but continue them by enriching practices in ways to produce better outcomes.

It is these things that we do not spend enough time on, that we don't celebrate enough, because it is easy to be adversarial, and one-dimensional and political advocacy thrives on reductionism. But it can't get us all of the way, and it certainly won't lead us to constitutional recognition.

What was overwhelming from the panel's work was that Australians have a deep sense of respect for the unique culture of Aboriginal and Torres Strait Islander peoples. This was borne out in our consultation process, and it is borne out consistently in polls and public opinion research and the Reconciliation Australia barometer. What is so often overlooked, as the Reconciliation Australia barometer establishes, is that there is much more that unites us than divides us.

Conclusion

Bill Wentworth contributed to this legacy in his advocacy for constitutional reform, in his foresight that without beneficial protection Aboriginal and Torres Strait Islander people would in the future be subject to unfavourable discrimination. Wentworth presents us with the story of the complex layers of the interactions between Indigenous and non-Indigenous Australia. AIATSIS embodies this.

I frequently get asked, 'How are you going to get this referendum up? How are you going to get Australians to engage in the technicalities and complexities of the Constitution? Why constitutional reform?' The question 'why constitutional reform?' is disarmingly simple and requires a similarly uncomplicated response. I would suggest that this is the conundrum of the constitutional reform project today. This is not 1967. We could never replicate those socio-political and geo-political conditions. This is the era of polling and public opinion research and social media that demand immediate assessments or expressions of public opinion. Those expressions of public opinion are delivered with characteristic opaqueness but are tangible enough to be translated back to the public through the subjective lens of politically charged opinion-makers and politicians. The reality of how things work in the media is no friend to the constitutional reform project.

I return to the question: 'How do you get Australians to engage with the complexity of the Constitution?' My only answer is that first you get the nation — Aboriginal and Torres Strait Islander people and the rest of the community — to engage with, recognise and understand the complexities and nuances of the relationships that they already have with one another.

References

Dodson, P, Leibler, MM & Expert Panel on Constitutional Recognition of Indigenous Australians 2012, *Recognising Aboriginal and Torres Strait Islander peoples in the Constitution: Report of the Expert Panel*, Commonwealth of Australia, Canberra.

Karvelas, P 2012, 'Tony Abbott holds race key, says Noel Pearson', *The Australian*, 10 February, viewed 8 March 2012 at <http://www.theaustralian.com.au/national-affairs/tony-abbott-holds-race-key-says-noel-pearson/story-fn59niix-1226267174423#>.

Macklin, J, Gillard J & McClelland R 2010, 'Expert Panel on Constitutional Recognition of Indigenous Australians appointed', media release, 23 December, viewed 8 March 2012 at <http://www.formerministers.dss.gov.au/13957/expert-panel-on-constitutional-recognition-of-indigenous-australians-appointed>.

Neilson, JS 1919, *Ballad and lyrical poems*, Bookfellow, Sydney.

Recognise 2011, *A national conversation about Aboriginal and Torres Strait Islander constitutional recognition*, discussion paper, May, viewed 8 March 2012 at <http://www.recognise.org.au/be-informed/discussion-paper>.

Recognise nd, *Terms of reference*, viewed 8 March 2012 at <http://www.recognise.org.au/downloads/1573e091bcdf7e2627c8.pdf>.

Sen, A 2006, *Identity and Violence: The Illusion of Destiny*, Penguin, Harmondsworth.

Legislation

Native Title Act 1993 (Cth)
Racial Discrimination Act 1975 (Cth)

Original lecture available at:
<http://aiatsis.gov.au/publications/presentations/recognise-or-not-recognise-place-aboriginal-and-torres-strait-islander-peoples-australian-constitution>

Index

Aboriginal and Torres Strait Islander Arts Board (Australia Council), 272
Aboriginal and Torres Strait Islander Commission (ATSIC), 272
abolition, 251
Aboriginal Artists Agency, 261–2
Aboriginal Cultural Material Committee, 49–50, 56–7
Aboriginal Folklore Act (proposed), 259
Aboriginal government, 59–72
  misrepresentation of, 63;
  politics of bestowal, 65;
  relationship between land, ritual and politics, 64;
  Western views of, 59–62;
  see also Aboriginal social organisation; Pintupi people
Aboriginal Land (Lake Condah and Framlingham Forest Act 1987 (Cth), 170
Aboriginal Land Act 1991 (Qld), 169
Aboriginal Land Grant (Jervis Bay Territory) Act 1986 (Cth), 169
Aboriginal Land Rights (Northern Territory) Act 1976, 119, 164, 168–9, 185
Aboriginal Land Rights Act 1984, 169
Aboriginal Law
  conflicts with European law, xviii, 125, 139–43;
  customary law practices, 125;
  use in remote communities, 141–2;
  see also land; policing
Aboriginal religious beliefs, 62–4

  relationship between land, ritual and politics, 64
Aboriginal reserves, *see* reserves
Aboriginal social organisation, 61–2;
  see also kinship rules
Aboriginal Studies, xvi, xxii
  as academic pursuit, 47–51;
  definition, 227;
  during 1961–85 era, 75–88;
  importance of imagination, 51–4;
  see also Indigenous Studies
Aboriginal Studies Working Group, 228
Aboriginalisation plan, 187
Aboriginality, 145–60
  accusations of essentialism, 158;
  artistic portrayal, 146;
  construction of identity, 154–5;
  defined by blood, 146, 147, 153;
  defined by difference, 146;
  historic constructions, 152;
  inaccurate representations of, 152–4;
  international indigenous criteria, 148–9;
  labelling, 147;
  'objective criteria', 148;
  'real' vs 'fake', 147;
  relationship with dominant culture, 155–7;
  self-determination, 150, 151;
  self-identification, xviii, 149–51;
  upsurge in 1970s, 43;
  see also doomed race theory; noble savage trope
Aborigines Progressive Association, 193

Aborigines Protection Act 1909–53, 154
Aborigines Protection Board, 192
Alice Springs community policing, 135
Allen, Jim, 18
Alligator River, 82
Anaya, James, 295
Anbarra Aboriginal community, 3, 8, 9
Anderson, Chris, 68
anthropology
  asking of questions, 28–31, 38–42;
  in Australia, 1–22;
  bone tools, 83;
  colonial dimension, 40;
  different accounts, 42;
  establishment of academic anthropology, 115–19;
  establishment of professional anthropology, 109–15;
  future of, 55–7;
  institutionalisation, 102–20;
  middens, 3;
  periods of development, 104–19;
  revisionist accounts of Aboriginal history, 86;
  role of philanthropy, 103, 110–12, 115;
  school kits, 44–7;
  sharing of information, 42–4;
  stone tools, 12–16;
  systematic research, 104–9;
  University of Sydney Chair, 77, 109–10, 112–13;
  untrained observers, 39–40;
  wooden tools, 83–4;
  see also Aboriginal Studies; Indigenous

Index

Studies; song cycles
Aranda people, 69
　Engwura ceremony, 69–70
archaeologists
　relationship with
　Aboriginal people, 85–6
Arkwookerum, Peret, xxi
Arnhem Land, 27, 44
　song productions, 30–1;
　stone tools, 15–16
art, *see* Indigenous art
Arts Law Centre
　Artists in the Black
　program, 270
Ashley, Djardie, 263–4
Aslin, GD, 85
assimilationism, 81, 194,
　197–8
Atkinson, Ellen, xxi
Aurukun, 63
Austin-Broos, Diane, 252
Australasian Performing
　Right Association (APRA),
　271
Australia 2020 Summit, 268
Australian Academy of
　Science, 77;
　Committee on
　Anthropological Research,
　77
Australian Institute of
　Aboriginal and Torres
　Strait Islander Studies
　(AIATSIS)
　as resource for freedom,
　xix, 159
*Australian Institute of
Aboriginal and Torres
Strait Islander Studies Act
1990*, 102
Australian Institute of
　Aboriginal Studies (AIAS)
　changing brief, 81;
　Eaglehawk and Crow
　Letter, 118;
　establishment, xvi, 25, 96,
　103, 117, 227;
　original aims, 48–9, 118;
　review and criticism, 76
Australian Law Reform
　Commission, xvii–xviii,
　125, 126, 131, 138
Australian National Research
　Council, 107

Australian Society of Authors
　(ASA), 271
autonomy, 242, 243

Bambegan, *see* Mammus,
　Billy
Barnes, John, xiii, 76
Barunga Satement, 168, 194
Barwick, Diane, xxi, 76, 86
Barwick, Justice Sir Garfield,
　291
Basedow, Herbert, 40
Bates, Daisy, 105
Battye, JS, 167
Baudin, Nicolas, 12
Beazley, Kim Sr, 76, 80, 186
Bednarik, RG, 85
Behrendt, Larissa, 294
Bell, Diane, xxi, 72
Bern, John, xvi, 64, 72
Berndt, Catherine, ix, 242
Berndt, Ronald, xv, xvi, xxi,
　168, 242
big man, role of, 63, 71–2
bilingual education, *see*
　education
Biraban, xxi, 204, 205–6
Birdsell, Joseph, 6
Bishop, Bronwyn, 160
Blainey, Geoffrey, 39, 94
Boomanulla Oval
　Statement, 194
Bowdler, Sandra, 11
Brandl, Eric, 265
Brandy judgment, 175
Brennan, Chief Justice Frank,
　285
Bridge, Ernie, 56–7
Bringing Them Home report,
　196
British Association for the
　Advancement of Science
　Meeting, 106
Brough, Mal, 290
Bulun Bulun, John, 262–4
bunggul ceremony, 185
Burbank, Victoria, 249
bureaucratisation, 94
Burke's Cave, 13
Burt, Judge, 167

Cambridge Anthropological
　Expedition to the Torres
　Strait, 105

Cape Keerweer people, 63,
　208
Carnegie Corporation, 115
Carpets Case, 262, 263, 267
Cassels, Richard, 17
celebration of identity, 168
chaos, 4
Chase, Athol, xvi, 71
Chester, Thomas, 206
circular migration, 252
Clark, Manning, 166
classificatory schemes for
　Aboriginal people, xviii;
　self-definition, xviii;
　see also Aboriginality
Cobern, Patricia, 39
Colbung, Ken, xvi–xvii, 247
Collmann, Jeff, 209–10
Communist Party Case, 293
Community Development
　Employment Project, 139
comparative morphology, 65
Conference on Aboriginal
　Studies (1961), 26–7,
　47–8, 79–80
conservation movement
　Aboriginal survival and,
　100–1
Constitutional recognition for
　Indigenous people, xxiv–
　xv, 198, 298–311;
　current process, 301–6;
　preamble, 304–5
Coombs, HC 'Nugget', 131,
　164, 259, 261
Cooper, Bill, 195
copyright, *see* Indigenous art;
　Indigenous culture; prior
　informed consent
Copyright Act 1968 (Cth),
　260
　amendments to include
　Indigenous communal
　moral rights, 267–8
Copyright Agency Limited
　(CAL), 271
Council for Aboriginal
　Reconciliation, xx, 195,
　196, 201
*Council for Reconciliation
Act 1991*, 200
cultural attribution, 277
cultural integrity, 277
cultural property rights, 258

313

Index

see also intellectual property rights
cultural revival, 168
culture, see Indigenous culture

dance, 98–9
Davenport, Charles, 110
Davis, John, 298
Davis, Megan, xxiv–xv
Dawson, Justice, 286
Day of Mourning and Protest (1938), xx, 192–5, 198–200
Deaf Adder Creek rock art, xxiii
Deane, Sir William, xiv, 294
deaths in custody, xvii
Deloria, Vine, 156
Devil's Lair (WA), 84
Dhakiyarr, 183
Dhanbul Association, 130
Dhupuma Aboriginal College (Yirrkala), 46
difference, 242
discrimination, 148
dispersal, 130
dispossession, 197
    bipartisan recognition of, 171
Dixon, Justice, 293
Djerrkura, Gatjil, 183
djuluru ritual (Eastern Kimberley), 42
Dodson, Mick, xviii–xvix, 258, 298, 299
Dodson, Patrick, xx–xxi
doomed race theory, 147, 153
Dow Dow, Mick, 208
Durkheim, Emile, 70, 105
Durmugam, Smiler, xxi, 204, 215–18
Dutton, Geoffrey, 60
dying race theory, 95 166, 228

education
    bilingual, xx, 186, 189–90;
    presentation of Aboriginal culture in schools, 45;
    support for schools, 45–6;
    Yolngu, 185–91
egalitarianism in Aboriginal society, 67–9
Elcho Island adjustment movement, 42
Elkin, AP, 48, 77, 82, 104, 115, 116
Elliot Smith, Grafton, 106, 107, 108, 110, 111, 112
Ellison, Ralph, 156–7
Embree, Edwin, 110, 111, 113, 114
entropy, 2, 4, 5, 17, 18
environmental change, 85
ethnographic present, 86
Eva Valley Statement, 194
Expert Panel on Constitutional Recognition of Aboriginal and Torres Strait Islander Peoples, 299, 300–6;
    development of methodology, 304–5;
    experience of consultation process, 307–11;
    new non-discrimination section 116A, 305;
    new recognition of languages section 127A, 306;
    power to make laws for Aboriginal and Torres Strait Islander peoples, 305;
    recommendations, 303–6;
    repeal of section 25, 303;
    repeal of section 51(xxvi), 303;
    response to recommendations, 306;
    terms of reference, 304
extinguishment doctrine, 173
Eylmann, Erhard, 105
Eyre, Edward John, ix; view of Aboriginal government, 59–60

Ferguson, Bill, 193
Fidock, Alan, 44
Fison, Lorimer, 104, 105
'Flash T-shirts' Case, 262–4
Flinders, Johnny, xxi
Flinders, Matthew, 12, 16
food sources
    Bogong moth, 19;
    Bunya pine, 19;
    Macrozamia nuts, 19–20
Fraser, Malcolm, xxiv
Frazer, Sir James, 105, 107, 108, 109, 110
Freedom Rides, 81
French, Chief Justice Robert, xix–xx, 291, 293

Galiwin'ku Community Justice Program, 126
Galligan, Brian, 171
Gallus, Sandor, 82
galtha, 188
    ceremony, 185
Galton Society, 110
Ganalbingu people, 263
ganma, 188
Garland, Alf, 147
garma, 186
    maths curriculum, 188–91
Gaudron, Justice Mary, 283
Gerritson, Rolf, 71
Gibbs, Pearl, 193
Gidjingali people, xv, 62
Gill, Edmund D, 82
Gillard, Julia, 300
Gillen, Frank, xv, 69, 77, 105
Gillespie, Danny, 252
Gleeson, Chief Justice Murray, 289
Golvan, Colin, 262
Gorton, John, 80
Gove land rights dispute, 168
Grant, Madison, 110
Grey, Fred, 183
Grimble, Arthur, 112
Grosvenor, Helen, 193
Gummow, Justice, 286, 291
Gunbalaya community policing, 135–6
Gurindji walk-off, 168
Gurrmanamana, Frank, 71
Gurungu Council community policing, 134

Haddon, Alfred, 105, 106, 107, 108–9, 110
Hamilton, Annette, 72
Harris delegation, 198
Hart, CWM, 65
Hawke, Bob, 194
Hayden, Justice Dyson, 289
Hayne, Justice Kenneth, 289, 291

Hercus, Luise, xxi
Hiatt, Les, xv–xvi, 15, 88
High Court of Australia, 281, 284–9
Hocart, AM, 112–13
Howard, John, xxi, 290
Howitt, Alfred, xxi, 77, 104, 105

incarceration of Aboriginal people, xvii, 128–9, 141
Indigenous art, xxiii, 98, 260
  agreements with communities, 264–5;
  appropriation of images, 261–4;
  Bulun Bulun equity, 264;
  copyright protection, 260, 261, 271–2;
  development of protocols, 270;
  fiduciary duty, 264;
  folklore, 261;
  oral dimension, 260;
  see also rock art
Indigenous culture, xxiii, 98, 260
  copyright protection, 260, 261, 271–2;
  folklore, 261;
  oral dimension, 260
Indigenous Land Fund, 174
Indigenous Law Centre (UNSW), xxiv
Indigenous music, 274
Indigenous Studies, xxi–xxii, 225–38;
  community pedagogy, 237;
  cross-disciplinary study, 228, 229;
  external knowledge production, 227–8;
  focus on contemporary society, 228–9;
  Indigenisation, 233–5;
  Indigenous academics, 229;
  Indigenous health worker education, 237;
  from Indigenous perspective, 225;
  influence of political activism, 228;
  international context, 230–1;
  intersections of knowledge, 235–6;
  involvement of Indigenous people, 228–9;
  narrative of cultural loss, 238;
  narrative of survival, 238;
  place of traditional knowledge in, 234–6;
  redefinition of, 229–38;
  reinstatement of Indigenous ontologies and epistemologies, 231–2;
  special programs, 229;
  support centres, 229;
  tension between academics and Indigenous communities, 226–7, 232;
  theoretical and methodological issues, 226;
  Western role in, 230–1;
  see also Aboriginal Studies
intellectual property rights, 258
  see also cultural property rights
International Commission of Jurists, 127
International Labour Organization Convention 169, 151

Jabiru Primary School, 46
Janke, Terri, xxiii
Jigalong Mission, xviii, xxii, 243, 246, 247
Johnston, Elliott, 126, 127
Jones, Rhys, xiii, xiv
Julalikari Council Patrols, 131–4
Justice French, 262
justice
  as fairness, 165, 170–1;
  meaning for Aboriginal and Torres Strait Islander people, 164–5;
  as natural law, 165

Kangaroo Island, 12, 82
Kartinyeri v The Commonwealth, 282, 287

Keating, Paul, 194
Keen, Ian, xvi, 69
Keilor, 82
Keith, Sir Arthur, 110
Kenniff cave, 82
Kimberley Institute, xx
Kinchela, Jack, 193
kinship rules, 61
Kirby, Justice Michael, xxiii, 286, 291
Kluckhohn, Clyde, 116–17
Kluckhohn, Florence, 116–17
Koonalda cave, 82, 84
Kow Swamp, 99
Kugu-Nganychara people, 63

Lake George, 13
Lake Mungo, xiv, 11, 13, 83, 84, 86, 99
Lambert, Jacquie, xiii
Lami-lami, Lazarus, xxi
Lampert, RJ, 12, 17
Land Act (Aboriginal and Islander Land Grants) Amendment Act 1992 (Qld), 169
land claims
  ethnographic substantiation for, 49
land
  distribution, 93, 95;
  management, 93, 94–5;
  reform, 93;
  relationship with ritual and politics, 64, 90–101;
  rites, 93, 96, 97–100;
  see also land rights
land rights, 90, 92, 95
  attitudes to, 170–2;
  evolution of statutory, 168–70;
  legislation, 169–70
Lang, Andrew, 105
Langton, Marcia, xvii–xviii, 88, 147
Larakia people, 184
Laura Early Man shelter, 84
Lévi-Strauss, Claude, 14
Lourandos, Harry, 18
Lyons, Joseph, 195

Mabo judgment, xxiii–xxiv, 163, 168, 172–4, 262, 285–7, 289, 300;

Index

principles of, xxiv, 172–3, 287;
reaction to, 170–1
Mackenzie, William, 212
Macklin, Jenny, 306
Maddock, Kenneth, 62
Mahkarolla, Harry, xxi, 204, 206–11
Malangi, David, xxiii, 261
Malinowski, Bronislaw, 107–8, 112–13
Mammus, Billy, xxi, 204, 211–14
Mammus, Jinny, 214
Mammus, Rosie, 214
Manzie, Darryl, 136
Maralinga Tjarutja Land Rights Act 1984 (SA), 169
Marcus, Julie, 214
Marett, Robert, 105
Marika, Dr, xxi, 180–91
Marika, Wandjuk, 182, 261
Martin, David, 243
Martu people, xviii, xxii–xxiii, 242–56;
autonomy, 243, 247, 250, 255;
education, 254;
gender relations, 250;
identity, 253;
impact of coming in from the Desert, 245;
Martu Law, xxi, 245, 248;
Native Title claims, 253;
paternalism, 246;
readiness to travel, 250;
religious practices, 248;
self-management, 246–9, 254, 255–6;
sharing and kin obligations, 249;
socialisation, 244;
urban settlement, 253;
vehicle ownership, 250
Mason, Justice, 285
Mathew, Rev John, 77, 105
Mathews, RH, 77, 105
Mawulan, 32
McColl, Constable, 183
McConnel, Ursula, xxi, 204, 206, 208, 211–14, 220
McGill, John, *see* Biraban
McHugh, Justice Michael, 286

McLean, Mick, xxi
McLeod, Billy, *see* Tulaba
Mee, Arthur, 166
Meehan, Betty, 3, 8, 15, 20, 252
Meggitt, Mervyn, xv, 61–2, 63, 65, 66, 67, 72
Menzies, Sir Robert, 283–4
middens
Galatea Bay, 3;
role in anthropology, 3
Milirrpum judgment, 185
milngurr, 188
Mimi Rock Art, 265
Moorundi, 59–60
Morgan, Lewis Henry, 104, 105
Morphy, Howard, 69
Mountford, CP, 206
Mulvaney, John, xvi, xvii, 14, 15
Munro, Jenny, 193
music, *see* Indigenous music
mutual obligations, 100
Myers, Fred, xvi, 66–8

Nakata, Martin, xxi–xxii, 310
Nambarra School, 187
Narogin, Mudrooroo, 157
National Association for the Visual Arts, 270
National Campaign Against Drug and Alcohol Abuse, 137
National Indigenous Arts Advocacy Association, 270, 272,
National Indigenous Arts Reference Group, 269
national Indigenous cultural authority proposal, 267, 268–75
National Label of Authenticity project, 272–3
National Native Title Tribunal, 174, 175
Native Administration Act 1936 (WA), 166
Native Title Act 1993, 163, 174–5, 301
reaction to, 70–1
native title, xix–xx, 163–78

country and, 177;
mediation, 176–7;
rights to country, 167–8;
see also land rights
Nelson, Topsy, xxi
Nelungaloo Pty Ltd v The Commonwealth, 292
Newcrest Mining (WA) Ltd v The Commonwealth, 291
Newman, 246, 253
see also Martu people
Ngalijibama, 20
Ngunnawal people, 192, 242, 258
Ngurruwutthun, Dula, 183
Nhulunbuy High School, 46
noble savage trope, xxiii, 145
see also Aboriginality
Noonkanbah people, 198
Northern Territory 'Intervention', xxiv, 281, 290–4
Northern Territory National Emergency Response Act 2007 (Cth), 290

O'Gorman, Anne, 214
Oakeshott, Rob, 300
Onus, Lin, 262
Ooldea Mission, 27, 38
Our Culture, Our Future report, xxiii, 258, 266–8

pacification, 130
Pambegan, Arthur Jr, 212
Pambegan, Arthur Sr, 212
Pambegan, Geraldine, 212
Pan Pacific Science Congress (1923), 107
Pandak, 215
Papua New Guinea
Wahgi Valley, xiv, 21–2
Paris Museum of Arts of Africa and Oceania, 261
Parker, Mrs, 105
Pastoral Award (1966), 81
paternalism, 165–8
Patten, Jack, 193
Pearson, Noel, 165, 252, 305–6
Perry, W, 108
personal responsibility, 164
Peterson, Nicolas, xvii, 7, 15
Phillip, Governor Arthur, 4

Pilbara strike, 198
Pilling, AR, 65
Pink, Olive, 206, 214, 220
Pintupi people
  political organisation, 66–8
Pitjantjatjara Land Rights Act 1981 (SA), 169
policing
  Aboriginal people and, xvii–xviii, 125–43;
  community policing, xviii, 125, 127, 134–6;
  suggested changes to, 142–3;
  Aboriginal relations with criminal justice system, 127;
  community justice mechanisms, 125, 127, 129–31, 141;
  Aboriginal initiatives, 129–30, 131–4;
  education, 129–30;
  Queensland police powers, 127;
  minor vs serious offences, 139–40;
  see also Aboriginal Law; Alice Springs community policing; Galiwin'ku Community Justice Program; Gunbalaya community policing; Gurungu Council community policing; incarceration of Aboriginal people; Julalikari Council Patrols; Tangentyere Social Behaviour Project; Yuendumu community policing
population densities of Aboriginal people, 6;
  Arnhem Land, 7;
  relationship of energy and population, 8;
  role of technology, 9;
  Tasmania, 6–7
prehistory of Australia, 10–14, 82–8;
  initial colonisation, 10–11;
  see also anthropology

prior informed consent, 275–7
Professional Association of Applied Anthropology and Sociology, 56
protectionism, 166–8

Quiggin, Robynne, 274

Racial Discrimination Act 1975, xix, 173–4, 301
Radcliffe-Brown, Alfred, 27, 61, 65, 78, 105, 212;
  appointment to Sydney University Chair of Anthropology, 77, 109, 112–13, 114
Raiwalla, xxi
reconciliation, 196–8
Reconciliation Australia, 310
Reconciliation Week, xx
Redfern Speech, 194
referendum of 1967, xx, 81, 195–6, 284
referendum of 1999, 300
Register of Native Title Claims, 175
remote communities as living museums, 251–2
research collaboration, 204–21;
  kin incorporation, 220–1;
  nature of relationships, 210–11;
  sharing of information, 219
Research School of Pacific Studies (ANU), 116–17
reserves, 93
  declaration of, xvi
Reynolds, Henry, 94
Ridgeway, Aden, 267
rights agenda, 199
Rigsby, Bruce, 63
Riptide Churinga, 265–6
Rivers, William Halse, 105
Roach v Electoral Commissioner, xxiv, 287–9
Robinson, George Augustus, 6
Robinson, Michael Massey, 5
rock art, xxiii, 84–5
  copyright issues, 265

Rockefeller Foundation
  funding for Australian and PNG research, 77;
  funding of anthropology, 110–12, 115
Roth, WE, 105
Rousseau, Jean-Jacques, 2, 20–1
Rowley, Charles, 78, 170
Royal Commission into Aboriginal Deaths in Custody, 126, 130, 196;
  Aboriginal Issues Unit, 127, 131;
  complaints, 126–7;
  Criminology Research Unit, 128;
  recommendations, 138–9
Rudd, Kevin, 294
Ruxton, Bruce, 147

Seaman, Paul, 56–7, 169
Seaman report, 169
Securing the Future report, 270
self-determination, 50, 196
self-management, 246–7
  see also self-determination
Shared Responsibility Agreements (SRAs), 255
Sharp, Lauriston, xv, 60–1, 63, 65
Shaw, Barbara, 137
Social Impact of Uranium Mining Committee (NT), 45, 48, 57
Social Justice Package, 174, 266
Social Sciences Research Council (SSRC), 78;
  Aborigines in Australian Society project, 78
song cycles, 30–2
  Djaŋ'gau song epic, 32–7;
  messages of, 37–8
Spencer, Baldwin, xv, 40, 69, 77, 103, 104–5, 106
Stanner, Professor WEH, xv, xxi, 75, 96, 116, 120, 204, 215–18
Steep Head Island, 17
Steward, Julian, xvi
stone tools, 86
  Arnhem Land, 15–16;

Kartan industry, 12;
Lake Mungo, xiv, 11;
role in anthropology, 12–13;
small tools, 14–16;
Tasmania, 17
Stopping the Ripoffs report, 266
storytelling
role in remembering, 194
Strehlow, TGH, 67
Strelein, Lisa, 299
Sutton, Peter, xvi, xxi, 63, 65

Tangentyere Social Behaviour Project, 136–8
Tasmanian Aborigines
absence of great religious ceremonies, 18;
myth of extinction, xix, 154;
social matrix, 18–19;
stone tools, 17
Taylor, Russell, 298
television
impact on Aboriginal audiences, 46
Tent Embassy, 168
Teori Tau v Commonwealth, 291
terra nullius, 197, 285
This is What We Said book, 294, 296
Thomson, Donald, xxi, 183–4, 206, 208, 220
Threlkeld, Lancelot, xxi, 204, 205–6
Tindale, Norman B., 12, 82
Tonkinson, Myrna, 246, 252
Toohey, Justice, 286
Torres Strait Islander Land Act 1991 (Qld), 169
Traditional Aboriginal Property Act (proposed), 259
treaty, 201, 202
Trucanini, xix, 154
Tulaba, xv
Ucko, Peter, 81–2
United Nations Declaration *on the Rights of Indigenous Peoples*, 266–7
United Nations Permanent Forum of Indigenous Issues, xxiv
United Nations Sub-Commission on Discrimination and the Protection of Minorities, 148
urbanisation, 99

Valadian, Margaret, xiv–xv
Vanstone, Amanda, 251–2
Vivienne, May, 166
Von Doussa, Judge, 263
von Sturmer, John, xvi, xxi, 63, 218

Waitangi Tribunal, xix, 176–7
Ward v Western Australia, 287
Warlpiri people, xvii
Warner, Lloyd, xxi, 183, 204, 206–11, 220
Wattie Creek, 81
Weld, Governor, 167
Wells, Rev, 184
Wentworth, William Charles, xiii, xvii, xxv, 1, 25, 75, 80, 96, 117–18, 151, 160, 163, 225, 242, 259, 281, 282–4, 289, 296, 299, 303, 310
Wentworth Lecture
choice of lecturers, xiii;
inaugural, xiii, xiv
West, John, 5
Western Desert Lands Aboriginal Corporation (WDLAC), 255
Western Desert people
concern for land, 27;
see also Martu people
white settlement of Sydney Cove, 5–6;
movement of Aboriginal people, 5–6
Whitlam, Gough, 81, 186, 259
Wik judgment, xxiv, 286–7
Wik people, 208, 211
Wild, Rex, 294
Willandra Lakes, 96
Williams, Don, 44
Williams, Nancy, xviii, 131
Wilson, JT, 112
Wissler, Clark, 110, 113
Wonggu, 183
Wood Jones, Frederick, 112, 113, 114
Woodward Royal Commission, 164, 168–9
Woodward, Justice Sir Edward, 94
Wurridjal v The Commonwealth, 281, 289–94, 296
Wurridjal, Mr, 290

Yir-Yoront people, 61
Yirrkala 182
community justice project, 130–1;
dream diaries, 31–2;
mission, 184
Yirrkala Bark Petition, 168, 184, 186, 194
Yolngu
community justice program, 130–1;
education, 182, 185–91
law, 181;
Macassan influences, xx, 182–3;
mathematical ideas, 187–91;
oral histories, 181;
people, 180–91;
values, xx
Yuendumu community policing, 135
Yumbulul Case, 262
Yumbulul, Terry, 261–2
Yunupingu, Dr M, 186
Yunupingu, Galarrwuy, 165